"Inspiration with a bit of pyromania. With his hair on fire, Eric invites you on his own thrill ride. Free-spirited and spiritual throughout, the pages share Eric's philosophy with both authenticity and depth. While reading, I was instantly inspired to evaluate my own life. This book is packed with stories that will make you both laugh out loud and reflect. Best of all, I was entertained while working on the best version of myself."

-John Gall
Stanford University Hall of Fame
All Time Pac 12 Hits Leader
2006 St. Louis Cardinals World Series Champion
2008 Team USA Olympic Bronze Medalist

"Eric is easily one of the most driven, passionate and enthusiastic people I know. The lessons he's learned in his life have all led him to where and who he is today. This book proves you can have failures without failing. I didn't play in the Major Leagues, my body fat percentage is much higher than Eric's and I've spent my entire life on the East Coast, but that's not to say that I can't relate to the lessons he presents in this book. This list proves you can accomplish anything in life if you learn from your mistakes and demand that you're better today than you were yesterday."

-Paul Severino
Emmy Award Winning Sports Broadcaster
Play by Play, Miami Marlins

"When the right person pens the right book, there's an honesty and vitality that should not be missed. *The F* It List* by Eric Byrnes fits that description. I've known Eric since we were 18 years old, and he has always lived the concept of getting out of the comfort zone. This book captures Eric's commitment while also calling the reader to action. Anyone looking to spark their adventurous spirit will love this book."

-Mark Shapiro, MD
Host & Producer, Explore The Space Podcast
Medical Director, Hospital Medicine at St. Joseph Health Medical Group

"The F*It List embodies everything the WEDŪ spirit is all about. The stories are incredible, and the lessons taken from the stories are something we can all use to survive and thrive."

-Lance Armstrong
Former Professional Cyclist
WEDŪ Founder

W9-ATZ-302

"Life's path is centered around pivotal moments and the decisions you make in those windows of time. Eric has powerfully laid out his story from childhood to fatherhood, thoughtfully chronicling the intense choices he made along the way. His words are a guidebook to effectively eliminate all the excuses that dictate our lack of progress and cast shadows on the dreams that lie within us. This book is inspiration in its purest form."

-Kelley James
Singer, Songwriter

"If you're looking for a book that motivates you to push yourself way beyond your comfort zone, you found it! Eric is a self-proclaimed guinea pig. His personal story is proof positive that the only limits to your potential are the ones you make for yourself. This book draws you into decision mode - you can either live a) an ordinary life or, b) not give a f*ck and stretch yourself to live an extraordinary life. Eric's story is a great example of someone who maximizes his life by using visualization, momentum, habit building tricks, and life-hacking to reach any goal he pursues while inspiring the reader to do the same. The book is filled with great anecdotes, a ton of heart and some truly applicable life-lessons. I strongly recommend it for everyone and anyone who wants to be inspired to keep moving. If that's you, start your own "F*It List!"

-Jennifer Cohen
Author, *Strong is the New Skinny*
Forbes Columnist

"I met Byrnsie in 2001 when he could barely catch a fly ball. I was the vet on the way out. He was the prospect on his way up. I was the teacher. He was the pupil. He would go on to have a Major League career that most of us would kill for. But as time has gone by, the roles have strangely reversed. Now, in our lives after baseball, he shows me. A true inspiration to me on a daily basis to live my life to the fullest. Every. Single. Day. While his career as a ballplayer was outstanding, his life after baseball is even better! This book is fantastic because it shows the world what I already know, that every day is a gift and we all need to live our lives to the fullest and... *The F*IT List* is a true inspiration and should serve as a guide for all of us."

-FP Santangelo
Former Major League Baseball Player
Current Color Analyst, Washington Nationals

"I was a huge fan of Eric Byrnes as a baseball player because his love of the game came through loud and clear every time he sprinted full out onto the field. I became an even bigger fan when he made the brutal transition from a fast twitch sport like baseball to take his body in an entirely new direction and become an ultra-marathoner and a multiple time Ironman finisher. I have had him on my radio show a number of times and that same passion from his baseball days still comes through loud and clear. After every interaction with the amazing Eric Byrnes, I'm always left wanting more and always left wondering how this guy is able to live every day of his life full-out? Fortunately, all of the answers are in this book and I guarantee that the book is as spectacular and unpredictable as the man himself. I loved every page!"

-Bob Babbitt
Co-Founder, Competitor Magazine
Co-Founder, Challenged Athletes Foundation
Host, Babbittville Rado
USA Triathlon and Ironman Triathlon Hall of Fame Inductee

"Eric Byrnes is one of the most unique individuals on the planet. His life is an action movie and it's not an act. The way that he went all-out for every fly ball in the outfield is the way that he approaches each day. Whenever I can learn from his routine and life lessons, I'm all ears. Mission accomplished with this book. Eric's ideals have steered him in a direction of positive enthusiasm and epic stories. Nobody has more energy and I felt that electricity through his words."

-Scott Braun
MLB & NHL Network
Emmy Award Winning Studio Host

The F*It List

Life Lessons from a Human Crash Test Dummy

Copyright © 2018 by Hustle Media

ISBN-13: 978-1986507172
ISBN-10: 1986507173

To learn more about Eric Byrnes, visit
EricByrnes.com

The F*It List
Table of Contents

Prologue

Shortly after my last season playing professional baseball, I began working at MLB Network. Once or twice a month, I would fly between San Francisco and New York City. On the 5-hour flight each way, I had plenty of time to reflect on many of my early life and professional baseball experiences. I eventually began writing down the stories and a few years later I had compiled a pretty epic collection of life experiences.

As you can probably imagine, many of the stories were comical to say the least, yet, no matter what emotion I felt reliving the experiences, the one thing I eventually realized was that each story carried with it some sort of invaluable life lesson. Then, as I transitioned into broadcasting, ultra-endurance sports, and fatherhood, the collection of stories continued to grow, and so did the lessons.

For a long time, I wasn't sure what I was going to do with the writings. My initial thought was to keep them in the diary form in which they were written, then one day pass them on to my kids.

In 2016, I had the opportunity to run the Western States 100-mile endurance run. A buddy of mine who had done the race before compared running the Western States to "living a lifetime in a day." He couldn't have been more right.

As I approached mile 97 of the race at No Hands Bridge, I had an epiphany. Maybe it was because earlier in the race I was sure I was getting stalked by a mountain lion or because I thought I saw an orangutan. It might have been the nasty fall I had around mile 20 or the fact that my feet were so jacked up with cuts and blisters, every step felt like I was running on glass. Regardless, I knew I needed to share what I had just experienced.

Then, in my delusional and incredibly emotional state, I also decided I wanted to share all of the stories I had accumulated. If for no other reason than if just ONE story, or ONE life lesson drawn from a story, is able to put a smile on somebody's face or motivate somebody to step outside of their comfort zone and challenge themselves, it will all be worth it.

When I was in college at UCLA, my roommates and I would playfully argue about who would get the most activities done in a day. Of course, that led to a competition where we got a big ass dry erase board and would actually chart our individual activities throughout the course of the entire day. No doubt, it was a pissing contest with 4 dudes that had way too much testosterone to burn but the list taught me a lot about myself. More than anything, the list taught me about the incredible value of a routine. For the past 20 years now, I have continued to develop and modify the daily list of activities in order to do everything I can to optimize my current lifestyle.

Its name... The F*ck It List.

Because Mom was mortified by the title, I promised to refer to it as The F*It List :)

When I played professional baseball, I had the tendency to fly around the outfield and run into a few walls. Early on in my career, Hall of Fame writer and broadcaster Peter Gammons gave me the nickname 'Human Crash Test Dummy'. It took a while for it to grow on me but just like any obstacle we face in life, we are always much better off embracing it.

So... To Peter Gammons, and all of the original F*It List participants: Mike Seal, Bryan Sidensol, Bob Angus, Eric Valent and Royce Valent... This title is for you dudes.

To Mom, Dad (Double Sky Point) and my sister Shea: Thank you for teaching me how to LIVE my life. Thank you for giving me an opportunity to make mistakes and fail. Thank you for your endless support and unconditional love.

To Tarah: Thank you for being the best wife and mother to our children I could have ever dreamed of. Thank you for your unwavering commitment. Thank you for accepting my many flaws and challenging me to become a better person on a daily basis. It has been a helluva ride...

To Chloe, Cali and Colton: Thank you for teaching me a love so deep I never thought possible. Thank you for continuing to fail and learn from your failures. Thank you for pushing limits and defining your own boundaries. There are only two things in life I will be able to give you that nobody will ever be able to take away: EDUCATION and EXPERIENCE. Always keep learning and NEVER STOP charging.

To everyone else along the way that has made my life difficult: Thank you for that. Without failure and the lessons we are able to learn from failure, we are nothing. Whatever successes in life I have been able to achieve are a direct result of leaping over hurdles. Thank you for being that hurdle.

No matter what I have done in my life, whether it was playing Major League Baseball, performing on TV, competing in Ironman triathlons, running 100 miles or in this case writing a book, I have been and will be critiqued and ridiculed by outsiders in just about every way possible. I am extremely grateful for that. These are the people who have helped me realize there is no sense ever wasting any sort of energy worrying about external opinions and events outside of my control. These opinions and events are what has allowed me to focus all of my effort and energy on what is actually within my immediate control.

When you learn to become comfortable with the uncomfortable and live a life of vulnerability, you will finally be authentically LIVING YOUR LIFE. As the 26th President of the United States, Teddy Roosevelt, so brilliantly pointed out...

"It is not the critic who counts; not the man who points out how the strong man stumbles, or where the doer of deeds could have done them better. The credit belongs to the man who is actually in the arena, whose face is marred by dust and sweat and blood."

F*It... Let's Go!

Intro

November 19, 2011 was a day that seemingly connected my past, present, and future, all at the same time. Possibly the most impactful day of my life...

It was 6:50 am and I had just jumped into Tempe Town Lake with an approximate water temperature of 62 degrees. Everyone around me was bitching about how cold the water was, but that was the least of my worries. Growing up on the rugged Northern California coast surfing in water that gets into the 40's was finally paying off. Quite honestly, between my extended experience in cold water and the fact that adrenaline was pulsating every vein in my body, it practically felt like bath water. I would use this as the only psychological advantage I had because basically that's all I could hang my hat on. 11 months earlier, I could not swim 25 yards without stopping, the only bike I owned was a beach cruiser, and I had never run more than 4 miles in my life.

This brings me to the obvious question: "What the F*CK was I doing about to attempt an Ironman?"

Barely a year removed from an 11-year Major League Baseball career, I was about to embark on a day in which I would swim 2.4 miles, bike 112 more, and run a 26.2-mile marathon. While some may believe there would be a seamless transition from MLB into the world of triathlon, that could not be any further from the truth. If I had been sitting on a couch for the past 15 years smoking weed and drinking beer, my prep would have been relatively equivalent. I spent years building an anaerobic base through playing baseball, which had me dialed in to run a hard 90 feet to beat out an infield single or chase down a fly ball in the gap. Going 1st to home was what I considered a "long run." I was treading water waiting for the famous Ironman cannon to sound. Looking around at 3,000 people in the water, I could not help but think what their individual stories were. What possibly drove them to the start line? Music was pumping but I was not really hearing it. There was a crowd of spectators that lined the lake and even hovered above on the Mill Avenue Bridge. I could tell they were cheering but the sound was faint, white noise. The sun then began to rise over the Arizona desert mountains off in the distance. We were about to swim directly toward it. Then, it happened...

I actually saw my Dad. I could even hear him. "Isn't this great 'E'! I am so proud of you. What a magical day!" The problem was that my Dad died 8 months earlier. I didn't have time to question or even reflect upon the encounter. BOOM. We were off...

This is my journey, this is my life, my lessons, my successes, and my many failures... in my own words.

This is my **F*It List**.

The F*It List is a lifestyle as much as it is an actual list of sh*t to get done. It is an attitude that bleeds into every aspect of your life. It constantly challenges you to question the norms of society and push the limits of the status quo. Specifically, your status quo. Most importantly, the F*It List forces action. It promotes energy and gives life. It allows you to stand up for what you believe but also helps give perspective on external situations and opinions outside of your control. It's not always comfortable and in many instances, it is downright scary. Yet, instead of searching for the meaning of life, you will be authentically living it.

Too often we put limits on ourselves, creating boundaries around what we believe we are capable of. We immerse ourselves in a fixed mindset and make every excuse along the way. "I'm too old. I'm too young. I'm too tired. I'm too shy. I'm too weak. I'm not smart enough. I'm not pretty enough. I'm not rich enough. I'm not a good enough athlete..." Bullsh*t! If there is one TRUTH that I have learned in life, it's that you get out what you put in. The question then becomes, are you willing to put in the work to challenge yourself to live your authentic life? Are you willing to say, 'f*ck the result' while completely embracing everything the process has to offer? It's not always that easy to say f*ck it...

*We need to say f*ck it in order to do things we don't think we want to do...*

*We need to say f*ck it because something tragic has happened in our life...*

*We need to say f*ck it and stand by our beliefs...*

*We need to say f*ck it and try to understand somebody else's...*

*We need to say f*ck it to make very difficult life decisions...*

*We need to say f*ck it because sometimes those difficult life decisions we made didn't work out how we thought they would...*

*We need to say f*ck it if we are going to attempt to do anything outside of our comfort zone...*

*We need to say f*ck it (or them) when somebody tells you NO...*

*We need to say f*ck it to attempt something we don't believe we are capable of doing...*

*We need to say f*ck it when we fail...*

*We need to say f*ck it when we succeed...*

*We need to say f*ck it because in 100 years from now we will all be dead...*

Lastly, it's very simple...

If you want to do EPIC sh*t with your life, start with F*CK IT.

Chapter 1
Remember Your Roots

"The most important thing in the world is family and love."
-John Wooden

My mom (Judy) grew up in Torrance, California, 20 minutes outside of Los Angeles. She was the third of Glenn and Annabel Mullin's six children. The family consisted of one boy, "Uncle Mike," and five wild girls — Patty, Judy, Janie, Sally, and Peggy... aka "the skirts." Their dad, my grandfather, was a hard-working longshoreman who was killed during a surfing accident when my mom was 18. My Uncle Mike quickly became the rock of the family, working long hours on the docks, teaching, and coaching basketball all in an effort to keep the family afloat. My mom ran track at Banning High School (50% African American at the time) and still to this day claims to have been the fastest "white girl" in school. Truly a free spirit and Southern California beach girl at heart, her aspirations to "travel the world" led her to a 20-year flight attendant position with Western Airlines. She then spent 10 years being the most incredible and supportive house mom a kid could have ever possibly asked for. When my sister and I graduated high school, she began a real estate career that she continues to thrive in today. My entire life, my mom has been very active as a tennis player, marathoner, and skier. Even today, in her 70's, she charges the mountains!

While working as a flight attendant, my mom was based in San Francisco where she met my dad. The first of three kids from John and Claire Byrnes (brother Mike, sister Claudia), he was born in San Francisco while his father was overseas serving in the army. My dad grew up playing hoops but athletics were secondary to the aspiring saxophonist. Both my dad and his brother Mike dominated the local music scene playing wherever and whenever they could get an audience. Uncle Mike eventually went on to play keyboard with the legendary Carlos Santana for years.

My great grandparents migrated from Ireland. At the time of my Dad's high school graduation, there wasn't a Byrnes in our immediate family that had gone to college. After the graduation ceremony, my grandfather insisted that my Dad join him in the sheet metal industry. Instead, my Dad decided to join the National Guard and was immediately deployed during the Watts riots. When he returned home, he made the very difficult decision to go against his father's will and go where no Byrnes had gone before - college. To his father, the idea of having to pay to do work was not easily grasped by somebody from an Irish immigrant family that had created their livelihood through intensive manual labor. Regardless, he enrolled at San Francisco State and, 4 years later, earned his Bachelor's degree. He then went on to earn an MBA and taught business courses for several years as he moved up through the ranks at Acousta-Lite (a global commercial ceiling & lighting company that was based in Redwood City, CA).

To pay for school, he originally started working in the warehouse of Acousta-Lite, driving forklifts and working graveyard shifts so he would be able to make his next tuition payment. Once he graduated, he moved into sales and eventually worked his way up the corporate ladder. When the longtime president stepped down, it was my dad who he handpicked to replace him.

How did a kid who was destined for a lifetime of hard labor become president/CEO and part owner of a global enterprise? I asked him that same question. His response? "I said f*ck it." He explained that the last thing he wanted to do was go against his dad's wishes but he knew in order for him to gain fulfillment in all arenas of his life he needed to create his own path.

My dad's ability to put in the necessary work while completely immersing himself in every step of the process allowed him to acquire an in-depth knowledge of the company from all angles. Most importantly, he knew how to communicate with everybody from the dudes in the warehouse to the top-level executives. The reward of running the company was simply a byproduct of him dedicating himself to each individual step along the way. Eventually, the company was sold and my dad transitioned into consulting and later built a successful real estate career in which he applied the same step-by-step principles. This was also the disciplined approach that earned him a 4th degree black belt in Kenpo Karate and allowed him to open a studio and teach karate for 20+ years.

Like all of us, my parents have not lived life without their flaws. For years, my mom thought she was Mario Andretti behind the wheel and my dad was personally responsible for keeping the Napa Valley wine industry thriving. Overall though, I was very fortunate to have a mom and dad set great examples as to how to live life. I realize that not everybody can say the same. Many people come from f*cked up backgrounds that they had absolutely no control over and are forced to find direction from other influencers in their lives.

Human Crash Test Dummy Life Lesson #1

The most important thing is to find a positive influence in your life that you are able to lean on. Then, do everything in your power to be that same positive influence for somebody else.

Understand that your words and actions are constantly setting the tone for the next generation. Hustle your ass off and commit to a lifetime of growth, learning, and educating. It's possible to go from the warehouse to the penthouse, but you have to stop at each floor along the way.

Chapter 2

March to The Beat of Your Own Drum

*"Do not go where the path may lead,
go instead where there is no path and leave a trail."*
-Ralph Waldo Emerson

January 31st, 1974, my sister Shea was born. Two years later, on the 16th of February, 1976, at Sequoia Hospital in Redwood City, CA, I was literally vacuumed out head first, joining the party. The first two years of my life we lived in San Carlos, a suburb of San Francisco 20 miles south of the city. While my memory of the time on Eaton Ave is vague, my mom still tells the story about when she got a phone call from family friends who found a towhead two-year-old riding a toy motorcycle more than a mile away from our house at 2 am. She still talks about the time I decided to climb a tree at the pre-school family party. It took the fire department and a double-extended ladder to get me down. Early on, my parents obviously realized they had their hands full.

We eventually moved a few miles southwest to a small town called Woodside. Think old, legitimate stagecoach town with generations of "cowboy" ancestors cohabiting with Silicon Valley's pioneers. It was quite the eclectic mix of people. The good thing was that I had more space to do stupid sh*t. I grew up on Old La Honda Road, known for its vast redwood trees and its steep incline that has made it an iconic Bay Area cycling "must ride." As a kid this was perfect for two reasons: 1) I could bomb down the road on anything with wheels — bike, skateboard, rollerblades, and even a make-shift soap box derby go-kart. 2) I could dress up in camouflage, hide in the trees, and smoke bikers and cars with water balloons. Before paintball days, my buddies and I would actually have BB gun wars with no face or eye protection. Our idea of being responsible was making above the shoulders off limits.

By the time my feet could reach the pedals of my dad's Yamaha motorcycle, nicknamed "The Yellow Banana," I was off. There wasn't a road or trail in Woodside I didn't navigate on either "The Yellow Banana" or while driving my dad's Ford Diesel F-250 truck. All accomplished by the ripe age of 13. A few reckless decisions did not come without consequence. I ended up in the hospital more than a few times — once after jumping from the second story of our garage, severely spraining both ankles, and again after sliding nearly 100 feet on asphalt and ripping several layers of skin off my leg, just about down to the bone. Then there was the time my partner in crime Eric Tallon and I flipped a go-kart and my ankle snapped.

As a father of three children now, I more than realize the magnitude of how over-the-top idiotic many of the things I did in my youth were. I also realize that some of those very same things created lasting memories which shaped my childhood and will stay with me for a lifetime. The greatest gift my parents gave me was the freedom to fail. From all of the failures throughout my childhood came the greatest lessons which have helped shape every one of my successes in life.

School at a young age was incredibly difficult. I started Ormandale School in Portola Valley for kindergarten and somehow made it through the 5th grade without getting expelled. Suspensions and after school yard work seemed to be part of the daily curriculum. The main problem was that I couldn't sit still long enough to make it through a class and I sure as hell couldn't keep my mouth shut. Yes, I get it, not much has changed. It got to the point where if I made it through a single day without getting kicked out of class, Mom was cooking Annabel's tacos (my favorite) as a reward that night. The school eventually ran an IQ test thinking a low score would be imminent and that I must have had some sort of learning disability. The exact opposite occurred; I scored in the 98th percentile of all 9-year-olds. I was eventually diagnosed with ADHD and prescribed the 1980s version of Adderall — coffee. At 9, I thought coffee tasted like sh*t so I was left to find a way to cope drug-free. The good thing about my form of ADHD is that I have always had an incredible ability to multitask. It's what allowed me to find a way to excel at school, on the athletic field, and now in the broadcasting world. Undoubtedly, when I was younger, it was a struggle. Over the years I have figured out a way to hyper-focus on the task at hand. I am literally sitting here right this moment peck typing my iPhone, watching the news, and Facetiming my kids on the iPad... all at the same time. The only way to make it work is to put your attention on the task at hand. My focus for the moment is typing, but when a story on the news peaks my interest, I will stop typing and focus my attention there. Then, if my kids ever answer the phone, that's where my full and undivided attention will go. It sounds a bit like a contradiction but in order to successfully multitask you have to stay present, attentive, and in the moment more than ever. I have figured out a way to use my hyper-focus abilities to my advantage.

Whether or not it was related to my ADHD, I wet the bed every night until I was 13 years old. I was absolutely terrified to go to sleepovers or overnight school field trips. The last thing I wanted was for somebody to find out and make fun of me for being a bedwetter. The anxiety I caused myself at an early age was overwhelming. Eventually, I came to grips with the situation and basically had to say f*ck it. I wasn't going to let wetting the bed dictate whether or not I was going to be able to sleep at a friend's house or go on a school trip. I simply became the most efficient washer and dryer operator in the world between the ages of 5 and 13.

Human Crash Test Dummy Life Lesson #2

Live your life and let kids live theirs. Letting them fall teaches them how to get their ass back up. Use what is perceived as your weakness and turn it into a positive. Also, make sure you don't let peeing the bed take away all of your fun!

Chapter 3
Root for The Home Team

"Keep the heart into everything."
-Ronnie Lott

From as early as I can remember, I would refuse to leave the house unless I was wearing a jersey or shirt with a number on it. When it came to participation in youth sports, there were very few that I didn't do. Football, basketball, baseball, soccer, tennis, karate, skateboarding, and surfing were the standard staples. As a kid growing up in the Bay Area during the 1980s, the 49ers and Giants were my world. Naturally, my earliest vivid memory as a child was January 10, 1982.

25 miles south of Candlestick Park in San Francisco, I was sitting on my dad's lap in the family room growing increasingly irritated. About 30 family members and friends had been glued to the television for the past 3 hours watching the San Francisco 49ers play in the NFC Championship Game against the Dallas Cowboys. San Francisco had the ball on their own 11-yard line trailing 27-21 with just a few minutes remaining. All I wanted was peace and quiet, but not surprisingly, my family would not shut up. I needed to get away. I needed space. This was not only the biggest moment in 49ers franchise history, this was the biggest moment of my life. I was 5.

I bolted to the only other room with a TV, my parents' bedroom. I then watched Joe Montana orchestrate a drive that put the 49ers on Dallas' 6-yard line with 58 seconds to go. I was so nervous I went for cover underneath the sheets on Mom and Dad's bed. I could not bear to watch. Then it happened... With my face firmly planted into the bed, I heard Vin Scully's legendary voice.

"For the upstart 49ers, they are 6 yards away from Pontiac..." Chills engulfed my body. "Montana... looking, looking..." I couldn't take it anymore. I needed to watch. I threw the covers off my head to see

Montana rolling to the right and blanketed by three Cowboy defenders including 49er nemesis Ed "Too Tall" Jones. Scully continued, "throwing to the end zone..." To this 5-year-old, it looked more like heaving the football in a desperate attempt to toss the ball away. I put my hands back over my face, barely peeking through my middle and index fingers. Then, as if Dwight Clark turned into Clark Kent, Superman flew out of nowhere. Scully uttered the words that will resonate with me for the rest of my life... "Clark caught it!"

I fired up out of the bed and ripped my shirt off, a move that would have made any European soccer player proud. I then began swinging it over my head as I screamed at the top of my lungs. I sprinted toward the family room to celebrate. Pandemonium had officially taken over Candlestick Park and the Byrnes household wasn't any different. I began to take a lap around the house throwing out high fives to whoever I ran into. I then saw Dad across the room pounding his chest. "E, E, E... Chest Bump, chest bump, chest bump!" I sprinted towards him and tossed a 'flying bump' that nearly knocked over the 4th degree Kenpo Karate Black Belt. Immediately I regained composure and motored back to the bedroom to kick the extra point with a decorative pillow that was shaped like a football, a ritual I had begun for each Ray Wershing kick. Just like the 49ers kicker, I would not look at the goal posts (my parents' headboard) as I lined up to strike the pillow that sat up nicely and did not require a holder. My kick was good... so was Wershing's. The 49ers were headed to Super Bowl XVI in Pontiac, Michigan.

In many ways, that was my introduction to life. I can vaguely remember certain things B.C. (Before Catch) but essentially every significant happening P.C. (Post Catch) is a clear memory in my life. The 49ers went on to beat the Bengals a couple weeks later, a dynasty was born and so was a lifelong 49ers fan. The next season, at 6 years old, I made my Candlestick Park debut. At that point in my life, I had been to Great America, Knott's Berry Farm, and the granddaddy of them all, Disneyland. Combine all 3 amusement parks and those experiences still didn't come close to the moment I walked through the swinging metal doors in lower section 22. The image of the fresh cut grass and painted red 49er end zones trumped meeting Goofy or any stupid teacup ride. As a matter of fact, if Mickey Mouse was there, I would have told him to kiss my ass.

Throughout the 80s, we had 2 season tickets to 49er games. More often than not it was my dad and I that headed to Candlestick on Sundays. We would take the Ford diesel F-250 truck and stop by Robert's Market on the way to load up on fresh cut meats, cokes, and red wine for the old man. When we got to "The Stick," the operation was simple: pull down the tailgate, fire up the charcoal BBQ, load up the meat, pop our bottles, and start chucking the football.

When we went inside, it wasn't exactly how you would envision a father and son watching a game together. We would both put on our headphones and listen to Joe Starky and Wayne Walker call the action on the radio. There was always plenty of time to reflect on the game during commercial breaks, halftime, and the ride home. After a 49er win, we would stop at Estrada's Restaurant in Daly City for their famous steaming tostada, a celebratory margarita for the old man, and a Shirley Temple for the kid. Throughout the years, Candlestick Park essentially became the centerpiece for significant events that in many ways defined a large part of my childhood.

I was there October 10, 1987 (NLCS Game 4 against the dreaded St. Louis Cardinals who the Giants and their fans absolutely despised). Mike Krukow went CG and Jeffrey Leonard went bridge to put the Giants ahead in the 5th. The "Hackman" then circled the bases with one flap down adding more fuel to the already intense rivalry.

I was there October 30, 1988. Steve Young had one of the most incredible runs by a quarterback in NFL history. Once everybody was on their feet during the run, Dad grabbed me and hoisted me on his shoulders just in time to see Young stumble into the end zone and score the game-winning touchdown against the Minnesota Vikings.

I was there October 9, 1989. Will Clark ended an epic battle with Mitch Williams by smoking a line drive single up the middle, clinching the Giants' first trip to the World Series since 1962. I understand why this would not make sense to most people, but I would not have traded my view from the nosebleeds in Section 62 for front row seats behind home plate.

I was there for the BB twirl in 1997. Fresh off an appearance in the College World Series and a summer spent in the Cape Cod Baseball League, I couldn't have asked for a better homecoming than a Giants/Dodgers series at "The Stick" with the NL West title on the line. To make sure we were able to get bleacher tickets, my boys and I arrived at Candlestick at 10 am for a 7 pm game. There are very few rivalries in sports that could match the electricity of a Giants/Dodgers matchup when both teams are relevant come late September. There was also something about Candlestick that seemed to make both the players and fans even more 'on edge.' I will never forget Barry Bonds hitting a ball so hard I can still remember hearing the echo through the metal seats below me. I imagine most people in the park followed the ball hit well over the right-field fence but for whatever reason, I never took my eyes off of Bonds. He stood at home plate to admire his work for a moment and then pulled off something I had never seen done on a baseball field — a pirouette! Shocked and going nuts celebrating with my fellow 'bleacher bums,' I actually slipped and fell back into the row of people behind me. Thankfully the fans caught me, then proceeded to body pass me halfway up the section as if we were at some sort of rock concert. #OnlyAtTheStick

I was there January 5, 2003. The 49ers fell behind 38-14 to the New York football Giants. The 49er quarterback Jeff Garcia then led a miraculous comeback with the 49ers eventually winning 39-38. I was playing for the Oakland A's at the time and told 49er/A's team photographer Michael Zagaris I would do anything to get onto the field for the game. "Z" man came up big. He got me a press pass and registered me as his assistant which basically granted me access well beyond a normal credentialed media member. I acted as "Z" man's shadow and carried his camera bag around the entire game, occasionally pretending as if I was snapping a couple shots myself. I'll never forget being inside the locker room and tunnel with the players right before the game. The entire 49er squad banging the walls and chanting as they walked toward the field. "We ready, we ready, we ready for Y'ALL." I just about dropped "Z" man's camera bag and charged the field with the team. After the game, as the stadium was going nuts, I found myself standing on the sideline next to my boyhood idol Ronnie Lott who was getting ready to do the postgame on TV. He looked at me with a huge smile on his face, slowly gazed around the entire stadium, then uttered one word... "Unbelievable!" Nothing more needed to be said. For the first time in my life, I was speechless.

I was there October 6, 2013. My final time at Candlestick Park. It was the Sunday night game against the Texans but for me it might as well have been a Wednesday daytime matinee against the Houston Astros in 1985, the year the Giants lost a franchise record 100 games. I wasn't there for the game. I was there for 'The Stick' and I was there to give my 3 young children the same experience my dad gave me 30 years earlier. I explained to my kids that the 49ers were going to get a new home next year and we are going to say goodbye to the old stadium that they are going to tear down. I purposely bought tickets in Section 62, the exact same seats I sat in, second row from the top on the aisle when Will Clark busted the Cubs' ass and sent the Giants to the '89 Series. I wasn't exactly sure how my kids, just 2, 3 and 4, were going to react but they stuffed their faces with cotton candy, rode the sugar high, and loved every minute of it. My girls kept dancing in the aisle and my boy would stand up on top of his chair, put both hands in the air, and scream "NOBODY" (a little trick Daddy taught him). After the game, my 4-year-old kept looking back at the stadium as we walked back to the car. Then when we drove out of the parking lot she began to cry. "What's wrong, Peanut?"

"Daddy, I don't want them to blow up the Candlestick!"

"Me neither, Peanut. Me neither." She wasn't the only one with tears in her eyes.

December 23, 2013. The final game at Candlestick Park. I was not there. I was at my home in Lake Tahoe watching the game in the living room with 30 of my family members who had come up for the Christmas holiday. As you could imagine the crowd was loud and I was growing increasingly irritated because my family would not shut up! I needed to get away. I needed my space. The game that seemed to be locked up took a turn for the worst. Atlanta scored late in the fourth quarter to make it a three-point game. The Falcons then recovered an onside kick and were on the doorstep of punching the football into the end zone and putting the 49ers' playoff hopes in serious jeopardy. More importantly, the send-off to the stadium that had given so many fans so many great memories was about to be closed out with one big kick in the nuts.

Then it happened. A deflected Matt Ryan pass ended up in the hands of 49ers linebacker Navarro Bowman. I sprung up off of the couch the same way I sprung up out of my parents' bed when I was 5 years old. I ripped off my jacket as Bowman crossed the 50. By the time he got into the end zone, my shirt was off and I was waving it above my head screaming at the top of my lungs. I then began a lap around the house, throwing out high fives to my wife, kids, mom, sister, aunts, uncles, and cousins. Unfortunately, Dad wasn't there this time for the chest bump; he had passed away 2 years earlier. Before I had time to get all nostalgic, I spotted my 2-year-old boy across the room. Just like his daddy and just like 'Great Pa,' his shirt was off as he was pounding his chest and screaming, "Daddy, Daddy, Daddy… Chest bump, chest bump, chest bump!" RIP Candlestick. I appreciate the generations of memories.

Human Crash Test Dummy Life Lesson #3

Scrap whatever obligation you may have and get your ass out to the ballpark. The bond that is created through shared experience with family and friends will last a lifetime. I feel like I have traveled to a lot of cool places and experienced a lot of cool sh*t, yet the authenticity of "The Stick" and my experiences there had as big of an impact as anything else in my life in defining who I am and what I value today.

The first personal autograph I ever received was from Ronnie Lott and very simply sums up the greatest lesson Candlestick Park ever taught me, "To Eric: Keep the heart into everything! Ronnie."

Chapter 4
Martial Arts is Life

"I fear not the man who has practiced 10,000 kicks once,
but I fear the man who has practiced 1 kick 10,000 times."
-Bruce Lee

My first love was Kenpo Karate. Under the tutelage of Larry Tatum and Ed Parker, at one point my dad was the 8th highest-ranking Kenpo Black Belt in the world. As a young boy, my father was my biggest influence. If he said it, I repeated it, if he wore it, I wanted to put it on, and if he did it, I damn well was going to do my best to do the exact same thing. Karate created a bond between the two of us that is hard to describe. He was my sensei; I was his student and his little buddy. He created his own studio and I became his shadow every step of the way. By the time I was 6 we were traveling every weekend to different karate competitions with the pinnacle event being the International Kenpo Karate Championship in Los Angeles. Trophies that were taller than I was began to stack up.

Yet the benefits of karate had nothing to do with winning trophies or learning advanced martial arts fighting strategies. The discipline, work ethic, and self-confidence I was taught was invaluable and still resonates with me in my everyday life. There is no other sport that I participated in as a kid that had a greater impact on the person I have become.

Today, the one sport that is mandatory for my three kids is karate. I basically look at it as if it is an extension of school. Eventually, I will let them decide if they want to keep going, but for now, it is not an option.

I kept competing at the highest level of karate until I was 12, and then the reality of an over-demanding school and athletic schedule took over. All of my friends were playing team sports, and I couldn't help but feel as if I was missing out. Ultimately, I decided to give up karate.

No doubt that must have been a dagger in my dad's heart, yet he never made it seem as if that was the case or even remotely questioned my decision. This is the exact reason why I will forever be indebted to both of my parents. They never once pushed me into doing anything I did not want to do and always supported and encouraged me in every one of my athletic pursuits and life ventures. They both understood the vital importance of letting my sister and I carve out our own paths in life. Their one rule when it came to athletics was: if you start a season, you finish a season. Quitting was not an option.

Human Crash Test Dummy Life Lesson #4

I don't care how old you are, it's never too early or too late to begin something new. If you are a parent, lead by example and give your kids every opportunity to follow in your footsteps. If you or your kids have not already been, get into a martial arts or basic self-defense program. The discipline and confidence obtained will carry over into every other sport and every other arena of your life. Ultimately, there is a time for children to make their own path. Let them go. The martial arts lessons will be ingrained; it's now up to both you and them to apply those lessons.

Chapter 5
Treat Each Day As If It Could Be Your Last

"When you arise each morning, think about what a precious privilege it is to be alive... to breathe, to think, to enjoy, to love."
-Marcus Aurelius

When I was 11 years old, my summer consisted of playing a full season of Little League Baseball and District 52 All-Stars. All the while, I was playing competitive tennis, which had me traveling throughout the entire state of California. There were days when I would finish a match, literally run off of the tennis court, Superman change into my baseball uniform, and get to the game just in time for first pitch. I loved every minute of it, but when I would have an off day from my structured activities, I enjoyed doing the normal unstructured sort of sh*t that kids usually do. I rode my bike, played commando in the woods, hit the skate ramp, or snuck out to Felt Lake (privately owned by Stanford and shut off to the public) to do crazy ass flips off the water tower. That summer I spent every spare minute I had with my best friend, Todd Wilbanks. We would ride our bikes together all over Woodside and Portola Valley, exploring new trails looking for crazy jumps and steep hills to bomb. If we didn't consider the jumps to be big enough, we would figure out a way to build them higher. Todd had two awesome older brothers, Matt and Doug, and a cute little sister, Wendy, that we would let hang out with us every now and again.

On a day I had a big tennis match, my mom was waiting for me as I came off of the court. I don't remember whether I won or lost or even the exact location of where the match was, but I remember the look on my mom's face and the crackle in her voice as if it was yesterday.

"Todd Wilbanks was killed today. He was riding his bike and got hit by a car."

I didn't know how to react. My defense mechanism and way of coping was to try to block it out. 11 years old is a volatile age to have to deal with any sort of tragic event, let alone the death of your best friend. Nothing in the world could have prepared me for this. My first thought was if I was with him that day, just as I was so many other days that summer, Todd would still be alive. For the past 30 years, I have passed the spot on Cañada Road where he was killed, usually while riding my bike. There has not been one time when I have passed that spot without feeling a rush of overwhelming emotions. I've cried, I've laughed, and I've cried and laughed at the same time. The one constant when I ride by that spot is Todd's presence — I have felt him there every time.

I still keep in contact with Wendy, who has had a very successful career in real estate, and I keep up with Matt & Doug through social media, who have beautiful families of their own now. It has been 30 years since Todd Wilbanks died, and there are certain memories that I have held on to that literally make it seem as if it was barely 30 days ago.

Human Crash Test Dummy Life Lesson #5

If you are fortunate to live long enough, f*cked up sh*t is going to happen throughout the course of your life. Be grateful for every minute that you get to spend on Earth. Be grateful for every opportunity you have to spend time with loved ones. We don't know when our time, or the time of those closest to us, will be up, so embrace each moment as if it may be the last.

Make sure to take a few minutes each day to reflect on everything in your life that you are thankful for. Recently, I have immersed myself in daily guided-meditations that have allowed me to really understand what it means to be in the present moment. We all live crazy hectic lives; slow down and embrace the NOW.

We cannot change the past, and the future is completely unknown. How we live our life in the present moment is the only thing we will ever have complete control of. Don't waste it; we don't know how long it will be here.

Chapter 6
Play Like Mac

"The important thing is to learn a lesson every time you lose. Life is a learning process and you have to try to learn what's best for you. Let me tell you, life is not fun when you're banging your head against a brick wall all the time."
-John McEnroe

Growing up, my mom and dad were both avid tennis players and my sister and I naturally followed suit. We typically would play at Alpine Hills Tennis & Swim Club in Portola Valley. Tennis during the 1980s was in its absolute heyday and Alpine Hills had a long-standing tradition of being the best club "team" in the Bay Area. It's tough to think about tennis as a team sport, but the program that legendary coach Chris Bradley had put together created an awesome team atmosphere. Year after year our teams brought home the "Gar Glenley Cup" state championship. Tennis was undoubtedly my passion. Eventually, I started competing with a group of badass elite players within the Northern California tennis world. Ironically, three of the dudes ended up playing at Stanford and one of the others, Cory Guy, also from Alpine Hills, was the #1 player at Santa Barbara. All 4 went on to play professionally. The issue with tennis was that it was one of the first sports that was considered a "specialty sport," basically meaning that even at a very young age, in order compete at a high level, a year-round commitment was mandatory. Once I reached that level, I had too many other interests to make that ultimate commitment.

Although my Wimbledon dreams crashed and burned by the time I was 14, much like karate, tennis provided me with a great athletic base and a kick-ass, no-prisoners style of play. It also provided me with a role model who eerily resembled who I was at that stage of my life – John McEnroe. Johnny Mac was a mess, but so was I.
I loved everything about him: the energy he played with, the way he questioned authority, and even his terrible temper. I loved the fact

that he acted like a 10-year-old crybaby; I loved that he played with his heart on his sleeve. While everyone else was appalled by his mannerisms and antics, I wanted to be him. His "I don't give a f*ck" attitude resonated deep inside me. On the court he wasn't there to make friends and neither was I. Johnny Mac not only shaped who I was on the court but he had an overwhelming influence on who I was as an athlete. Not only in tennis, but every sport I played. Just like Mac, I played with a fire that at times would give me an extreme edge over my opponent, yet at other times it would act as a severe detriment.

Human Crash Test Dummy Life Lesson #6

Sometimes in life, we have to make a difficult decision and give up something if we want to get something else. My decision to give up both karate and tennis at an ultra-competitive level allowed me to focus on football, basketball, and baseball. But it was karate and tennis that gave me the athletic foundation, and more importantly, the mental fortitude, to excel in the other sports.

Bottom Line: Play as many sports as possible and emulate the passion of John McEnroe in every one of them.

Chapter 7
Be an Entrepreneur

"Happiness is not in the mere possession of money; it lies in the joy of achievement, in the thrill of creative effort."
-Franklin D. Roosevelt

When I was in the 5th grade, without our parents knowing, I took a train to San Francisco with two of my best friends, Luke Clebsch and Bryan Sidensol. Sidensol and I eventually became roommates at UCLA. We quickly made our way around town, either on foot or jumping cable cars, eventually landing on Broadway in the middle of all of the Adult XXX rated stores and a plethora of Gentlemen's Clubs. Despite our best efforts as curious 11-year-olds to sneak into the strip shows, our imaginations were left wondering from the outside. We did manage to make our way into one of the XXX stores. Ever the entrepreneur that my businessman father ingrained in me at a young age, I spent my $20 allowance for the week on pens that had a woman dressed in a bikini on them. That was, of course, until you hit the top of the pen and the ballpoint came out and the bikini came off! I thought it was the greatest invention since electricity and felt the pens needed to be shared with the rest of the young men of Ormandale School in Portola Valley. My next day at school, I set up a shop in the bathroom during lunchtime. Within minutes I sold every one of the pens.

Just as I was planning my return trip to the city to restock the supply, I got called into the principal's office. To my surprise, when I walked in, both of my parents were in the office. The principal had called them that morning in a panic saying that they needed to come in immediately. He told them that I was selling illegal goods out of the bathroom during the lunch hour. Obviously frantic and fearing that I was selling drugs, my dad walked out of a board meeting to join my mom at school. When I walked in the principal had not yet told my parents exactly what I was selling, but he was holding one of my pens. Once I sat down he proceeded to tell my mom and dad that I had been selling the pen that he had in his hand. My dad then asked to take a look at it. After the principal handed it over, Dad intently studied the woman dawning the full bikini. He then hit the top of the pen and whoosh, bikini off! My dad's eyes instantly lit up. He then turned to me and gave me a hard stare before he turned back to the principal and asked how much I was selling the pen for. The principal indicated that I had sold the pens for $2 each. My dad then asked me how much I bought the pens for. I told him they cost me $1 a piece. My dad then stood up, reached into his pocket, and grabbed two $1 bills and tossed them on my lap. He then turned to the principal as he walked out of the room. "Seems like a pretty good deal to me!" He kept the pen.

Human Crash Test Dummy Life Lesson #7

Discipline your kids when necessary, but also have their back every chance you get. From that day forward, my relationship with my dad went to another level. I still got in plenty of trouble, but I also stayed out of a lot more because I didn't want to disappoint my parents. When I had kids, he passed on his favorite phrase he used to tell people all of the time, "Make sure you catch your kids doing something RIGHT."

Chapter 8
Change a Kid's Life

"The delicate balance of mentoring someone is not creating them in your own image, but giving them the opportunity to create themselves."
-Steven Spielberg

Considering the ADHD, the temper, and the rebellious attitude inherently ingrained within me, I was a good kid, but I needed direction. There was only so much my parents could do, and them giving me a long leash, believe it or not, probably prevented me from going over the edge. I was a punk ass 9-year-old kid who tried out for Alpine Little League "Majors" that generally was reserved for mainly 11-12 year olds. I remember talking to all the coaches at the tryout except one, Coach Tom Sutter from Peninsula Building Materials, aka "Morey's." I had heard the horror stories about him, and quite frankly, he scared the sh*t out of me and just about everyone else involved with the league. The mere sight of the robust man with the tan skin, white hair, and mirrored aviators absolutely freaked me out. He dressed in all black, his language was choice, and his voice would boom to such a high level that oftentimes it could be heard through the hills that set the backdrop of Ford Field in Portola Valley. "You Bet" was his famous catchphrase. For years, parents tried to get him removed from the league because he was "too hard" on the kids or he made them practice "too much." To top off the mystique of the man and the team, Morey's wore pinstripes and never lost. If there is such a thing as a dynasty in Little League Baseball, "Morey's" was it and Tom Sutter was the reason why.

A week later, when my mom told me that my new Little League coach was at the door, forgive me if I ran and hid in my room when I saw who it was.

The reality of the situation is that Tom Sutter was the greatest coach I ever had. Was he a disciplinarian? Of course. Was his choice of words and tone a bit overwhelming for 9 to 12-year-old boys? Sure.

Did we stretch the rules of how often we were supposed to practice? Probably. Did he once make me throw the ball to Nathan Anderson after the game 100 times in a row because I botched a double play? "You Bet." But he was exactly what a 9 year old with extreme ADHD and an overwhelming desire to be the best needed. People talk all the time about the 4-year period of their life in which they became a man. Often times it's usually high school or college. For me, it was 9 to 12 years old on the Little League diamond. Coach Sutter was a drill sergeant, a father figure, and a friend all at the same time. We lost one game in 4 years. Shockingly, in a town that was more known for geeky kids with high test scores, three of us that played on that one Alpine Little League team went on to play professional baseball. Two in the Major Leagues.

Coach Sutter helped me develop as a baseball player and as a person. He gave me a vision of the future, which for the first time in my life, emphasized the importance of education. Both of Coach Sutter's kids had attended St. Francis High School, the perennial powerhouse in high school athletics in the greater San Francisco Bay Area. By the time I was 12 that was the only school I wanted to go to. The issue? I was not a good student. It was tough enough for me to stay in the classroom without being sent to the principal's office, let alone excel academically.

I have always been a person with an incredible ability to apply myself and focus if there is something I am interested in or if I had a vision of something I wanted. It became very simple — I wanted to go to St. Francis, so I became interested in school. By no means was I a great student, but all of a sudden, I found myself making it through entire days without having to visit the principal. (Hey, I had to start somewhere!) Then in the 6th grade, we began to switch classrooms and teachers for whatever subject was being taught. At that point, I completely changed as a student. There was no doubt the constant change of scenery catered to my ADHD and had an incredible impact on my ability to focus. Whatever it was, all of a sudden I made school a competition. In math class, I wanted to solve the equation correctly before anybody else. In English class, I always wanted to get the highest grade on my essay. In history, I wanted to learn more than you, then tell you intricate details about the life and legacy of our 25th President, William McKinley. I also had an incredible desire to learn Spanish. There was nothing better than coming home and answering my mom's pertinent questions in a language she could not understand. I thought science sucked, but what young, curious kid did not like cutting open dead animals and dissecting their insides?

The desire to win, the desire to be the best, and my thirst for competition is what drove me as a kid. So just like karate, tennis, baseball, football, basketball, soccer, etc., school became a game, and miraculously, I became an "A" student. I am sure a lot of people, including every teacher I had leading up to my Junior High School years, truly felt as if hell had frozen over.

Without Tom Sutter in my life, I am not sure where I would be today. He taught me life principles and discipline on a baseball field, which eventually carried over to every other aspect of my life.

Human Crash Test Dummy Life Lesson #8

Be a coach, be a mentor, and change a kid's life. There is no need to act like their parent or be their best friend, but you can greatly influence a kid's life by teaching them the essence of hard work and holding them accountable for their actions. At some point, all kids need to hear an influential voice other than their parents... Be that voice.

Chapter 9
Invest in the Future

"If you want your children to be intelligent, read them fairy tales. If you want them to be more intelligent, read them more fairy tales."
-Albert Einstein

Even though my dad never played baseball, he chucked enough ninja stars that he easily figured out a way to throw me batting practice. Every free minute I could get of his time, we would head down to take whacks at the Portola Valley Town Center. By the time I was 12, my dad realized that as much as I loved to hit and as hard and as often as I wanted him to throw, his arm was destined to fall off. Between the endless pre-game trips to Malibu Grand Prix with my mom, and the abuse I put on my dad's arm, my parents got smart. On my 13th birthday, after a traditional French toast breakfast on the special red birthday plate, Mom and Dad explained that they had gotten me a new friend for my birthday. "He is waiting for you down by the shed. His name is Mike." They both could not get enough of themselves as they began hysterically laughing. Obviously, something was up, but I wasn't exactly sure what was going on. My dad then led me to the backyard where we walked down to an area not visible from the house. Sitting there was a big, blue iron-pitching machine. Its name... "Iron Mike!"

I am not sure if my parents or I realized it, but the day I met "Iron Mike" was the day I became a big leaguer. Over the course of the next 4 years, I lived in that batting cage. Year-round, rain or shine, I would wake up and hit before school then come home and continue to take hacks until the last ray of sunlight was gone. From the get-go, I cranked it up to 90 mph. At first, I could not touch it; I had no chance. I then slowly began making contact and eventually got the timing down. Before long, I was absolutely crushing balls.

When people talk about being in "the zone," they usually speak of how the game seems like it is in slow motion. After spending countless hours and seeing thousands of 90 mph pitches, the ball firing out of the big blue machine seemingly slowed down to a snail's crawl. Then, when I was a sophomore in high school and got called up to the varsity, I faced Serra High School's first-round draft pick, Dan Serafini, throwing 94 mph from the left side. Most of the other juniors and seniors didn't have a shot against him, yet I ended up hitting three BULLETS back up the middle. I don't even think I had hair on my balls yet, but I could RAKE 94 mph like I was a 10-year, grizzled Major League veteran. Of course, there was an element of natural talent involved, but I didn't have any more talent than other top players in the league. I just found an efficient way to work and will my way to be the best. It's that simple.

Based on the fact that I ended up getting college paid for, my parents would always say "Iron Mike" was the best investment they ever made. I will undoubtedly tell you the single day that helped me become a Major Leaguer more than any other day in my life was the day Mike arrived.

Human Crash Test Dummy Life Lesson #9

Give your children every opportunity possible to succeed. That doesn't mean they need a swing coach at seven years old, but it does mean that you provide an environment that allows them to work on their craft. At the same time, make sure you provide yourself with the right environment that will enable you to get the most out of whatever your passion is. Find a way to create a workspace that will encourage you and your kids to GO GET IT.

Be there for support along the way, but always remember that whether or not your kid will be great at something ultimately is not up to you — it's up to them. It's up to them how much they love to work and how big of a fairy tale they believe they can live.

Chapter 10
Make Failure the Path to Growth

"You build on failure. You use it as a stepping stone. Close the door on the past. You don't try to forget the mistakes, but you don't dwell on it. You don't let it have any of your energy, or any of your time, or any of your space."
-Johnny Cash

Although I had become a much better student, I still had an adventurous side that unquestionably walked the fine line of reckless. On a typical weekend night in the 8th grade, Bryan Sidensol came over to spend the night. We had found out the girls in our class were having a "tent sleepover" at Katie Dismyer's house and that obviously meant one thing — we wanted to crash the party. I asked my dad if it would be okay if we rode our bikes down to Katie's to "scare the girls." He gave it some serious thought, then eventually realized how furious he would be if a group of punk boys snuck up on my sister and her friends in a similar situation. A firm "NO" was the final answer. Very suspiciously, I did not argue and told my parents that we were going to bed. The two of us went straight to my room and very strategically planned our escape. The more time we waited for my parents to go to bed, the more elaborate our plan became. I was 13 years old at the time and my sister was 15. She was just a few weeks away from getting her driver's license, and with the help of my parents, she had already purchased her first car, a Nissan Pulsar. My dad had made the deal with us when we were younger that whatever money we would be able to save for a car, he would match. So after a lifetime of working, my sister's prized new possession sat in our driveway, just days away from her being able to drive. My sister was spending the night at a friend's house, so once my parents went to bed, the temptation was too sweet to pass up. The two of us decided that the new car needed a test drive and where better to go than Katie Dismyer's house? I quietly grabbed the keys in the kitchen, and then we snuck out the window of my bedroom. I fired up the Pulsar, which was parked far enough away that I believed there was no chance my parents could hear the car start or us drive away. A few hours later, after some innocent fun of shaking the tent from the outside and freaking the girls out, we returned home. I flawlessly delivered my sister's car back to the exact spot and angle it was parked before. We then climbed back through my bedroom window, and then quietly celebrated as if we had just won Game 7 of the World Series. We had a vision, we had a plan, and we executed it without any hiccups. The sense of pride and joy was overwhelming.

After a while, we finally calmed down and got ready to go to sleep. Sidensol was the first to open the covers of his bed that we had so brilliantly stuffed with pillows before we left. All of a sudden, Sidensol looked up as if he had just seen a ghost. It wasn't a ghost, but it might as well have been. It was a life-sized version of the Easter Bunny lying in his bed. I then frantically whipped the covers off of my bed, which we had perfectly stuffed as well. Lying there was a life-sized version of Santa Clause, which had been in our family for years. There was a note on Santa Clause's mouth that read, "YOU LIED, YOU STOLE, YOU'RE CAUGHT, YOU'RE GROUNDED!"

I could deal with whatever wrath was coming my way. I knew I f*cked up, and it obviously wasn't the first time. My larger concern was with Sidensol. Once his parents found out that we stole my sister's car and used it to go scare a bunch of 8th grade girls, there was no way they would ever let him hang out with me again. Because I was a cocky, borderline arrogant little prick at times, I didn't have a ton of friends. Not being able to hang out with Sidensol would be detrimental. In an agreement to not tell Sidensol's parents, we negotiated a deal with my dad. Both of us would have to complete 20 hours of manual labor, either around the house with yard work or in the warehouse of Acousta-Lite, my dad's business. We had 1 month to complete the 20 hours. Every weekend for the next 4 weeks, we worked several hours a day, eventually completing our commitment and undoubtedly learning our lesson. As long of a leash that my parents gave me, there was absolutely no reason to sneak around and try to deceive them. I was taught at a very young age that family is the most important thing in the world, and there is absolutely nobody who will understand and forgive the way your family will, so long as you are honest. My dad's favorite line that is still applicable in just about every aspect of my life was "let your behavior reflect your commitment." Ironically, Sidensol continued to work for my dad well after he completed his 20 hours of service. He eventually moved from the warehouse into the sales division at Acousta-Lite, which helped shape his career as a successful baseball product business owner.

We obviously f*cked up, but the key was that we both learned from our mistake of being dishonest. The punishment eventually became an opportunity for Sidensol, and he and my dad built a relationship that lasted a lifetime.

Human Crash Test Dummy Life Lesson #10

Don't ever strive to fail, but when it happens, because it will, learn from your mistakes. So long as you are able to learn the valuable lessons failure has to offer, those life mishaps have the potential to become stepping-stones to new opportunities. Ultimately, long-term sustained growth depends 100% on your ability to accept responsibility for your actions and properly react to both your minor and massive f*ck-ups.

Chapter 11
Be Humble or Get Humbled

"Real genius is nothing else but the supernatural virtue
of humility in the domain of thought."
-Simone Weil

My sister helped pave the way 2 years before, but when I got into St. Francis, the joy was overwhelming. Not necessarily for me, who always believed it would happen, but for my parents who, just a few years earlier, were told I needed to be put into a school with other juvenile delinquents who constantly undermined authority. As one would expect, the transition to St. Francis was difficult. Think about it... I was a 14-year-old kid going through puberty who came from a liberal, public school system to a very conservative, private Catholic institution. My 8th grade graduating class had 40 kids in it. My freshman class had 400. Before St. Francis, my wardrobe consisted of shorts and t-shirts. After St. Francis, it seemed like the only things I had in my closet were the mandatory khaki pants and polo shirts. Athletically, I went from being the best athlete in my school to wondering if I was going to be able to make a team.

Freshman football was my first taste of reality when there were 100 guys at the tryout. Half got cut, leaving the number at 50. I had no experience playing organized tackle football and considered myself very fortunate to be one of the 50 guys that made the team. Then, of course, there were only 11 who could be on the field at the same time. The extent of my freshman football contribution essentially consisted of relaying in the play calls. I was the wide receiver who would rotate with two other guys bringing the play call to the QB. On defense, I was part of the 3-man rover squad that brought the defensive alignment to the linebacker. As a "starting" wide receiver in a veer/option offense, I caught one pass all year. On defense, I played about one down per defensive series. Needless to say, my first experience with high school football didn't go exactly how I had envisioned it. I did realize that this was St. Francis. Here were many of the best athletes in the Bay Area. It is what I asked for and it is what I got. For the first time in my life, though, I began to doubt whether or not I was a good enough athlete to compete with St. Francis' best.

In most arenas in life, you are not going to have the most experience, and you are not going to be the best. I had never played tackle football, and I was a pimple-faced freshman going through an awkward physical time. The only thing you can do is bust your ass, learn as much as possible, and strive to be your best. A phrase we use in baseball all the time is, "there are those who are humble and those who will be humbled." I was humbled.

Human Crash Test Dummy Life Lesson #11

To get humbled is a good thing. It allows us to look at our situation from an outside perspective and lets us evaluate where we are and what we have to do to get to where we want to go. Being humbled does NOT mean that you have a defeatist mindset. A humbled person has a realistic mindset of where they are right now with an ultimate vision of growth, work, and opportunity.

Make sure to always evaluate without judgment. Then, figure out exactly what it is going to take to get you to where you want to go. After that, it's up to you to DO THE WORK.

Chapter 12
Names Don't Matter... People Do

"What's in a name?
That which we call a rose by any other name would smell as sweet."
-William Shakespeare

After football season, I had a very difficult decision whether or not I was going to play basketball. Hoops was definitely a love of mine, and still to this day, I would argue that the 56 points I scored in an 8th grade basketball game would rank as the greatest accomplishment of my athletic career. Ultimately, my decision was made based on the fact that I felt baseball was my better sport and the basketball season would run several weeks into the start of baseball. Not to mention, if I wanted to make the team, and play more than a few courtesy innings, I needed to get to work and prepare for the upcoming season. Baseball tryouts brought out nearly 50 aspiring freshmen. Only 15 would make the team. The tryout started off with playing catch for 10 minutes, five ground balls, five fly balls, and then five pitches to hit off of a pitching machine. I froze up and took the first one; I swung and missed at the second, swung and missed at third, popped up the fourth, then hit a chopper on the fifth. I figured that was the first-round and we would no doubt get some more pitches to hit.

I'll never forget freshman baseball coach Dave Fererra hollering out after I took my feeble cuts, "That's it, you can go home now. The list will be posted tomorrow at 8 am on the south entrance door to Raskob Gym." That's it? That's all? You have got to be kidding me!!! There are 50 dudes out here and that's how you freaking knuckleheads are going to make a decision? I was doomed. I had no chance.

I hopped in Mom's WGN4KID license plated station wagon (no, that's not a joke) and I started to cry like a 2 year old. All of my hopes and dreams of playing baseball at St. Francis just went by the wayside with five stupid-ass pitches. I wanted out, and I wanted out now. The competition was too much, the athletes too good, and the selection process too ridiculous. "Drive me to Woodside High School (the public school in the area), Mom. I didn't make it." Once the tears stopped I came around to tell her the actual team would not be posted until the morning, but my fate was sealed. I agreed to at least wait until the morning to make sure my name was not on the list, but I was so sure that I actually left all of my St. Francis books at home.

My sister had her license, and on a normal morning, I would have ridden to school with her. But this was not a normal morning. I discussed with my parents the night before, and they both agreed to let me transfer immediately if I did not make the team. When we pulled up to the backside of the gym at 7:58 am, the list was not posted. Then came Coach Fererra with the white paper in hand with 15 names written in blue sharpie. An entire heard of insanely insecure freshman boys anxiously awaited their fate. I stayed toward the back and could only see first names from where I was standing. Matt, Kenny, Ryan, Brendan, Zack... I continued to scour the list all the way to the 15th name, Chris. No Eric. I had already prepared myself for this moment. I was going to be OK.

This was my way out of St. Francis. This was my chance to get back to a public school where I didn't have to wear khakis and a dumb-ass collared shirt every day. I was now going to be able to hang out with all my friends I went to grade school with. The athletic competition would not be the same, but at this point, that didn't matter to me anymore. I was going to get an opportunity to play, and that was the only thing that I cared about. I was going to be a Woodside Wildcat, and I was pumped. I would walk back to the WGN4KID with my head held high and my chest out, but first, there was just one last piece of unfinished business I needed to take care of. I wanted to look at the 15 names, so I could remember who those guys were, and use them as motivation throughout the course of my entire pursuit toward playing in the Major Leagues. Matt Doyle, Kenny Fluharty, Brendan Royer, Zack Walz, Ryan Tollner. All the way down to the last name... Chris Byrnes... "Who?" We were in the spring quarter now, and I sure as hell would have known had there been another Byrnes in the freshman class or even at the school for that matter. Could they have screwed up my first name? Could they have screwed up somebody else's last name? Coach Fererra was still in sight. I sprinted towards him, 100 yards away, as he headed to the track to get his 8 am P.E. class going. "Coach Fererra!" I screamed storming up behind him; he swiftly turned around... "What can I do for you, Chris?"

Human Crash Test Dummy Life Lesson #12

Even if the odds are stacked against you, focus on what is in your control. Numbers can be intimidating, but the more you focus on the odds, the less you are able to focus on the task. Commit to the process and eventually they will learn your name.

Chapter 13
Embrace the Obstacle

*"The only use of an obstacle is to be overcome. All that an obstacle does
with brave men is not to frighten them but to challenge them."*
-Woodrow Wilson

I eventually won the Co-MVP award of the freshman baseball team.
The competition did not get any easier as I went into my sophomore
year. There were several sophomores that were invited to work out
with the varsity team once practice started; I was not one of them.
Getting ready for the JV season on my own, I was taking ground balls
with the Royer twins, Brendan and Brian, two legendary Redwood City
athletes that had gone to St. Francis but transferred to Woodside
High School. After fielding a ball, I was walking back to my position
when I heard Brian scream "heads up!" I immediately put my hands
on the back of my head and then BAM!!! The intended ground ball to
Brendan ended up being a line drive directly at my dome. The ball
broke my right hand.

Before the season, the goal was to make the varsity team. Even
though the plan as to how I was going to make the team needed to
change, the goal did not. Over the course of the next several weeks, I
worked my ass off doing anything I could do to stay ready. Six weeks
later, after plenty of one-handed drills, I was able to start the season
with the junior varsity team.

After just a few JV games, I got called up to the varsity team for the
Knights of Columbus Easter tournament held at the College of San
Mateo. The "plan" was that I was supposed to be up with the varsity
team only for the tournament, but after I hit the first pitch I saw off
the right-center field wall, and endeared myself to Chris Bradford, St.
Francis' legendary varsity baseball coach, the "plan" changed. I
ended the day 2-2 with two doubles and two walks. The next 2 games
of the tournament I did not make an out. After the final game, Coach

Bradford informed me that I would be staying with varsity for the rest of the season.

I was so excited to tell my family the good news that I raced home in my Ford Bronco as fast as possible. When I got off of the exit to go to my house, I was pulled over by a California Highway Patrolman. Apparently, I was going 30 mph over the speed limit and made an "unsafe lane change." According to the officer, the duo was considered criminal reckless driving. The officer had me step out and put my hands on the roof of the car. While I was being frisked, he pulled batting gloves and some Bazooka bubble gum out of my back pocket. I was then cuffed and stuffed into the back of the police car, all while wearing my St. Francis baseball uniform. I was nervously sitting in the back of the police car trying to figure out whether I should be laughing or crying. The officer then asked why I was in such a hurry.

"I just made the varsity baseball team, sir. I was trying to get home as quickly as possible to tell my family." To which the officer replied, "Tough to relay that information from behind bars." He then proceeded to lecture me on the dangers of speeding for the next 10 minutes, explaining the harm I was not only putting myself in but other drivers as well. Eventually, he pulled me out of the back seat, took the handcuffs off and said, "Congratulations on making the varsity team, kid. Drive home safely."

Human Crash Test Dummy Life Lesson #13

Just because you may be dealing with an injury does not mean you have to stop working. Challenge yourself to find other ways to improve. Work on whatever you are capable of working on and eventually, when you are back at full strength, you will be better than before. Whatever the "plan" may be, always remember you have the ability to force somebody to alter their plan by outperforming expectations. What many perceive as an obstacle can undoubtedly be a major opportunity for learning and growth. Lastly, don't drive like a dumb ass no matter how excited you are.

Chapter 14
Just Because You Hear Does Not Mean You Have To Listen

"Any fool can criticize, condemn, and complain - and most fools do."
-Benjamin Franklin

I spent the summer in between my sophomore and junior year playing endless amounts of baseball and hanging with the Royer twins. The 3 of us played on the Peninsula Mets, a traveling baseball team comprised of many of the Bay Area's best 16 year olds. Travel ball teams at that time were very rare and essentially were reserved for the very best and most dedicated players in the area. We spent the summer playing whoever, wherever, and whenever we could find competition. Playing for the Mets was no doubt my first taste of what professional baseball would be like. We traveled from one obscure town to another all throughout the state of California. Playing for 2 epic dudes in their own right, Gary Tagliafico and Jerry Berkson, we played over 75 games in a 3-month period, ultimately qualifying for the Junior Olympics.

Playing that many games, we developed a serious archrival with the dreaded Folsom Flames. The Flames were another one of the few travel teams in Northern California, and we had probably played them at least 15 times throughout the course of the season. Tension had been building between the 2 teams for a while, and it finally came to a head. From the 1st inning, our starting pitcher was getting harassed by the Flames' bench. Basic sh*t talking was pretty common, but you could almost sense a perfect storm brewing. Our pitcher was struggling mightily, and the verbal jabs the Flames were chucking were the gasoline on the fire. Eventually, he was taken out of the game. He then walked back to the dugout, put down his glove, grabbed a drink of water, then calmly headed straight over to the Flames' dugout and punched the first dude he saw.

Mayhem then erupted as just about every player on both sides began throwing punches. In all my years of playing baseball, I was involved in a few other bench-clearing melees, but nothing ever like this. This made the infamous Braves/Padres brawl in 1984 look like a tea party. It eerily resembled a scene out of *Gangs of New York*. Everybody had broken off and was individually fighting one another in different areas of the field. When I realized what was going on, I came charging in from right field and headed to where the majority of the skirmishes were taking place in front of the first base dugout. While in the process of pulling one of the Flames players off of one of our Mets guys, I was punched in the back of the head. I quickly turned around, pinned the dude on the ground, and began playing pepper with his face. The fight was eventually broken up by parents, police officers, and the sirens of an ambulance. The kid that was originally punched by our pitcher fell back and hit his head on the concrete step of the dugout; he was out cold. He spent significant time in the hospital but eventually made a full recovery. Our pitcher who began the brawl was one of the first visitors to the hospital, and needless to say, he was incredibly remorseful. Nonetheless, our season was over. We were officially disqualified from the Junior Olympics.

This entire debacle started over dumb ass name-calling. Get control of your emotions and understand that your opponent is trying to get into your head and rob you of your inner peace by talking sh*t. When you react, all you are doing is stooping to their level and opening up an opportunity for disaster.

Human Crash Test Dummy Life Lesson #14

Always stay committed to your plan by focusing on the work you have to do to be successful. Negative outside noise will always be there, and oftentimes, no matter what you do, you are forced to hear it. Yet, it is solely up to us whether or not we want to listen.

Chapter 15
STOP. Don't Quit!

"It always seems impossible until it's done."
–Nelson Mandela

The summer playing for the Peninsula Mets was a big-time growing up experience for me in a lot of ways. I was driving for the first time, working construction in the mornings, and playing baseball in the afternoons. It was also the summer when I began chewing tobacco regularly for the first time. Most people have the story of their first dip where they ended up getting the spins, swallowing the spit, then puking their brains out. For me, that was not the case. Not even close. As a matter of fact, when I put in my first dip, I felt a euphoric feeling throughout my entire body. I experienced a tingling sensation that had me wanting more immediately. As a kid who was naturally wound very tight, the relaxed, calm, and focused feeling created by the large amounts of nicotine was awesome in every sense of the word. One dip and I was hooked. By the time I got to college, chewing tobacco had become a major part of my life.

Then there was the harsh reality surrounding the death of Tony Gwynn.

As we continue to celebrate the life and legacy of Tony Gwynn years after his death, I can't help but think that we lost one of the greatest players, and most brilliant minds, that ever played the game way too soon. The reality of the situation is that Tony Gwynn died from oral cancer most likely caused by years of chewing tobacco. On the surface, it makes one believe that Gwynn's death very easily could have been prevented. Habitually, I chewed tobacco for nearly 15 years. I can tell you with great conviction, there would have been nothing easy about it.

I took my first chew of Red Man tobacco when I was 12 years old. I took my first dip of Copenhagen when I was 16. By the time I was 22 and playing professional baseball, I began chewing nearly a can a day. When I woke up in the morning, I would have a cup of coffee, then put in a dip. After breakfast, I would put in a dip. After my workout, I would put in a dip. After lunch, I would put in a dip. When I got to the ballpark, I would put in a dip. During batting practice, I would put in a dip. When the game started, I would put in a dip. After each time at bat, I would put in a dip. On the way home from the ballpark, I would put in a dip.

What started as something I would do to pass time turned into a full-blown addiction. To this day, chewing tobacco is the only thing I have ever encountered in my life that I had absolutely no control over. In a sense, I was helpless.

Throughout the course of my entire baseball career, MLB did a very nice job of warning players about the dangers of smokeless tobacco. During spring training every year, it was mandatory for all players to watch a video that detailed the harsh reality of all of the health risks associated with chewing tobacco. I didn't quit.

My dentist and lifelong family friend, Len Vinci, still sends me articles and personally lectured me on several occasions about chewing tobacco. I didn't quit.

Joe Garagiola, whom I had as much respect for as anybody in baseball, led a public charge against chewing tobacco for years. He pulled me aside several times when I was with the Diamondbacks encouraging me to give up the potentially deadly habit. I didn't quit.

With tears in her eyes, my own mother pleaded for me to stop. I didn't quit.

At no point was I dumb enough to think that I was invincible or immune to the potential dangers. I didn't quit because I couldn't. Copenhagen had become such a big part of my life. Like air, food, or water, I felt like I needed chewing tobacco to survive. I never denied my addiction; it just took me a while until I finally did something about it.

March 2, 2011, my dad unexpectedly passed away. Over the course of the following weeks, my chewing tobacco use hit an all-time high. After the service on St. Patrick's Day, March 17th, 2011, I sat back in a lounge chair in my backyard, looked up to the stars, then fired in the fattest pinch of Copenhagen I could possibly fit into my mouth. That was the last dip that I ever took.

Why then? I don't exactly know. I didn't plan for it to be. I didn't tell anybody I was going to stop or that I even wanted to stop. I just did. At the time, I had a 2 year old, a 1 year old, and my wife was pregnant with our third child. I do know that I realized I was no longer living life just for myself. Sometimes it takes a tragic event in somebody's life for that person to make a major, life-altering decision. Unfortunately, I had to deal with the tragic event. Fortunately, I finally made the life-altering decision.

It has been years since I last took a dip of Copenhagen. There is not a single day that goes by that I don't think about it. Every time I finish a meal, take a long drive, step on a golf course or a baseball field, it is on my mind. I am not a quitter. I never have been, and I never will be. I simply have stopped. I am not going to chew tobacco today. Day-by-day, hour-by-hour, minute-by-minute is the only way I have been able to get through the most difficult battle of my entire life.

I am not writing this as a PSA to try to get people to stop chewing tobacco because I know it's not possible. There is nothing I or anyone else can say or do that will get you to stop. I am simply telling you my experience with one of the most addictive and deadly vices in the world. Take it however you want. Ultimately, it is your decision; ultimately, it is your life.

That said, here is what worked for me: Stop. Don't quit!

Quitting sounds so permanent. Don't quit. Just stop. The first step is wanting to stop; the second step is finding an alternative. Whatever the habit is, it becomes so much a part of our daily routine that we feel like we need it as much as food or water. So when we stop doing something, we will continue to go back to it unless we have something else to go to fill that void. FILL THE VOID.

I started replacing my dips with Nicorette gum. Typically, I would have 4 to 6 pieces of gum a day, and I would put the gum in my mouth the same way I would put in a dip. I would chew it about 10 times, and then pack it away between my cheek and gums. Every 10 minutes or so I would give it another 10 chews and pack it away again. Each piece would last me about an hour.

Eventually, the Nicorette gum caused such severe heartburn that I couldn't do it anymore. I weaned myself down to about a piece or two a day. Then when Tony Gwynn passed away, I said F*CK IT. I was done with nicotine altogether. To this day, I still chew mints constantly through the course of the day and hold whatever mint I am chewing in the exact same spot I would put my dips.

Other times, I attempted to quit with marginal success by limiting the number of dips I would have in a day. At my peak, I took about 6 to 8 dips a day, so I would try to lower that to 4 to 6, then 2 to 4, then 1 to 2. This strategy worked, but ultimately, the number would blow back up after an 0-4 day at the plate or a long night partying.

Another way to stop that worked well for friends of mine is through hypnosis. I used hypnosis throughout the course of my career but never to try to quit dipping. Knowing the effect that hypnosis had on my baseball career, I would highly recommend it to anybody.

Human Crash Test Dummy Life Lesson #15

We as human beings are creatures of habit. If you have a habit that you want to STOP, replace that habit with something else. I realize it may not seem possible; I have been there, but you will realize the possibility through a day-to-day, hour-to-hour, minute-to-minute commitment to STOP.

Chapter 16
Play with the Big Kids

"To be the man, you got to beat the man."
-Chase Utley

The WCAL (West Catholic Athletic League), consisting of St. Francis, Bellermine, Serra, Mitty, Riorden, St. Ignatius, Sacred Heart Cathedral, and now Valley Christian, has long been known for producing top talent. Barry Bonds, Lynn Swan, Jim Fregosi, Doug Cosby, Gregg Jefferies, and Dan Fouts all played in the WCAL, just to name a few. The time period when I was there proved to be no different. Serra had a left-handed hitting catcher with big-time power and an absolute cannon for an arm that was destined for stardom. Bellarmine had a quarterback that could throw a football and hit a gnat in the ass from 50 yards away with a perfect spiral. I am just not sure that I would have predicted the quarterback from Bellarmine, Pat Burrell, would go on to hit over 300 home runs in the big leagues, and the catcher, Tom Brady, would go on to be arguably the greatest quarterback in the history of the NFL.

Brady went to Serra where he played quarterback on the debunked Padres football team and was the catcher of the historic baseball program that had a rich tradition of producing Major League players. It was obvious that Brady was a good quarterback, but it was difficult for him to throw the football from his back. Playing against Serra and Tom Brady my senior year, we steamrolled them 62-6 and future NFL'er Zack Walz and I sacked Tom a combined 6 times, 3 a piece. Trust me, we more than realize Brady has gotten the last laugh!

The baseball diamond was a much different story where we would fight Serra and Bellarmine every year for WCAL supremacy. I remember our entire team marveling at Brady's quick release from behind the plate during pre-game infield practice. Ironically, the furthest ball I ever saw hit in a high school game came off the bat of the future NFL Hall of Famer. The ball cleared the 360-foot sign in right field, and then traveled across two lanes of the road and landed on top of the Planned Parenthood building across the street. Not sure if the irony runs deeper with the homer hit by Tom Brady being the furthest I have ever seen in a high school game, or the fact that there was a Planned Parenthood across the street from my Catholic high school.

There is no doubt in my mind that competing against the best competition brings out the best in everybody. I was lucky to go through high school competing with and against several MLB and NFL players, which undoubtedly elevated my game to the next level.

Human Crash Test Dummy Life Lesson #16

Find the best competition available and they will help raise your game to the next level. Beating up on marginal athletes feeds the ego but does very little to push you to the top. Be grateful for your competition and feed off of their skills. To be the best you must learn from the best. Watch, analyze and then apply what works for you. Immersing yourself in an ultra-competitive culture will bring you to the precipice of maximizing YOUR abilities.

Chapter 17
Chase Your Dream

"Freedom is the only worthy goal in life.
It is won by disregarding things that lie beyond our control."
-Epictetus

I grew up 10 minutes from the Stanford campus, and beginning when I was 9 years old, I spent 2 weeks every summer attending Stanford's baseball camp. Under head coach Mark Marquess, Stanford had become a national powerhouse, winning back-to-back College World Series titles in 1987 and 1988. At a young age, I began going to Stanford baseball games at Sunken Diamond, and that was where the dream of attending Stanford University and playing baseball was born. By the time I was in high school, Stanford had an invitational "All-Star" select camp that I was invited to and attended after my sophomore and junior year. Throughout the years, I forged a very close relationship with Stanford hitting coach Dave Esquer, who was committed to do everything in his power to make sure I became a Cardinal. During the fall of my senior year, I made my first "unofficial" trip to Stanford where I was paired up with two Stanford baseball players, Todd LaRocca and Brody Van Wagonan.

I had followed Stanford baseball as closely as the San Francisco Giants, so neither one of these guys needed an introduction. LaRocca, or "Rock," as they called him, was selected in the 3rd round by the Dodgers out of high school, but like so many others, elected to put his big league dreams on hold while he received a Stanford education. He was a shortstop-turned-pitcher from Atlanta, Georgia, but most importantly, "Rock" was the life of every party. Van Wagonan, the starting right fielder, wore #6 (my HS #) and had a smoking hot swimmer girlfriend named Molly and "Hollywood" good looks of his own.

The day started very casual as Rock and Brody introduced me to many of the other Stanford baseball players. Then festivities picked up before the football game as Rock introduced me to the beer bong. The night ultimately ended with keg stands and pizza back at the Sigma Chi house. Rock and Brody definitely refuted the stigma that Stanford guys didn't know how to have fun. As good family friend and Stanford baseball alum, Vince Sakowski, always likes to declare, "Work hard, play hard, study hard, party hard!" There was no other place that I wanted to go to college; Stanford was it.

The overall success of Stanford students beyond Major League Baseball and athletics was by far and away the main attraction for me. Growing up close to campus, I fully understood the magnitude of a Stanford education and what that would mean well beyond my years of playing baseball. Not shockingly, Vince Sakowski runs a very successful venture capital firm, Van Wagonon is a leading baseball agent, and LaRocca is one of the top financial advisors in the world.

Two weeks after my "unofficial trip," I was back on the Stanford campus for my "official" visit. A.J. Hinch, the All-American catcher from Oklahoma (and 2017 World Series Champion as manager of the Houston Astros), was my host. Hinch truly was the golden child and the poster boy for Stanford baseball. The weekend was a bit more subdued than the Rock/Van Wagonon debacle but enlightening nonetheless. I grilled A.J. with every question I could think of having to do with the university, baseball, and life. He gave me the official campus tour, and I was mesmerized by the tradition of the school and the success of the baseball program. What was once a far-off dream of attending Stanford and playing baseball was officially becoming a reality. It became very difficult to control my excitement. Never in my life had I wanted anything more. That evening, we had dinner with Dean Stotz, the recruiting coordinator, and head coach, Mark Marquess, at Sundance Steakhouse. They explained to me that in baseball there are 30 guys on the team and only 11.7 scholarships to go around. Coach Marquess then offered me a 50% scholarship, which was way more than I expected.

Getting into Stanford was the last piece of the puzzle. I had become a "good" student, but Stanford's academic standards generally go well beyond "good." It was not a secret that I was going to need help with the admissions process. Ironically, Susan Marquess, the wife of Stanford's head baseball coach, was my high school counselor at St. Francis. Susan and Coach Marquess both felt that if I maintained my GPA and achieved a certain number on the SAT, I would have a very good chance of getting admitted.

Not only did I maintain my GPA but I improved it significantly. I then took the recommended number on the SAT and surpassed it by 90 points. As much as I wanted to go to Stanford for the obvious academic and athletic excellence, I wanted to show gratitude to my parents for dealing with all of my misadventures as a troubled youth. I wanted to go to Stanford to show that somebody with an extreme learning disability as a kid can persevere to the highest level academically. Ultimately, I wanted to go to Stanford so I could stick my middle finger up to all my grade school teachers that thought I was a lost cause and doubted that I would ever graduate high school, let alone graduate from one of the most prestigious universities in the world.

Ever since I had the vision to attend Stanford and understood what it would take, I made a commitment to control what was within my control. First it was getting my game to a high enough level that they would even consider me; secondly, it was getting the necessary grades and test scores; and thirdly, it was interacting and being respectful to all of the people within the Stanford baseball program. I felt like I did my best to control what I was capable of; the rest was out of my hands. I understood that and never fretted Stanford's decision.

Human Crash Test Dummy Life Lesson #17

So long as you do everything in your power to succeed, you will be able to put your head on the pillow at night and be satisfied with your effort regardless of the ultimate result. Be humble, be respectful, toss out positive vibes, and you will be welcomed by any team. Lastly, chase your dream. The chase is always the best part.

Chapter 18
Share the Love

"A dream you dream alone is only a dream.
A dream you dream together is reality."
-John Lennon

I had trips scheduled to UCLA and Santa Clara, but so long as I was going to get into Stanford, those trips were simple formalities. The only reason I was even offered a trip to UCLA was because they had heard from a good family friend of ours, Jack Gifford, that I had a scholarship offer from Stanford. Jack and my mom were best friends since they were 7 years old. They went to grade school and high school together before Jack went on to UCLA, where he majored in engineering and played baseball, obviously a very rare combo. Jack went on to start multiple semi-conductor companies including Maxim Integrated Products, making hundreds of millions in the process. Undoubtedly though, Jack's first love was baseball, and he was UCLA baseball's largest supporter. Jack followed my career at St. Francis, and when he heard that Stanford was interested, he wanted to check out exactly how good Judy Byrnes' kid was. Jack came over to the house to hit with me in the batting cage. Not just to watch me hit but to actually hit with me.

Jack still played 1st base and hit 2nd for his Maxim baseball team which was comprised of former college All-Americans and professional players. They traveled around the world with similar accommodations to a big-league team, playing in top amateur tournaments. Jack and I spent 3 hours in the batting cage taking whacks and talking ball. By the end of the session, I had made Jack Gifford a believer. Translation: Jack told UCLA, even though they had never seen me play, to make sure I took an official visit to the Westwood campus and also make sure there was some sort of scholarship available.

Not surprisingly, I loved everything about UCLA: the guys on the team, the campus, the college co-eds, and the rich tradition of UCLA greats, like Jackie Robinson, Kareem Abdul-Jabar, Bill Walton, Troy Aikman, Jackie Joyner Kersee, and of course the most legendary coach in the history of college athletics, John Wooden. As a matter of fact, I was so enthralled with UCLA that when I got home I told my parents that if you take baseball out of the equation, and I could choose any school in the country, UCLA would be my top choice. The combination of academics, athletics, social life, co-eds, city, proximity to home, and the near-perfect Southern California weather... In my opinion there was not a better school in the country for what I was looking for. My mom's friendship with Jack Gifford, and then his belief in me, single-handedly created an opportunity to attend a school that had all the makings of being a perfect fit.

Human Crash Test Dummy Life Lesson #18

Use your connections to your advantage. Who doesn't love helping people, and who doesn't love helping friends even more? No need to beg for their assistance and don't ever ask for any sort of handout. There are 4 very simple things to do when seeking guidance...
1) Share your story,
2) Ask for advice,
3) Show genuine gratitude,
4) Always reciprocate the love.

Chapter 19
Keep Moving

"You can only lose what you cling to."
-Buddha

The early signing date for baseball was November 11 of my senior year. Coach Marquess at Stanford had mentioned that he would let me know as soon as he got word from the admissions department if I would be accepted in early admissions. As the 11th approached and I did not hear from him, I began to worry.

I finally got a call on the 10th. Coach Marquess wanted to come over to the house. I wasn't sure but I figured that was a pretty good sign. I thought to myself that he must be coming over to drop off the letter of intent. I'll officially sign it tomorrow then drop it off at Stanford on my way to school (maybe even pick up a hat at the student store to sport my new school colors). There was very little chance in my mind that he was coming over to tell me I did not get accepted to the school.

Mark Marquess walked into the house and then proceeded to shatter the biggest dream that I held onto since I was 9 years old. He claimed my GPA and SAT scores were adequate, but I had not gotten into the school because of my class rank. Every year, Stanford received nearly a hundred applications from very qualified St. Francis students, yet most years they would accept no more than 5 kids. Those 5 were hardly ever outside of the top 10 in the class. Of the approximate 400 students in the graduating class, apparently my class rank was not sufficient. Coach Marques explained that I could wait until the winter admissions and the scholarship would still be there if I were to get into the school at that point.

I did not want to hear it. I felt duped. I got the grades, I got the SAT score, and then I got a big fat Stanford Cardinal kick in the balls. It was bullsh*t. Word on the street was that the baseball program submitted a list of 10 guys that they would like to get into the school. They then ranked the 10 guys in order of importance to the baseball program. Admissions then makes a judgment based on GPA, SATs, and where the kid is ranked on the "list." In order to get in to the school, I was going to need help and be ranked towards the top of the list. Supposedly, I was toward the very bottom.

I let Coach Marquess finish speaking, and when he asked if I had any questions, I stood up and walked out of the room. I felt nauseous. I went to my room and grabbed my "binkey" that was tucked away in the back of my closet. This was the very same "special" blanket I had had since I was a year old, complete with pee stains and bite marks. These days it would only come out on my most emotional, challenging occasions of young adulthood. Now was definitely one of those times. I curled up on my bed and sobbed.

Ten minutes later, I stood up, walked over to the mirror, wiped my tears away, and slapped myself in the face. I could in fact wait until winter admissions and press my luck with Stanford, or I could simply put an end to the heartache and move on. I could still hear Coach Marquess in the other room talking to my parents when I picked up the phone and called UCLA head coach Gary Adams. Earlier that week, Coach Adams had called to tell me that I had been accepted to UCLA. Now, it was me calling Coach Adams to tell him that I would be proud and honored to become a UCLA Bruin.

Gary Adams was shocked. They had figured that I was going to go to Stanford. Jack Gifford is the only reason I was ever even contacted by UCLA. I am not sure if Gary or Vince Beringhele (the head recruiter for UCLA at the time) would ever admit it, but I think they were pissed or at least annoyed that I was forced on them. Nonetheless, our UCLA recruiting class was ranked #1 in the country and for good reason: Troy Glaus, Jim Parque, Tom Jacquez, Brett Nista, Pete Zamora, Jason Green, and myself. Everybody in the class went on to play professional baseball, and 4 of us spent a significant amount of time in the big leagues.

Human Crash Test Dummy Life Lesson #19

We can do everything in our power to try to make something happen, but oftentimes for whatever reason, sh*t just doesn't work out: A job, a relationship, or in this case for me, admission into a school. You have two choices: 1) Make excuses, sulk, and cast blame on everybody and anything you can think of besides yourself, or 2) Move on.

I chose to move on.

Losses in your life are going to hurt, but if you are able to charge on without hesitation, you immensely shorten the painful healing process. As far as I am concerned, it's pretty simple... keep F*CKING moving.

Chapter 20
You Don't Get Style Points

"For something to be beautiful it doesn't have to be pretty."
-Rei Kawakubo

I finished my baseball career at St. Francis as a high school All-American on a team that at one point was ranked #1 in the country. Playing for legendary football coach Ron Calcagno, I switched to running back and linebacker my sophomore year and was part of 3 consecutive Central Coast Section CIF championship teams. My junior year, we went 13-0 with an average margin of victory of nearly 40 points. Hands down, it was the best team I have ever played on in any sport, at any level. I earned All-Northern California honors my senior year and received a good amount of attention from major D1 universities regarding football. The good thing was that I had already committed to UCLA to play baseball, so football anywhere other than UCLA was not an option. The issue with walking onto the football team at UCLA was that I would have had to miss fall baseball, making it nearly impossible to start as a freshman. I actually loved football every bit as much as baseball, but I realized my best chance of playing professionally was undoubtedly going to be on the diamond.

My senior year of high school wrapped up with the Major League Baseball draft. I had not really attracted much attention from scouts until about half way through my senior season when our team started 20-0. We were ranked by Cal-HI Sports as the #1 team in the State and were also ranked as the #1 team in the country by USA Today, and 8 of 9 regular starters went on to play Division 1 baseball, while 2 of us ended up in the big leagues. When I originally got called up to varsity my sophomore year, I played third base and right field. The problem was that I was way too erratic as a third baseman, and in right field, the ball would bounce on me every time I ran down a ball in the gap or down the line. That's really where my career began to have some promise. Our head coach, Chris Bradford, obviously noticed my troubles catching a ball in the outfield, but it wasn't until we were doing base running drills that the solution became obvious. I actually interrupted a conversation Coach Bradford was having with a scout from the Baltimore Orioles when I was running down the baseline. THUMP, THUMP, THUMP. Bradford and the scout immediately pulled me aside and explained that the ball was moving on me in the outfield because I was running on my heels.

The next day, Coach Bradford instructed me not to come to baseball practice. Instead, I was to report to the track and work with Coach Dozier, the track and field coach. That was where I learned the basic fundamentals of running. That was also where I realized my true speed potential. Coach Dozier had me over-exaggerate running on my toes and corrected my body position so I could run with a good forward lean as opposed to running straight up and down. Throughout my entire career, other players, coaches, and fans would make fun of the way I ran. "Twinkle Toes" wasn't exactly the nickname a high school kid was looking for. As much as you would think name-calling and criticism would have had an adverse effect on the psyche of a young man at a vulnerable stage in his life, all it did was fuel me. I returned to baseball practice the following day after my track tutorial, and to my amazement, the ball wasn't moving on me in the outfield anymore. Then at the end of practice, Coach Bradford and the scout had me run from home to first. I had never known my times down the 1st base line, but apparently, I was a pretty consistent 4.4 seconds. They had me run 3 times as fast as I could with my new running form. Every one of them was under 4 seconds. From that point on, I went from a kid who couldn't field and ran okay to becoming a legitimate prospect. Ultimately, after an 11-season Major League Baseball career predicated on speed, "Twinkle Toes" sounded just fine.

When it came to the draft, I was what scouts would describe as extremely "raw." I played several different positions but none of them great or even good for that matter. I was the "Jack of all Trades" and the master of none. My senior year, we didn't have a catcher so I volunteered to go behind the plate. Ironically, I was drafted as a center fielder, which along with 1st base was the only position I had never played. I was the 38th round selection of the Los Angeles

Dodgers in the 1994 draft. There were 37 guys picked ahead of me on 30 different teams. Basically, I was roughly around the 1150th pick of the draft and I didn't give a f*ck. The fact that I went from being a kid that thought he got cut from the freshman baseball team to getting drafted by an MLB team was one of the greatest honors I could have ever asked for.

The only way I was able to succeed at St. Francis was because I was willing to accept the growing pains. I was willing to understand that I was not the best, but I also learned what I needed to do if I wanted to be the best. I worked and willed my way from being an awkward athletic kid begging to make a team to an awkward athletic MLB draft pick.

Human Crash Test Dummy Life Lesson #20

Be willing to let down your guard if an opportunity for improvement arises. Throw whatever bullsh*t people want to talk completely out the window. Stay true to yourself and your commitment to improve; that's all that matters.

Chapter 21
Go Where Everybody Knows Your Name

"Everything I am, everything I've been allowed to do, career-wise, has come out of the opportunity I had with 'Cheers'. I think it's one of the funniest shows ever. They are some of my best friends."
-Ted Danson

The Dodgers never officially offered me a contract. Instead, they considered me a draft and follow, meaning that if for whatever reason I had decided to go to junior college instead of UCLA, they would have been able to sign me any time before the next year's draft.

No offense to Cañada College or College of San Mateo, which are both elite junior college programs in my area, but forgive me if I wasn't tempted to bail out on UCLA. However, the Dodgers could still sign me up until my first day of classes at UCLA. The summer after my senior year was one of the best times in my life. In previous summers I had played for the Peninsula Mets, a traveling select baseball team comprised of many of the Bay Area's best players. We traveled from border to border in the state of California, playing whoever and wherever we could find competition. Although it was fun and no doubt very helpful in my development as a baseball player, it was a grind. So, when many of my buddies that I played with at St. Francis and other friends that I grew up playing little league with decided to play for the local "Joe DiMaggio" team, I was in.

The exposure was not nearly the same, but I had already signed to play at UCLA, and I had already been drafted by the Dodgers. In a lot of ways, I felt like my work was done, so why not enjoy my last opportunity playing a kids' game with the same kids and many of my best friends I played little league with? The Menlo Park Brewers was the name of the team, and it was said to have earned the "Brewers" nick name. The legend goes that apparently on the very first road trip, the Menlo Park Joe D players were trying to come up with a name for the team. During the debate, they somehow figured out a way to sneak a keg of beer onto the bus and stash it in the bathroom. When the players were fighting for a shot to get to the back of the bus, head coach Jim McAlpine quickly figured out what was going on. "Well, at least you guys finally figured out what to name yourselves. Go Brewers!"

Coach McAlpine, or "Mac," as we called him, was everything you would want in a coach of 18-year-old boys on the verge of becoming men. He was very baseball savvy and an eternal optimist yet very stern when he needed to be. Most importantly though, he was one of the guys. I was going through a very difficult part of my life and having "Mac" to lean on during that time period was huge. I was about to leave home for the first time and my dad had just been diagnosed with prostate cancer. Because he did not want to disrupt anything that I had going on, my dad did not break the news to me until the night before he went into the hospital for surgery. 20 years ago, prostate cancer surgery was much more complicated than it is today and there were no guarantees that they could remove the cancer or that he would even make it out of the surgery alive. This was the first point in my life that I thought about life without my dad. I was upset he did not tell me earlier, but now, as a father, I fully understand his position.

That summer, our Menlo Park Brewers team went 44-2. The first loss happened when several of us went on our senior trip to Cancun. The second was the first game in the State finals in Yountville when the whole team spent the night before carrying on the "Brewer" tradition. Good thing for us, we had to be beaten twice on that final day and we sobered up before the second game. Amazing to think that 9 guys from that local Joe DiMaggio team went on to play top-level college baseball, and 3 of us, including Gary Johnson (Angels) and John Gall (Cardinals), ended up playing Major League Baseball.

There is no doubt that this group of dudes pushed each other, but what was special about this team was that we were not some travel ball squad that was thrown together for the summer. We had played with and against each other since little league and had gone to school together since grade school. The chemistry and bonds that were built throughout the course of the years allowed all of us to have an absolute blast, which then directly translated to success on the baseball field. During a very difficult time in my life, which was full of uncertainty and change, spending just about every day that summer with my family and best friends prepared me for what is ahead.

Human Crash Test Dummy Life Lesson #21

If you have an opportunity to move forward with some of your best friends, take it. So long as your crew is all pulling in the same direction, each one of you will individually be better for it. In life, we typically perform our best, and the team performs its best, when we are having fun. Enjoy your squad!

Chapter 22
Charge Change

"Life is a series of natural and spontaneous changes.
Don't resist them; that only creates sorrow. Let reality be reality.
Let things flow naturally forward in whatever way they like."
-Lao Tzu

After surgery, my dad spent weeks recovering at home, and I could tell he was becoming increasingly irritated. Unfortunately, it put a huge strain on his relationship with my mom. They would argue at times when I was growing up, but it began to reach new heights. It is often said that cancer will bring a family together. Unfortunately, in my family's case, it completely tore us apart.

I wanted to go away to UCLA for many selfish reasons, but I did not want to leave my dad. Even more so, I did not want to leave my mom. She has been and always will be my angel. My mom was the one who fought for me when my grade school principal wanted to put me into a "juvenile delinquent" school. She was the one who would take me 30 minutes out of the way to Malibu Grande Prix before my little league games so I could take batting practice. She was the one who made sure I had my 2 Jack in the Box "home run" tacos, and yes, they were 99 cents in 1988 too. When I was playing tennis and had visions of becoming the next John McEnroe, it was Mom that was driving me all over the state every weekend. There wasn't a karate competition, tennis match, basketball, baseball, or football game that she missed, ever. My mom was the one that would run me from one tutor to another so I could reach my full potential in school. I was terrified how she would react with my sister, who was already at Boulder, and me away from the house. I was worried what would happen if my mom and dad were left alone.

When it came time to leave for UCLA, I never imagined it would be so difficult. My dad had been declared cancer-free and things seemed to have stabilized at home a bit, but like most 18-year-olds leaving home for the first time, I was scared. I hopped into the Bronco and made the 6-hour trek south to Westwood with Mom riding shotgun. After moving in and getting settled, I dropped my mom off at the airport and played it cool as could be. "I'll be fine Mom. I love you. I already told you that 9 times. I'll call you every day. Bye, mom. You are going to miss your flight!" Then the door closed and she was off.

I didn't get 10 feet away before my tears became so overwhelming that I actually had to pull over so I didn't crash. I thought this bullsh*t macho front was going to make the day easier, but the truth was that I was just another 18-year-old Mamma's boy that was scared to death to be away from my family for the first time.

My transition to college life was made much easier when Sidensol and I found a way to manipulate the system and become roommates in Rieber Hall. For 250 square feet, we undoubtedly made the most of our space. Old school Nintendo was set up on our 22 inch VHS/TV so we could wager the few bucks we had in our pockets on RBI Baseball or Techno Bowl. We had a mini fridge filled with Coors Originals and a brass spittoon was the centerpiece for the room. Liars dice, poker, and putting "action" on games were all staples in our nightly rituals.

Human Crash Test Dummy Life Lesson #22

We are often scared of change because we want to hold on to the past and are freaked out by the uncertainty of the future. The great thing is that it is the memories, lessons, and relationships of the past that actually allow us to bravely take on what the future has in store. There is also no doubt that the best and most meaningful relationships in life will last a lifetime, regardless of constantly changing life circumstances. Life is change and change is an important reminder that you are still alive. Don't run from change, charge at it.

Chapter 23
The Spirit Lives

"When we meet real tragedy in life, we can react in two ways - either by losing hope and falling into self-destructive habits, or by using the challenge to find our inner strength."
-Dalai Lama

When I was 10 years old, a new house was being built across the hill from where I lived. I used to go exploring the construction site looking for leftover wood to build a skate ramp. I got to be friends with the workers and they would set aside scraps that I could take home. As the house was getting close to completion, I rode by one day and found the perfect piece of plywood in the scraps pile. I tossed my bike into the bushes, threw the piece of wood on my back, and began to haul it off. Just as I was making my way off the property a booming voice came out of nowhere. "Hey!!! Where you going with that plywood kid?" Nervous as could be, I responded, "Going to build a skate ramp, sir. I was told it was okay to take the wood in that pile over there." The guy walked over, inspected the wood, and then gave me the okay to take it home. Meanwhile, the family that was moving into the house appeared out of the front door and headed toward their car. There was the mom and dad, a son that appeared to be a few years older, and the most beautiful looking thing that I had ever seen in my 12 years of life. Amanda MacDonald.

At the time, I wasn't into girls, but then again, I had never met a 12-year-old princess. The next day, my mom and I made cookies for me to take over to the house. I was too nervous to drop them off by myself, so I convinced my other neighbor, Liz Castleman, aka "Punky Brewster," to come with me to drop them off. When we knocked, Amanda answered the door. I stood there with a plate of cookies in my hand and a huge smile from ear to ear. I knew what I wanted to say; I had even rehearsed it in front of the mirror nearly a hundred times. "Hi, I am Eric and this is my neighbor Liz, we wanted to give you these cookies to welcome you to the neighborhood."

Instead, nothing came out. This was the first and one of the very few times in my life that I was 100% speechless. Liz finally interjected. "Hi, I am Liz and this is Eric, here are some cookies for you; you want to hang out with us?"

Over the course of the next few years, the three spent a lot of time together, and Amanda and I eventually became very close. We would ride bikes, shoot hoops, skateboard, go hiking in the hay fields, and watch movies. We would talk about school, sports and life in general. Our favorite topic? What we wanted to be when we grew up. I was having a tough time deciding between a baseball player and a bridge toll taker. Amanda went to the private school in the area so the only time I would get to see her was usually late in the afternoon after school or on the weekends. She was my first kiss; she was my first love; she was my first heartbreak. By the time we both got into high school and took on more responsibilities in life, the time we spent together dwindled. Amanda went to Menlo High School while I went to St. Francis. Our paths would cross at parties every once in a while, and even though we were far removed from the innocent puppy love days of our youth, I do know that the feelings I had for her never left. Although we both went our separate ways, I always believed that one day I was going to marry Amanda MacDonald.

Ironically, Amanda went to the University of Colorado and was in the same sorority as my sister. I would keep regular tabs on her and ask how my "future wife" was doing. In March of 1994, Shea and Amanda were planning to take a trip home, but something changed; Amanda decided to stay in Boulder. That night she went out to a party with a group of friends in the mountains surrounding the Boulder campus. Ever the adventurer, Amanda was "car surfing" (riding on the roof of the car). The driver was intoxicated and speeding. The car flipped. Amanda MacDonald was killed. She was 18 years old.

I was still a senior in high school at the time. I had just finished playing a baseball game at St. Francis when my sister told me the news. I walked to the outfield, fell to my knees, and began uncontrollably sobbing. There is no way to describe the pain I felt.

I was now just 18 years old, and I had dealt with the loss of my best friend and my first love. I did everything I could to distract myself from actually realizing the magnitude of each loss. I went about my life and used school and baseball as an outlet to hide my emotions. Looking back now, I don't think I had much of a choice. I have to imagine that if I did not have major outlets to refocus my emotions, both losses could have very easily had life-long detrimental effects. I still think about the Willbanks' and MacDonald's families all of the time; the pain that they must have been feeling at the time, and the pain that they still feel today.

I searched the internet trying to recall some of the details of Todd's life and figured there most certainly would have been something on his death. Sadly, it was as if he never existed. I could not find a single thing about the gregarious 11-year-old kid and not a mention of the accident that fateful summer day. The way it was explained to me, Todd was hit coming out of a side street onto Cañada Road, which happened to be as major of a road that you will find in the town of Woodside. Shortly after Todd's death, a stop sign was put in. Like I mentioned earlier in this book, I have traveled past that stop sign hundreds if not thousands of times since Todd's death. Not one time have I gone by without saluting him in some way.

If you google Amanda MacDonald, you will find her name in a couple articles talking about her tragic death that led to a fraternity house getting shut down. You will also read something about Mothers Against Drunk Driving putting up a cross at the site where she died, which created debate about the symbol of the cross and whether or not it was appropriate for a group such as M.A.D.D to use the cross as a form of remembrance.

What you won't read about is that Amanda's father went on a crusade, traveling around college campuses warning students of the danger of drinking and driving. The amazing thing, he traveled to each of these seminars with the kid that killed her. Just recently, my kids had a karate tournament at Menlo School. While walking back to the car after the tournament, my 9 year old daughter pointed to what appeared to be a brand new building, and said, "Daddy, don't you know her?"... I looked up and front and center on the building it read: "Amanda Macdonald Student Activity Center." My heart dropped. I had no idea it was there.

Human Crash Test Dummy Life Lesson #23

Tragic events are inevitable, grieving is natural, and moving on is necessary. Find outlets to remember and find outlets to move forward. Both were mandatory coping mechanisms that helped me get over the unimaginable. Todd and Amanda are both physically gone but their spirit has lived through many people and is alive and well today. When you deal with the loss of somebody major in your life, the greatest thing you can do for that person, and for yourself, is live your life how they would want you to. Live their spirit.

Chapter 24
Sack Up

"Start running."
-Gary Adams

When I arrived at UCLA, I was part of the #1 rated recruiting class in the country. As a matter of fact, I was most likely looked upon as the bottom dweller of all the freshman class. Fall baseball started and within a couple practices, I immediately knew where I stood. I was put into the batting practice group that was relegated to taking BP in the cage. Once inter-squad games started, my place on the UCLA depth chart of outfielders became very clear. The 1st game, I sat through 9 innings and never came off the bench. The 2nd game, the exact same thing. I was beginning to become increasingly pissed about every inning that went by without me getting a chance to play.

The next day, we had a double header. Surely this would be my opportunity to finally get a chance to show Coach Gary Adams and the staff what I could do. I was not in either lineup for game 1 and again sat all 9 innings. 27 innings into the fall-ball season and I had yet to play one of them. Worse off, all 10 other outfielders had played at some point. I had tried to stay positive and realize as a freshman I was going to have to bide my time, but when my name wasn't in either lineup for the 2nd game of the double header, I completely lost it and mentally checked out. What was internal rage turned eventually to apathy by the 3rd inning. I had sat through 30 innings of baseball over the course of 3 days and there was not a guy other than me in a UCLA uniform that had not gotten into the game.

I had enough and decided to kick my feet out and put my hat down low over my eyes, my version of a silent protest. "Hey Eric," Coach Adams said in his ever so distinguishable voice. "Finally," I thought to myself, this silent protest may have actually worked and I am about to get my shot. "Yes, Skip," I replied. "What was the last pitch?" "I don't know." "Why not?" "Because I wasn't paying attention." "Why not?" "Because I'm bored." "Why?" "I just sat through 3 games and I'm the only guy who hasn't been on the field, Skip." "Oh, ok, you want to go on the field?" "Yes, sir" "Get up and start running around the field, I'll tell you when you can stop."

I started running in the 3rd inning and did not stop until after the game was over. Looking back at it now, that was my first introduction to the endurance world. Apparently, Coach Adams was a marathoner and was impressed by my ability to run for nearly 3 hours. The next day I was leading off and playing right field.

The childish silent protest was me being an immature 18-year-old kid, trying to get the attention of a coach so he remembered that I was on the team. The way I was trying to communicate was stupid, but the message was not.

Human Crash Test Dummy Life Lesson #24

Have faith and believe in yourself to want that next opportunity. Even more, get some balls and ask for that next opportunity. From there, it's up to you to take advantage of that shot. At some point, you are going to have no other choice but to SACK UP.

Chapter 25
Go Get It

"Look,
If you had one shot,
One opportunity,
To seize everything you ever wanted,
One moment,
Would you capture it,
Or just let it slip?"
-Eminem, *Lose Yourself*

When I finally got my opportunity I ran with it (pun intended). In my first at bat I crushed a ball off the right-centerfield wall and never looked back. I ended up being the starting right fielder and leadoff hitter as a freshman. Knowing that I had done the work throughout the course of my life gave me the confidence for that one moment of opportunity. With my antics the day before, I knew that moment of opportunity could be short lived, but I asked for the test because I had studied. Confidence is fueled by preparation, and I had spent my entire life preparing for that one moment.

Now, as the starting right fielder for UCLA, I felt like I had a score to settle with Stanford. The school I grew up dreaming of playing for, only to have my heart broken at the last minute. The first chance I had to play against them was at UCLA. I homered on the first pitch I saw. I ended the 3-game series 6 for 12 with 2 home runs. A few weeks later, I went home to play at Sunken Diamond in front of over 100 family members and friends. I had 9 hits in 12 at bats. My communication skills at that point in my life were still developing, but my success on the field against Stanford throughout my entire college career seemed to be my personal way of telling the Cardinal to go F*CK themselves.

To further spice things up, toward the end of the 2nd game of the 3-game series, I was on first base when there was a routine ground ball hit to the short stop. As usual, I went hard into second base trying to beat the throw. Stanford 2nd baseman, Brian Dallimore, caught the ball for the final out. Then as my back was turned and I was facing the outfield, something hit me in the helmet. Stunned, not realizing what had happened right away, I turned around and watched Dallimore sprint off the field. It actually wasn't until the next morning at breakfast when long time big leaguer Doug DeCinces, whose son Tim was our catcher, explained exactly what had gone on. After Dallimore caught the 3rd out, he turned around and rocketed the ball from point blank range off my coconut. Apparently, he took exception to my hard slide at second base. I asked Doug what he thought I should do. He said it was very simple... "When you hit a double today, tell Dallimore that you thought guys at Stanford liked to play hard, and then ask him why he acted like a baby." In my 3rd at bat, I hit the double and asked Dallimore exactly that... His response... "Wait till you get into the box next time..." My response... "If I get hit, I am coming for you."

Kyle Peterson, Stanford's highly touted freshman pitcher, was on the mound when I came up for my next at bat. The first pitch hit me square in the ass cheek. Without hesitation I charged right passed the pitcher's mound and headed straight for Dallimore at 2nd base. I was in a full sprint approaching the cut of the infield grass when I got absolutely smoked from my right side. It felt as if I was a wide receiver going across the middle and Ronnie Lott had just blind-sided me. Vince Behringhele, our first base coach, had come from the first base coaches box to relive his Loyola High School football glory days. He then did his best WWE impersonation, pinning me to the ground until I was able to calm down. Although I never reached my destination, I have to figure there is a good chance that was the first time in baseball history that somebody charged the 2nd baseman after getting hit by a pitch.

Kyle Peterson was an influential freshman pitcher and was simply delivering a message. There was no need to waste time with him when I knew where the message was coming from.

Human Crash Test Dummy Life Lesson #25

When you get your opportunity, make sure you are prepared to take advantage of it. Put in the work. The work is what will give you the confidence to succeed. Also, too often in life we don't address the root of the problem. Always make sure to cut through the bullsh*t and go after what, or who, really matters.

Chapter 26
Failure First

*"Success consists of going from failure to failure
without loss of enthusiasm."*
-Winston Churchill

I ended up my freshman season at UCLA a 1st team All Pac-10 player and a 1st team freshman All-American. I had been invited to play in the prestigious Cape Cod summer baseball league, so immediately after finals, I headed back east for the summer. I played for the Chatham A's and lived with a host family, the Gallops, along with 4 other dudes from different universities across the country. I was 3000 miles away from home, playing in a wood bat league against the very best college baseball had to offer. I was homesick, my girlfriend from back home dumped me, and I was completely worn down from the long college season. Not surprising, it wasn't long before my ass was handed to me on a silver Cape Cod platter.

Never in my life had I struggled like I was struggling in Cape Cod. I wanted to go home, and I wanted to go home badly. My dad came out to visit and that definitely helped, but hitting .200 did not. To make matters worse, every one of my struggles was well documented, as our team was followed around the entire season by a Hollywood film producer who was going to make a movie about the Cape League. 5 years later, the world was treated to Freddy Prince Jr. and Jessica Biel starring in "Summer Catch."

What is probably shocking to most, the movie was actually spot-on when it came to some of the extra-curricular activities. Eric Brubaker, a pitcher from Pepperdine University, was my roommate. He eventually helped work on the film in an attempt to make it as accurate as possible. Brubaker even has a character, Billy Brubaker (played by Matthew Lillard), named after him. Yet if you have ever seen the movie or happened to live the summer of '95 in Chatham, Massachusetts, for the good, the bad, the and ugly, Billy Brubaker's character was very much based on my very own Cape Cod League experience.

I never wore her thong but there is no doubt that my summer completely turned around when I met the real-life DeeDee Mulligan. Freddy Prince Jr. (Ryan Dunn), the local Cape kid who gets the rare opportunity to play in the Cape league, is loosely based after one of my very best friends still to this day, Peter Princi. Ironically, Princi actually played for Cotuit and Hyannis but never the Chatham A's. As far as some of the other details in the movie, nobody ever burnt down the press box but big parties were a regular occurrence, there was a dude on our team that loved fat girls, and there was a guy, actually two, who were banging their host moms. The Hollywood ending is obviously a bunch of sh*t... If any player ever left the mound for a chick in the middle of a no-hitter, he would have gotten his ass kicked.

My experience in Cape Cod not only prepared me for professional baseball, but it prepared me for life well beyond the game. Cape Cod taught me how to manage a life on and off the field and how to develop relationships with guys from all over the country who come from all different walks of life. Most importantly, the Cape taught me how to manage failure. I will never accept failure, but learning how to productively react to things that don't go my way has ultimately been the main reason I have been able to experience personal success and happiness in life. On the field that summer, I undoubtedly had plenty of opportunities to work on failure management.

I returned to the Cape the next 2 summers with the Hyannis Mets, and after learning from my failures of the past, ended up leading the league in home runs. I also had the opportunity to wear a Scott Proctor 94 mph fastball off the face. I sucked lucky charms out of a straw for the next month, but I did steal second the next pitch and never missed a game.

The best thing about the Cape was that the players became part of the fabric of the community. Whether you worked at a grocery store, pulled crab pots out of the ocean, or mowed lawns, just about everybody on the team had a summer job. I happened to luck out and got what I considered the best job on the Cape: working baseball camps for kids. A bunch of 6-12 year olds were basically being led by somebody that acted in the 6-12-year-old range. It was a natural fit. I still visit Princi on the Cape at least once a year, and now we have an awesome opportunity to share the cape experience with our families.

Human Crash Test Dummy Life Lesson #26

If you are willing to accept failure for all it is worth, the potential success you will have beyond that is immeasurable. All of my greatest moments in life, be it socially, financially, school, work, baseball, triathlon, and ultra-marathon, have all had failures from which I was able to learn and grow. The only way you will ever genuinely appreciate your successes in life is by going through failure first.

Chapter 27
Lost Love

"In three words I can sum up everything I've learned about life: it goes on."
-Robert Frost

At the first football game I went to my sophomore year, there was a new cheerleader that I had not seen before. She had red hair and the biggest smile I had ever seen in my life. Most impressively though was the fact that she was doing double back flips through the air twice as high as any of the other girls who were struggling to do a single. Julie Anne Sommers was her name and I immediately fell in love. She happened to be a sorority sister of a girl that I went to high school with, Melissa McKale. I quickly began begging for an introduction. Of course, the first few times we met, she wanted absolutely nothing to do with me. I was down but not out. I stayed persistent yet did my best to avoid stalker status. My big break came when Julie Anne did not have a date to a sorority party at Gladstone's on the beach in Malibu. As a favor to Melissa, she agreed to take the annoying baseball player that would at least be good for a couple laughs. Julie Anne and I then started going to lunch at both of our favorite sandwich spot, "Sandbags," which was owned by UCLA Hall of Fame basketball player Don McClane. Lunches became dinners and pretty soon we were basically inseparable. We would head to Westlake Village and stay with her parents during the weekends, and I eventually brought her home to meet my family in Northern California.

When I began playing professional baseball, the difficulty of maintaining a relationship clearly became evident. All of the time spent traveling from one obscure city to another definitely did not help the cause. To Julie Anne's credit, she was not into me for the potential money I could make or any sort of fame that would be associated with me becoming a Major League Baseball player. She was as innocent and pure as any individual I had ever met in my life. On several different occasions, she would say that she wished I had a normal job. The problem was that I didn't. Had I done anything other than play baseball, I most likely would have gotten engaged and then married very soon after college, fired out a couple little ones, put up a white picket fence, and lived happily ever after. The reality was that I did play baseball, and in a lot of ways, in order to succeed to the utmost of your ability, you need to be a selfish prick. I say that in the sense that if you want to be the best at what you do, your craft needs to be your number one priority. All else including family, friends, and relationships need to take a back seat and are merely complimentary figures in your life. You are the king; they are the pawns.

Yes, I realize how jaded it sounds, but it is the exact reason you see so many athletes' marriages fail. It is the reason why you hear tales of athletes not being good husbands or fathers. It is also the exact reason you see so many athletes fall on serious hard times when they are done playing. Whatever leftover time I had for Julie Anne was not nearly enough to keep her happy; she wanted and deserved a lot more.

Immediately after college, Julie Anne got her master's in education from Pepperdine and began teaching kindergarten. Her life was essentially the antithesis of mine: secure and stable as opposed to questionable and volatile. She wanted me to be there both physically and emotionally and I couldn't. I had become so consumed by baseball and making it to the big leagues that I had a very hard time keeping things outside of that world in perspective. One of the most difficult things I have ever experienced in my life was dealing with the breakup of the girl that I unquestionably thought I was going to spend the rest of my life with. Not surprisingly, she moved on and seems to have an awesome family of her own, but it's interesting to think how a game completely changed the direction of my life.

Human Crash Test Dummy Life Lesson #27

Things don't always work out the way we envisioned them. Life situations bring people together and can pull people apart. We have to accept change to move forward and that change may be letting go of somebody you love. So long as you are here on this earth, life as we know it goes on. Mom used to always tell me, "Better to have loved and lost than to have never loved at all." She's right.

Chapter 28
Mother F*ckers Win

"Pain is temporary. It may last a minute, or an hour, or a day, or a year, but eventually it will subside and something else will take its place...
If I quit, however, it lasts forever."
-Lance Armstrong

Over the course of my athletic life, I have had the opportunity to meet and interact with some of the greatest athletes of all time; Tom Brady, Barry Bonds, Steph Curry, Phil Mickelson and Lance Armstrong just to name a few. The one common denominator that all of these dudes possess is what my doctor in Palo Alto likes to describe as the "mother f*cker" gene. Yes, it is real.

The way they express themselves are all very individual and very different, but the deeply embedded competitive nature in each and every one of them is above and beyond anything I have ever seen in my life. I have played with and against all sorts of great competitors in all different sports throughout the years, but what separates these dudes beyond their obvious natural athletic talent is a competitive spirit, drive, and will to be the absolute best at all costs.

Barry and Lance were the best at their craft well before either one was ever tied to PED's. I imagine what possibly drove them down that path was having to watch inferior athletes excel because of artificial enhancements.

I'll never forget one summer day when I was with a bunch of buddies playing a pick-up basketball game at the Pacific Athletic Club. On the court beside us was Brady wearing special moon boot shoes, doing sets of lunges and plyometric exercises for the entire duration of the one-hour basketball game.

Phil has such a confidence about him that he had me pull the flag from 50 yards out; then drained it.

When I had an opportunity to spend time with Steph, he had a quiet and very humble confidence about him. Never before in my life had I been around a more polite and gracious superstar. Nonetheless, just from my experience watching Curry on the court for years, this dude is a f*cking assassin.

Please don't take this literal but Lance, Barry, Tom, Phil and Steph would slit your throat if it meant getting to the top of the mountain first. Yes, there are some adverse effects to being the ultimate competitor, but the good thing about the crew above is I feel like afterwards they would patch you up to try to stop the bleeding.

Human Crash Test Dummy Life Lesson #28

Do you want to get to the next level or get to the point where you are striving to be the very best in the world at your craft? Let your inner "mother f*cker" gene come out. Use your competitive spirit to fuel your work ethic, which will in turn fuel your confidence, allowing you to perform at the very highest level of your capabilities and stand up to whatever competition or obstacle is in your way.

Chapter 29
Light the Match

"Motivation is the art of getting people to do what you want them to do because they want to do it."
-Dwight Eisenhower

My sophomore year at UCLA got off to a slow start. I'll blame it on the Cape League hangover. I think I had to remember what it was like to hit over .300 again. About 2 weeks into the season, we were playing a weekend series at home when I continued to suck it up. I was terrible in the Friday night game and then again on Saturday. I was undoubtedly frustrated but at no time did my confidence ever wane. I was always a notorious slow starter, and I realized it was just a matter of time until I found my groove.

Coach Adams, on the other hand, felt like it was time for a change. On Sunday, I was not in the lineup, for only the 2nd time in my college career. Obviously upset, I torturously sat through the game, then took off back to my apartment immediately after. I wanted to go in and tell Skip how I felt but decided it would be better to wait and calm down before I said something I would later regret.

About a half hour after I got home my phone rang. It was Skip. He wanted me to head back to the stadium, "NOW!" When I arrived at his office, he wasted no time absolutely laying it on me. "I see you out there every day grunting away on every swing, trying to hit the ball 9 miles. You are the fastest guy on the team and you never bunt or use your speed like you should. You need to be putting the ball in play way more than you do. You are wasting your 'God-given' talent and I can't watch it anymore. I am going to continue to sit you on the bench, and I have no idea when or if you will play again."

He made some valid points, but I was still fuming and I couldn't help firing back. "One thing I do know is that I do not have it in me to sit on the bench. Not at this point. Not less than 2 weeks into my sophomore season coming off a 1st team All-Pac 10 and freshman All-American year. I have given too much to this team for you to give up on me now. This is bullsh*t." To which Skip responded, "If you want to leave school go ahead. Go to Pepperdine, go to LMU, go to Fullerton, I don't care." I felt like I had no other option. "F*ck you, Skip. I'm done."

I headed back to my apartment and started strategizing with my roommates what my next move would be. I did not want to leave UCLA, but at this point, I had no choice. I had just told Gary Adams, the head coach of the UCLA baseball team, and who many would describe as one of the nicest guys in the world, to F*CK OFF!

Word spread quickly about the blow up that Skip and I had. Zak Ammirato, our team captain, wanted to hear the details so he had me come by his house the next day. I spent the morning on the phone with a counselor figuring out what I would need to do to transfer schools immediately and whether or not I would be eligible to play. That afternoon I went by Zak's thinking I was just going over to talk to him.

The entire team was there. I rehashed the story for everybody and really got more laughs than anything else. For the most part, Skip was a relatively mild-mannered dude, so guys were undoubtedly amused by his antics. The players of course also found humor in me telling Skip, who is essentially like your easy-going, happy-go-lucky grandpa, to go f*ck himself. Bottom line was that I had the ultimate support of my teammates and they were willing to go to Skip on my behalf and smooth things over.

Throughout all my years of playing baseball I had never been more gracious and humbled by the actions of every one of my UCLA teammates. Even if I had to sit the rest of the season on the bench, it did not matter. Because of the love that they showed me, so long as they could convince Skip to let me back on the team, I was going to remain a Bruin no matter what. The loyalty and support of my peers has been and always will be the most important thing to me.

Sometimes things happen in life that ultimately give you a much larger lesson than you could have ever imagined.

I learned one very big lesson: the respect and admiration of my family, teammates and friends is larger than the game of baseball. A lesson that would serve me well in my decision-making processes throughout the course of my entire career.

Without any apologies on either end, I showed up at practice the next day as if nothing happened. Skip and I had gotten along well before the infamous blow-up, and we got along even better after. Years later, when I was in the big leagues, we finally spoke about that night. Skip realized that I was somebody who was motivated by lighting a fire under my ass. Not surprisingly, he was simply sparking the match.

Human Crash Test Dummy Life Lesson #29

Don't be afraid to light somebody's match in your life, maybe even your own. We all respond to different triggers so figure out which trigger is going to light the fire. No two people are the same and not all motivation is created equal. By spending time getting to know somebody, you will be able to better understand what motivates that person.

Chapter 30
Action Speaks

*"There are a lot of squirrels that became road kill
by refusing to make a decision which way to go."*
-Bathroom graffiti at Coffee Bar in Truckee, CA

Just when I thought my 2nd year at UCLA could not get any more whacked out, it did. It was Friday of Spring Break and we had just played USC that night in the first game of the weekend series. I lived with 3 other guys: Sidensol, Bob Angus, another buddy from the same Northern California area where we grew up, and Mike Seal, my mentor at UCLA who was my teammate my freshman and his senior year. Mike was back in school finishing his degree. All 3 of those guys had gone out that night partying. I was a notorious light sleeper, so when they stumbled through the door at 2 am, that was my first wake-up call. As soon as the commotion settled down, I was able to fall back asleep. My 2nd wake-up call came 2 hours later when I heard another noise. My drunk roommates had long been passed out so this was a bit more disconcerting. I awoke to a large dude standing over my desk, which was positioned at the foot of my bed. I turned to see if Sidensol, who I shared the room with, was still asleep; he was. I then immediately assessed the situation. There had been a number of break-ins in the area recently, including a stabbing just up the street a week prior.

There is a relatively large f*cking dude standing at the foot of my bed rummaging through sh*t on my desk. He could have a gun, a knife, or a f*cking machete for all I know. Option 1, continue to lie in the bed and do nothing, hoping he doesn't completely clean the place out. Option 2, confront the intruder, ask him what he was doing in our apartment and hope to make a new friend. Option 3, jump his ass and ask questions afterwards. Considering the circumstances, option 3 seemed to be the appropriate choice.

As discreetly and quietly as I could, I curled up into a ball on the bed, positioning myself to strike like a cobra. Then, without any sort of hesitation, I leaped toward the intruder with a monster flying right hook. Because of my dad, I have an extensive background in martial arts and essentially spent my childhood sparring in and out of the karate studio. I was never out looking for fights, but because of my aggressive nature and unwillingness to back down, there were several scuffles that I could not avoid. Of all of the melees I have ever been involved in, I have never in my life landed a cleaner flying right hook. Then again, I am pretty sure I had never attempted such a thing either.

Immediately, the intruder hit the ground. I rushed to turn on the light and then grab a baseball bat that I had strategically placed by the door to our room. When Sidensol finally woke up, I was standing over the dude lying in a puddle of blood with my Easton Black Magic loaded up in launch position. The interrogation then began.

"What the f*ck are you doing here?"

"I'm here for the party man."

"No party here, dude."

"Sidensol, you know this guy?"

"Nope."

At this point, Seal and Bob had both gotten up and come in from the room across the hall.

"You guys know this f*cker?"

"Nope"

I then stood his ass up, put him against the wall, and then frisked him. I found seven wallets with no ID's, a bunch of cash, and hot chocolate packets the dickhead stole from downstairs. Bob called 911 immediately, so within a few minutes, campus police arrived, put the guy in hand cuffs, and sat him down in our room upstairs. A few minutes later LAPD arrived, took over, and it was on. They immediately began questioning the dude, asking for basic info such as his name and where he lived.

Intruder's response? "Let's go!"

LAPD tried one more time for the information they were looking for. The intruder's response again was, "Let's go." The LAPD officer responded, "You want to go? We will go my f*cking way,"

They then took the dude with his hands cuffed behind his back and tossed him up against the wall, THUMP! After that, all we heard was, THUMP, THUMP, THUMP, THUMP, THUMP!

They tossed the intruder halfway down the cement staircase! Then we heard another big THUMP against the wall, followed by THUMP, THUMP, THUMP, THUMP. . . BAM!

They chucked him down the rest of the staircase until he got to the bottom and crashed into the front door. We then watched LAPD toss him face first into the cruiser, which we could see from the bedroom balcony upstairs, where the LAPD had told us to stay as they provided the beat down.

The next day was pretty much a blur. I had slept no more than 2 hours that night before heading to the field to prepare for the day game against USC. I had a couple hits, including the game-winning double. By the end of the game, the story of the intruder had spread. The LA papers provided very limited coverage on college baseball. Usually a box score on the very last page with a 2-sentence game recap if we were lucky. The next day, the headline on the front page of the sports section read: "BYRNES KO'S INTRUDER THEN USC."

It's Hollywood, they couldn't resist.

I finished my sophomore season with All-Pac 10 honors once again, but most importantly, we made a regional for the first time in years. We traveled to Austin, Texas, where we lost early in the double elimination tournament to Southwest Missouri St. We then reeled off a bunch of victories and ultimately eliminated Texas in front of 12,000 lunatic Longhorn fans to get a chance to play Miami in the regional finals. UCLA had not been to the College World Series in 29 years and we were now 1 game away. Unfortunately, that was as close as we were going to get and we got blasted by Pat Burrell and the Canes. Nonetheless, we got invaluable experience that would give us the confidence to become the best team in college baseball for a large part of the next year.

I am 20 years removed from that wild night when the dude broke into our place, but people will still often ask me about the story. Just the other day, we were reminiscing and a buddy of mine asked if I would do the same thing if I was in the same exact circumstance right now.

NO F*CKING DOUBT.

Human Crash Test Dummy Life Lesson #30

The greatest mistake anybody can make is that of indecision. When you are put in a difficult situation, slow the game down, commit to a plan, then ACT.

Chapter 31
Let The Dogs Run

"Life is like a dogsled race...
If you ain't the lead dog the scenery never changes."
-Lewis Grizzard

My 3rd year in college was an absolute sh*t show. We came out blazing on the baseball field, winning our first 16 games and then spent most of the season ranked as the #1 team in the country. The first 5 spots in the lineup included Jon Heinrichs, myself, Troy Glaus, Eric Valent, and Pete Zamora. Together we totaled well over 100 homers and along the way gave ourselves the nickname "Death Row." Behind the pitching of future big leaguers Tom Jacques and Jim Parque, we finished up winning more games than any other team in the history of UCLA. At that time, because of the limited seating, Jackie Robinson stadium was not considered equipped to host a regional, so we had to travel to Stillwater Oklahoma as the #1 seed. It was a terrible draw and almost screwed us. We lost our very first game to Harvard, whose team featured two future assistant GMs that I would later play for: David Forst (A's) and Peter Woodfork (Diamondbacks). We then had to win out the rest of the way. We ended up pulling out 6 consecutive victories, including beating Oklahoma State twice in the championship. The end result was UCLA's first trip to the College World Series in 29 years.

"2 and Q." That's the term for a short-lived stay in Omaha. Two quick losses and it was time to BBQ. We lost an extra inning heart breaker to Miami and then handed Mississippi State the victory. Although a National Championship would have been ideal, the entire season and the Omaha experience was truly a dream come true. It was also my first chance to play in front of 28,000 people and a national television audience, a natural high that I undoubtedly realized I wanted more of.

I still believe the 1997 UCLA team was one of the greatest teams I have ever been a part of. What made that team so good was the ability to feed off of one another. When one guy got going, you couldn't stop us. Everybody fed off of everybody else. Of course, we were all confident as sh*t, but because there were so many great players (6 big leaguers off that one team), it kept every one of us extremely humble throughout the process of some serious ass-kicking. The internal competition created a game within the game in a positive and non-egotistical way.

Human Crash Test Dummy Life Lesson #31

Promote healthy internal competition. Make people understand that everybody is working towards a common goal and then let the dogs run! The dogs are all pulling the same sled but it's not always the same dog up front.

Chapter 32
Walk It Out

"Sometimes walking away has nothing to do with weakness and everything to do with strength. We walk away not because we want others to realize our worth and value, but because we finally realize our own."
-Unknown

The Major League draft happened the day after we got eliminated from the College World Series while we were on a flight back to LA. This was the first time I was eligible to be drafted since high school It's a rule that I agree with, and one that the MLB implemented to make sure guys are not "one and done" like you see all the time with college hoops. This benefits the school by assuring the player will stay for at least 3 years or until he turns 21. It benefits the MLB teams by oftentimes weeding out guys who most likely would have failed miserably at the Minor League level. It also provides more seasoning for the kids and in just about all cases gives the player a much better shot at succeeding in professional baseball. It also allows the player 3 years to develop physically, mature as person, and receive an education that will last a lifetime.

I was so caught up in the moment of the College World Series that I can honestly say I really had not focused too much on where I would be selected. Not because I didn't care but because I was so dialed into the moment that I completely blocked it out. I had talked to several teams, but really had no idea, other than the fact that I was pretty sure I would go before the 38th round, where I was drafted in high school. There was one scout in particular, Doug Deutsch from the Houston Astros, that seemed overly exuberant. Every scout I had ever talked to refused to say what round they would attempt to draft me in, and I did not blame them. For the most part, my relationships were with area scouts that had little control over what the cross checkers or scouting directors were ultimately going to decide.

Doug Deutsch was different. He flat out told me he recommended to the Houston Astros they select me with the 17th overall selection. I could not get another scout to make a commitment within the first 5 rounds and this guy is telling me he believes I should be a first-round pick. Forgive me if I was skeptical, but I absolutely loved his attitude. Doug Deutsch helped give me a belief in myself that I was a "first-rounder" regardless of where I ended up being selected. "You are not very pretty to watch, EB, but you are a legitimate 5-tool player." The 5 tools Doug was referring to are speed, ability to throw, field, hit for average, and hit for power. It is the basic measuring tool used by scouts for generations when grading out prospects.

I still knew the first round was a long shot and draft day confirmed my belief. Two of my teammates, Troy Glaus and Jim Parque, both found out they had been selected in the first round before we took off on our flight back from Omaha. When we landed in LA, I headed to the field to clean out my locker, and then eventually back to our condo. There was a note from Sidensol waiting for me on the coffee table right next to the signature golden spittoon. "Call Doug. You are a Houston Astro."

"Byrnesie," Doug exuberantly exalted. "We drafted you in the 4th round. . . Not as high as I wanted to get you but I am happy we got you. As of now, they gave me $90,000 to offer you, and that may go up but I cannot guarantee it. It all depends what happens with our other draft picks."

This is exactly why I loved Doug. He never once bullsh*tted me. The problem was the Astros' first-round draft pick was a kid out of Rice University that they had not anticipated dropping to them with the 17th pick, Lance Berkman. That said, it took more money to sign him than they had allotted for that spot, which meant everybody else was going to experience a trickle-down effect. Doing all the research myself, I figured out that the average amount of money 4th round guys had signed for the previous year was $135,000. I called Doug to tell him given that the approximate annual increase in signing bonuses per year has been about 5%, $141,750 is the fair number that will get me playing professional baseball.

2 weeks later, after hearing crickets from the Astros, I decided to jump on a rare opportunity to head to Cape Cod for a 3rd summer in a row. I actually became one of the very few players who have spent 3 summers playing in the Cape League. The first week I was there, the Astros scouting director was in town. I saw him at a couple of my games but for whatever reason he seemed to be avoiding any sort of communication with me. I found it odd. Finally, after about 4 or 5 games, I figured I should introduce myself. "Hello Mr. Scouting Director, I am Eric Byrnes, your 4th round draft pick." We went to breakfast the following day.

The scouting director was waiting with another Astros scout when I walked into this sweet little breakfast spot in downtown Hyannis. Before I could order a cup of coffee and an orange juice, both dudes proceeded to tell me everything they did not like about my game. Specifically, they did not like my tendency to pull the baseball and they said my circus act in the outfield was difficult to watch. They then proceeded to tell me that $90,000 was their final offer. I did my best to break down the situation from my perspective:

"So, let me get this straight. You guys are offering 40% less than what everybody else is getting in the round. Let's say I do accept the offer. I immediately give half the money back to Uncle Sam, then spend whatever is left over on a truck I would need to haul my ass from one po-dunk Minor League town to another. No doubt I would need to throw some 36-inch Mickey Thompson mudslingers on the bad boy to keep up with every Tom, Dick, and Harry in desolate America. At the end of the summer, after I drop buckets of coin on tires, gas, rent, and extra-curricular activities to keep me sane, I figure financially I would be right back where I am now, a broke-ass college student with no degree who still can't cut the umbilical cord from his parents' bank account. Also, why in the f*ck would I want to start my professional career with my back against the wall with an organization that thinks I suck donkey balls? I am not sure exactly what you dudes were trying to accomplish but for future notice, you dumb asses might want to think about taking a different approach when you try to sign your

other draft picks. I appreciate the offer but I am going back to UCLA."
I got up and walked out.

That was that last conversation I had with anyone affiliated with the Houston Astros front office. Amazingly, they did not sign their 2nd or 3rd round picks either. I have got to believe they are one of the only teams in the history of Major League Baseball to not sign their 2nd, 3rd, and 4th round picks in the same year. If you are an Astros fan, go ahead and hang your 10-gallon hat on the fact that at least they didn't f*ck up their first-rounder and the 'Stros are now your 2017 World Series champions.

Human Crash Test Dummy Life Lesson #32

Don't be afraid to walk away from a situation that doesn't feel right. My dealing with the Astros had way more to do with how I felt they negatively perceived me than it ever did about money. Feel the situation and do your best to analyze the scenario from an outside perspective. If it doesn't feel right, walk, even if it means leaving breakfast on the table.

Chapter 33
Clothing Optional

"If you're not making mistakes, then you're not doing anything. I'm positive that a doer makes mistakes."
-John Wooden

Figuring I was going to sign a professional contract after my junior year, I had not made living arrangements for my senior year. Sidensol, who had been my roommate since my freshman year, had become President of the Sigma Nu Fraternity. I was not a member of Sigma Nu, but I had attended several "gatherings" there during my time at UCLA and had gotten to know a bunch of the guys. That said, Sidensol and I made a proposal to the house that actually ended up going to a vote. I would be the first non-Sigma Nu member to live in the house and stay in Sidensol's big-ass presidential suite. In exchange, I would pay $500 a month that would go into an "emergency slush fund" to be spent on nothing but kegs and strippers. The vote passed unanimously.

Shocking to many I am sure, I actually had done extremely well academically at UCLA. I was a history major and was working towards a specialization in business administration. I have an incredible appreciation and passion for US history and ended up writing my senior thesis on Jackie Robinson and how him breaking the color barrier in baseball helped transcend race relations across the country and ultimately helped abolish any sort of legal segregation. I ended my career at UCLA winning the "Academic Excellence" award four years in a row. The "Academic Excellence" was an award handed out to the player with the highest GPA in his class. I had come a long way since my grade school principal was ordering IQ tests and wanted to banish me to a school for "troubled" youths.

On the baseball field, we had lost a bunch of our major contributors from the College World Series team. Gone was the 2nd overall pick in the draft, Troy Glaus, our 2 best starting pitchers, Parque and Jacquez, and our dual-threat, sh*t-talking sensation Pete Zamora. Yet Eric Valent continued to emerge as one of the best players in college baseball, and 2 freshmen, Chase Utley and Garret Adkins, made my senior season more enjoyable just by getting a chance to watch those dudes absolutely rake.

I struggled mightily during the first half of the season. I was trying so hard to prove that returning to school was the right decision that my drive and passion actually worked against me in this case. The harder I tried, the worse it got. At the half way mark of the season, I was hitting .290 with 1 home run. Discouraged and feeling sorry for myself, I asked my dad to come and help put things in perspective.

"Just think, 'E.' you could be sucking it up in the Minor Leagues right now, riding buses from one sh*tty town to another thinking you should have stayed in school. At least this way you are getting a great education and get to be around all the hot UCLA coed's." Nothing like a little levity from the old man. From that point on, I hit over .400 with 14 homers.

I finished up my career at UCLA as the all-time leader in hits, runs scored, and doubles, but unfortunately, no national championship. It has always been fun to follow the Bruins throughout the years since I left school. Although it wasn't until a couple years ago when Jack Gifford passed away that I really immersed myself back into the UCLA program. Jack's presence was so instrumental both financially and psychologically to the Bruin family that there was no way anybody was going to replace him. My goal was not and is not to replace Jack, but just simply be there for the Bruin program as much as I can so the current players understand that the Alumni care.

So, when the Bruins came to play at Stanford in late May of 2013, I threw a big BBQ for the boys after the last game of the series. One of my promises that day was that if they got to Omaha, I was going to be there. Not only did they get to Omaha, but they breezed through the tournament, getting to the Championship series against Mississippi State. True to my word, I hopped on a flight to Nebraska and watched the Bruins win their first ever National Championship in baseball. Unfortunately, I was one of the very few UCLA baseball alums to be there and witness the College World Series title. Other than UCLA athletic director Dan Guerrero, who also played baseball for the Bruins, I believe I was the only one there and gosh damn did everybody else miss out! The following is an email that I sent to several of my former UCLA teammates the next day after the title:

Last night the Bruins won their first baseball National Championship and I am proud to say that I was there... Being on the field with the players after the game hopping up and down holding the national championship trophy was one of the coolest experiences of my life... After the celebration we headed over to the "Mattress Factory" where I proceeded to open up a tab and buy drinks for the entire city of Omaha... The epic back and forth sh*t talking with Mississippi State fans somehow turned into beer drinking contests, pounding endless shots and me standing on top of the bar leading 8 claps... I do not remember how I got back to my hotel but I was awoken in the middle of the night by the security guard... Apparently I had passed out in the hallway in front of my room... Buck ass f*cking naked!!! Go Bruins!

I was inducted into the UCLA Hall of Fame in October of 2013. No telling if the selection committee got wind of the story and whether or not it helped seal my immortality as a UCLA Bruin.

Human Crash Test Dummy Life Lesson #33

Whenever you are struggling, lean on a trusted recourse to help give you a much larger perspective on your situation. Keep in touch with your school, teammates, and friends. Celebrate school and life successes on all fronts. Relationships are just like any other aspect of life; you get out what you put in. Invest in your relationships, clothing optional.

Chapter 34
Mom's Got Your Back

"My Mother had a great deal of trouble with me but I think she enjoyed it."
-Mark Twain

My parents had gotten divorced my freshman year of college. My mom took it very hard and used my UCLA baseball games as a way to help divert her attention. She would follow me both at home and on the road every weekend during the baseball season. By the time I was a senior, my mom had spent so much time around the baseball diamond that she began dating one of the only other people that was at Jackie Robinson Stadium as much as she was: a scout for the Oakland A's, Rick Magnante.

I actually was very happy for my mom. She broke out of her shell and finally began the process of moving on beyond my dad. I had known Rick for a couple years, and along with Doug from the Astros, they were by far and away my two favorite scouts. As much as a scouts' job is to project who will be the next great super star in the game of baseball, it is also their responsibility to figure out who the over-hyped frauds may be. Scouts are inherently critical and judgmental. Talking sh*t about a player's deficiencies is the norm in nearly every conversation they engage in. Doug and Rick were both very different. They were always very positive and complimentary. The only thing that would be weird was if the Oakland A's drafted me. I figured I had a 29 out of 30 chance of that not happening. Sure as sh*t, who comes calling on draft day?

Rick Magnante and the Oakland F*CKING A's.

Because I was terrible for the first part of my senior year at UCLA when the majority of the scouts come out to evaluate players, I expected to drop in the draft, and I did. I took solace in the fact that Magnante wasn't doing me any favors. The A's selected me in the 8th round, 4 rounds after I had gone the year before. Apparently, Mom making out with Rick only took me so far. Not wasting any time and not wanting to make the situation any more awkward than it already was, I signed as quickly as I could. My big signing bonus? A bus ticket to Medford, Oregon.

Ironically, as weird as the situation may have seemed on the surface, it wasn't weird at all. Rick was nothing but a gentleman and awesome figure in both my life and my mom's.

Human Crash Test Dummy Life Lesson #34

You never know where you may find guidance so get over whatever insecurities and perceived outside perceptions you may have. Be open and accepting to ALL people who have your best interest in mind. Especially when Mom is involved :)

Chapter 35
Just Get In The Lineup

"Be happy you aren't hitting 10th."
-Greg Sparks

When I arrived in Medford, we had 2 days of workouts before our first game in Portland. It gave me an opportunity to meet and get to know my teammates. Growing up in the San Francisco Bay Area, there have been very few times in my life in which I have ever been "culture shocked." This was one of those very rare times. From California to New York to Florida to Venezuela to the Dominican Republic, Puerto Rico, and everywhere in between, our team seemed to have representatives in Medford. There literally were guys from all different locations, vocations, and walks of life. Some had just signed out of high school, junior college and 4-year universities. Others had been playing professional baseball since they were 16 years old. There were white guys, black guys, Asians, and a ton of Latin American players that comprised nearly 50% of the team. There were kids that seemed to come from affluent backgrounds and others that grew up without electricity and running water. Regardless, everyone was there chasing the same dream and that dream could not have seemed any further away. The first 2 dudes I latched onto were a slugging first baseman out of Southwest Missouri State, Jason Hart, and a pitcher from the University of Minnesota, Jason Dobis.

Before the first game, Greg Sparks, our manager, posted the lineup: 9) Byrnes 9. I understood the 9 by my name, which represented right field, the position I would be playing, but 9th in the batting order? I immediately went into Sparky's office. "9th? F*cking 9th? That's some bullsh*t, Sparky. I have never hit 9th in any batting order in my life." Sparky fired back, "Be happy you aren't hitting 10th!"

Wanting to prove Sparky wrong so badly, I struggled throughout the first series. 2 hits in 12 at bats over the 3-game series. Maybe Sparky was right? Maybe I wasn't cut out for professional baseball? I had heard the numbers. Over 95% of all Minor League players never see a day in the big leagues.

For the first time since my freshman year in high school, doubt began to creep into my head. When we got back to Medford, I called my dad discouraged and mentally questioning my ability. "I don't know, Dad. This is different. Nobody seems to care whether we win or lose. At times it feels as if some players on the team enjoy seeing guys fail, the manager thinks I suck, and I am starting to think he may be right." Dad then asked, "How many games have you guys played?" "3." "Well if you want, you can come home and drive the fork lift at Acousta-Lite, we actually just had a spot open up."

Once again, nothing like a little perspective to ignite a hot streak. The next day: 2 hits, then 2 more, then 3 hits. All of a sudden, I had moved from the 9th spot in the batting order to 8th, then to 7th. We then made a road trip to Everett, Washington, just north of Seattle. As we were passing the old Kingdome, I couldn't help but think of how close we would be playing to a big-league stadium, yet how incredibly far we actually were.

The Northwest League was essentially the lowest level of A ball. To give you a gauge, there were 2 other A ball teams in the Oakland A's organization above our Southern Oregon team, then AA, then AAA. Of the 5 levels of the Oakland A's Minor League system, we were at the very bottom. It is pretty obvious that the task could seem daunting at times.

As we pulled into the Everett Stadium parking lot, there was a sign above the left field wall that read, "Ken Griffey Jr.'s 1st professional home run." Then there was a mark on the sign where the ball had hit. I turned to Jason Dobis, the quick-witted Minnesotan sitting next to me. "When I drill that sign tonight do you think they will put my name next to Griff's?" "Sure, Byrnesie, if you happen to hit that sign then get traded to the Seattle Mariners and hit 500 homers in the big leagues they might think about putting your name next to his." The 500 homers obviously never happened, but I sure as sh*t hit that f*cking sign that night for my first professional home run. Then, for good measure, I hit a 2nd homer that flew way over the sign, which upon returning to the dugout, I told Dobis, "F*ck Griffey, he can kiss my ass!" Years later, Ken Griffey Jr. was a teammate of mine in Seattle in what happened to be both of our final years. He is a great dude and got a good laugh out of the story.

After that game, I was moved up to the 3rd spot in the batting order and never looked back. A month later, I was promoted to Visalia in the California League. There are a few stretches in my baseball career where I can look back now and say that I was a BAMF (bad ass mother f*cker), and this undoubtedly was one of those times. I hit .420 for the month and a half I played for the Oaks and seemingly hit the ball hard nearly every time I was up to bat. The game seemed to me as if it was in slow motion.

The Mental Game of Baseball is a book written by Harvey Dorfman and Karl Kuehl. Ever since my freshman year of high school when I received the book as a Christmas present, it had become my bible. They refer to the "zone" several times in the book and give you keys to help you get to that sacred spot every athlete dreams about. I lived that dream in the summer of '98. I no longer questioned whether or not I was going to play in the big leagues. It was just a matter of when I was going to get there and how long I was going to play. Confidence is a powerful tool.

I think back to what Sparky told me at the beginning of the summer: "Be happy you are not hitting 10th." He couldn't have been any more right. Figuring there are only 9 spots in a batting order, hitting 10th obviously would have meant not hitting at all. Looking back, I am grateful for the opportunity to hit 9th and show that I was deserving of moving up.

Human Crash Test Dummy Life Lesson #35

It doesn't matter what position you are in at the moment. Completely commit to the process and all promotions will take care of themselves. So long as you are in the lineup and not hitting 10th, you've got a shot.

Chapter 36
Family First

"In our family we don't hide crazy,
we put it on the porch and give it a cocktail."
-Unknown

As I mentioned earlier, my dad's father was not a major player in my life, and my dad's mom passed away when I was in the 4th grade. My mom's dad was killed in a surfing accident when she was 18 and her mom died just a few years after I was born. My grandparents' direct influence in my life was relatively non-existent, but their spirit was kept alive and well through all of my crazy aunts, uncles, and cousins! I was incredibly blessed to have my mom's brother, Uncle Mike, and my Aunt Jean show me more love and support than I could have ever asked for. While at UCLA, I am not sure if they missed a game at home or on the road in 4 years. When I was in the Minor Leagues, they actually showed up in Little Rock, Arkansas. That should say it all.

I was also overwhelmed with the love and support of my Great Uncle Wayne and Great Aunt Nancy, who showed up to many of the exact same places as Uncle Mike and Aunt Jean. Wayne and Nancy didn't miss a Spring Training throughout the course of my entire 12-year career. Uncle Wayne just recently passed away and I was put in charge of giving the eulogy. I have done many public speaking engagements in my life but never anything like this. I wanted to make sure I put my thoughts and feelings into words that would explain the overall impact that my Great Uncle Wayne had on my life and pay tribute to one of the more accomplished men who has ever lived.

Today we live in a day and age where just about everything we do is documented. Personally, I very rarely get through the day without posting something that is going on in my life or something I have an opinion on. Facebook, Twitter, LinkedIn, Instagram; I am guilty of all four.

I have heard many people say that social media has completely changed the way we live our lives, but I disagree. I don't think social media changed the way we go about our daily activities but rather social media has simply allowed us to be able to instantly share those activities. A plethora of information typically not available pre-21st century now immediately becomes public with a "like" or "tweet." I am of the opinion that we as a society are constantly changing and generally progressing for the better. However, with the overload of information that we now receive, our imaginations are not nearly as challenged as they once were and the humble oppression of great accomplishment is virtually non-existent.

Enter my great "Uncle Wayne" Alexander. Uncle Wayne was my great uncle, my grandmother Claire Byrnes' brother. Claire passed when I was young and I think for whatever reason, Uncle Wayne felt inclined to take me under his wing. From the time I was in little league until my last game played in the Major Leagues, Uncle Wayne's overwhelming support was there every step of the way. He and his wife Nancy made just about every road trip while I was at UCLA. When I got into professional baseball, their commitment continued to grow as they followed me around from one obscure Minor League city to another. As a little extra incentive for the starving college student/bush leaguer that I was, Uncle Wayne would give me a $20 bill for every home run I would hit. Incredibly, it was a tradition that spanned over 26 years and even carried on throughout the course of my 11 Major League seasons. Not surprising, he even dropped me a $20 after I hit my first home run playing for the Dutch Goose softball team after I retired.

In our family, when Uncle Wayne spoke, everybody would listen and for good reason. He was quite possibly the most legendary storyteller I have ever come across in my life and he had plenty of tales to tell. He grew up swimming routes in the San Francisco Bay and Pacific Ocean; most people didn't even realize that swimming in many of these locations was even possible. He fought on the front lines in the South Pacific during WWII, originally leaving on a boat from North Carolina with well over 300 men. Uncle Wayne was 1 of 3 to come home. He then went on to put in 33 more years of public service with the San Francisco and San Mateo fire departments. Because of sub-par and unsafe working conditions, Uncle Wayne, along with 3 others, pioneered an effort that eventually led to the unionization of fire fighters across the country. He also was one of the pioneers of the Fire Fighter Olympics, which set new standards regarding the physical fitness levels of firefighters and still goes on today.

Following his father (my great grandfather) Constantine "Tex" Alexander's passion, Uncle Wayne began distance swimming in the San Francisco Bay at a very young age. Family legend says that Tex was the first person to swim from San Francisco, around Alcatraz Island, then back to San Francisco. A young Uncle Wayne wasn't too far behind. Apparently, whenever the father/son duo would get too close to the prison's shore, guards would fire off warning shots.

Uncle Wayne continued to push the envelope when he set out to complete an incomprehensible Farallon Islands to San Francisco swim. The Farallon Islands sit 27 miles west of the Golden Gate Bridge in the middle of the Pacific Ocean. Because of the huge population of elephant seals, the islands are most famously known for being the mecca of the Great White Shark's feeding ground. It is a place where an average person would most likely be uncomfortable in a boat, let alone the 52-degree shark infested water with no wetsuit, greased with Vaseline, and wearing a banana hammock. Records indicate that 2 swimmers in 1967 were the first to accomplish the feat and it wasn't done again for another 47 years. According to Uncle Wayne, he completed the swim long before 1967, and I would love to give you some sort of documentation but there is none. The way Uncle Wayne described it, he did not think the 13-hour journey was that big of a deal. If the current generation is described as the "look at me" generation, Uncle Wayne, born in 1925 shortly before the Great Depression, is the poster child for the Teddy Roosevelt legacy motto, "Speak softly and carry a big stick."

Judging by the multiple medals around his house, Uncle Wayne was no doubt a decorated Marine. From 1943 to 1945, he was under heavy fire at Guadalcanal, Saipan and eventually Iwo Jima. According to Uncle Wayne, he was present for both the first and second flag raisings on Mount Suribachi. The controversy and debate over both flag raisings still remain heavily contradicted and Uncle Wayne's story just adds fuel to the fire that has been burning for almost 70 years. I am not sure anybody knows exactly what took place that day but my great uncle would tell you that he held a .45 caliber pistol to a photographer's head, threatening to pull the trigger if a Marine was killed in the process of re-raising the flag.

I have no physical proof about what happened at Iwo Jima or whether or not Uncle Wayne actually completed the Farallon Islands swim years before 1967 as he claimed. There were no Instagram shots or Twitter timelines I can go back and check out. I can tell you though that there is absolutely no reason to discount him or his stories. So much of history has been brilliantly documented over hundreds and even thousands of years but reflecting on my Uncle Wayne's life makes me think of how much history has actually never been properly documented.

On April 10, 2014, Uncle Wayne walked over to his famous chair in the living room of the simple 2-bedroom house in San Mateo he had lived in with his wife Nancy for the past 50 years. He closed his eyes, went to sleep, and never woke up. I can't help but think that as Uncle Wayne died so did one of the last great story tellers from the greatest generation from which storytelling actually meant something. Tales were detailed scripts that allowed our imaginations to create our own images and perceived reality.

Excuse me, I need to go post this on Facebook and then fire out a tweet after I get a cool old pic of Uncle Wayne pinned up on Instagram all while making some new connections on LinkedIn that may be able to add insight to the legendary life of Wayne Alexander:

Two active marines were at the service to play "Taps" and deliver the American flag to my Aunt Nancy. The San Mateo Fire Department was well represented; they must have had nearly 50 current and former fire fighters. The chief delivered an awesome speech and the ceremonial ringing of the last bell laid to rest a true patriot.

Between Wayne and Nancy, Mike and Jean, my Aunt Kathy and Uncle Mike, Aunt Claudia, Aunt Sally and Uncle Jeff, Aunt Peggy and Uncle Terry, Aunt Janie and Uncle Chris, Aunt Patty and Uncle Don, Cousins Danny, Todd, Sherri, Gloria, Janet, Brian, Cher, Kristen, Carrie, Amy, Haley, Sean and Valerie, the family love and support I have felt throughout the course of my entire life has been hugely influential in all of my success. I am very grateful to all of my aunts and uncles who created this family first atmosphere and a bond that will last a lifetime.

Human Crash Test Dummy Life Lesson #36

Your family is a team. We oftentimes don't communicate nearly as much as we should. We have plenty of drama and not everybody gets along perfectly all of the time, yet the best teams and the best families learn from their successes and their failures. Ultimately, it is nice to know that your family will always have your back. Family first.

Chapter 37
You Have No F*cking Clue

"Do you know what it takes to play in the big leagues?"
-Karl Kuehl

Next stop was instructional league at the Oakland A's Minor League complex in Arizona. "Instructs" is generally reserved for an organization's top 30 prospects. You practice in the morning then usually play games in the early afternoons. While there, they have mini-seminars teaching players about professional baseball and all of the things that may lie ahead. One of the days, Karl Kuehl — yup, the same Karl Kuehl that co-authored *The Mental Game of Baseball,* gave a talk about what it takes to play in the big leagues.

"Hey guys. You are all here because you were the best in your high school or college. How many All-Americans do we have in here?" Hands go up all around the room. "How many Minor League all-stars do we have?" A bunch more hands were raised. "You guys have all had a lot of success. You gentlemen got a pretty good idea what it takes to play in the big leagues?" Heads around the entire room nod in agreement.

Then he broke into the scene right out of Bull Durham when Kevin Costner described to the other minor leaguers what his experience in "The Show" was like. "You hit white balls for batting practice, the stadiums are like cathedrals, you don't have to carry your own bag, women all have long legs and brains." Everyone in the room has big smiles on their faces.

"You guys get it. You all know what it's like to play in the big leagues, you were born for this. Right?" Now everyone in the room is smiling and nodding. I couldn't help but think to myself, "You are gosh damn right, Karl!" He then proceeds, "Let me tell you something boys. YOU HAVE NO F*CKING CLUE WHAT IT TAKES TO PLAY IN THE BIG LEAGUES!!!

Look around the room, gentlemen, look at the guy sitting to your left, look him in the eyes, look at the guy sitting to the right, look him in the eyes! There are 30 guys in this room and percentages say that only 3 of you will ever play a single F*CKING day in the big leagues! Who's it going to be?"

It became so quiet you could hear a pin drop. Total silence. I then did what Karl asked us to do. I looked to my left and right; my two roommates and two of my best friends, Jason Hart and Burt Snow, sat there with a bewildered look on their face. Hart was the big slugger from Springfield Missouri and Snow a filthy right-handed pitcher out of Vanderbilt with a devastating slider. I then broke the silence, "Well boys, since there is going to only be 3 of us, you f*cks coming with me?"

Not exactly the direction I thought the author of the book that preaches eternal optimism and positive thinking was going to go, but effective nonetheless. This was real talk. We didn't have any clue what it was like to play in the big leagues, and ironically, there were exactly 3 guys from instructional league 1998 that ended up playing in "The Show." Karl Kuehl served as a huge mentor of mine throughout the course of my entire career.

Human Crash Test Dummy Life Lesson #37

Have a realistic perspective on your situation and then immediately get back to work. It is the work that will give you the confidence to look around the room and ask who's coming with you.

Chapter 38
Win the Weakness

"My attitude is that if you push me towards something that you think is a weakness, then I will turn that perceived weakness into a strength."
-Michael Jordan

After instructional league, I got a call from Juan Navarette who was the roving pitching instructor for the Oakland A's at the time. He offered me a spot to play for the Los Mochis Caneros in the Mexican Pacific League. I had made $700 a month my first season in A ball. During instructs, we got 20 bucks a day for our meals and that was it. So, when I found out that Los Mochis was going to pay me $3000 a month to play winter ball, I hopped on the first plane to Mexico.

This had already been the most baseball I had ever played in my life, having logged over 200 games since the start of the college season. I was fried but I needed some spending cash. Once I got down there, I immediately latched onto J.R. Phillips, who I had watched as a kid when he came up with the San Francisco Giants and was a Mexican League American legend. He took me to the restaurants that were safe to eat at, showed me the streets to avoid passing through, and helped teach me how baseball is played the "Mexican" way. Essentially sh*t balls, sh*t balls, and oh yeah, more sh*t balls.

That's exactly how Mexican pitchers would treat American players. They would throw curveballs, sliders, change-ups, split fingers, screw balls, or anything else they could invent before throwing an American a fastball. My first game was in Obregon, a natural rival to Los Mochis and I quickly found out J.R. was not f*cking around. My first at bat with nobody on base: curve ball, slider, change-up, all balls. 3-0 count. Curve ball again for a strike. 3-1 slider, groundball to shortstop. Bienvenidos a Mexico!!! 5 pitches, not one fastball. Two more at bats went by and still not one fastball. I came to the plate 0-3 with 2 outs in the 9th inning and the scored tied. Slider, strike 1, spit finger, strike 2.

Figuring I had now gone almost an entire 4 at bats without seeing a fastball, what happened next was undoubtedly nothing short of a small miracle. On an 0-2 pitch with the game on the line, I got my first fastball in the Mexican Pacific League, belt high, right down the middle. So incredibly excited to see a straight pitch, I absolutely unloaded on it and watched it disappear into the Mexican night for the game winning home run. We returned to Los Mochis that night on a bus. By the time I had woken up the next morning, I was an instant hero. Not surprisingly, my Mexican fame was incredibly short-lived. With just 3 more hits in the next 3 weeks, my ass was sent packing. Nothing personal to Mexico or the Mexican Pacific League, but I was completely worn out and quite honestly, I could not have gotten out of there any sooner.

Overall, the Mexican League was a great experience. I understood in a hurry I needed to make an adjustment. I could hit a 100 mph fastball with ease but very few guys there even threw 90. The constant off speed exploited a part of my game that I knew I needed to work on. I went home and focused on hitting curve balls, sliders, and change-ups. By the time I got to Spring Training, I felt like my game had completely developed to the next level.

Human Crash Test Dummy Life Lesson #38

Sometimes it takes getting your ass handed to you to understand exactly what you need to work on to get better. Embrace your weaknesses, and then put in the work to improve. You don't need to be perfect; you just need to be better. Win the weakness.

Chapter 39
Confessions of a "Steroid Era" Career

"Sacrifice, discipline and prayer are essential. We gain strength through God's word. We receive grace from the sacrament. And when we fumble due to sin - and it's gonna happen - confession puts us back on the field."
-Lou Holtz

I played parts of 11 seasons of Major League Baseball from 2000 to 2010. I never used steroids and there is absolutely no reason why you should believe me. As a matter of fact, there is no reason why you should not question any player who played from the mid 1970s to every one of the current players today.

1970s you ask? Yup, that is the time when steroids became prominent at local gyms and were used recklessly by body-builders and all sorts of other athletes looking to get an edge. You can actually trace steroid use all the way back to the 1940s when the Soviet Union and other Eastern Bloc countries were looking for ways to enhance the strength of their Olympic weight lifters.

Disturbingly, not long ago I was having dinner with a former long-time Major League player that spoke about the steroid use of a prominent Hall of Famer that played the majority of his career in the '70s and '80s. Ha! Not like I was shocked but damn. So many members of the Hall of Fame, including this character, have recently spoken out and condemned guys who have had ties to performance enhancing drugs, saying there is no place for "cheaters" in the HOF. I just wonder how many of the other guys in the "Hall" were actually cheaters themselves?

Depends on your definition of cheating. I can guarantee you just about all of them at one point either stole signs, doctored a baseball, used a corked bat, or loaded up on some sort of amphetamine. Steroids, because of the adverse health effects, public perception, and terrible message it sends to our youth about what it takes to succeed, has always been looked at differently, and I believe it should be.

I can also make an argument though that steroids actually saved the game.

After the 1994 strike, many fans had turned their back on baseball. It wasn't until the famous home run chase of 1998 that MLB once again reclaimed the national spotlight. It seems a bit hypocritical to me that the guys that we marveled at and worshiped because of their ability to hit baseballs to places nobody thought possible, later became ostracized from the very game that they helped put back on the map, and for the most part, became somewhat exiled by society in general. We all had suspicions, yet nobody during that time period acted on them. Not that I condoned their performance-enhancing drug use, but let's remember there was no drug testing program in place at the time, and in my opinion, the 2 guys were simply products of a much bigger problem: an entire Major League drug culture.

I signed out of UCLA in 1998 with the Oakland Athletics and played my first Major League game with them in August of 2000. Years later, the "Mitchell Report" came out and I was shocked to read many of my former teammates' names tied to PED's. I was not ignorant to the situation, but one way I describe it is that the steroid culture was very much like the cocaine culture. You go to a club, everybody is dancing and having a good time, and you just assume everyone has that same good alcohol buzz that you do. Then you notice some dude's eyes popping out of his head or a chick that won't stop talking and looks like she is continuously picking her nose. I was not ignorant to the obvious in the "boom shooka boom boom" club and I sure as heck was not ignorant to the obvious in a big-league clubhouse. The similarities of steroids and cocaine continue; not once in my entire playing career was I ever offered steroids, and not once in my younger and wilder club-going days was I ever offered "blow." These were two very secret societies that kept to themselves

For a long time, I just accepted the "steroid era" for what it was. It did not bother me that much, and I didn't necessarily feel as if I was getting cheated. The main reason is because I did not feel as if I needed to get bigger, stronger or faster. I needed to lay off the 2-2 slider in the dirt. As a matter of fact, if I had chosen the steroid route, I would not have felt as if I was cheating. I would have been doing what a large percentage of other guys around the league had made habitual within baseball.

My decision to not use steroids was by no means a holier-than-thou attitude either. Actually, it was very selfish. I had no desire to deal with the common side effects: pre-mature balding, back acne (backne, as I like to refer to it), and shriveling testicles. I also watched a kid at my high school get so heavy into steroids that soon after graduation, his heart exploded.

Another major deterrent was that as much as I loved baseball, I refused to let the game define me as a person. So many guys put their entire self-worth into baseball; thus, they lived under the guidelines of "whatever it takes." Even as a kid, I always had many different interests. I figured that I would put my heart and soul into whatever I was doing at the time, and then when I was done for whatever reason, I would simply move on and ask myself, "What's next?"

I generally don't blame the guys who used performance-enhancing drugs prior to 2003 when the drug-testing program was finally implemented. They were simply victims of a PED culture that was ultimately fueled by the silence of the players, coaches, teams, and the media as well.

My first year out of the game, I ran into a borderline HOF-caliber player and the issue of steroids came up. He proceeded to tell me that he played his entire career steroid-free until he realized his time was coming to an end and he became willing to do anything to hang on. For the final 2 years of his career, he used performance-enhancing drugs. He said the main difference that he noticed was how well he could SEE THE BASEBALL! Immediately, I thought to myself it was a good thing I didn't find that out until after I was done playing. Throughout the course of my career, there were definitely times that I felt like I would have done ANYTHING to lay off that gosh damn 2-2 slider in the dirt!

As I am now years removed from playing the game and well into a broadcasting career, I hold a much different view. In 2013, 14 players tied to Biogenesis in a lot of ways was the final straw for me. For years, dirty players have been screwing clean players out of opportunities and potential financial prosperities. For whatever reasons, the clean players simply have just kept their mouths shut and continued to be okay with getting cheated. Based on the recent comments of many current major leaguers, times are definitely changing, and I encourage more to speak out. There is no greater influence than that of your own peers.

Concerning is the fact that not one of the players was suspended because of their link with biogenesis, and with the exception of Ryan Braun, not one of them ever tested positive for PED's. Here we are several years after the drug-testing program was implemented, and obviously guys are still beating the system. Chemists seem to be a least 2 steps ahead of the testers. Now, new forms of fast acting testosterone that can leave your system within hours seem to be the recent drug of choice.

So long as the reward of multi-million dollar contracts outweighs the risk of an 80-game suspension for 1st time offenders, players will continue to try to beat the system. For the sake of the game, current players need to encourage the players' union to make the penalty so severe for 1st time offenders that it actually serves as a real deterrent. My suggestion: a one-year suspension for the 1st positive test, and you also give the team the option to cancel a player's contract, figuring that player signed the contract under false pretenses. The players' union will never want to agree to this because players' contracts are essentially what keep them in business. The players must remember though, it is the PLAYERS' union and ultimately their opinions and voices are what run the entire operation.

2nd offense: Lifetime ban. Players must also continue to chastise cheaters, making them feel embarrassed and ashamed for their actions. This is now an opportunity for current big leaguers to stand up for all the clean players, active and former, who have been wrongfully cheated out of opportunities and jobs throughout the course of the past 30 plus years.

Human Crash Test Dummy Life Lesson #39

Every year we advance as a society and baseball advances as a sport. Instead of casting blame on individual players, baseball as a whole needs to accept responsibility for an entire era plagued by performance enhancing drugs. I encourage all of us to be accountable for our actions and learn from the mistakes of the past, which will in turn lay the foundation for a much better future.

Chapter 40
Fight Your Cause

*"First they ignore you, then they laugh at you,
then they fight you, then you win."*
-Mahatma Gandhi

The big question amongst baseball historians is what to do with an entire 20-30 year era that was no doubt tainted by performance enhancing drugs. Surefire first-ballot Hall of Famers Roger Clemens and Barry Bonds (in my opinion the best pitcher and hitter of that generation) were denied entry into the Hall in their first several eligible years. These are 2 guys who have obviously been linked to steroids, but if you are going to deny entrance to anybody from that era because of their link to PEDs, you must deny entrance to the entire 20-30 year time period that has become known as the "steroid era." We cannot expect or give the Baseball Writers Association of America (BBWAA) the right to conduct their very own witch hunt every year trying to figure out who they thought juiced and who they thought was clean. I am of the opinion that you either have to take that entire "Steroid Era" off of the ballot or you must let in all deserving candidates. I can write a book, just as I am doing, proclaiming I never touched performance-enhancing drugs, but because I played in that era, I am as guilty as the next dude. Guilt by association in this case is bullsh*t but there is just no possible way to decipher between who actually used and who played the game legitimately clean.

For me personally, the Hall of Fame should be about the best players of a generation and that's it. There is no way to compare Ty Cobb to Barry Bonds, Babe Ruth to Willie Mays, Hank Aaron to Joe DiMaggio, or Ted Williams to Mike Trout. Statistically, the only way to compare players is if they played within the same time period. Even as much as I believe in the sabermetrics world, adjusted statistics based on eras don't do it for me. Simply put, if you want to be considered the best, then that means you were statistically one of the very best of your generation.

The Sad Joke That Has Become The Baseball Hall of Fame:

First and foremost, I want to say how much baseball has been an incredible part of who I am. As a matter of fact, ever since I can remember, my life has been consumed with the game. As I kid, I would spend my days pitching a tennis ball against the garage and then picking up a bat and whacking the rebound. When "The Natural" came out, I went to see it with my mom in the old Belmont Theatre on the El Camino. I loved it so much I would not leave. I made her stay so we could watch the next showing an hour after the first one ended. After I saw "Major League" the first thing I did was go and buy a Cleveland Indians #99 jersey. I watched "61" so many times I actually became a quasi-Yankee fan. I would fall asleep to Ken Burns' PBS documentary "Baseball" almost every night, even when I played professionally.

I collected baseball cards as a kid and spent every dollar I earned pumping gas at the Chevron and slicing meat at Melina's Deli on improving my collection. Nolan Ryan, Rickey Henderson, Wade Boggs, Don Mattingly, Ken Griffey Jr., Jose Canseco, Cal Ripken Jr., Daryl Strawberry, and Dwight Gooden "Rookie" Cards — I had to have them. As for the Mark McGwire and Will Clark 1984 Olympic cards, no doubt I needed the whole set. At one point, there was not a Will Clark card that existed that I did not own. I even splurged for the famous "F-Face" Billy Ripken card; I was the envy of every 12-year-old kid in my neighborhood.

To be able to then play parts of 11 Major League seasons with 5 different teams was beyond a dream come true. Even now, working for the Major League Baseball Network, there is not a single day I don't realize how fortunate I am to have my professional life entrenched in something that I have had so much passion for throughout the years.

I have prefaced you with all of this because what I have to say next may be viewed as somewhat anti-Major League Baseball, and that is not the case. We all, including myself, have plenty of imperfections and MLB is not any different. Replay should have been implemented 30 years ago, it took a catcher nearly getting killed before they finally changed the rule about collisions at home plate, and a one-game wildcard playoff to decide a 162-game regular season still seems asinine to me. Yet I am not sure anything upsets me more than when a game that prides itself on history and tradition, above all else, fails to recognize some of its greatest players because Major League Baseball has decided to morally judge certain individuals based on circumstances and actions that many would argue Major League Baseball helped facilitate. Over 500 writers have a difficult enough time deciding who to vote for without asking them to play "moral police."

What I am trying to say is that I think the Hall of Fame has become a sad joke. The only person with 7 MVP awards and the only person with 7 Cy Young's in history haven't stood a chance for admittance because of their ties to PED's. Yet over the last several years, other guys who have been linked to performance enhancing drugs have gained admittance. We might as well throw Barry Bonds and Roger Clemons in the same category as Pete Rose. They are three of the greatest players of all time that all of a sudden people want to forget ever even played the game. There is part of me that sympathizes with the writers, part of me that sympathizes with the players, but there is not a single bit of me that feels sorry for the Hall of Fame that makes the voting decision incredibly difficult for everybody involved.

The Hall of Fame is listed on Wikipedia as an "American History Museum and Hall of Fame." How can the Hall possibly be considered an "American History Museum" when it attempts to turn its back to baseball's historical past? There are plenty of things in our history that we as Americans are not proud of, but the great thing about this country is that we recognize our mistakes of the past and move on to correct those mistakes for the betterment of the future.

The Hall of Fame's motto is "Preserving History, Honoring Excellence, Connecting Generations." By not recognizing the "steroid era" in general and honoring the greatest players in that time period is failing to do any of the three. Baseball facilitated a culture for many years and now is trying to do its best to pretend like that entire era never existed. Three managers of that time just unanimously got elected to the Hall of Fame. How many games did those managers win with the help of juiced up players? Obviously, the Hall of Fame Veterans Committee did not hold those managers accountable for their players' actions when deciding their HOF fate, and they shouldn't have. Yet if we are willing to forgive the "steroid era" managers, why would we not forgive the "steroid era" players? Especially when we have no idea who did what and when they did it.

The Hall of Fame Veterans Committee was amended in 2001 to include current Hall of Fame members and other "honorees" including executives, baseball historians, and media members. The intention of putting the vote into the hands of living players in the HOF seemed to be a good one but there is one major problem. The more guys that are elected into the Hall, the more a current Hall of Famer's brand is potentially diminished.

In 2007 after 3 consecutive years of electing nobody, Hall of Famer Mike Schmidt admitted such, "The same thing happens every year. The current members want to protect the prestige as much as possible and are unwilling to open the doors."

So, the question now becomes how do we fix the problem? First and foremost, I want an entire section built in the HOF explaining the "steroid era" and what sort of affect it had on the history of baseball. Let's also make sure current members of the HOF have nothing to do with any sort of selection process. The conflict of interest is too great. The next thing that needs to be done is the Baseball Writers Association of America needs to limit the number of voters to those who actually follow the game, actively write about it and care about the historical meaning of what the Hall of Fame is supposed to represent. The original concept to grant the writers the power to decide the game's greatest players of all time was to hopefully get unbiased opinions and votes. That has never been the case. The issue is that members of the BBWAA are actual human beings, and just like the rest of us, they have never been unbiased. They continue to prove that year in and year out when a seemingly no-question, slam-dunk first-ballot Hall of Famer gets denied votes. Babe Ruth, Ty Cobb, Willy Mays, Hank Aaron, Nolan Ryan, Greg Maddux, and every other elected Hall of Famers have all been victims of blatant wrongful omissions on the ballot by members of the BBWAA.

You would think that when it took Joe DiMaggio four tries to get inducted, that's right, four freaking tries, the HOF would have said enough is enough and they would have figured out a different election process. About the only semi-logical reason to keep the standard HOF vote solely in the writers' hands is because that's where it has always been. We all know baseball prides itself on tradition, but whether we like it or not, this world is about learning from our mistakes of the past and eventually changing for the overall well-being of the future. The time has come for the Hall of Fame to make that change.

I propose an annual rotating panel of voters comprised of members of the BBWAA, noted baseball historians, and former MLB players, managers, and executives NOT in the Hall of Fame. Who better to judge the best players of an entire generation than the actual people that signed, managed, and played against them, as well as those who documented their every move?

The Hall would also need to make sure as many different eras as possible are represented. I would also propose that a small portion of the vote comes from the actual numbers themselves. In the sabermetrics world that we now live in, I would trust a computer telling me who a Hall of Famer is just as much as a baseball historian or a certain player who may hold certain prejudices for whatever reasons. Trust me, I have no intention of eliminating the human element of the process; I just want to let the hard numbers have their say.

The final group that baseball has no right keeping out of the selection process is the consumers who keep the entire business of baseball in operation, the fans. The Hall must then make sure all of these groups have the appropriate education and understanding of what classifies a Hall of Famer.

In 1945, when the Hall came up with its official rules for election, it asked voters to consider candidates based on "overall playing ability, integrity, sportsmanship, character, their contributions to the team on which they played and to baseball in general." This was the final product of qualification standards that were amended several times between 1936 and 1945. In order to eliminate gray areas and individual biases and judgments, I propose the HOF eliminates the "integrity, sportsmanship and character" portion. For me personally, I really don't care what kind of guy you were or are. I just want to know if you were the best. The Hall of Fame selection process will never be perfect, there will always be controversy and debate, but it is the Hall of Fame's responsibility to make sure we simplify the selection process and eliminate subjective opinions as much as possible. There are already liars, cheaters, and drug users in the Hall of Fame; what's wrong with a few more?

Overall, my biggest problem with the Hall of Fame is that they don't let enough guys in. Growing up in the San Francisco Bay Area, Will Clark defined an entire era of baseball for me and many other Bay Area baseball fans in the mid-1980s and early '90s.

The Curious Case of William Nuschler Clark:

When I watched Roger Kieschnick make his major league debut in 2013, I could not help but feel an overwhelming discomfort as the former 2008 3rd round draft pick stepped into the box for his first major league at bat. It had nothing to do with Kieschnick or his ability. It was just that there was another lefty, one with the prettiest swing I have ever seen, that I could not get out of my head. A guy who happened to make his major league debut 27 years earlier and donned the same number Roger Kieschnick was wearing: 22.

Growing up a die-hard sports fan in the San Francisco Bay Area in the 1980s, there were two local athletes that defined my childhood and served as role models in my life. They helped shaped me as an athlete and as a person, the first being Joe Montana, the other, Will Clark: The gritty southerner out of Mississippi State that spoke with a Louisiana twang and played with an intensity and drive that resembled exactly who I was in my youth. Will Clark defined an entire era of San Francisco Giants baseball, and more importantly for me, he helped influence who I became as a baseball player through the course of my entire amateur and professional career.

"Thrill," as he was known since his Jesuit High School days back in Louisiana, blasted on the scene (literally) and lived up to his nickname by taking Nolan Ryan deep in his first at bat in the big leagues. The next season, in 1987, he went on to lead the Giants to the playoffs for the first time since 1971, hitting 35 homers and turning in a .951 OPS. In 1989, he introduced himself to the world in the National League Championship Series against the Chicago Cubs when he hit .650 with 3 doubles and 2 homers, including a memorable grand slam at Wrigley Field that proved to be the turning point in the series. Then came the clinching hit against the Cubs flame-throwing left-hander, Mitch Williams. I was sitting in the upper deck in Section 62 in center field that day at Candlestick Park. I am now a 40-year-old grown man who happened to play parts of 11 Major League seasons, and I still get butterflies thinking back to the feeling that went through my body when Thrill smoked the ball back up the middle, driving in the game winning runs. Obviously, Will Clark was named the NLCS MVP as he single-handedly carried the Giants to their first World Series since 1962.

In 8 total seasons with the Giants, he was a 6-time All-Star and finished top 5 in MVP voting 4 times. Clark then went on to play for the Texas Rangers, and in his first season there, propelled them into the playoffs for the first time in the organization's history. After a very productive 5 years with the Rangers, Thrill ended up in Baltimore in 1999, then in 2000, his final year, Clark was traded from the Orioles to the Cardinals and once again guided another team down the stretch and into the post season hitting .345 with an OPS of over 1.000. Will Clark retired at 36 years old with plenty of baseball left in him. He undoubtedly could have continued to play for several more years but made the selfless decision to put his family first. Will's son,

Trey, was diagnosed with autism, so he decided to hang 'em up and put the same emotion that he played the game of baseball with into helping full time with Trey's development. He finished his career with 2176 hits, a batting average of .303 and an OPS of .880. He hit 284 home runs and drove in over 1,205 runs.

In 2006, Will Clark's name was on the Hall of Fame ballot for the first time. He received 4.4% of the vote, not meeting the 5% threshold needed to remain on the ballot for future consideration. Not exactly sure why HOF voters penalize a guy that didn't play until he was hobbling around in his mid 40's in search of hit #3000 or home run #500 (both long considered HOF benchmarks)? Forgive me if I don't recognize the Hall of Fame's legitimacy as much as other baseball purists.

For me, a Hall of Fame player is somebody who was one of the best players over a 10+ year period. Will Clark was exactly that, but for 15 years. Also, if the Hall of Fame wants to continue to morally judge players and leave guys out of the HOF based on the "character" clause, shouldn't they consider the noble decision of Will Clark to walk away early for the greater good of his family and actually award somebody for their character?

Will Clark will never get into Cooperstown, but quite frankly, I am not all that concerned with the hypocrites that vote for and constitute the Hall of Fame. Their issues go far beyond Will Clark. What I am concerned with is that there are currently 10 numbers that have been retired by the Giants organization. #3 Bill Terry, #4 Mel Ott, #11 Carl Hubbell, #20 Monte Irvin, #24 Willie Mays, #27 Juan Marichal, #30 Orlando Cepeda, #36 Gaylord Perry, #44 Willie McCovey, and #42 Jackie Robinson, which is universally retired around baseball. Will Clark's #22 is painfully absent from this list. The common denominator of each of these guys is that they have all been inducted into Cooperstown.

This is now the Giants' chance to stand up and not let the Baseball Hall of Fame dictate who the most important players are in the storied franchise of the New York and San Francisco Giants. The

Giants have a responsibility to recognize one of the fiercest competitors and greatest players in the history of the organization by making sure his story continues to be told to future ballplayers and fans for generations to come. When my dad used to take me to Candlestick Park, I would always ask him about the numbers hanging from the right field chain link fence, and he always had detailed stories for me about the former Giants greats. Now, I feel it is my obligation to share stories with my 3 children about the greatest Giants who ever played. I would love nothing more than to go to AT&T park, have one of them point to #22, and give me the opportunity to explain to my kids the legend of one William Nueshler Clark.

I began a campaign effort a few years ago and even got an opportunity to explain to Larry Baer my sentiments. A petition was created by fans to make it happen, attracting several thousand signatures of dedicated Giants fans, yet still no ceremony. The only thing we can continue to do is pressure Giants ownership and front office to do the right thing, properly recognize one of the greatest players who ever put on a Giants uniform by retiring the number 22.

Human Crash Test Dummy Life Lesson #40

Don't be afraid to stand up for what you believe. Whatever your cause may be, the most important thing is to authentically believe in the change you are trying to create. Remember, no great change is made without great efforts. Keep grinding.

Chapter 41
Play Your Game

*"From good people you'll learn good,
but if you mingle with the bad you'll destroy such soul as you had."*
-Musonius Rufus

I went to my first Spring Training not knowing what to expect. I started out with the AAA team in camp where I was introduced to an entire group of dudes that basically were a bunch of bitter pricks that all had a bullsh*t sob story on how and why they were getting screwed out of a big-league job. It is very normal to start camp at least 1 or even 2 levels above the team you would actually break camp with because of the excess players in Major League camp that eventually get demoted, causing a trickle-down effect. Basically, I was the only first-year guy with a lot of older dudes who had not been invited to big-league camp or who had already been sent down. The last thing they wanted was to get shown up by some punk in his first Spring Training looking to take their job.

Well, that's exactly what I did. I would diligently go through the plyometric stretching routine, bust my ass on every base running drill, and chase down every fly ball I could get to in batting practice. The harder I went, the more pissed these guys would get. I definitely wasn't making any friends and I didn't give a f*ck.

The first day of camp, we broke off with our teams and went through a "fitness test." It was 4 laps around the field, approximately 1 mile, that had to be done in under 7 minutes and 30 seconds; otherwise, it was to be repeated for the following days until the time could be achieved. The majority of the guys ran in a group that would have them come in together just under the allotted time. I finished in under 5 minutes, which was a full minute and a half ahead of the next AAA guy. I lapped nearly the entire team. Of course, all of the veteran Minor Leaguers were talking sh*t. "Who's this f*cking guy think he is? Hey Prefontaine, settle down you are making us look bad." Essentially there were two directions I could have taken in regards to the general sentiment of the team: 1) being it was my first time in camp, I could slow up a bit and try not to make things too hard on myself when it came to making new friends, or 2) being it was my first time in camp, I could send a message that I am going to approach Spring Training with my nut sack hanging out of my pants and I don't give a f*ck what you think.

I decided to go with number #2.

Through all of the abuse that I took, I stayed true to myself. I did not let the pressures to be cool, lazy, or average affect me. That wasn't who I was and that was not who I was going to be. I started the year with Modesto, the high-A team in the California League. That team quite possibly could have been the best team I played on in my professional career. We ended up winning over 100 games in the Minor League season, which consist of only 142 games as opposed to 162 played in the Major Leagues. Bob Geren was the manager, and we were led offensively by guys like Ryan Ludwick, Esteban German, Jason Hart, and Oscar Salazar, all of whom played in the big leagues. Yet our best player that summer was Jacque Landry, a 27-year-old Minor League journey man out of Rice University whose famous phrase, "What's up tho" became the team rallying cry. Our pitching staff was anchored by Jesus Colome throwing 100 mph nearly every pitch, Jon Adkins, the easygoing hick from the back woods of West Virginia, and Jim Brink, the Stockton kid out of University of Nevada Reno. The first 2, Colome and Adkins, pitched several years at the big league level. By August, the final month of the Cal League season, I was leading the league in hitting and was promoted to AA in Midland, Texas.

Human Crash Test Dummy Life Lesson #41

It is always important to maintain a growth mindset and do not conform to a way of thinking, acting, or playing because you are trying to please others or because that's the way it has always been done. By no means am I advocating disrespecting anybody, but stay true to your beliefs and style of play regardless if others take offense.

Bottom line: Play your f*cking game.

Chapter 42
The F*ck You Effect

*"Can you see the 'f*ck you' in my smile?"*
-Unknown

Other than the 2-week debacle in Mexico, AA Midland was the first time in pro ball that I got a pretty good taste of failure. I hit under .240 for the month of August as I was rudely introduced to cities like Shreveport, Louisiana, Jackson, Mississippi, and the beautiful summer weather. Never before had I made any sort of excuse because it was too hot or too cold.

This was different, way different. Playing in 100-degree heat with a heat index in the 120's was flat out miserable and I found myself bitching to anyone who would listen. It basically got to the point where I wanted to annex a good part of the south from the rest of the United States. I was f*cking miserable and my play on the field was just as bad.

For the most part, my month-long experience in the Texas League was a lost cause with the exception of one night in Midland. Eric Gange, the Texas League pitcher of the year and crazy-ass Canadian with a high 90's fastball and devastating off-speed pitches to go with it, was on the mound for San Antonio. Throwing a self-pity party as I struggled to get to the end of the season, I needed some sort of wake-up call and Gange gave it to me.

Gange liked to work quick so I wanted to be sure I was ready to hit before he threw the pitch. I came up with a runner on base, fouled off the first pitch, then stepped out of the box to regroup and get the signs from Tony DeFrancesco, our manager and 3rd base coach. That's when I heard a booming voice coming from the pitcher's mound. "Get in the box!" I looked out towards the mound and Gange was standing there motioning toward me with his glove to get back into the batter's box. My blood began to boil a bit but I kept my mouth shut. He was

Eric Gange, Texas League pitcher of the year, and I was just some scrub hitting .200 that just got called up from A ball. The next pitch came directly at my head upwards of 95 mph.

Now, I no longer cared who the f*ck he was. Dude just intentionally tried to throw a baseball in my earhole. My immediate reaction was to get up, run out to the mound, and do my best to detach his head from his body. Instead, I just froze, my heart rate increased, and my pupils dilated. We exchanged words back and forth until the umpire and the catcher stepped out in front of home plate to act as a shield between the two of us.

The next pitch was a fastball over the middle of the plate at eye level. To this day, I still have no explanation how I was able to hit a mid-90's, head-high fastball further than any other ball I had ever hit in my life. It was also the first time in my career that I stood at home plate to admire my work. I then proceeded to slowly round the bases until I touched home plate for my one and only AA home run that summer. I faced Gange several times after that and thankfully nothing more ever developed. I have seen him several times at a golf tournament in Pebble Beach and always keep close tabs on his whereabouts just in case he finally decides he wants his payback.

I recently read a book by Matt Fitzgerald called How Bad Do You Want It? The book's main premise is that people are motivated to ultimately reach their full potential by various factors. The crowd effect, the country effect, the team effect, the fear effect, and so on. I will refer to this one as the "f*ck you" effect; seems appropriate.

Human Crash Test Dummy Life Lesson #42

No matter how difficult the circumstance, save your complaints and self-pity party. Neither are productive avenues to move forward. If and when you become consumed by emotions, let that energy positively work for you. The "f*ck you" effect is real. Think about applying a 'controlled aggression' and use it to your advantage.

Chapter 43
Think Outside The Box

"Being generous often consists of simply extending a hand. That's hard to do if you are grasping tightly to your righteousness, your belief system, your superiority, your assumptions about others, your definition of normal."
-Patti Digh

After the AA season, I was fortunate to get an invite to the prestigious Arizona Fall League, where organizations generally send their top 5 or 6 prospects. This was the first time that I realized I actually played for the Oakland A's organization, as each player donned the Major League uniform of the team that they were with. My team, the Phoenix Desert Dogs, was managed by John Mizerock, who was with the Kansas City Royals organization at the time. The screwy thing with the fall league was that your playing time was generally dependent on where your team slotted you based on level of importance.

For example, I played about every third day, so I assume that I was probably the 5th or 6th guy that the A's prioritized. Basically, I was at the bottom of the list. It was tough to get into a groove playing infrequently, so my struggles from my first short stint in AA continued into the fall league, right up until my mom came into town for 3 games. The first game I did not play. This was not something she was used to; as a matter of fact, this was probably the first baseball game she had ever been to in her life in which I did not play. I tried to explain to her how the system worked. Her response was that she wasn't quite sure how the Arizona Fall League playing time situation works, but she had a pretty good handle on how the rest of the world works.

"What does he like?"

"What do you mean?"

"Does he like chocolates? If so, I'll bring him some See's candy. Does he like wine? If so I'll bring him a nice bottle."

"Mom, this isn't little league. This is the gosh dang Arizona Fall League with Major League Baseball's top prospects. You can't bribe your way into playing time around here."

"You never answered me, what does he like?"

"I don't know... He drinks Budweiser's and smokes Marlboro Red's."

That night after dinner, my mom had me take her by the 7-11 to get some aspirin, or so she said. She walked out with a 30 pack of Budweiser's and a carton of Marlboro Red's. "Give these to your coach tomorrow and tell him your mom would LOVE to see you play."

The next day, I walked into the clubhouse with the case of beer in one hand, a carton of cigarettes in the other, and an embarrassingly huge smile on my face. I dropped them on "Rock's" desk in his office as he gave me this bewildered look. "My mom says she would LOVE to see me play." I figured at the worst, I could play it off as a joke and get a few laughs from Rock, who seemed like a guy who would find humor out of such a ridiculous proposition. "Your mom is a very smart person. You are leading off and playing left field." He then opened up the carton of cigarettes, grabbed a pack, walked outside, and lit up a smoke. Ironically, I had 3 hits that game, and the next game I was in the lineup again and hit my first home run of the fall. Rock continued to find a way to get me into the lineup long after Mom went back home. I played way more than I should have that fall and hit well over .300, putting myself on the map as a legitimate Major League prospect. All thanks to my mother, a case of beer and a carton of smags.

Human Crash Test Dummy Life Lesson #43

Even if it is not "normal," go ahead and do something small for somebody you are working with. So long as you don't EXPECT something in return, there is absolutely no downside. At the very least, it shows that you are a thoughtful person and a ridiculous gift could be just the thing that molds a relationship to create a better work environment.

Chapter 44
Commit to the Journey

"God grant me the courage to accept the things I cannot change, the courage to change the things I can and the wisdom to know the difference."
-Reinhold Niebuhr, *Serenity Prayer*

The next season, I started back in AA Midland where I had finished the last month of the previous year. The weather in the Texas League and my attitude were much better in April and May as opposed to the previous August. Not surprisingly, so was my play on the field. At the halfway point of the Minor League season, I was called up to AAA Sacramento where I continued to play very well. By mid-August I was hitting nearly .370 with 11 home runs in just over a month of playing in Sacramento. Then on August 21, 2000 at Raley Field in Sacramento, I came up with 2 outs and nobody on in the 9th inning with our team trailing by 2 runs. I hit a blooper down the right field line that I saw the right fielder loaf after knowing he was not going to be able to catch the ball. Going full speed as soon as I left the batter's box, I thought there was no way he would be able to throw me out at 2nd base, so I attempted to slide in for a double.

I was wrong. I had just committed an ultimate baseball sin: ending the game on the base paths when I was not the tying or go-ahead run. Immediately, longtime-Yankee Roy White, who was our hitting coach, found me as I made the long walk back to the clubhouse that was situated beyond the left field fence. Roy was the most easygoing guy that I had ever dealt with in professional baseball. So, when I saw the stern look on his face, I knew he was pissed.

"Bob wants to see you in his office, NOW!" The Bob he was referring to was Bob Geren, who I had played for in A ball in Modesto and now was the AAA manager in Sacramento. We always had a very good relationship, but bone-head plays, like getting thrown out going for a double when your team is down by 2 runs in the 9th inning, he would not tolerate. I walked into his office.

"Shut the door. What were you possibly thinking? You know way better than to get thrown out at 2nd in that situation. I know I have taught you better than that. I know you know better than that. Whatever you do, don't make the same mistake in Cleveland tomorrow night!"

"Cleveland? Who's playing in Cleveland?"

"The A's are and you will be in the lineup. Congratulations, you are going to the big leagues!"

I went back to my place in Sacramento and immediately called my mom. "Mom, remember all the trips to the batting cages and the stops at Jack in the Box for 'home run' tacos?"

"Of course, did you hit a home run tonight?"

"No, but hopefully I will in Cleveland tomorrow."

"Cleveland? Oh no! Did you get traded to Cleveland?"

"No, Mom! The Oakland A's play in Cleveland tomorrow. I got called up to the big leagues!" She immediately began to scream and then cry, which I think all of a sudden made me realize the magnitude of the situation. I then had a flashback to the days when I was 4 years old firing the tennis ball against the garage then quickly picking up a bat and whacking the deflection into the redwood trees behind my house. I thought about when I was 7 years old playing tee ball for Melina's Deli, getting upset with the other kids who could not catch the ball. I thought about when I was 9 years old and playing on Morey's, chasing fly's in the outfield in between pitches and crying every time I struck out. I thought about my dad, throwing countless hours of batting practice to me at the Portola Valley Town Center. I thought about my sister and my cousin Brian, who I spent my childhood telling them that I would one day play in the Major Leagues. I thought about that day at St. Francis when I looked at the names of the kids on the board who had made the freshman baseball team (Chris Byrnes). I thought about Tom Sutter (little league), Chris Bradford (St. Francis), Gary Tagliafico and Jerry Berkson (Peninsula Mets), Jim McAlpine (Menlo Park Joe D), Gary Adams and Vince Beringhele (UCLA), Sparky, Tony D, Keith Lippmann, Dave Hudgens, Karl Kuehl, and Bob Geren (A's). I thought about Coach T who taught me the value of training "the right way." I thought about every one of my coaches and mentors who, along the course of a 20-year period, helped me get to this point in my baseball career. I began to cry, then laugh, then cry, then laugh some more. After I called my dad and sister, I did everything I could to try to get some sleep. No chance, so I grabbed a 40 of Mickey's, sat down in front of the TV, and watched Seinfeld re-runs until it was time to head to the airport at 5 am.

I started the season with the idea of trying to prove myself at the AA level. When I was first promoted to AAA, there seemed to be at least 3 outfielders ahead of me on the depth chart. Then, after a dumb ass mistake, I assumed I was being summoned to the manager to get absolutely blasted and possibly fined or benched. Instead, I got called up to the big leagues.

Human Crash Test Dummy Life Lesson #44

If you spend too much time focusing on the destination, you won't ever live the dream. Stay committed to the process of what is in your control and all the other sh*t will take care of itself. The journey is the dream.

Chapter 45
Dreams Become Reality

"Welcome to the big leagues, kid."
-Art Howe

August 22, 2000: I took off from Sacramento on a Southwest flight and landed in Denver for my Delta connection to Cleveland. That's where I ran into a couple familiar faces waiting at the gate for the same flight I was on: my mom and my sister. I was too tired to really put things in any sort of coincidental perspective at that point, but I was ecstatic that they had made the trip. I had not slept in over 30 hours and my first taste of the Major Leagues happened as soon as I got on the plane and plopped my ass in a first-class seat. Within minutes I was out and slept the entire flight.

When we finally landed in Cleveland and got to the ballpark, it was past 6 pm. I then had to spend several minutes convincing the security guard at Jacobs Field to let me inside the stadium. I did not have any sort of Major League credentials, and I had lost my Minor League player's card, so all I had was a California driver's license and my word that I had just been called up from AAA. The security guard called to verify my identity, but apparently, my name was nowhere to be found.

After 20 years dreaming of making it to the Major Leagues, I had finally arrived and I couldn't get into the f*cking stadium. So, there I was, standing outside the back gates of Jacobs Field begging for the security guard to let me in. The game started at 7 pm, and at this point, it was well past 6. Panic and desperation were beginning to set in. I was trying to call Mickey Morabito, the traveling secretary for the A's, but because he was already in the stadium and underneath in the clubhouse, his cell phone would not go through. I finally lost it on the security guard. "Listen, dude, I have worked my entire life to get here, and we are 45 minutes away from my first Major League game. I am begging you, PLEASE let me into this stadium."

The guy didn't seem like he had any intention of budging, so I finally walked away and decided the only way I was going to get into the stadium was to buy a ticket. Just as I began looking to scalp a ticket, I ran into a Cleveland Indians fan and baseball card collector that recognized me. Shockingly, he had my Minor League baseball card on him. I immediately explained the situation to the guy and asked him if I could borrow the card to bring to the security guard. At this point, the security guard agreed to walk me down to the clubhouse, where there was another security guard that walked in and found Mickey who came outside to greet me with a big smile. "Hey Byrnesie, was wondering if you were going to make it. Welcome to the big leagues!"

Mickey quickly took me into Manager Art Howe's office. I had actually played and lived with Matt Howe, Art's son, in Medford and in instructional league my first year so I had met Art a few times before.

"Welcome to the big leagues, kid, you're DH'ing and hitting 7th. Have fun."

I thanked him for the opportunity and headed for my locker, where I found my road-grey Oakland jersey hanging up with the #22 and BYRNES stitched across the back. I got the chills. Obviously well documented, Will Clark was my favorite player growing up, so seeing #22 hanging in my locker magnified the already surreal experience. This was not the time to get all emotional or sappy, but I definitely took it as a positive omen.

Usually when a guy gets called up to the big leagues, he had already spent some time with the Major League team in Spring Training and is relatively familiar with guys on the team. For me, that was not the case. I had only been to 2 Spring Trainings and both of them were in the Minor Leagues. The only guys I knew were Barry Zito, the stud left-handed pitcher from Southern California who I had roomed with in AA earlier that year, and Adam Piatt, the Texas league player of the year who I played with the season before. Other than that, I knew who all of the guys were, but I had not met or played with any of them. As I was putting my uniform on, guys were coming up to me and introducing themselves: Eric Chavez, Tim Hudson, Ben Grieve, Matt Stairs, and Jason Giambi to name a few. The A's at that point were becoming known as a fun group of characters that liked to play hard on and off the field; I figured I would have no problem fitting in. Ever since little league though, I had always worn my socks high, and at the time, there was not one A's player that wore their socks up. They all had the long pants that literally tucked over the shoes. I thought it would be appropriate to ask Giambi, who along with Stairs was the unofficial captain of the team, if it would be okay to wear my socks up. Giambi's response? "Go for it, dude, this is the Oakland A's, bro, do whatever the f*ck you want to do, bro!"

By the time I was dressed and ready to go, it was game time. I walked into the dugout then out onto to the top step. I did a complete 360 as I took in all of my surroundings. I couldn't help but think of Karl Kuehl's famous instructional league speech about knowing what it takes to play in the big leagues. The Indians were perennial winners and had actually sold out Jacobs Field over 400 consecutive games. The sight of the stadium, the Major League players, and all the fans suddenly freaked me the f*ck out! I basically began uncontrollably shaking. I decided to do what has always helped me calm down in the past and busted full speed out of the dugout all the way to center field where I went through my normal pre-game stretch routine. Remarkably, after 2 flights, 2 hours of sleep in a 48-hour period, and a case of the nervous shakes, my legs felt awesome. I then went back underneath the dugout where there was a tee and a net and took a few swings. The bat had never felt so light. Sexy would be the most appropriate word to describe the sensation I was feeling at the time.

We were facing All-Star left-hander Chuck Finley, who I had actually spent a lot of time watching on TV when I was at UCLA and he was pitching for the Angels. Finley was a tall lefty who threw hard with good 2-seam movement and a good change-up and breaking ball to go with it. Ever since high school, whenever I would watch a game on TV, I would pretend as if I was in the batter's box facing whatever pitcher was on the mound. In my mind, I had already hit against Chuck Finley several times. Every time I stepped into my imaginary box with my air bat and went through an entire at bat against an imaginary Roger Clemens, Pedro Martinez, Kevin Brown or Chuck Finley, my boys would take jabs and get a good laugh. I simply would tell them to go f*ck themselves and one day it would pay off. Apparently, today was going to be that day.

This time I stepped into the real batter's box at Jacobs Field, leading off the top of the 2nd inning. It was almost as if this was the final exam that I had been preparing for over the course of the past 20 years. Like any test in school, when I had studied and done my homework, there was nothing to be nervous about. The first pitch was a fastball low and outside, the second, another fastball for a strike on the outside corner. I swung and foul-tipped the 3rd pitch into the catcher Sandy Alomar Jr.'s glove. Then with the count 1 and 2, down to my final strike, Finley threw another 2-seam fastball that he left over the middle of the plate. I absolutely smoked it right back up the middle for my first Major League hit. The umpire got the ball and threw it to Miguel Tejada on the top step of the dugout, who then appeared to toss the ball into the stands.

The switch-a-roo was a common baseball trick. Somebody would get the first-hit ball and quickly switch it out with another ball, then throw that ball into the stands making people believe you just tossed away the dudes first-hit ball. Whatever the case was, I never saw the first-hit ball again. No joke.

My next 2 at bats, I lined out to Kenny Lofton in center field and hit a ball up against the wall in the left-center field gap that Lofton ran down once again. My 4th at bat, I drilled a ball to left field for my 2nd hit of the day. My 5th at bat came against right-handed, side-winding Indians relief pitcher Steve Reed. He threw a first pitch slider that replicated a cement mixer, slowly spinning toward the plate that should have had a fat-ass "hit me" sign on it. I took a huge cut and fouled the pitch off directly behind me. I did not hear him, but apparently, Reed took exception to the big swing and said something to me and then looked into our dugout. The next pitch hit me square in the left shoulder. Our dugout erupted. Ignorant to the situation, I ran down to first base where I finally grasped what was going on. The next half inning, in retaliation, we hit Sandy Alomar Jr., which then cleared the benches. As I was running onto the field, it almost seemed like I was in some sort of weird dream. 2 hits, 2 runs scored, a stolen base, and a near benches-clearing brawl that started because Steve Reed didn't appreciate how hard I swung the bat. I wanted to make sure I was on the front line when I got out there, but I did not want to act as the aggressor in any sort of way. Not surprising, I found myself face to face with a guy that was known as the baddest dude in Major League Baseball, David Segui. Not only was he an absolute physical specimen with veins popping out of his ears, but he also happened to be a black belt in some form of martial arts. On top of that, it practically felt as if I was squared up against a raging bull. Segui was breathing so heavily it seemed as if he had steam coming out of his nostrils. Matt Stairs quickly got between the two of us and began litigations. I then found myself toe-to-toe with Omar Vizquel, who I had watched and admired for years. All I could think was damn, that is Omar Vizquel. I eventually could not help myself. "What up, Omar, big fan." That seemed to break the ice as we both got in a good laugh. "What's up, kid?"

Obviously, it was quite an eventful first day. When I got back to the hotel, I finally had an opportunity to look at my phone for the first time, 73 voice messages. I made one phone call to my dad who got stuck back in the Bay Area, and that was it. My mom, sister, and Mike Sasson, my agent, all surprised me by making the trip. The 4 of us sat around the hotel room and did our best to rehash the events and amusements of the past 24-48 hours. After about a half hour, the hotel phone in my room rang. "Byrnes, it's Stairs. Get your ass down to the hotel bar NOW! "

Obviously, I did not have much of a choice, but if I did my ass would have been there anyway. "I will be right down."

When I got downstairs, Stairs was waiting with shots lined up on the bar. We then threw back a few beers and headed to Cleveland's most famous gentlemen's club, Christy's Cabaret. This was my first experience of going out with "big leaguers" and it was everything and more than I expected. We immediately were escorted past a long line out in front of the club and into a private VIP area inside. From there it was bottomless Coors Lights, a few more shots, and endless lap dances performed by Cleveland's finest. I was not sure exactly how long this whole big-league thing was going to last, so I just assumed I might as well enjoy every minute on and off the field.

Human Crash Test Dummy Life Lesson #45

You can dream and envision all you want but the reality is that it's the spontaneity of life that makes it worth living and the spontaneity of the game that makes it worth playing. Oftentimes in life, we are overwhelmed or taken aback by situations. That's when you take a deep breath, look around, and realize this is amazingly f*cking real, very real. What was once a dream is no longer; it is your reality. Enjoy the moment! You worked your ass off for it.

Chapter 46
Be Here, Now.

"Wherever you are, be there totally. If you find you're here and now intolerable and it makes you unhappy, you have three options: remove yourself from the situation, change it, or accept it totally. If you want to take responsibility for your life, you must choose one of those three options, and you must choose now. Then accept the consequences."
-Eckhart Tolle

Turned out my stay in the big leagues did not last long. When we got back to Oakland I was sent back down to Sacramento to make room for a pitcher. This became a common trend over the course of the next year and a half. As a matter of fact, between August of 2000 and late April of 2002, I got called up and sent down 9 times. Let me re-write this bullsh*t just so whoever might be reading this realizes this is not a typo. I got called up and sent down a total of 9 F*CKING times. The most frustrating part was that despite continuing to put up good numbers in the Minor Leagues, I never got the opportunity to start more than 2 consecutive games at the Major League level during that time period. If I had gotten an opportunity, gave it everything I had, and puked all over myself, I could live with that. But not getting a chance and spending a ridiculous amount of time sitting on the bench was f*cking terrible.

The novelty of the big leagues wore off by the end of the 2000 season, and my frustration actually got to the point where I would have rather been playing in the Minor Leagues as opposed to sitting my ass on the bench in the big leagues. Pinch running, coming in as a defensive replacement, and getting a start every lunar eclipse at the big-league level was for the birds. I found out in a hurry that the worst job in baseball was being an American League bench player. Unlike the National League, the pitcher does not hit, so that immediately eliminates any pinch-hitting for the pitcher and the double switch. I would go several days and sometimes even weeks in between at-bats and starts.

I cannot and will not bullsh*t you. Every day I sat on the bench was torture. I wanted to be out on the baseball field so badly I would actually get a pit in my stomach each day right before first pitch. I did everything I could to hide my frustrations and be the best teammate I could be, cheering on the other guys and preparing myself to play just in case I got an opportunity to get into the game. The reality was that my playing time situation at the big-league level was absolutely eating me alive.

At certain points in life you may be a yo-yo. Basically, you and your livelihood are at the mercy of someone else's subjective opinion. I didn't want to accept being a yo-yo, so I tried to fight it, but that's a tough battle to win from the bench and all that fight did was cause myself more frustration and anxiety. Looking back, I should have realized it's okay to be a yo-yo. You may go up and down a bunch but the string will always stay attached. I wanted it all and I wanted it fast.

Human Crash Test Dummy Life Lesson #46

Being at the mercy of another person or an organization can be extremely demanding. Accept your role so long as the opportunity for growth is there for you. There is no sense wasting time and energy on other people's opinions and decisions you have absolutely no control over. Continue to focus on being present and commit to all of the things within your immediate power, work ethic, execution and attitude. Be here, now.

Chapter 47
A & E

"Success depends upon previous preparation, and without such preparation there is sure to be failure."
-Confucius

In 2001, the night before the first game of the Bay Bridge series in Oakland, I knew that Shawn Estes, a left-handed pitcher, was starting for the Giants. I spent my evening praying that I would somehow be in the lineup. This was my first opportunity to play against the team I grew up rooting for. Anticipating I would get the start, I actually left over 100 tickets for family and friends.

When I walked into the clubhouse and looked at the lineup card my heart sank. BYRNES was listed where I had become all too accustomed to finding it: under the RIGHT HANDED RESERVES column. This was the only game the Giants were scheduled to throw a left-hander and pretty much my only opportunity to play in the series. Oh yeah, and did I mention I left over 100 f*cking tickets? Every day during batting practice they would open the gates at the Coliseum just in time for the last group, generally the reserves, to hit. On a normal day, there might be a few hundred people that roll in, but this day was different. Thousands began to fill the stands and they were fired up; "LET'S GO OAKLAND" and "LET'S GO GIANTS" chants began immediately. I had flashbacks to all the different Bay Bridge series I had attended in my life, none more memorable than Game 4 of the 1989 World Series at Candlestick Park when the A's closed out the sweep. At this point, I realized how fortunate and blessed I was just to actually be a part of this rivalry. I instantly fed off the emotion of the crowd and took the best batting practice of my life, launching one ball after another over the wall. After our batting practice was over, I stayed in the dugout and just took in the moment as the stadium quickly began to fill up.

Oakland was known for having the greatest 13,000 fans in baseball, but the Bay Bridge series is different, way different. The series not only brings out the die-hard A's and Giants fans, but casual Bay Area sports connoisseur's all of a sudden become incredibly passionate about either the black and orange or green and gold. "Mt. Davis," the area above center field that Al Davis demanded be built upon returning the Raiders from Los Angeles to Oakland, was covered with a tarp for every other series except this one. Nearly 60,000 seats in the stadium were sold, creating an NFL-type atmosphere.

My excitement during and after batting practice completely drowned out any negative thoughts about not being in the lineup. So what if my 100+ family and friends were going to be disappointed not to see me play? The Bay Bridge series is way bigger than me or any other individual for that matter; overall, this was one of the few times a year when West Coast baseball could rival the heart and passion of East Coast fans.

When I did not start, which was often, I had an entire routine I would do 30 minutes before the game. I would switch off between the hot tub/cold tub for 15 minutes and then stretch naked in front of my locker. It was always nice to get a few laughs right before game time. I would then watch the first 3 innings of the game from the dugout before heading up to the weight room where I would hammer the elliptical for 10 minutes then head up to the batting cage. 10 swings off the tee to right field, 10 to left, then 10 to center followed by 20 more off Old Faithful, the Iron Mike pitching machine. The entire routine would usually take 2 innings and I was generally back in the dugout ready to rock by the 5th. Then, in between every half inning, I would sprint up the staircase from the dugout into the locker room to make sure I stayed loose. I sure as sh*t was not the best bench player by any means, but if I was going to fail it was not going to be because of lack of preparation.

3 minutes in the hot tub, then 3 minutes cold, 3 minutes hot, 3 minutes cold... Just as I jumped into the hot tub for the last 3-minute session, Ken Macha, our bench coach at the time who would later become the manager of the A's, stuck his head into the room. "Byrnes,

get some f*cking clothes on, you are starting in right field." Olmeado Saenz, who was the DH, had some bad Taco Bell and had spent the last hour on the can. Jeremy Giambi, who was in right field, became the DH and I was in business!

Beyond excited, I fired out of the hot tub, began doing some naked calisthenics in the locker room, threw on my uni, grabbed my glove and bat, then headed down to the field just in time for the national anthem. At that time, Shawn Estes was one of the better left-handed pitchers in baseball. My first at-bat was just about as surreal as my first at-bat in the big leagues. It was almost as if I had that same sort of floating sensation I had felt in Cleveland the previous year. I took a couple healthy cuts at fastballs, and then he dropped his signature, big 12-6 curve ball that I thought I was right on and about to demolish. The end result was a "Massey" cue ball shot right back to Estes that only the best pool players in the world would be proud of. My next at-bat, I had no interest in waiting around for Estes' nasty "Uncle Charlie." I swung at the first-pitch fastball up in the zone toward the inside part of the plate. I knew I hit it well, but I wasn't quite sure if I got enough of it, so I came blazing out of the box and just about ate sh*t before rounding first base. I eventually looked up and saw the ball bouncing off the staircase beyond the left field fence. I had just hit my first Major League home run, in the Bay Bridge series, in front of 100 of the most important family members and friends in my life, in a game I was not supposed to be playing in.

Human Crash Test Dummy Life Lesson #47

Prepare every day as if you are in the starting lineup. Many times in life, we are unexpectedly put in positions that can have a huge impact. A & E (Attitude & Effort) are the two main things that are in our immediate control. Make the effort to prepare and approach each day with an attitude of gratitude. Be thankful for whatever opportunities you are presented with.

Chapter 48
Know What You Stand For

"Waste no more time arguing what a good man should be. Be one."
-Marcus Aurelius

I ended the 2001 regular season with 3 Major League home runs in 38 at-bats. The majority of my season was played in AAA Sacramento where I hit 20 home runs and stole 25 bases. After going up and down 4 different times through the course of the season, once September rolled around and the rosters expanded, I was back in the big leagues. My role was relatively undefined or I guess you could say pretty non-existent. I may have gotten a start or two, but for the most part, I would sit my ass on the bench and be a cheerleader until it was time to pinch run for one of the several base cloggers in the A's regular lineup.

We were in a battle with the Seattle Mariners for the American League West title but all of a sudden everything that was happening on baseball fields across America became completely irrelevant. It has been nearly two decades since the morning of September 11th, 2001, yet I could describe the day from start to finish as if it was yesterday. I, like so many people, was essentially in a state of shock as I watched the Pentagon on fire, both World Trade Centers crumble to the ground, and a plane heading to San Francisco crash in Pennsylvania.

As the reports came in I immediately understood the magnitude of the situation and realized life as we knew it was going to change. I also realized there was a good chance that with the thousands of deaths that were being reported; somehow, I would be directly affected. Sure enough, as the morning became afternoon, my mom called me with the news that Andy Garcia, the dad of one of my best friends growing up, was on the flight that crashed in Pennsylvania.

Rage is the first word I can think of that described my feelings. I wanted justice, and I wanted it in a hurry. All Major League Baseball games were postponed indefinitely. I headed to the stadium that afternoon and continued to sit in front of the TV in the locker room for hours. That night, I went to hang out with childhood friends in San Francisco; we all reminisced about Mr. Garcia and reflected on the day's events. Common questions we all wanted answers to were: Who did this? Why did they do it? And how long are we going to have to wait until we can bomb the F*CK out of them?

We ended up at Bar None on Union Street where there was a pretty big crowd considering the day. No doubt it was a somber crew that made it out, who probably much like me and my boys were hoping a little alcohol might somehow calm the emotions and bring some sort of perspective. Right about midnight you could have heard a pin drop and the place was packed. Several different quiet conversations taking place until some dude stood up on top of the bar, put his hand over his heart, and began to sing the National Anthem.

Everybody looked stunned at first, and then within second, there was not a soul in the bar that was not singing at the top of his or her lungs. That was the first time I realized that everything was going to be okay. Americans generally are a bunch of type A, selfishly driven people who constantly scratch and claw their way to the top in any situation. There is a reason we made it over here, then miraculously took down the world's largest army to win the right to become our own nation. We don't like being told what to do or how to live our lives. We typically march to the beat of our own drum and we don't like being f*cked with. Flick our ear and we will punch you in the face. This is the attitude that has defined who we are through the course of history.

Before 9-11, many baseball players and baseball fans will tell you that the National Anthem was simply a formality before games that oftentimes was looked upon by many as an inconvenience. This obviously would no longer be the case. The Star Spangled Banner took on an entire new meaning for an entire generation of Americans.

More likely than not, this is one of the main reasons you see so many people upset over the current National Anthem protests. The National Anthem has always been something that draws unity among American citizens, not something that divides us.

My first reaction to Colin Kapernick sitting down during the national Anthem was an extreme feeling of disappointment. I had the opportunity to interview Kap when I was working in radio, and I truly believe he is a good kid and he has a big heart.

I also agree with a lot of Kap's message. I believe that there is a disturbing amount of social injustice within our country and even more so around the world. There is no doubt that ACTION needs to be taken.

The problem is that sitting down during the National Anthem is a divisive action, and I truly believe the only way to fix social inequality is through UNITY, NOT DIVISION.

Kap has a unique opportunity to use his voice and his actions to bring people together. If he wants to make a real difference, he needs to take a big-time leadership role in different community outreach programs. He should use every free moment he has to speak and moderate town hall meetings across the country, bringing inner city youth and police officers together. This problem needs to be fixed at the root. Spread a message of togetherness and love, not division and hate.

The National Anthem was and still is a time where I am able to stand up, place my right hand over my heart, bow my head, and show gratitude for the sacrifices others have made for me to be able to play or watch a game that I love.

I am sure the National Anthem and the American Flag are symbols that mean something different for each individual, but there is no doubt that both represent the democratic society that we created some 240 years ago. Over the years, our country has continued to develop and grow, most of the time in a positive direction, while other times we have experienced serious setbacks. Regardless, the anthem continues to play, the flag continues to fly, and just about all continue to stand.

Yet, the greatest thing about our country is that Colin Kapernick or anybody else does NOT have to stand for the National Anthem or salute the American flag. He has the freedom of speech and the right to express his message without getting thrown in prison or executed.

Ultimately, Kap and many others have made the decision to sit through the National Anthem and many have articulately expressed their reasons for doing so.

Me, I am going to stand:

I stand for democracy.

I stand for those who have fought and continue to fight for our country's freedom.

I stand for all branches of the military.

I stand for those killed in action protecting your ass and mine.

I stand for their families.

I stand for the values and principles our nation was founded on.

I stand for our founding fathers.

I stand for our forefathers.

I stand for our government structure.

I stand for George Washington, Abraham Lincoln, Teddy Roosevelt, FDR, JFK, and Ronald Reagan.

I stand for all U.S. Presidents and the sanctity of the Presidential office.

I stand for Alexander Hamilton.

I stand for Geronimo, Sacagawea, and Sitting Bull.

I stand for Lewis and Clark.

I stand for John Muir.

I stand for Martin Luther King, Fredrick Douglas, and Rosa Parks.

I stand for Jim Thorpe and Mohammed Ali.

I stand for Jackie Robinson.

I stand for Pat Tillman.

I stand to express my gratitude for working people who continue to make our country safe and operational.

I stand for public servants and government officials.

I stand for teachers.

I stand for fire fighters.

I stand for police officers.

I stand up because Colin Kapernick, and every other American citizen, has the right to sit down.

Human Crash Test Dummy Life Lesson #48

Know why you stand.

Chapter 49
Champion Champions

"Passion makes life interesting, ignites the soul, fuels our love, carries our friendships, stimulates our intellect and pushes our limits."
-Pat Tillman

As you sit around the BBQ next Memorial Day weekend, surrounded by family members and friends enjoying burgers, dogs, a big slice of apple pie, and an ice cold Budweiser, take a minute, or several, to remember the very real sacrifice that Americans have made in order for us to enjoy life as we know it within the United States. Then, go ahead and make sure you find a kid, could be yours or somebody else's, and explain to them the significance of Memorial Day beyond getting a day off of school and stuffing their faces with ice cream.

It is our responsibility to teach our children the very harsh realities of life. We celebrate Memorial Day because American soldiers have been killed defending our country. Have them understand that those soldiers died fighting for our freedoms, liberties, and the future well-being of the exact kid you happen to be talking to. Teach them that Memorial Day is our way to honor, give thanks, and celebrate the lives of those who made the ultimate sacrifice.

September 11, 2001 hit me hard like it did just about every other American. Immediately, I questioned the life that I was living and thought about how I could possibly help protect the future of our country. My great grandfather, grandfather, and father all served in the military to help ensure future generations of Americans will be able to live in a free and democratic society. Now, here I was, representing the future generation that they had fought so hard for and I hadn't done sh*t. Ironically, shortly after 9-11, I saw an interview with a guy that I had always respected and admired that virtually shared the exact same sentiment, Pat Tillman.

I first learned about Pat from watching High School Sports Focus, which was a local Bay Area TV show that would run high school football highlights on Friday and Saturday nights. Pat was a running back and linebacker for Leland High School in San Jose. Basically, he was unstoppable on both sides of the ball, but what made him different was the flare and style in which he dominated. He was by no means an imposing figure physically, but add in Pat's unbelievable quickness, long golden locks flowing out of his helmet, and his jut jawed chin, he might as well have been some sort of Greek god playing amongst a bunch of mere mortals.

My sophomore, junior, and senior years, I played on a football team that won 3 consecutive section championships and had several guys go on to play D1 football, yet for whatever reason, just about every single guy on our St. Francis football team was mesmerized by the mysterious surfer looking dude wearing #42, single handedly winning football games for a school with a relatively underwhelming football pedigree. For insecure teenage kids to idolize a peer on another football team was unprecedented, or at the very least, extremely rare. Pat had become so much of a football icon in the area that when a group of my teammates and I were at a high school basketball tournament and spotted Tillman on the other side of the gym, it literally became some sort of dare to see who was going to sack up and go introduce themselves to the iconic high school legend. Ironically, that guy was Zack Walz, the same dude who 5 years later would become Pat Tillman's teammate with the Arizona Cardinals. After the chance encounter, Tillman went on to become the Pac 10 defensive player of the year at ASU while Walz became the Ivy League defensive player of the year at Dartmouth. Walz was then selected in the 6th round of the 1998 draft by the Cardinals, with Tillman getting selected in the 7th.

The two immediately became great friends and training camp roommates. I signed with the Oakland A's that same year and was sent to instructional league in Phoenix where I shacked up on Walz's couch. It was during that fall that I had a chance to finally meet and hang out with the guy that I had looked up to for years. People talk about the "it" factor whether referring to an athlete or a person.

Generally, "it" can be described as an aura, confidence and demeanor carried by somebody clearly playing their sport or living their life on a different level. Both on and off the field, Pat had "it."

Although I was emotional after 9-11, I eventually put aside any thoughts of joining the military in any sort of capacity that actually would have had a direct impact on the immediate and future safety of our country. I talked about how cool it would have been to join the Navy Seals. I talked about what it meant to be an American. I talked about how I would be willing to do anything to protect our freedom and liberties. Yet, at the end of the day all I did was talk. Like many other people, I had great intentions but I did not follow through; quite frankly, I wasn't even close. I was way too wrapped up in my selfish world of chasing a lifelong dream of playing Major League baseball, a dream made possible only because of the generations before me that sacrificed their individual dreams for the collective dream of our country.

Pat did much more than talk. Despite a multi-million-dollar contract offer on the table, he walked away from the NFL and joined the Army Rangers. I became so enthralled with his story that I intensely followed what was happening with Pat and his brother Kevin, who joined the Rangers as well. Both were assigned to the second battalion of the 75th Ranger Regiment based in Fort Lewis, Washington. Through Walz, who was one of the very few in contact with Pat during this time, I would get updates. Originally, they were about the rigors and challenges of becoming an Army Ranger and eventually the updates detailed the brothers' trips to Iraq in 2003 during Operation Iraqi Freedom and Afghanistan during Operation Enduring Freedom. The last briefing I got from Walz was in early 2004 when he showed up at my house with a set of Tillman's dog tags that Zack had begged Pat to send him. According to Walz, the plan was for Pat to finish out his 3-year commitment to the Rangers and then return to the NFL.

Unfortunately, Pat never got that opportunity. April 22, 2004, while in Afghanistan, Pat's unit was ambushed while traveling through rugged Eastern Afghanistan canyons. In a heroic effort to provide cover for his men, Pat Tillman was killed. I have listened to stories, read books, and watched documentaries that have detailed Pat's death by friendly fire and the massive cover up that ensued. I am still not sure exactly what to believe, but what I am sure about is that we lost one of the greatest Americans who ever lived.

After Pat's death, I made sure I spoke about him and the sacrifice he made every opportunity I had. My goal has been and always will be to keep his name and legacy at the forefront of American culture.

In 2006 while I was playing for the Arizona Diamondbacks, Richard Tillman, Pat's youngest brother, reached out to me to invite me to Pat's statue unveiling at the new Arizona Cardinals stadium in Glendale. It was there that I had an opportunity and pleasure to meet the entire Tillman family. From that day on, I knew I wanted to focus my individual fundraising efforts throughout the course of my entire life on the Pat Tillman Foundation. Without getting all nostalgic, between my connection to Pat through Bay Area high school sports, Zack Walz, and playing baseball professionally in a city in which he became an icon, I felt as if it was something in my life that I was meant to do; my small way to finally do more than just talk. The foundation was founded on the basic principles that encompassed everything Pat Tillman represented: Education, leadership and loyalty. "Leadership through action" was the foundation's original rallying cry. The Tillman Military Scholar program was eventually formed and has been expanded throughout the years. Today, the program is now responsible for putting over 300 Tillman Military Scholars and their spouses through schools of higher education.

While with the Diamondbacks, I hosted several fundraising events benefiting the Tillman Foundation. I have since been able to continue my fundraising efforts through the different Ironman triathlons and ultra-marathons that I have competed in, each time crossing the finish line with Pat's Arizona Cardinals #40 jersey flying high above my head.

What I have enjoyed more than anything is the opportunity to talk about and reflect on the significance of Pat's life. It has been years since Pat's death and there is now an entire new generation of kids that have no idea who Pat Tillman was. I relish every opportunity I have to teach my children about the selfless nature of Pat's decision to walk away from the limelight of the NFL in exchange for the front lines of combat. Pat's story speaks for itself and by no means needs me or anybody else to sensationalize it. The reality is that there have been so many others, just like Pat, who walked away from other life opportunities and ultimately were killed in action protecting your ass and mine. We all should take every opportunity we have to honor those who don't just talk about what it means to be an American, but they show us what it means to be an American.

Human Crash Test Dummy Life Lesson #49

"Champion" was a word that Pat often would use to describe people who lived their life in an authentic way that had a vision of impacting society beyond themselves. Take every opportunity in your life to make sure you champion champions.

Chapter 50
For The Love of The Game

"The game doesn't stink Mr. Wheeler, it's a great game."
-Billy Chapel

When I started playing organized baseball at 9 years old, I fell in love with the sport. For the next 25 years of my life, baseball became my identity; it defined who I was as person. All too often my mood was dependent upon whether or not my name was in the lineup or how many hits I had that day.

In 2010, I was released by the Seattle Mariners. That was the third time I had been released in my career and the second time within a 3-month period. Mariners General Manager Jack Zurdinzick offered to make phone calls to other teams on my behalf, but I politely declined. I was done.

I was 34 years old and was finally healthy after 2 years of dealing with a hamstring that I tore off the bone and a broken hand that was shattered by a Scott Feldman 2-seam fastball. I was coming off a Spring Training in which I played very well, and I truly believed I had plenty of good baseball still left in me. Physically I was fine. Yet, after 25 years of emotionally giving baseball everything I had, I no longer loved the game.

Despite several offers to continue to play, I walked away from the sport. I felt like it was finally time to find my own sense of self-worth that was not reliant on playing time or a box score. I spent the entire summer of 2010 soul-searching in a sense. I surfed, golfed, played beer league softball, and began training for Ironman triathlons. Most importantly, I finally took the time to truly learn what it meant to be a good dad and embraced all of the diaper-changing responsibilities that came with it.

The next year I began working for MLB Network and quickly realized how much passion I still had for the sport. I realize this may be difficult for many to believe but I can honestly say that I have had just as much fun sitting at the desk of MLB Tonight as I did playing baseball. Being able to naturally react to live action of 15 games being played on any given night is an absolute rush. Then to have the ability to instantly break down a play and teach young fans the inner nuances of the game only enhances the experience that much more.

In 2015, I was approached by the San Rafael Pacifics, an independent league baseball team just north of San Francisco, about suiting up and playing two games as some sort of promotion. The idea was laughable. I had not seen a pitch or stepped onto a baseball field without wearing a suit and tie in more than 5 years. The preparation it would take to not embarrass myself would entail hours of batting practice, throwing, and taking fly balls. Between my family commitments, work schedule, and triathlon training, it seemed nearly impossible to find that extra time.

When the idea was eventually pitched for the games to be a platform to help raise money for the Pat Tillman Foundation, I became intrigued. I basically figured if there was one kid in the stands that got to learn about Pat willingly walking away from a lucrative NFL contract to enlist in the Army Rangers and fight for the liberties and values of our county, it would be well worth me making an ass out of myself.

I began my preparation in June and utilized all of my available resources to get ready. I took several whiffle ball batting practice sessions before, after, and during MLB Network shows on the miniature baseball field in Studio 42. I also even took meaningful cuts off of my 2-year-olds tee in which the ball is actually attached to a string. I hit with the Truckee High School baseball team while vacationing in Lake Tahoe and made it back to my St. Francis High School Alumni game for the first time since I graduated. In order to fire up the fast twitch muscles again, I incorporated a lot more speed work into my triathlon training sessions. To get my arm back in shape, I would go out to a creek by my house with my kids, find baseball size rocks, and chuck them into the stream. The alternative approach towards preparing for the two games wasn't exactly what a Major League team would prescribe.

When I arrived at Albert Park on August 5th, I really did not know what to expect. The Pacifics were in a pennant race and every game for them was meaningful. I very easily would have understood if the players had been upset with me barging in on something they had been working towards all season. Fortunately, that was not the case, not even close.

What I found was 23 dudes who welcomed me with open arms. Independent ball is typically comprised of a very eclectic mix of players. Some of the guys are fresh out of college, many have played affiliated ball with a Major League organization, and even a few have seen time in the Major Leagues. Regardless of their background or their story, they are all there for one reason; they love playing baseball.

Every one of the players has an off-season job in which their main goal is to make enough money to be able to survive the season. Most players live with host families and barely make enough money to eat decent meals and pay for the gas to get them to away games. Yes, they are responsible for their own transportation. No disrespect to Albert Field, but the Pacifics play in a beat-up OLD ballpark with no showers and makeshift dugouts created by a portable plastic fence. I am also pretty sure it is the only field in professional baseball that has a dirt softball infield smack dab in the middle of centerfield.

The greatest thing about the realities and hardships of life in the Pacific Baseball Association is that when the players get in-between the lines, none of it matters. We could have been playing on an obscure sandlot, a concrete parking lot, or a big-league stadium; it would not have made one bit of a difference. When the games start, it is all about baseball, nothing else.

Not one bit surprising to me, there were players on both teams that could very easily play in the Major Leagues right now. Over the course of the two games, I was undoubtedly reminded of how difficult the game is. I had personally vouched $500 for every ball I caught in the outfield, $1000 for every hit, walk, run scored, stolen base, and RBI, $10,000 for a homer and $100,000 if I happened to hit a grand slam. I donated my Pacifics salary and the Pacifics donated $1 for every ticket sold over the course of the two days.

No grand slams or home runs were hit, but I did manage to scrap out 3 walks, 3 runs scored, 7 fly balls caught, and my first professional hit in 5 years. Together, we raised nearly $14,000 for the Pat Tillman Foundation, and I know there were at least 3 kids that got a lesson about the life and legacy of Pat Tillman. Those same 3 kids also got to watch their Daddy play baseball for the first time.

After the second game, I ordered a big BBQ spread and beers for the guys. For over an hour, the entire team sat around in the smelly-ass, Cracker-Jack-box Pacifics locker room and talked shop. I wouldn't have wanted it any other way. I explained to them my relationship with Pat Tillman, the impact he has had on my life, and the reasons I continue to champion the foundation. We talked about approach at the plate, the evolving world of sabermetrics, and who the nastiest pitcher I ever faced was. I did my best to leave them with a message of hope and belief. I recounted Daniel Nava's path from getting cut by the Chico Outlaws to hitting a grand slam in his first Major League at-bat and eventually becoming a world champion with the Boston Red Sox.

Ultimately though, whatever lessons I could have taught them paled in comparison to the simple reminder they left with me. I love the game just as much now as I did when I first started playing baseball over 30 years ago.

Human Crash Test Dummy Life Lesson #50

Whatever it is that you do in life, remind yourself of why you do it. Remember what drove you to it and exactly what lit the spark that fueled the passion. It could be a job, a hobby or even a relationship. Push yourself to dig deep and rediscover that authentic passion for the love of the game.

Chapter 51
Relentless Forward Progress

"Without a struggle there can be no progress."
-Fredrick Douglas

When the San Rafael Pacifics approached me about returning the following summer to celebrate the second annual Pat Tillman Foundation nights, I immediately began brainstorming different ways in which we could appropriately honor Pat's memory.

By all accounts Pat was a very forward thinker. He was somebody who would constantly challenge society's norms and status quos frequently levied upon us. Just because things have always been done a certain way was absolutely no reason to not find a better or more efficient way to accomplish the same feat.

We as a society are constantly evolving with the ever-changing technological world that we live in. For well over a decade we have had the ability to accurately call balls and strikes with an automated system using 3 different cameras which track the ball 40-50 times from the time the ball leaves the pitcher's hand until it crosses home plate. This technology has now been implemented into almost every single television broadcast as well as on the Internet.

Something to me seems disturbingly wrong with the fact that anybody in the world can see whether or not a pitch was a ball or a strike by the true definition of the strike zone immediately after it crosses home plate EXCEPT the person actually having to make the call.

This is unacceptable and a major injustice within the game of baseball. The moment I realized this technology was available, I have begged and pleaded for the automated system to be installed.

When I brought up the idea for us to automate the strike zone for the two Pat Tillman Foundation games, the Pacifics were all for it. Then, when Sports Vision agreed to set up their technology, my dream became a reality. For the first time in the history of professional baseball, balls and strikes would be determined by a computer, not a human.

Of course, it was a bit awkward for everybody involved. Both catchers tried to consistently frame pitches. The home plate umpires couldn't help themselves by making strike calls, and players needed to get used to what exactly is the true definition of the strike zone. Pitchers benefited by the total height of the zone while hitters definitely benefited by the width.

Overall, the two #RoboUmp games could not have gone more flawlessly. To keep the spirit of the games at the forefront, I donated $100 to the Tillman Foundation for every strikeout and walk, totaling $4600 over the course of the two days, while the Pacifics donated $1 for every ticket sold.

Umpires at the major league level are the best in the world at what they do. They continuously have a ball/strike success rate of well over 90 percent. Ironically, the umpires use the exact same technology to grade themselves that was implemented in the two games with the Pacifics.

The major difference between any MLB game and the two Pacific League games was that the ball/strike success rate of the Independent League games was 100%. There are many baseball traditionalists who think above 90% is good enough and they enjoy the "human element" of the game. For me, the human element I fell in love with as a 9-year-old kid has been and always will be the players, not the umpires.

In August of 2015, Kevin Plawecki was leading off the bottom of the 3rd inning and worked the count full before walking on a borderline pitch up in the zone. Immediately, every single viewer watching on TV at home or on the Internet could tell that instead of ball 4, the pitch should have been called strike 3. The next two guys were promptly retired, which should have been the end of the inning. Instead, Curtis Granderson stepped up and hit a two-run home run giving the Mets the lead. That was followed by a Daniel Murphy homer, a Yoenis Cespedes single, and then a Lucas Duda homer. What should have been an easy 1-2-3 inning turned into a 5 run, 3 homer barrage.

All because of one missed call.

Scenarios like this happen on a nightly basis. As a matter of fact, umpires change the dynamic of the game on a pitch-by-pitch basis. Imagine a simple 1-1 count in the 3rd inning of a tie game. For the sake of this example, let's say that the bases are loaded. A borderline pitch is called a ball. The count then goes to 2-1. Harmless mistake, right? WRONG. Because of the 2-1 count, the pitcher throws a fastball for the next pitch, instead of the wipeout slider he has in his arsenal. The ball is then crushed for a grand slam. The team's chance of winning that game went from about 50-50 to 95-5 on a seemingly innocent 1-1 blown call. On Base Percentage + Slugging Percentage (OPS) is the single most accurate statistic I would use to evaluate the overall effectiveness of a hitter. The difference between a 2-1 count and a 1-2 count has an OPS delta of nearly 400 points! Most people will usually bitch about the bad strike 3 call or bad ball 4 call, but obviously, the 1-1 call can be just as impactful if not more. Basically, the fate of just about every game is left up to an umpire's guess. That's not fair to the players, fans, or umpires.

We repeated the experiment in 2016, and this time, HBO Real Sports documented the entire process. We also took it a step further when I got behind home plate and acted as the home plate umpire. I had an IFB device in my ear and each ball and strike was verbally relayed to me immediately when the ball crossed the plate. Sports Vision also installed a light in centerfield that would light up on every strike. The experiment went flawless.

Ultimately, I have absolutely no desire to get rid of the home plate umpire or any other umpire on the field. Just like instant replay, the only thing I would like to do is give them the necessary tools to get the call right every time. Once the umpires' union realizes that an automated strike zone will make their job easier and potentially create another on-site umpiring job opportunity, I don't see any reason why MLB and the MLBPA would not agree to immediately begin using the automated system to determine balls and strikes.

If I were to have written a book such as this 150+ years ago I would have been limited to an ink pen and a piece of paper. Then, in order to get people to read it, I would have had to stand on a city block handing out duplicated copies.

Fortunately, as in many other arenas in life, technology has prevailed. Around the middle of the 19th century, the typewriter was invented and eventually became available for widespread use. The copy machine was created by Chester Carlson in 1938, and then by the 1980s, word processors and personal computers took reign.

Today, I am currently writing this on my 3-inch mobile device 37,000 feet somewhere above middle America. Upon completion, I will publish and send out a link on my Twitter account, which directly connects to Facebook where it will be published as well. Between the two, this will reach nearly 50,000 people with the click of one button.

As much as I appreciate good calligraphy and social interaction with people on the street, forgive me for utilizing the 21st century world of technology. MLB should give it a try with the strike zone, it makes life a lot easier.

Human Crash Test Dummy Life Lesson #51

Change is difficult and uncomfortable for a lot of people. I do realize that not all change is good, but I also realize forward progress is mandatory. When we have an opportunity to improve, it is vital that we take advantage of it. Although it is important to respect the history and authenticity of a product, it is necessary that we continue to improve that product when presented with the opportunity. We are living in an incredibly progressive technological time, so let's make sure we use that technology to further enhance what we already have.

Chapter 52
It's Not About You

"New York, New York."
-Frank Sinatra

After the 2001 season resumed following 9-11, the Mariners did not slow down, winning an AL record 116 games. We won 102 games and were the Wild Card team, drawing a first-round matchup with the New York Yankees for the 2nd year in a row. Unlike the previous year, I was on the playoff roster this time around, and I was there for one main reason: to RUN. As I mentioned before, the one thing this A's team lacked was speed, so the big reason I was even on the roster was to pinch run in any sort of critical situation late in the game. Despite the incredible atmosphere in Yankee Stadium, we somehow won the first two games of the series in New York. Then in Game 3, with a chance to close out the Bronx Bombers, a situation arose late in the game when Jeremy Giambi reached 1st base with 2 outs. It was the bottom of the 7th inning with the score still 0-0. Anticipating that this could be a spot where manager Art Howe could use me to pinch run, I undoubtedly was all lathered up ready to rock and roll.

I sat at the end of the dugout with my helmet in hand, getting ready to make the mad dash to first base. All I needed was my cue. I could see Art talking with Ken Macha, the bench coach. Then Macha turned to me. "Byrnes, you ready?"

With sweat dripping from my forehead from sprinting up and down the stairs to the clubhouse 35 times, I responded, "Believe it!" Then there was more discussion between the two. Jason Giambi was sitting next to me on the other end of the dugout. "Byrnesie, let's go, get your ass in there!"

"F*ck, G, I would love to but it ain't my call." A few pitches later, Whack! Terrance Long hit the ball into the right field corner and Jeremy Giambi was off to the races. I first knew we were f*cked when he rounded 2nd base. I was sitting directly in line with 2nd and 3rd base and could see the extremely wide turn he took, which was for sure going to significantly slow down his time to home plate. Then it happened.

We had caught a break when they missed the cutoff man and the ball seemed to be headed for foul territory where it should have come to rest, allowing Jeremy to easily score. Instead, Derek Jeter, playing shortstop, came out of nowhere to retrieve the ball near the first base line and then back handed it to Jorge Posada who applied a swipe tag on Giambi just as his foot was touching home.

"OUT."

A few things I need to get off my chest about the play; first of all, it was not a slam-dunk pinch run scenario, which is the exact reason Howe and Macha had such a difficult time making the decision. Jeremy had been swinging the bat well and it was still only the 7th inning, which made it very possible his spot in the order was going to once again come up, or possibly, I would have been of better use in the 8th or 9th inning pinch running for one of the other turtles. The other thing is all the grief that Jeremy Giambi gets for not sliding is bullsh*t. In my opinion, the tag and Giambi's foot touched home plate at the same time, which the umpire really could have called either way. If Jeremy had to slow down and slide feet first, which is the only way I had ever seen him slide, he would have been out by 3 feet.

The Yankees ended up riding the momentum of the infamous Jeter play and went on to beat us that night and the next day, forcing a Game 5 back in New York. The crowd, which we completely took out of play in the first 2 games, was not going to be denied at this point and neither were the Yankees. Both had endured too much over the last month not to complete the comeback. With 2 outs in the 9th inning and down by 2 runs, I heard, "Byrnes, grab a bat." The fate of the Oakland A's season was now in my hands, going up against the greatest closer of all time, Mariano Rivera.

Before stepping into the batter's box, I glanced up at the 56,000 fans on their feet, making so much noise I could not here myself say "hello" to Jorge Posada or the home plate umpire. I had no other choice than to soak in the moment. Barely a month after 9-11, this was a city that had been waiting to passionately cheer about something and now was their time.

Thinking back to that moment as I am writing this, I still get the chills. I tapped myself on the helmet with the bat as I always did as part of my routine, stepped in the box and said, "F*ck it, nothing to lose." I battled as well as I could, taking a couple monster cuts in the process, but eventually ended up foul-tipping the 3rd strike into Posada's glove and that was it. "Start spreading the news…" Sinatra immediately began playing over the loudspeaker and 56,000 New Yorkers began to sing "New York, New York" in unison. Still to this day, I have never heard a louder stadium in my life.

When people speak about their favorite big league moment, they typically will recall a home run or talk about winning a huge game. Mine was a strikeout at Yankee Stadium and that moment had absolutely nothing to do with me.

Human Crash Test Dummy Life Lesson #52

Sometimes in life you win, sometimes in life you lose, sometimes in life the moment becomes much larger than either outcome. Make sure to immerse yourself in that moment.

Chapter 53
Immerse Yourself In Their Culture

"I love you because you love my country."
-Juan Marichal

After the 2001 season was over, I immediately headed to Santo Domingo to play for the Licey Tigres in the Dominican Winter League. I didn't know exactly what to expect other than many of the best baseball players in the world came from the small island southeast of Cuba. I had also heard that the Country's passion for the game was second to none.

When I arrived, I was greeted at the airport by a Dominican dude named Johnny that didn't speak English and was holding a sign that read "ERICK BYRENESE." At this point, it was a good thing I had taken Spanish every year in school from the 6th grade on and was as fluent in the language as I could be without living in a Spanish speaking country.

I hopped into the "Licey" minivan, which essentially was a blue box with a steering wheel, an engine, and 3 rows of bench seating, seat belts non-existent. Then, as we headed down the highway, it didn't take long to realize I was no longer in the United States. To my left were the most gorgeous palm trees and crystal blue water I had ever seen. To my right were shacks, people carrying large baskets on top of their heads, and wild dogs roaming freely. Johnny, just the same as every other driver on the road, drove like a f*cking wild maniac, weaving in and out of traffic with one hand on the horn at all time. Think New York City in the middle of rush hour with no laws.

The most incredible sight though was the amount of mopeds and motorcycles that were on the freeway; helmets apparently had not yet been introduced on the island, but even more amazing were the 5 people that were stacked on many of them. FIVE!!!

Johnny dropped me off at the Hotel Plaza Naco, which was located right in the heart of Santo Domingo and secured by 2 guys strapped with 9mm and holding sawed-off shot guns, sitting on fold out lawn chairs. Not exactly the luxurious beachfront property I was expecting. I checked into my room, which was not terrible, other than the fact that it smelled like foul mildew, and crashed out after a long day of travel. I then woke up in the middle of the night to what I thought were fireworks or an M-80. Pop, Pop, Pop! I immediately hopped out of bed towards the window to try to see where the noise had come from. At this point, I gazed out at the Santo Domingo skyline, and thought about all my boys back home surfing and playing golf, then wondered, "What the f*ck am I doing here?"

The next morning, I woke up and headed downstairs to the lobby. When I came out of the elevator I immediately saw that there was yellow tape surrounding the entire front desk area. Then as I looked closer inside the tape, there was a body outline that I had only ever seen on TV or in movies. Come to find out the Pop, Pop, Pop noise from the night before was the security guard shooting one of the hotel guests as he tried to get a girl up to his room. In the Dominican, most hotels will not let you bring a non-registered guest to the room. The rule is mainly in place so men can't bring prostitutes to what hotel operators considered an upscale or classy establishment. Essentially, it is the hotels way of making sure they don't become known as a whorehouse. The guest apparently would not take no for an answer, pulled out a gun, and pointed it at the hotel receptionist, at which point the security guard unloaded 3 rounds and killed the dude. Bienvenidos a la Dominicana!

In general, Dominicans are very family-oriented and incredibly happy people. Many have learned to get by with no electricity or running water, which immediately made me think of how spoiled we are in the United States. We often take many things for granted and view them as essentials or necessities. Dominicans view many of those same items as luxuries and will get by just fine with or without them. There was nothing better or more humbling than making the mile or so trek from the hotel to the stadium through the streets of Santo

Domingo and seeing the kids on the street playing baseball with a stick, a rock, and using milk cartons for gloves.

The actual baseball was everything and more than I expected. "Licey," the team I played on, is known as the New York Yankees of the Dominican League. Year-in and year-out, they generally are the best team. Licey has won the most championships and will spend the most amount of money to attract top foreign players. All of this adds up to Licey being the most revered and hated team in the Dominican Republic.

The style of play in the league suited my game well. I never met a fastball I didn't like and I've never met a Dominican who didn't love throwing one. The games were f*cking nuts. Fans would blow horns and ring bells from the first pitch to the last. Hard alcohol was sold in the stands and many fans' common practice was to bet money on nearly every pitch. As a matter of fact, gambling got so bad that the league implemented a rule that only American umpires can work home plate because they were having a problem with Dominican umpires fixing games. Power outages were regular occurrences, one time happening while I was up to bat with the pitcher in the middle of his windup.

Yet, nothing tops the time I was playing centerfield and heard this incredibly loud thud behind me. The cameraman had fallen a good 15 plus feet from the TV stand above the outfield wall and landed on the warning track. He was lying there motionless; I thought he was dead. Immediately two dudes, who were not paramedics, ran out onto the field and grabbed him by all 4 limbs and ran off with the cameraman. Apparently, the dude was infamous for drinking large amounts of rum during the game and that was not the first time he had fallen off of the stand. He was back in action the next night!

Another eye-opening experience in the Dominican Republic came during the All-Star game. I was selected to participate in the Home Run Derby against some of the Country's biggest and baddest. At the time, I was leading the Dominican Winter League in homers and this was my stage to validate my thump. La Romana was the site of the game, which was anything but a bam box. It was arguably the toughest park to hit homers in the league. These dudes went up there and made La Romana look like Williamsport. Balls were flying out of there like I had never seen. One thing I noticed was that the guys who went before me kept passing the same bat to each other. When my turn came up, Izzy Alcantara tried to hand me the bat that everybody else was using. I politely declined. Why would I possibly swing somebody else's bat in a home run contest? I crunched a couple balls and they were barely reaching the warning track. There was a collective laughter amongst all of the other Dominican players. Alcantara came back out offering the bat a second time. This time I grabbed the bitch and went to whacking. The bat was more loaded than a .45 in a cop's holster. Still to this day, I don't know what was inside the bat, but we might as well have been swinging an aluminum rocket launcher. I was too late to the party to win the contest, but it didn't matter one bit. For a kid who grew up watching the Natural countless times, I dreamed of one day having that Roy Hobbs moment when he shatters the lights in the outfield, making it look like a 4th of July fireworks show. Well, this was that moment. I bamboozled a ball off the light standard in left field, busting out one of the bulbs. Although I would love to say it looked like a full-blown Independence Day celebration, it actually looked more like a little spark from a baby firecracker.

All of our games were on TV, and as I continued to play well and we continued to win games, my popularity in the country quickly began to grow. I soon became known as "Capitan America" because of a newspaper column that stuck me with the nickname. During the winter of 2001-2002, I became the first American in over 20 years to win the Dominican Winter League Most Valuable Player award. It actually got to the point where it became very difficult to eat at a restaurant, go out to a club, or even walk the streets without being stopped by a mob of people. It also didn't help that I was a white dude with a huge mop of blonde hair that could have been easily spotted amongst any Dominican crowd. This was the first time in my life I ever had to deal with anything like this. I completely embraced the culture, the people and the language, speaking only Spanish to everyone with the exception of the other American players. In a sense, I had become a f*cking rock star and I enjoyed every minute of it.

Human Crash Test Dummy Life Lesson #53

If you want to have success in a foreign land or in any industry, you need to completely immerse yourself in their culture. Speak their language, eat their food, and understand their ethics. Ultimately, it comes down to respect and trust. If you respect their culture, you will earn their trust. If you earn their trust, you will have their respect. If you have their trust and respect, it will give you every opportunity to thrive within their culture.

Chapter 54
Present Your Case

*"When the sword is once drawn,
the passions of men observe no bounds of moderation."*
-Alexander Hamilton

After a Licey Dominican League championship and string of wild celebrations, I had 2 weeks to rest and prepare for camp. Physically I obviously was in great baseball shape because I had been playing all winter. I also had my trainer T come out to the Dominican for the entire month of January to ensure my off-season workouts were not compromised. Mentally though, I was absolutely fried. The off-season was non-existent. I had been playing baseball for nearly 12 months and it was starting to take its toll. I started off sluggishly for the first couple weeks. Realizing I needed to get my ass in gear if I wanted to make the team, I started to pick it up offensively. With a week to go I finally hit my stride, hitting 3 homers in the week and taking one good at bat after another. This was it. I finally was going to make an opening day roster as I traveled back to Oakland with the team for the annual Bay Bridge series. I had no doubt done everything in my power. I was able to put up a very nice year in AAA the previous season while spending 4 different stints in the Major Leagues where I held my own enough for them to put me on the playoff roster. The team suggested that I go play in the Dominican and I returned as the first "gringo" to win the MVP award in 20 years. The last order of business I needed to take care of was spring training, which did not start out great by any means, but ended as well as it could have. As far as the outfield situation, Terrance Long was slated to be the CF, Jeremy Giambi in RF, and they signed David Justice to play LF. There were at least 2 outfield reserve spots, maybe even 3 if you consider the DH option; one was going to go to Adam Piatt, and the other I had every intention to put into my back pocket.

I was confident my work was done and I looked forward to standing on the 3rd baseline during pre-game introductions to experience my first opening day ceremony at the Major League level. Then it was as if it was Christmas Eve, and all of a sudden somebody told me Santa was not going to be coming to the house. With the Ebenezer Scrooge look on his face, clubhouse manager Steve Vucinich came by my locker and said the 5 infamous words I had become all too accustomed to hearing, "Skip wants to see you."

I walked into Art Howe's office and I could tell by the look on his face that this was different than the other 8 times I had been sent down. He always had a way to optimistically put a spin on the situation and generally had me feeling as good as I could before I hopped back on the shuttle to Sacramento. This time he had his head down, took a deep breath, and said, "Sorry, kid, you have done everything you needed to do. This isn't my choice, talk to Billy."

If I didn't have a leg to stand on I would not say sh*t, but this was different and even the manager knew it. I had been the Oakland A's f*cking yo-yo despite continuing to put up good numbers in AAA and playing as well as I could in limited action at the Major League level. They wanted me to go to the Dominican and I ended up putting together one of the best seasons in the history of the league. Including the past 2 spring trainings, this was the 9th time I had been sent down and I had never complained. There is just so many times though that a person is able to get punched in the face and kicked in the balls before he starts to fight back. The "sword" was officially drawn. This was my time to throw some punches of my own; I realized it was not a fight I was going to win but you better believe I was going down swinging!

I picked up the phone in Art's office and called Billy. His receptionist answered and said he was not in but would be returning shortly. "Eric, would you like me to have him call you? " To which I replied, "No, thank you. I'll wait for him in the parking lot." "Oh, oh my. Okay."

I packed up my gear, went outside and waited over an hour until Billy finally pulled into the parking lot. "I have been sent down 9 times now and I have never asked why until now... Why?"

"You don't walk enough, you had 1 walk in about 50 spring training plate appearances."

"Are you serious? You are really going to base this off 50 spring training AB's?"

"That's my latest sample size."

"F*ck your bullsh*t sample size! I got a sample size of Minor League numbers that say I f*cking deserve to be in the big leagues. Check the walk rate, check the strikeout rate, check the average, on base percentage, slugging percentage. Check the Dominican MVP numbers. I've busted my ass to get to this point Billy. I earned this f*cking chance."

With a smirk on his face, Billy responded, "Enjoy Sacramento, you will probably be back soon."

Human Crash Test Dummy Life Lesson #54

Know the facts, present your case, then accept your fate and move on. There was not a doubt in my mind that I knew that I earned a spot on that team. I presented the reasons why I felt that way and then I accepted my ass going back to AAA.

Chapter 55
Puppy Love

"If you want a friend in Washington, get a dog."
-Harry Truman

I was so irate at this point that I decided I was no longer going to let baseball continue to control my life. I needed a companion, somebody who was going to be there and listen to me when I needed to vent my frustrations, somebody who was going to love me unconditionally, understand and have the same sort of belief in me that I had in myself. I needed someone that was not going to judge me based on my walk rate in 50 plate appearances, someone who would be able to comprehend exactly who I was as a player and as a person. I needed somebody to snuggle with when times were tough and gosh dang it, if I wanted a big fat smooch on the lips with a little tongue every now and again, it wasn't going to be an issue.

Emotional times generally call for instinctively emotional reactions. I went out and did what I felt was very logical for somebody to do in my position. I bought a bulldog puppy and named him, Bruin.

From that point on, that little sh*t, figuratively and literally, did not leave my side. Outside of the road trips I would go on, I brought him with me everywhere I went. I even made a nice little home for him in my locker at Raley Field in Sacramento, complete with food, water, and toys. We definitely battled over several issues, including when and where it was appropriate to lift a leg or drop a deuce. I had to explain that if I wanted to get back to the big leagues, the manager's office was not okay. There was also a problem with this back at my boy Eric Brandan's (EB's) house, where I was very lucky he let both me and Bruin stay with him. For whatever reason Bruin kept thinking the fireplace was his own personal play pen. Regardless of what I would do to block off access, he would somehow figure out a way around whatever barricade I contrived. Bruin would paw at the glass fireplace door to pry it open, then roll around in the ashes, come out almost completely black, then proceed to stop, drop, and somersault around every other part of the house, leaving a trail of soot which generally led to under EB's bed, where he would hide and not come out for hours.

These times would pass, and Bruin's and my relationship grew to insurmountable heights. I loved that dog as much as I have loved anything in my life. In 2007, the two of us ended up in a kayak in McCovey Cove during the All-Star game working for Fox. Somehow, we ended up on a boat and I tossed a ball into the Bay for Bruin to fetch. He hopped into the water but started swimming the wrong way. He was headed out toward the Bay Bridge. Full recon mission ensued and we finally got him back into the boat. In reality, this was just one of our many epic adventures, but this one just so happened to be captured on national TV in front of millions of people.

There is no doubt a dog is man's best friend. Their unconditional love is something all humans can learn from. Whether I was 0-4 or 4-4, he would be waiting for me at the front door with his nub tail wagging every night after a home game. He would then get cozy and sleep on my head while he would press his slobbery cheek up against mine. There were many mornings when I literally would have to pull back his cheek, which was stuck to mine because the slobber had dried up.

Bruin went to doggie heaven a few years back, but that one bulldog has led us to own a total of 7 throughout the years. He also drew several family members and friends into either buying or rescuing bulldogs as well. It's incredible to think of the long lineage of the Bruin Family Tree. He literally is the gift that keeps on giving (in a good way)!

Human Crash Test Dummy Life Lesson #55

Dogs can be a small part or a big part of our lives, depending on our other commitments or current mood. The greatest thing you can remember is that we are everything in the dog's life. Treat them with the love and respect of the most loyal person in your life, because that is exactly who they are.

Chapter 56
Attitude Adjustment

"A positive attitude causes a chain reaction of positive thoughts, events and outcomes. It is a catalyst and it sparks extraordinary results."
-Wade Boggs

When I originally got to AAA, I noticed how everyone was always bitching and complaining about something. Generally, guys felt sorry for themselves because they were not in the big leagues and it was always everybody else's fault but their own. For the first time in my career, I had become that guy. Not surprisingly, my play on the field suffered dramatically. Bob Geren, who was my manager in Modesto and was also the manager of the Licey Tigres during the past winter, was now the manager in Sacramento. There was not a person in professional baseball that knew me, or my game, better than Bob. There was also not a person who had a greater impact and influence on my professional career to that point. So, when he saw me struggling and mopping around the clubhouse he had seen enough; it was the first time in our relationship together that he became a father figure.

He called me into the office and said, "I realize you're disappointed you're not in the big leagues but get over it. There are 24 other guys in that room that feel like they should be in the big leagues too. Also, there is no way you are going to get back there if you continue to mope around and feel sorry for yourself. I am going to bench you for two days. I want you to get back to being the person I know you are first, then we will worry about getting you back to the player you and I both know you are."

Tough pill to swallow but Bob was right. We were in Nashville, Tennessee, so I took the liberty to go out on the town with Jason Hart, my best friend and running mate all through the Minor Leagues. Jason was the bigger prospect and the reigning Texas League MVP, but he had yet to see a day in the big leagues. Something he no doubt reminded me of as we listened to country music and pounded beers through the course of the night. Soon, it became very easy to put things in perspective. I know it sounds corny, but all of a sudden, I realized just how lucky I was to be playing baseball for a living.

The next day I sat and watched us kick the sh*t out of Nashville. As far as I could remember, this was the first game in my entire Minor League career that I didn't start and I hated every minute of it. Stoked for my boys who went off that night, but damn it was tough not being able to get out there. I did not want to have to sit through another game and endure that torture again. Normally, as a visiting player, I would show up at the ballpark around 3:30 pm for a 7 o'clock game. Managers and coaches generally arrived around 2 pm. My ass was there at 1 pm to make sure I was there before Bob could write out the lineup. Just like a scolded school kid, I told Bob I had learned my lesson and then begged my way into the lineup. He obliged and I did not let him down. Homering off Pirates top prospect Bronson Arroyo in my first at bat, I finished the game with 3 hits. In the week that followed, I went on an absolute terror, hitting 4 home runs and raising my average 160 points. That was the last official week I spent in the Minor Leagues for the rest of my baseball career.

Human Crash Test Dummy Life Lesson #56

We try to be perfect and say and do all the right things, but oftentimes, we get overruled by our emotions and lose perspective of what it's going to take to move forward. Hold yourself accountable with constant self-evaluations and attitude checks. Remind yourself of why you began doing what you do and ask yourself tough questions. "Is this the best way to get the job done and is my attitude beneficial to the forward progress of both the team and myself?"

If the answer is no to either of these, figure out what exact changes need to be made to regain the proper perspective that fosters success. Adjust the attitude.

Chapter 57
Let's Go Streaking

*"Any minute, any day, some players may break a long standing record.
That's one of the fascinations about the game, the unexpected surprises."*
-Cornelius McGillicuddy, Sr.
(1862 – 1956, better known as Connie Mack)

When I arrived back in Oakland, it was almost as if it was a "be careful what you wish for" situation. I played almost every day, but the problem was my game typically would not start until the 7th inning or later. David Justice was the left fielder, and I was his designated defensive replacement "caddy" whenever we had the lead. Of course, I wanted to start every game, but as the season progressed, I realized that there was something special about this team and I became very content with my role.

Tim Hudson, Mark Mulder and Barry Zito were at the top of their game, but it was the late Corey Lidle that really solidified the best rotation in baseball. Offensively, Miguel Tejada was the leader on the field and eventual AL MVP. On August 13th, 2002, we won a game in Toronto and did not lose again for over 3 weeks. It was one of the most incredible streaks in the history of sports. Even having a small role, I would consider the winning streak one of the greatest accomplishments of my athletic career. Once the streak reached 10 games, players began to take notice but only because ESPN actually began showing Oakland A's highlights at the beginning of Sports Center. The greatest thing about the streak was that some dudes were so incredibly oblivious to what was actually going on. I remember being in the food room eating with Corey Lidle after our 12th victory when the guys on TV were talking about how rare of an accomplishment 12 wins in a row actually was. Then, completely shocked, with a bewildered sort of look on his face, Lidle asked, "Damn, have we really won 12 in a row?"

Professional sports can be a brutal business and in baseball's case, oftentimes you will get 25 guys with their own agenda. Guys play for their own livelihood and future contracts. Because of the harsh reality of the business, it is tough to blame them. The earning potential for professional athletes is generally very short-lived. The length of the average Major League Baseball career is under 3 years. The Team concept is taught at a young age and it slowly deteriorates as you move up through the ranks, regardless of the bullsh*t sound bites professional athletes want to feed you about how it's "all about the team" or "all about winning a championship." So, to say that for over the course of almost an entire Major League season it felt like we had 25 plus guys that genuinely cared about one another and pulled for each other is beyond rare. Oftentimes you would see guys rooting against one another in hopes that somebody else's failures would lead to their next opportunity. I saw it all the time and it made me absolutely sick. I attribute a lot of the selfless attitude of the 2002 Oakland A's to David Justice. To this day, he is the coolest character I have ever met in the game of baseball. DJ was playing his final year of baseball, and truly, all he wanted to do was win. No bullsh*t; no other agendas. This attitude then became infectious amongst the rest of the young and incredibly talented Oakland players.

September 3, 2002: we were riding a 19-game winning streak and playing the Kansas City Royals with Tim Hudson on the mound. The 20th victory would set a modern-day baseball record and over 50,000 people showed up to watch history take place. We came out banging, scoring 11 runs in the first 5 innings. With an 11-0 lead, it was tough to blame anybody who thought consecutive win #20 was undoubtedly in the bag. KC then started to chip away and made the score 11-5. I came into the game for DJ in LF at that point in the top of the 7th inning. KC was relentless; in the top of the 9th inning still leading 11-8, with 2 on and 2 out, Mike Sweeney hit a ball over my head in LF and it seemed like the entire play happened in slow motion. The ball actually started out in foul territory, and then as I went back toward the wall, I could see it coming back into fair territory. I scaled the wall but there was no chance. The game was now tied and we were about to be known not as the team who broke the modern-day win streak record, but rather the team that blew an 11-run lead with an opportunity to do so. After we got the 3rd out I realized I was set to lead off the bottom of the 9th inning. As soon as I saw Jason Grimsley, a right-hander running to the mound for Kansas City, I realized Scott Hatteberg was going to pinch-hit for me. Most dudes in my situation would probably be upset because they would want an opportunity at the glory. As far as I was concerned, I would have told Hatteberg to hit for me if Art Howe had not. Grimsley at the time was one of the filthiest right-handed relief pitchers in baseball, and Hatte, a left-handed hitter, was the much better match up.

One pitch later, Hatte unloaded on a Grimsley 95 mph sinker and euphoria set in as I watched the ball sail over the right field wall. Scott Hatteberg had just won the 20th consecutive game for us, and I celebrated as if I was the one who hit it, jumping up and down like a crazed lunatic, eventually ending up on the back of Billy Koch greeting Hatte at home plate. It was one of the proudest moments in my entire athletic career and I had absolutely nothing to do with it. After a night off, we headed to Minnesota and finally lost. The 20 victories were a modern-day baseball record and held for 15 years until the 2017 Cleveland Indians won 22 consecutive games.

When Cleveland was approaching the record, there were a lot of publications that reached out wanting to know my thoughts on the streak. The obvious question was whether or not I was rooting for them. I can honestly say that winning 20 consecutive games was such a surreal and special experience that I wanted the group of dudes on the 2017 Indians to be able to experience the exact same thing. I was 100% rooting for them and I am stoked that they have now set a new mark that another team in the years to come can collectively come together and GO GET!

Human Crash Test Dummy Life Lesson #57

The only way to achieve greatness is by collectively working together with your entire team. Internal competition is a beautiful thing that will most always elevate everybody's game to another level. Streaks are simply byproducts of a complete and total dedication to the small details that make history happen.

Chapter 58
Spin the Wheel

"Eat your betting money but don't bet your eating money."
-Horse racing proverb

When players in baseball talk about having good team chemistry, one of the things they often refer to is guys going out to dinner and hanging together outside of the clubhouse. On the 5 teams that I played on, I would say that a large group generally consisted of 8-10 dudes. When we would go to dinner with the 2002 Oakland A's, there was oftentimes over 20 guys, nothing I had ever seen before and nothing I have ever seen or even heard of since. We had just flown into Seattle to play the Mariners and we actually had 23 guys at Capital Grille. This was not a mandatory team function and if you ever did not go it was no big deal. The fact was that guys liked being around each other. It was as close to a little league, high school, or college team that I ever played on at the professional level. What was always interesting was who would pay. Because we went out often and our groups were so large, it wasn't just the veteran who was making the most amount of money that would pay every time. Outside of David Justice, we did not have a lot of older players, and with the A's limited payroll, we didn't have guys making a ton of money. Because of my perpetuity for gambling, credit card roulette always seemed to make things exciting. That night in Seattle we had 23 guys drinking cocktails and fine wines, eating appetizers, and steak and lobster entrees. This was going to be a big one!

The way the game would work is that each guy would throw his credit card into a hat, and then the waitress would pick the credit cards one by one. The drama would build with every one of the cards that was pulled out. Eventually it would come down to two cards left in the hat and a large dramatic production would ensue. On this night, the final two happened to be two dudes making the minimum: myself and Mark Ellis. Even though it could potentially cost me nearly a paycheck, I loved the drama! Ellis on the other hand is not a gambler;

he grew up in South Dakota with an incredibly humble and conservative background. Every dollar he earned he did his best to save. The car he drove in 2002 was so old and beat up, it was a legitimate safety hazard. I said everything I could to try to convince him to buy a new car so he could "protect his investment" (himself), but to absolutely no avail. He bumped around in that little red piece of sh*t for two years!

So, as I was getting my blood boiling over the credit card roulette process, Ellis was freaking out. By the time we got down to the two of us, his palms were sweating and it looked like he had seen a ghost! Dudes were literally jumping up and down with excitement over one of the two rookies having to wear the bill. Then the waitress pulled out the final card. "Mark Ellis." To be honest I was totally unfazed; of course I did not want to have to suck on a several-thousand-dollar bill, but to be able to see the panic, and then eventual relief, on Mark Ellis' face was damn near worth every penny.

After I signed out and while we were walking back to the hotel, David Justice came up from behind and nearly tackled me. He then pulled out the copy of the $8,000 receipt I had just signed. "I got you Byrnesie, you took it like a champ! They just refunded your credit card!"

Human Crash Test Dummy Life Lesson #58

So long as it is not going to cost you a relationship or jeopardize the roof over your head, don't be afraid to spin the f*cking wheel. Scared money doesn't ever make money. Also, accept responsibility with a smile on your face and maybe David Justice will save your day!

Chapter 59
Get Up

"Perseverance is failing 19 times and succeeding the 20th."
-Julie Andrews, Marry Poppins

Early 2003 tested my patience and overall mental fortitude. When I went to Spring Training, I wanted to leave no doubt in Billy Beane's mind as to whether or not I should be on the team. I had again spent the winter in the Dominican to supplement the lack of at bats from the previous year. Spring went incredibly well, but just as I had learned the previous season, there were obviously no guarantees. I made my way north with the team for the final Spring Training series, this time against the Rivercats in Sacramento. I kept waiting for head clubhouse man Steve Vucinich, aka the "Axe Man," to tell me to go see Ken Macha, the new manager, in his office. Everywhere I walked the entire day, before and after the game, I kept one eye on Vuc. Although Vuc is one of the nicest guys in the game, I even went so far as to tell him to stay the f*ck away from me. I couldn't take it anymore. I finally approached the "Grim Reaper" right after the game. "What the f*ck, Vuc? Do I stay in Sacramento or drive back to Oakland?"

"You should probably show up tomorrow night in Oakland, unless you want to stay here and have somebody else take your spot?"

That was how I found out I had made my first opening day roster.

Opening night 2003 was definitely one that I will never forget, everything from the National Anthem and the fly over to just putting on the uniform with the opening day patch on it. I had already played in 2 playoff series but there was something about my first opening day in the Major Leagues that was beyond special. Considering what I had experienced the year before, I had an incredible appreciation very similar to my first day in the big leagues.

I had been knocked down (sent down) 9 times, so when I finally landed on my feet on opening day 2003, the experience was overwhelming.

Human Crash Test Dummy Life Lesson #59

It takes getting knocked down multiple times if you want to reach your full potential. You don't always have to understand how or why you got knocked down; you just need to get your ass back up, and you will be better for it each time.

Chapter 60
I x V = R

"Image x Vividness = Reality."
-Kirk Gibson

The 2003 season can best be described by the title of the Clint Eastwood movie, *The Good, the Bad, and the Ugly*. The season saw plenty of all three.

I spent the first several weeks in my standard role of coming off the bench to pinch hit, pinch run, or play defense with the occasional start against a left-handed pitcher. I was growing increasingly frustrated but continued to do everything in my power to keep a positive outlook and believe that my opportunity would come at some point. The Detroit Tigers were in town and one of my favorite players growing up, Kirk Gibson, was on the coaching staff. After our batting practice before the first game of the series, Gibby was on the field hitting fungos, so I snuck over and asked him if I sent over a bat to the visiting clubhouse, would it be possible for him to sign it for me and send it back? He hit one more ball then turned around and stared at me as if I just interrupted him during his at bat against Dennis Eckersley in Game 1 of the 1988 World Series. He eventually fired back, "Send it over." He quickly turned around and continued to hit fungos. Not exactly the warm reception I was looking for, but I had heard all the rumors of how intense he was so I did not let it bother me. As a matter of fact, it actually made me like him even more.

I sent the bat over and Gibby signed it and had the bat returned to me before the game even started. Mikey Thalbaum, the visiting clubhouse manager, wrapped it in a long sanitary sock. I kept the bat in the sock for protection and took it home. The next day when I was taking BP, Kirk Gibson came up to me this time.

"You get the bat?"

"Yes, sir, thank you very much."

"Have you read what I wrote?"

"No, I took it home but I haven't taken it out of the sanitary sock yet."

"Take it out, read it, figure out the meaning, understand it, then apply it."

When I got home after the game, I immediately grabbed the bat and pulled it out of the sock. "To Eric, I x V = R." What could that possibly mean? How was I supposed to decipher this mysterious equation?

I asked everyone I encountered the rest of the day and got nothing; nobody had any idea what it meant. The next day was a day game, so we were not taking BP on the field but the Tigers were. I absolutely could not take it anymore! I needed to know the meaning of I x V = R!

As soon as I got to the stadium I went down to the dugout and essentially stalked Kirk Gibson until he came out onto the field. When he showed, despite being surrounded by several other Tigers coaches and players, I immediately bombarded him.

"I take it you read the bat?"

"Yup, I have asked almost everyone I know in the last 24 hours the meaning but nobody has a clue."

"Not many people do. I X V = R, Image x Vividness = Reality. The more vividly you are able to imagine something the more likely it is to become your reality. This equation changed my career and it will yours as well."

I immediately went up to the clubhouse and wrote it down.

Ironically, that very same day, Jermaine Dye hurt his knee in the outfield. Terry Francona, who was the bench coach in 2003, told Adam Piatt, another reserve outfielder and former Minor League player of the year, to grab his glove. As Piatt was getting ready to run out to replace Dye, Macha intervened, "Byrnes, get your ass out to right field." Assuming Piatt was going in, I had to scurry to find my glove then sprint out to right field completely disheveled but fired up to be in the game.

At this point, I just kept repeating, "I x V = R, I x V = R, I x V =R..." I then visualized seeing the ball well at the plate, taking good swings, and making plays in the outfield. I ended the day with three quality at-bats and two hits, one of which ignited a rally that eventually helped us win the game. I got the start the next day and laid out a couple more hits in another win, buying myself another start.

I now made visualization a part of my routine. I would watch video of the next day's starting pitcher and completely etch him in my mind, studying the different pitches he throws and the mechanics he used to throw them. Then, right before I would go to bed I would visualize all of the pitches I was going to see. A fastball inside for a ball, a fastball inside for a strike, a fastball over the middle for a ball, and a fastball down the dick (middle) for a strike. A fastball outside for a ball and a fastball outside for a strike. I would then repeat the same thing with all of the other pitches the pitcher had. I would also repeat this routine in the batting cage, whacking all of the visualized strikes off a tee 20 minutes before the game.

By the time I stepped into the batter's box to face Greg Maddox or Roger Clemens, because of my vivid imagination, I felt like I had faced these guys and had success off of them several times already. Amazingly, I was in my 4th season and had yet to start 3 consecutive games, but thankfully that was about to change. One way to hold a team hostage and force them to play you is by playing at such a high level that you don't give them a choice. That's exactly what I did. 3 games became 4 and then 9 games became 10. I didn't realize it until I got to 10 because I was so focused on the moment and doing everything in my power to stay in the starting lineup, but I had also hit in 10 consecutive games. At that point, I figured so long as I kept the hitting streak going, Macha would have to continue to write my name in the lineup.

Human Crash Test Dummy Life Lesson #60

The brain is the most powerful tool that we possess. Use it to your advantage. Visualization does not guarantee success, but I will guarantee you that you will be more comfortable and confident in a situation that you have already played out in your mind. Comfort and confidence will in turn give you your best chance to succeed. As Gibby laid it out for me, the more vividly you can imagine something the more likely it is to become your reality.

Chapter 61
Consistency is the Path to Greatness

"There is always some kid who may be seeing me play for the first time, I owe him my best."
-Joe DiMaggio

When I was a kid, I used to sit around with all of my buddies and we would ask the question: if you could break one baseball record, what record would it be and why? Roger Maris' 61 home runs in a season? Hank Aaron's 755 home runs in his career? Ted Williams' .406 average?

These were all great accomplishments, but in my opinion, there was one answer and one answer only. Joe DiMaggio's 56 game hitting streak.

The streak represented the ultimate gold standard of consistency. As I grew older and got an opportunity to play professional baseball, my fondness for a hitting streak continued to grow exponentially. After I signed with the A's the message was sent loud and clear that the biggest difference between a Minor League player and a Major League star was the major leaguer's ability to perform on a consistent basis. What better way to measure consistency than a hitting streak? When I got to 15 games, I realized I had something good going, but most importantly, I now felt like so long as I got a hit in the previous game, I was going to get a chance to play the next one. In regards to playing time, for the first and probably only time in my career, I had the A's by the balls, so long as I continued to get hits.

We had a road trip that took us to Kansas City where I collected 2 hits Friday night to stretch the streak to 20 games, the longest I ever had at any level. Then came a Saturday day game. I had gone 0-4 in my first 4 at bats and I felt like absolute sh*t. I was having a very difficult time seeing the ball, and for whatever reason, I felt as if the game had completely sped up on me overnight. Dudes who were throwing

88 mph appeared to be throwing 95 mph. So, when Mike McDougal, Kansas City's All-Star flame throwing closer that year, came into the game in the 9th, I wasn't exactly beaming with confidence. There were 2 outs, a man on first base in the top of the 9th inning, and we were down by one run. The game and the hitting streak were on the line. I was telling myself, "Slow it down, slow it down, slow it down, see the ball, see the ball, see the ball."

The first pitch was a two-seam fastball that started over the inside part of the plate and then ran inside for ball one. Wow, what a difference! I saw it great. I thought to myself that maybe McDougal, who normally threw in the high 90's, did not have his best stuff that day? The next pitch literally seemed like it was in slow motion. I could see the ball come out of his hand, this time starting over the middle of the plate and then running to the inside corner. Without trying to do too much, I simply dropped the head of the bat to the ball. I could not feel the ball come off the bat so I wasn't sure how well I hit it, but the ball headed towards left field. "Get up, get up, get the f*ck up!" I screamed as I sprinted down the first base line.

My head was down as I was rounding 1st base and by the time I looked up, I could not see the ball. Either the left fielder had caught it or the ball had somehow gone over the left field fence. Then, judging by the reaction of the home crowd's silence, I knew it was gone.

We had just taken a one run lead and I extended the hitting streak to 21 games. The streak was at 22 when we went into Florida to play the eventual World Champion Marlins. Josh Beckett, who was considered the nastiest right-handed starter in baseball at the time, was on the mound for the Fish. In my first at-bat, I smoked a curveball down the line that I felt like was going to be a double off the bat. But for whatever reason, the left fielder was playing me deep and right on the line, making the catch seem relatively routine. They say that in baseball you get 1 good pitch per at-bat to hit; you don't want to miss that pitch. Similarly, I feel like you generally have one good shot to get a hit in a game against an elite pitcher. That was my shot, and it got caught; 3 at-bats later the streak was over.

When I first signed with the A's, under the tutelage of Karl Kuehl, Keith Lippman, and Dave Hudgens, I developed a routine. Routines are easy to maintain because you don't show up at the park searching for what you are going to do; you just do it. Tee work, 10 balls up the middle, 10 to right, 10 to left, 1 handed drill, walk up drill, up and in drill, soft toss, iron mike. That was it. I showed up every single day and that was the first thing I would do. Being consistent with my routine and getting consistent playing time allowed me to be consistent on the field.

I nearly got a hit almost every day for a month and barely got halfway to Pete Rose's National League record of 44. I cannot even imagine Joe DiMaggio's 56 consecutive games with a hit; it is completely incomprehensible to me, especially in today's game. The problem with maintaining a hitting streak today is that the game is managed much differently now than it was in the 1940s. Starters are no longer expected to go 9 innings. Typically, if a manager can get 6 innings out of a guy, they then turn it over to a 7th, 8th and 9th inning left-handed or right-handed matchup specialist that is paid to do one thing: get you out, once. The 56-game hitting streak is the most hallowed streak in all of sports, and in my opinion, of all the records it will be the last to fall.

Human Crash Test Dummy Life Lesson #61

Consistency is a trait the greatest in any industry possess. The ability to do something at a high level for an extended period of time is extremely difficult in an ever-changing world. Celebrate and learn from those people. Effort and routine lay the foundation for consistency. Be consistent with your effort and develop and maintain a routine.

Chapter 62
Fuel the Fire

"What's the matter with Byrnes? He's a bum."
-San Francisco Giants' fans in OF bleachers

Although my streak ended, I had played well enough to the point where for the first time in my Major League career, I was able to come to the ballpark and have some comfort in knowing that I would be in the lineup. June 29, 2003 was the final game of a 3-game series against the Giants at Pac-Bell Park. My day started with my 2 boys, the Royer twins, calling me on my way to the ballpark to tell me they would be sitting in the front row of the outfield bleachers. Their intended plan: talk sh*t to me the entire game. "That's fine. Just make sure you dick heads hold on to the ball I hit into the bleachers. I'll sign it for you f*cks." Obviously, this was harmless fun, sh*t-talking with my boys, but make no mistake about it, they lit my fire for the day.

Leading off the game I hit a check-swing excuse me single, my 2nd at-bat I hit a double, and then in my 3rd at-bat, right after I discreetly flipped them the bird, I sent my boys a present! The ball actually flew just to the left of where they were sitting. I was now 3-3 with a single, double, and a homer. A triple was no doubt on my mind for my fourth at bat just because of "triples ally" in right center field; otherwise, I don't even think I would had paid it any attention. I hit a double off the left field wall and was now 4-4. I approached my 5th at-bat as relaxed as could be when I took a low and outside slider from Felix Rodriguez and dumped it into centerfield for what I thought would be a single to cap off the first ever 5-hit game of my life. Then something very weird happened, Carlos Valderamma, the Giants center fielder, slipped, and the ball bounced over his head. I was off to the races and ended up standing on third base, completing the first ever cycle in Pac-Bell/AT&T Park history. It was also the first time in my life I had ever accomplished the feat at any level.

"You crazy ass mother f*cker. Look at them people, they cheering for you!" Ron Washington, our third base coach, was never a guy who was lost for words, and I didn't expect him to be at that moment. The first thing I noticed was all of the guys on our team who had made their way to the top step of the dugout and seemed genuinely fired up. Then, just as Ron Washington said, I looked up into the stands and noticed the majority of the San Francisco fans out of their seats and applauding. The inning completed, and as I ran out to left field, all of the fans, including all of my boys who had been talking trash the entire game, rose to their feet to give me a standing ovation. There really is no way to appropriately describe exactly what I was feeling because I had never experienced the way I felt at that moment in my entire life. I had flashbacks to all the Giants games that I went to growing up, cheering and heckling alongside many of the same fans that were in the stands that day. I was extremely humbled, grateful, and for whatever reason, I actually felt embarrassed. The day started with innocent trash talking and ended with the first ever 5-hit game and cycle in my life. Trust me when I say I never needed any extra motivation to play in a big-league game, but whenever I was able to draw on something new, I went for it.

Human Crash Test Dummy Life Lesson #62

Figure out what fuels your fire and then seek it. Motivation comes in all forms and the key to consistent success is maintaining a purposeful drive that forces you to perform at or near your maximum potential.

Chapter 63
If My Aunt Had Balls,
She Would Be My Uncle

*"Sh*t happens."*
-Forrest Gump

Following the game in which I hit for the cycle, there was a huge push for me to play in the All-Star game, which was just 2 weeks away. Although I was left off the original roster, I was put on the first ever ballot that allowed fans to vote for the final guy. I ended up receiving over 1,000,000 votes but came in 2nd to Boston Red Sox catcher Jason Varitek.

Between the hitting streak, the cycle, and now the All-Star push, I was becoming a bit overwhelmed. So, it was not a huge surprise when I hit a wall in the second half of the season and pulled off one of the most epic slumps in the history of Major League Baseball: 9 hits in 95 at-bats. That was not a typo. 9 hits in 95 f*cking at-bats!!!

Needless to say, I was back to reality in a hurry. I was able to pick it up a bit toward the end of the season and came into the playoffs feeling good. We were AL West champs and faced Boston in the first round of the playoffs. Just like 2001 we jumped out to a 2 games to none lead in the series. The series went back to Boston with us just having to win one game to move on to the American League Championship.

With the score 1-0 in the middle of the game, I led off the inning with my 2nd of 3 hits that I ended the day with. I promptly stole 2nd base and then moved to 3rd base with 1 out. Miguel Tejada was at the plate and hit a slow roller down the 3rd base line. I broke for home and felt like there was no chance the 3rd baseman would be able to throw me out at the plate. When I was three-fourths of the way home, I focused on catcher Jason Varitek as he stood far to the left of home plate, acting as if the 3rd baseman would either throw to first or just hold onto it. I had seen the deke play all too often to fall for Varitek's acting, so I continued full steam ahead. Varitek left the entire plate open so I proceeded to slide toward the outside of home plate.

At the last second, Varitek stuck his leg out in front of the plate without the baseball, tripping me over the plate and causing me to do a full summersault in the air. My immediate thought was that my knee was blown out. As the pain set in, my second thought was that I wanted to rip Varitek's f*cking head off. I got up, and Varitek happened to be standing right in my face, so I pushed him out of the way and headed back to the dugout. Amongst all of the commotion, I never realized I had not touched home plate. Varitek picked up the ball that he never had possession of and tagged me out.

I accept full responsibility for not touching home plate. Always throughout the course of my career before and after, if there was ever any doubt, I would always make sure I retouched the plate. In this case, I was in such a daze because of my knee that I simply blanked. Regardless of the situation, there is no excuse. I f*cked up.

We went on to lose the game but had another chance to close out the series the next day. I came up in my first at-bat in Game 4 with the bases loaded. I drilled a ball off veteran right-hander John Burkett down the right field line that landed just beyond Pesky's Pole. The ball was ruled foul. After watching the video replay several times, I still could not tell one way or another if the ball was fair or foul. Nonetheless, I was within inches of a grand slam that would have changed the dynamic of the entire series.

We went on to lose Game 4 in extra innings and then lost Game 5 back in Oakland. I ended the season on 3rd base as the tying run in the bottom of the 9th. There is no guarantee things would have worked out differently had I gone back to touch home plate or if the ball down the right field line stayed fair, but undoubtedly, both plays would have been game changers. Figuring Varitek was blocking the plate without the ball, the play at home plate would have for sure been overturned if the current replay system had been in place or if the umpires made the proper ruling. Then again, if my Aunt had balls she would be my Uncle...

Jason Varitek became known throughout his years as a dude who would bait a player into thinking he was going to give you home plate and then at the last second stick his leg out to clip you. There is a rule that you cannot block home plate without the ball and essentially that became his signature. It would be one thing if he stood in there waiting for the ball and willing to take the impact, but in his case, he stood to the side of home plate, and before catching the ball or even making an attempt to catch the ball, he stuck his leg out covered in a protective shin guard to deliberately trip a runner. I was not the first player it happened to and by no means was I the last. Umpires around the league never called him on his actions, which essentially gave him free reign to continue his dirty play. For the rest of my career, I literally prayed for an opportunity to blow his ass up at home plate. By all accounts, I have heard that Jason Varitek is a good dude, and as I am sure the leg trip was not personal, my intentions at retribution were not personal either. I simply wanted to deliver a message that sticking your leg out in front of the plate to deliberately trip a base runner was bullsh*t. Regardless, I was in the wrong for not being aware of the fact that I had missed the plate, and ultimately I accept sole responsibility for my f*ck up.

Human Crash Test Dummy Life Lesson #63

Sh*t happens in life. Sometimes you f*ck up and as much as you want to go back in time and change the past, there is absolutely nothing you can do about it. Accept responsibility, learn from your mistakes and move forward.

Chapter 64
Mind Games

"The greatest discovery of my generation is that human beings can alter their lives by altering their attitudes of mind."
-William James

I came into 2004 knowing damn well what was at stake. I was heading into my 3rd full season, meaning at the end of the year I would be eligible for arbitration. Arbitration is a process in which you are evaluated as a player and compared to players of years past to figure out monetary compensation for the following year. Essentially, it is the first time players really get paid. Once again, I was scrapping for playing time during spring training but this year was different. I had a confidence and "get the f*ck out of my way" attitude about me from the 1st day of Spring Training. I wanted redemption for the way 2003 ended, and I wanted to prove to myself and the A's that I was capable of being a very consistent baseball player after a roller coaster ride the previous year.

I have always appreciated and understood the importance of the mental game of baseball. Yet it wasn't until after the 2003 season that I realized I needed to make a psychological adjustment if I wanted to reach my full potential.

The Mental Game of Baseball, written by Karl Kuehl and Harvey Dorfman, became my bible. I dissected it cover to cover, and then personally reached out to Karl Kuehl for more advice on how to specifically apply the book's lessons to my situation. I also delved into several different martial arts books my dad gave me that he used to mentally put him over the edge in the process of becoming one of the highest-ranking black belts in the world. What was amazing through all of my readings was how the message of "staying in the moment" resonated as the key ingredient in reaching your full potential. Too much time spent gloating or dwelling on what has already happened was no doubt detrimental to your progress. Too much time spent fantasizing about the future or fearing what lies ahead is wasted energy that hinders your ability to be your best in the here and "NOW." It all made perfect sense, and I focused my entire off-season on training myself to stay in the present moment. Breathing exercises became a daily practice, and not coincidentally, surfing became part of my workout regimen. Of all the activities that I have done in my life, surfing is the one that brings my ADHD ass into a Zen state in which the past and future become completely irrelevant. I figured the more I got to experience that feeling, the better chance I would have to eventually apply it to my baseball career.

At the end of the off-season, I continued my alternative form of training by climbing a killer mountain adjacent to Squaw Valley with a peak of over 9,000 feet. Physically and psychologically, I had never felt more ready for a season. Once again though, I didn't have a job when I showed up for Spring Training, but this time I didn't give a f*ck; I was going to take one.

Human Crash Test Dummy Life Lesson #64

Spend just as much time training your mind as you do your body. You can have all the physical talent in the world but if you don't have the proper mental fortitude you will never realize that talent.

Chapter 65
Amor Fati

"The impediment to action advances action. What stands in the way becomes the way."
-Marcus Aurelius

At the end of spring training, we traveled to San Francisco for the annual Bay Bridge series. I had a great spring up to that point yet still no starting job. I came into the game late as a replacement left fielder and in my first at-bat faced a hard throwing Dominican right-hander. The first pitch sailed out of his hand and was coming directly at my head. I did everything I could to escape but I was f*cked. Bam! The ball hit me right where the skull and bill of the helmet meet.

Immediately I went down. The umpire and catcher hovered over me, and then I could see panic set in on their face. I quickly tasted why. Blood was spraying from my head, onto my face, and into my mouth. Larry Davis, our head trainer, came out and applied pressure to the cut above my left eye. After a minute or so, I felt fine and I wanted to get up. Larry demanded I stay down. "Stay right here, Byrnesie, we have a cart coming to get you."

It's one thing that I just got hit in the f*cking head and was bleeding profusely from my dome, but it's a whole other thing when you want me to get on a cart on the way out. "Larry, I don't need a f*cking cart!"

"Byrnesie, I don't care what you think you need, you are getting on the cart."

As I was being driven off down the left field line, I was receiving the courtesy cheer from Giants fans. So often you see guys give a thumbs-up sign on the way out to let family, friends, and fans know that they will be all right. I possibly gave the first ever thumbs down sign in the history of sports. I had just gotten plunked in the melon on the 2nd to last Spring Training game, I did not want to be taken out on a cart, and this more likely than not cost me a chance of getting my first opening day start.

When I got back to the visitor's locker room, my entire family was waiting outside. I could see tears in the eyes of my mom and my sister; the exact reason I did not want to take the f*cking cart! I proceeded inside the locker room where it took 12 stitches to close the gash in my head. 2 days later it was opening night in Oakland against the Texas Rangers. Doctors were worried about a possible concussion, but I felt no lasting symptoms other than the stitches.

Fortunately, I was not put on the DL, but I was also not put in the starting lineup. In the bottom of the 8th inning though, trailing by a run with 2 outs, the Rangers brought in left-hander Ron Mahay. Unlike "Moneyball" when it was "Byrnesie, grab some bench," this time it was, "Byrnes, grab a bat!"

We would sell out the Coliseum 4 times a year: the 3 regular season series games against the Giants and Opening Day. 50,000 plus fans in the seats, 2 runners on base, down by 1, bottom of the 8th. I realize it was not the World Series, but these are the sort of opportunities I dreamt about as a kid. The first pitch I saw I drilled into the left field corner, scoring the tying and winning run. Just 2 days earlier, I was lying on a cart with blood profusely spewing from my head, wondering when would be the next time I would be able to play baseball.

Now, I was standing on 2nd base watching my teammates and 50,000 people go absolutely berzerk. Pretty f*cking cool experience.

Human Crash Test Dummy Life Lesson #65

Things don't always go as planned, and oftentimes, we are presented with obstacles. It is up to us to use those obstacles to propel us forward. Embrace all situations and take them as stepping-stones in the journey of life. Amor Fati is a saying that was embraced by ancient stoic philosophers. Its meaning: love your fate. Love everything that happens to you in your life and use it as an opportunity for growth and development.

Chapter 66
The Man in the Arena

"It is not the critic who counts; not the man who points out how the strong man stumbles, or where the doer of deeds could have done them better. The credit belongs to the man who is actually in the arena, whose face is marred by dust and sweat and blood; who strives valiantly; who errs, who comes short again and again, because there is no effort without error and shortcoming; but who does actually strive to do the deeds; who knows great enthusiasms, the great devotions; who spends himself in a worthy cause; who at the best knows in the end the triumph of high achievement, and who at the worst, if he fails, at least fails while daring greatly, so that his place shall never be with those cold and timid souls who neither know victory nor defeat."
-Theodore Roosevelt

I eventually played my way into the starting lineup and turned in my most consistent season as a Major Leaguer, hitting .283 with 20 home runs and 17 stolen bases. The season eventually came down to a 3-game series in Oakland against the Angels for the chance to make the playoffs. We got beat handily in the Friday night game, meaning we needed to win the next two games. We fell behind early on Saturday then scratched and clawed our way back into the game. With 2 outs in the bottom of the 9th inning, the Oakland A's season was left in my hands.

I came to the plate against one of the best closers of all time, flame-throwing right-hander Troy Percival. Before I got into the box, I kept repeating to myself my favorite mantra in big time situations, "Slow it down, slow it down, slow it down." That mantra was the key to any success I have ever had against guys who throw in the mid to upper 90s. When Percival released the first pitch, my positive affirmations of the moment and my year-long commitment to the mental aspect of baseball paid off. The ball actually seemed as if it was in slow motion; I could visibly see the rotation. I then took my best swing, hitting the ball right on the sweet spot of the bat, and then watched it sail deep towards the left center field bleachers. Generally during the day, the ball would carry much better than at night in the Coliseum. The issue at times though is as the late afternoon sets in, the wind usually picks up. Because of the enclosed stadium, the wind typically will swirl, thus at times helping a ball get over the fence and knocking it down at others. I immediately looked at Angels left fielder Jeff DaVanon who had turned his head and sprinted towards the high wall in left center field. DaVanon, with his back now against the wall, looked up and watched the ball fall from the Oakland sky and into his glove ending our season. I felt as if somebody had ripped my heart out of my chest.

Two years later when I played with him in Arizona, I finally got a chance to ask DaVanon about his perspective on the play. He said he felt as if the ball was literally over the fence and was then blown back onto the field of play at the last second. Nice to know but didn't exactly make me feel better.

Within a 2-year period, I was on some kind of crazy roller coaster ride. I finally got my shot to play every day in the Major Leagues, went on a 22-game hitting streak, received over 1,000,000 votes for an All-Star game, went into a 9-95 slump, didn't touch home plate in the playoffs, hit .462 in those same playoffs with a 1.000 OPS, and hit what would have been a grand slam in that same series that most likely would have put the nail in the coffin (but instead the ball went foul by inches, apparently). The following year I had my most consistent season as a big leaguer (hitting 20 tanks and swiping 17 bags), and then a would be home run that would have kept our season alive (but got swatted down by a late afternoon breeze). A lot of highs, a lot of lows.

One thing I have always done pretty well in my life is keep things in perspective. I realized how fortunate I was to be in the situation I was in and to experience both the good and bad. Through all of the adversity in my career, I rarely ever let it affect my overall emotional state, especially away from the field. When I got into my car after the game, and all of the realities of the past 2 years set in, I became very emotional and began crying uncontrollably. I wasn't exactly sure what I was crying about other than dealing with a lot of sh*t in a relatively short period of time. The experience I gained within those 2 years would give me a blueprint on how to deal with life's challenges, successes, and failures. It has been said that 10 percent of life is what actually happens to you, and 90 percent of life is how you react. Although very challenging at times, I was learning how to react.

Human Crash Test Dummy Life Lesson #66

Control what is in your control and accept the things that are not. It's that simple. You can't control the weather; you can't control random events; you can't control other people's actions or their perceptions of you. There is no sense worrying about what may happen or even fretting over something that did happen. The only thing you can control is your reaction to those events. The sweat and the blood is yours. You've done what you can do. Humbly wear your efforts as a badge of honor. You are the f*cking man in the arena.

Chapter 67
Know Your Value

"Risk comes from not knowing what you are doing."
-Warren Buffet

The off-season in 2004 was spent going through the arbitration process for the first time. My agent, Gary Wichard, was primarily a football agent. Through the agent selection process, many people advised against hiring Wichard because he wasn't a "baseball" guy. One meeting my dad and I had with him eliminated any doubts about his competency. There was not another guy out there that I would rather have had represent me in an arbitration hearing or free agent negotiation. Gary was one of the smoothest, most badass dudes I have ever been around, and I was more than honored to have him on my side. Michael Sasson, a Bay Area kid who was the equipment manager while I was at UCLA, and a good buddy of mine, was working for Wichard, which made the situation ideal.

For the most part, arbitration is basically a numbers game. A player's numbers are compared to other players with equal service time that have played the same position in recent years. A player's projected salary is determined by other guys' salaries of years past, as well as current comparable players and market conditions. Where the process gets interesting is when the player and team exchange file numbers. The player files the number that he feels he is worth based on all of his comps, and the team files the number that they feel like the player is worth. From there it becomes a game of chicken. If the negations are not settled and the process ends up in a hearing, the arbitrator picks one number or the other. There is no middle ground.

In my situation, the player that we used as our comp was Tori Hunter, who made $2.4 million in his first year of arbitration with the Twins. The player that the A's used as their comp was Jay Payton who made $1.85 million in his first year of arbitration with the Rockies. The strategy then became trying to figure out where the team was going to file so that we could file an appropriate number to set a midpoint at which we knew we could prove I was worth $1 dollar more than. I spent a large percentage of the off-season at Gary's office in Pacific Palisades with him and Sasson, completely immersing myself in the process. I absolutely loved it. We eventually filed at $2.5 million. The A's filed at $2 million setting the mid-point at $2.25 million. We knew that I did not quite have the numbers to prove that I deserved even the $2.4 million that Tori Hunter got, but we did not have to. We just needed to prove that I was worth more than the mid-point of $2.25 million.

I am a gambling man by nature, so I did what any good gambler would do. I calculated my odds. The largest offer I had from the A's was $2.1 million. Even if I lost the arbitration hearing, so long as I was not released by the A's before the start of the season, I was going to make $2 million dollars. So basically, I stood to lose $100,000 if I went to arbitration and lost. If I went to arbitration and won, I would make $400,000. The next question was what were my odds of winning the case? Over the previous several years, teams had easily won the majority of the hearings. Obviously, each case is individual of one another, so although that was not a promising trend, it did not serve as a major deterrent. The key question was whether or not my true value was greater than $2.25 million? The answer that Gary, Mike, and myself all came up with was NO.

Yet, we all agreed that $2.25 million was the actual number that we felt was right. Still with that said, we all felt like I had at least a 50 percent shot of winning the case. So, you are telling me I am getting 4 to 1 odds on a coin flip bet. Who the f*ck is going to turn that down? Not me!

Within just a few days of exchanging numbers, the A's raised their offer to $2.25 million. I felt the risk was still worth the potential award, but on the principal of that being the number that we actually felt like I deserved, I signed the deal and avoided going to an arbitration hearing.

Human Crash Test Dummy Life Lesson #67

Know your value. Honestly assess the situation that you are in and have an idea of your exact worth at the moment and your potential worth going forward. That gives you a baseline for the sort of compensation you should agree upon with your employer or partner. Your goal should not be to take advantage of the system. Outside of that being unethical, it will cause resentment among everybody else involved. Know your role; know your value.

Chapter 68
Go Beyond The Numbers

"Computers, like automobiles and airplanes, do only what people tell them to do."
-Bill James

Now that I was no longer playing for near the league minimum, I became immediately expendable to the A's. Every day there seemed to be a new rumor as to where I was going to be traded. New York, Pittsburg, Colorado, Baltimore, and several other cities were mentioned. It got to the point that when I returned from the Dominican after another season of winter ball and another Licey championship, it seemed more likely that I would be going to Spring Training with a team other than the A's. It was actually very uncomfortable not knowing or having any control of where I was going to be playing. I normally would arrive to Spring Training at least 1 or even 2 weeks before the official report date. There seemed to be no immediate reason to head to Arizona based on everything I was hearing. Of course, hardly anything ever happens when you hear about it, so when spring training started, I was still a member of the Oakland A's.

As the '05 season got going, I did not have a starting job again despite hitting .283 with 20 home runs and 17 stolen bases in '04. It was almost comical at this point but obviously something I was used to. I started the first part of the season off slowly and rarely playing. I then scraped together a nice little run that got me back to respectability, and I was no doubt pushing the envelope for more starts against right-handed pitching. It's not that match ups were new to baseball, but Billy Beane was an extremist. So much so that I actually saw Olmaedo Saenz, a right-handed hitter, hit a rocket double in his first at-bat, and then a mammoth home run in his second, both against the left-handed starter. By the time Olmaedo's third at-bat came around, the starter had been knocked out of the game and replaced with a right-handed pitcher. Saenz got pinch hit for!

I am all about the numbers, and I totally get how and why if you are a general manager or manager you would want to play percentages, but sabermetric geeks need to remember that the game is not played by robots. I guarantee you that there was not another guy on our team that had a better chance at the plate than Olmeado Saenz did at that moment. There is no way to put a number on an internal feeling of confidence that comes to a player after the 2 at bats that Olmeado had just put together

---

Human Crash Test Dummy Life Lesson #68

Know the overall numbers but know the niche numbers as well. Most importantly, know the player. Understand what sort of situation each individual player will thrive in and what sort of situation that player may struggle with. Understand the intricacies of each situation that may contribute to the success or failure of the individual. All of this will help us understand the broad numbers on a much more intimate level.

Chapter 69
Position, Opponent, Boundaries

*"Without debate, without criticism,
no administration and no country can succeed."*
-John F. Kennedy

After a miserable April, I finally got my ass going and felt like I had some nice momentum heading into a series at Fenway Park. I got the start on the final game of the series against right-hander Matt Clement. I took good at-bats all day against the tough righty with a filthy slider. Down by 1 with 2 outs in the 9th, I came up for my final at-bat with a runner on first against All-Star closer Keith Foulke. After a long battle, I finally caught one and smoked it over the green monster to give us the lead. Given the entire scope: my current playing time situation, my history with the Red Sox, and my history with Jason Varitek, it was one of the most rewarding hits of my career. Right up until Jason "F*CKING" Varitek came up in the bottom of the 9th and hit a 2-run homer to win the game. No f*cking joke, you can't make this sh*t up! Forgive me if I don't buy him a drink if I ever see his ass at a bar.

The next game we were back in Oakland facing the Yankees and Kevin Brown. I got the start again against another tough right-hander. We got smoked but I finished the game 2-4 with the only 2 runs batted in. Just when I figured I had bought myself another start against another right-handed pitcher the next day, kaboom! We called up a kid by the name of Matt Watson, took me out of the lineup, and put him in my place. Matt was a left-handed hitting outfielder, a solid player, and a great guy, but after finally getting into a groove over the past several games, I was f*cking steamed. I walked right into Ken Macha's office, and just as I began my tirade about not being in the lineup, he pointed to the phone and said call Billy. I picked up that f*cking phone and called Billy.

His secretary answered, "Billy Beane's office how can I help you?"

"Hi, Mam, this is Eric Byrnes, is Billy around?"

"No, Eric, he just stepped out, would you like to leave a message?"

"Yes, can you please tell him to come down to the clubhouse when he gets a chance and explain to me why the F*CK I am not playing left field today? Thanks!"

20 minutes later Billy shows up, "You wanted to see me?"

"Yup, I have kept my mouth shut this entire year about playing time mainly because I did not have a leg to stand on. I have always lived by the motto 'put up or shut up.' Early in the season I did not put up for sh*t so I kept my mouth shut. The past couple weeks, and specifically the past few days, all I have done is put up when given the opportunity, so I am ready to run my f*cking mouth now. Why am I not playing Billy?".

"You are not playing because we are facing Mike Mussina and you have a sh*tty OPS against right-handed pitching, so we called up Matt Watson to hopefully get more production."

"My OP (f*cking) S wasn't so sh*tty against Matt Clement or Keith Foulke the other day, or it wasn't so sh*tty against Kevin Brown last night. Was it?"

"Do you want to play every day?"

"F*ck yes I want to play every day."

"Okay, I will send you to AAA and you can play every day there."

"Perfect, thank you!"

"You really want to go to AAA?"

"So long as I get to play every day, yes."

"That's stupid."

"No, you paying me over 2 million dollars to play in AAA would be stupid."

We both cracked up at this point. For the several blowouts that I had with Billy over the years, I have to say I enjoyed each and every one of them. I also don't think there is any doubt that Billy enjoyed the confrontations every bit as much as I did, if not more.

Have a leg to stand on if you are going to be defending a position. Have factual results that are quantifiable. The first encounter I had with Billy I was coming off a good year in AAA, a Dominican Winter League MVP and a great last week of spring training. This time, I had the recent huge games that should have been fresh in Billy's memory.

Human Crash Test Dummy Life Lesson #69

It is important NOT to burn bridges and NOT to make it personal. It's okay to attack somebody's position, but it is not okay to personally attack that person. It can be an incredibly fine line between the two. It is also important to know who you are talking to and what tone is acceptable. I believe the key to any debate can be summed up by knowing 3 main things:

1) Know your position.
2) Know your opponent.
3) Know your boundaries.

Chapter 70
Action Speaks

"You may never know what results come from your action. But if you do nothing there will be no result."
-Gandhi

I got the start the next day against Randy Johnson, of course, a left-handed pitcher. In Oakland in the 2005 season, we were dealing with fans running onto the field on almost a daily basis. It had gotten to the point where it was becoming extremely disruptive and quite frankly, dangerous. Sometime in right about the middle of the game, two guys came running onto the field. One had a diaper on, no shirt, and a pacifier in his mouth. The other a black shirt, yellow shorts, and some dress shoes. At first I stood at my position in right field, watching the two dudes do figure 8's in center field around Mark Kotsay as security tried to haul them in. As the minutes passed, security finally hauled in "Diaper Boy," but the other dude was still on the loose.

Suddenly, he was headed in a dead sprint straight towards me. I kept waiting for him to veer off but he stayed right on course. I did not move and he kept coming. When he was finally about 10 feet from me, I decided that there was no way that I was going to give this guy a huge, running head start and the go-ahead to barrel into me. So, I chose to go right back at him.

As soon as I made the move towards him, we were like two trains on the same track destined for a head-on collision. At the very last moment, he made a hard left and headed towards the outfield wall. Instinctually, I continued to go after him as he proceeded to climb the wall. He had actually made it to the top of the 8-foot-high right field wall and was hoisting his body over the top of the wall when I jumped up and snatched him by his waist and ripped him off of the wall, slamming him back onto the dirt warning track. Immediately, Coliseum Security was there along with the Oakland Police

Department to cuff and stuff him. The large crowd on hand that day went absolutely nuts! I had no premeditated intentions of interacting with a crazy-ass fan that ran onto the field. But as soon as this f*cker came heading towards me, I felt threatened and was by no means going to give him any sort of free shot. I was sick and tired of the bullsh*t idiots disrupting our games for their 2 minutes of fame, and quite frankly, right or wrong, I had no problem sending the message that if you step onto our workplace, there will be consequences. I also felt in this situation that fans or other players could have been in danger.

Immediately when we came back into the dugout, Ken Macha was pissed. He didn't say anything, but he was shaking his head and giving me a death stare. I paid little attention to Macha, grabbed a bat, and headed to the plate where Roy Steele, the famous PA announcer of the Oakland A's, announced me as, "Now batting, linebacker, #22, Eric Byrnes."

I ended up getting a base hit to left field off the future Hall of Famer. My next at-bat, Randy Johnson was out of the game and a right-handed reliever was in. Despite still being early in the game and with 2 solid at-bats, I got pinch hit for in favor of a left-handed batter. After the game, when the media asked Ken Macha about my apprehension of the fan in right field, he said that I should have let security do their job and he planned on talking to me about it. When the media relayed the message to me, still steaming from getting pinch hit for, I fired back with, "I don't really care what my manager thinks, I am going to do what I need to do to protect myself on and off of the baseball field. If he wants to talk to me he knows where my locker is."

Obviously the "I don't really care what my manager thinks" card is the one in which the media ran with, and when Macha read the quote, he was f*cking irate and rightfully so. I have said some stupid sh*t in my day, but this was flat-out dumb and disrespectful.

Regardless if I was upset or not about getting pinch hit for or my playing time situation, I disrespected Ken Macha as a man. When my own dad saw it, he was pissed. He was actually the first one to call me and demanded that I immediately go sit out in front of Macha's office until he got to the stadium so I could apologize and explain that I got caught up in the heat of the moment. I got to the stadium early and headed for Macha's office, where before I could even get a word out, he absolutely laid into me and he had every right to do so. I picked my battles through the course of the years and this was not going to be one of them. I was wrong and I knew it.

I sat there like a puppy dog with his tail between his legs and his paw out begging for forgiveness. Truth was that I had all the respect in the world for Ken Macha, but the competitive fire that burned so deep inside of me caused me to snap. It was a compilation of many things. I was pissed about going up and down 9 f*cking times; I was pissed about my overall playing time situation since I first got to the big leagues; I was pissed about not starting the day before; I was pissed about getting pinch hit for, and I was f*cking pissed that he tells the media he is going to have a talk with me when I was there all game and he didn't say sh*t to me. Nonetheless, Macha had only a small part in everything I just mentioned, and I unfairly took out my frustrations on him. I was 100% in the wrong and I knew it.

I approached Susan Slusser, the Chronicle beat writer for the A's, and wanted to make sure that it was made clear that I obviously cared what my manager thought and that my comments were solely regarding what happened on the field with the fan.

Look, this is exactly why you don't say dumb sh*t. Once it's out there, it is out there and regardless of how hard I tried to clean it up, it was still a huge f*cking mess. It was now my job to try to earn back the respect of my manager.

Human Crash Test Dummy Life Lesson #70

Two simple lessons to learn from this entire scenario:

1) Choose your words wisely.
2) If you feel threatened or you feel somebody else may be in danger, do something about it. Action always speaks loudest.

Chapter 71
Rocky Mountain High

"Perhaps love is like a resting place, a shelter from the storm, it exists to give you comfort, it is there to keep you warm, and in those times of trouble, when you are most alone, the memory of love will bring you home."
-John Denver

By the time the All-Star break came around, I felt like my relationship with Ken Macha was the best it had ever been in 5 years. He is a very intelligent and witty man who I actually found hilarious once the barriers between the two of us were broken down. I had also finally settled into a role. I wasn't exactly the "everyday" player that I argued to Billy that I should be, yet I was much more than the platoon player that he had pegged me as. It wasn't exactly a compromise or any sort of concession from Billy or myself but probably just the reality of who I was as a player and who we were as a team at the time.

In years past, my All-Star break pretty much consisted of trips to either Lake Tahoe or Las Vegas. In 2005, I decided I was not going to go anywhere. I spent the entire weekend with family and friends at home and decided to head to the Coliseum the day before our mandatory workout to review video of the first half of the season. I probably spent more time than anyone in the video room hanging with video coordinator Adam "Puddin" Rohden. So much so, I actually had my name etched above the back-corner seat I would always sit in. For the most part, my time spent there had little to do with video and more to do with escaping the locker room, which generally is cluttered with media and is the furthest thing from any sort of sanctuary for players. I also had my own individual way to view video.

Early in my career I obsessed over how and why I would make outs. I oftentimes spent way too much time figuring out what I was doing wrong, as opposed to figuring out what I was doing right in the at-bats where I would have success. Essentially, I grew tired of watching the same bullsh*t and decided to ignore it. Many people say that the act of hitting a baseball is the single hardest thing to do in all of sports. Hall-of-Famers fail nearly 7 out of 10 times. So, I deemed it pointless to focus on something that no matter what I did or changed was still going to happen. Instead, I would watch what my man "Puddin" would refer to as my "dig me" tape.

The "dig me" tape was basically all hard-hit balls and any base hits. I figured the more positive reinforcements I could implant in my mind, the much better off I would be, both physically and psychologically, while playing a game based around failure. My other focus when it came to video was on the opposing pitchers. I would find right-handed batters similar to myself and see how the pitcher would attack that particular batter. I would also spend time on an opposing team's bullpen, particularly left-handed relievers that I knew I would have a good chance to potentially face late in the game if I was not in the starting lineup.

As I was sitting in my usual spot, David Forst, the assistant GM, popped his head into the room. "Hey, Eric, can I speak to you for a minute?" I immediately knew something was up when he called me by my first name. I began to get that big nervous pit in my stomach as I made my way to Ken Macha's office where I had been summoned.

"We traded you to Colorado. Billy wanted to be here to tell you but he couldn't make it."

Wow, 7 years in an organization and that was it. I felt like the husband that always thought the relationship was going great. Sure, we had some bumps in the road like every other couple, but I did not expect to come home and find all of my sh*t waiting for me on the front porch while my wife was inside already banging her new boyfriend. I did not have a chance to say goodbye to my teammates because it was the All-Star break, but I am Irish and we suck at goodbyes anyway. It was hard to describe my original emotions because it was a cluster of everything: angry about being thrown to the curb by the A's, excited about the Rockies wanting me, sad about leaving home yet happy about a new opportunity in a new city.

Logistics also quickly began to set in; I needed to get to Cincinnati the next day in order to start the 2nd half of the season with the team. Who do I need to contact about the flight? How will I get all of my gear there? How do I get my car to Denver? Do I need a car in Denver? Where am I going to stay in Denver? Who do I need to call to tell them that I got traded before they find out in the news and get their feelings hurt that I did not tell them first? How is Mom going to take it? Do I know anybody on the team? Who is the manager? Who are the coaches? What place are they in? What position am I going to play?

Just a few of the questions rolling through my mind at the time. Needless to say, I did not necessarily have time for a huge emotional reflection about my time in Oakland. I called my mom, dad, sister, girlfriend, and T, my off-season trainer and one of my very best friends. I had plans to meet some buddies for dinner over at the "Dutch Goose" and then head to the BBC in Menlo Park for a few cocktails. I no doubt was going to cancel. All of a sudden, I became so overwhelmed by the events of the past few hours; I figured bullsh*tting with my boys at the "Goose" with a few cold beverages was exactly what I needed. The "Goose" it was.

Some burgers, beers and bullsh*t with my boys definitely calmed my nerves a bit about the upcoming journey I was about to embark on. Later in the night I got a call from Billy Beane, thanking me for all I gave to the organization. I thanked him for giving me an opportunity to live out my dream of playing Major League Baseball. I hung up the phone and I finally lost it. I cried the same way I had when I left home for UCLA for the first time. The Oakland A's organization had become my family, and the thought of not having them in my life hurt.

Overall, I could not have asked for a better organization to start my Major League career with than the Oakland A's. Although sustained success has become more difficult as other teams have caught on to the A's philosophy, they still continue to thrive as one of baseball's best-run organizations from top to bottom.

Human Crash Test Dummy Life Lesson #71

Change in life is inevitable and change often hurts for a period of time. Oftentimes we have no idea when change is going to come, but so long as we are prepared and accepting of an uncertain future, we will eventually be able to charge forward. Home is always where the heart is.

Chapter 72
Trading Places

"A lot of people in our industry haven't had very diverse experiences. So they don't have enough dots to connect, and they end up with very linear solutions without a broad perspective on the problem. The broader one's understanding of the human experience, the better design we will have."
-Steve Jobs

When I arrived in Cincinnati to meet my new Colorado Rockies team, I was extremely excited by the prospects and direction of where the Rockies were heading. They had a superstar who was their quiet leader in Todd Helton, some young stud position players including Matt Holiday and Garret Atkins, a couple of very good starting pitchers in Aaron Cook and Jeff Francis, and a lock down closer in the bullpen by the name of Brian Fuentes. The team was in last place in the NL West at the time of my arrival, yet there seemed to be this overwhelming sense of optimism amongst the team and the entire organization. One of the main reasons why was their manager, Clint Hurdle.

From the first time I met Clint in his office in Cincinnati, I knew I was going to love playing for him. He was energetic, perpetually positive, and loud. My kind of guy! We started out with a 10-game road trip with 3 in Cincinnati, 3 in Washington, and 4 in Pittsburg. By the time we got back to Colorado, I was finally starting to get settled with the team. I had never played at Coors Field and was absolutely taken aback by how beautiful of a stadium it was. I met general manager Dan O'Dowd, who seemed like a very nice man and genuinely happy to have me in Colorado. He just about assured me that I was going to be a Rocky for a long time unless, for whatever reason, somebody gave them an offer they could not refuse.

I got off to a slow start with the team, but I also felt like Clint Hurdle or anyone else in the organization had in no way given up on me. After spending almost 3 weeks in a hotel room, I began to look for condos by the ballpark. I really liked Denver. After the 15th game I played with the Rockies, only 5 at Coors field, I was sitting at a Mexican restaurant in the SODO neighborhood of Denver when I noticed a 707 number pop up on my cell phone. The place was loud so I did not answer. The number immediately called again; this time they left a message. I went outside to check my voice mail.

It was Dan O'Dowd telling me I had been traded to the Baltimore Orioles.

However crazy my year had gone so far, it just got more nuts. The deal was actually supposed to be a 3-way deal that would send Larry Bigbie from Baltimore to Boston and catcher Kelly Shoppach from Boston to Colorado. The agreed-upon deal was dependent on Boston's ownership approval, which was not supposed to be a problem. It was a problem and the trade of Bigbie to Boston never happened, leaving the Rockies irate. Nonetheless, I was a Baltimore Oriole.

The first day I arrived at Camden Yards, the Orioles were still very much in the hunt for an AL East championship. They were 4 games back and baseball fever had finally hit a baseball town thirsting for something to cheer about after several years of futility. I walked into Lee Mazzilli's (the manager of the Orioles) office when I arrived after taking a red eye from Denver to Baltimore. Lee was sitting there with a stack of pancakes and eggs in front of him and a cigarette in his mouth. In his awesome New York accent, he said, "Grab a seat, kid. I have three rules, be on time, play hard, and steal every f*cking time you get on base. I've wanted to get you here for a long time. You are my everyday left fielder, have some fun!"

What more could I ask for?

As I sprinted toward left field in the top of the first inning, I got a standing ovation from all of the fans down the left field line and in the bleachers. There was a chill that went through my body that I definitely had rarely ever experienced. Welcome to East Coast baseball! No disrespect to the fans out west, but there is just simply more years of history and tradition, specifically in the northeast, which translates to more emotional fan bases that oftentimes live and die with their teams.

I had not slept in about 36 hours and I felt as if I was flying. I came up to bat with a runner on 3rd base and a chance to properly introduce myself to the city of Baltimore. I smoked a double down the line, giving us the early lead and again received another standing ovation, this time from the entire packed house at Camden Yards. I stood on 2nd base and I could barely feel my legs. All of a sudden, I snapped out of la-la land and remembered the 3rd rule given to me by Lee Mazzilli: "Steal every f*cking time you get on base."

I was going to go on the first pitch but never got the opportunity. White Sox pitcher Freddy Garcia must have got wind of my meeting with Lee and picked my happy ass off 2nd base before he ever threw a pitch! Much different than my start in Colorado, I hit in my first 11 games as an Oriole but the team was struggling. Nonetheless, it was incredibly comforting to play for a manager who I knew was going to give me every opportunity to succeed.

After the first couple weeks in Baltimore, everything seemed to be going great. I was even approached by Jim Beattie, one of Baltimore's dual GM's at the time, telling me that he looked forward to me being a Baltimore Oriole not only for the 2005 season but for many years to come. After years of trying to establish myself with the A's, and then getting traded to Colorado only to have them trade me 15 games later, that was music to my ears. I began looking for places in Baltimore and found a kick-ass penthouse unit in a brand-new building on the inner harbor. I figured since I was probably one of the only big-leaguers that ever lived at home with his mom during the regular season, it was okay for me to splurge a bit. I also was beginning to fall in love with the city and for good reason was optimistically thinking I would be a Baltimore Oriole for at least another year. I signed a 12-month lease on a 3-bedroom place that would allow my family and friends to stay with me when they would come to visit, making a trip from California to Baltimore much more enticing.

Right about the same time I inked my name on the dotted line, Lee Mazzilli (the main reason why I ended up in Baltimore) got fired. For me individually, it was all downhill from there. Soon after, we went to Oakland in the middle of August for my first return home. I wanted to beat the f*ck out of those dudes so badly I ended up puking all over myself, 0 for 13 in the series, or "0 for Oakland" as I like to refer to it. I spent the entire month of September platooning, starting mainly against left-handed pitchers. My final line in Baltimore was not pretty: .192 with 3HR and 11RBI.

During the last series of the season, Sam Perlozzo, who took over for Lee as manager, went around and talked to all the players, telling them what he expected out of them heading into the off-season and into Spring Training the following year. I pretty much knew that my fate was sealed as an Oriole when Sam told me he would give me "a shot" to make the team out of Spring Training. Trust me, the way I had hit in the second half of the season, "a shot" to make the team was all I deserved. The problem was that there is no way they were going to tender me a contract and commit to paying me at least $2.5 million unless they looked at me as a sure thing to make the team and be a major contributor. I knew I was gone. There was no communication between my agent and the Orioles all the way up until the night before the tender date, when we found out I would not be tendered a contract. I was released and became a free agent.

After spending the first 7 years of my career with the Oakland A's organization, I got traded twice and released within a 3-month period. Welcome to the reality of a professional baseball player's world.

I recently ran into Lee Mazili in Spring Training when he was working for the Yankees as a special instructor. Lee's first words to me: "Yo Byrnesie, I haven't seen you since you got me fired from Baltimore!" We both had a good laugh.

Human Crash Test Dummy Life Lesson #72

Life can turn on a dime; as soon as you think you are settled, it can change again. The most important thing is to maintain perspective on whatever situation you are presented. Change can be intimidating and overwhelming if you let it be. Yet, if you properly perceive change as an invaluable experience, it can be the lifeblood of forward movement and success. Let your life experiences help broaden your perspective and open your mind to what possibilities the future may present.

Chapter 73
Bet on You

"You have to let fear go. Another lesson is you just have to believe in yourself; you just have to. There's no way around it. No matter how things are stacked against you, you just have to every time."
-Venus Williams

Toward the end of the '05 season, I was approached by ESPN about coming to Bristol to work for ESPN Radio's late night show during the World Series. After a year that was beyond sub-par, I knew that this was an opportunity I could not pass up. From my very first day in professional baseball, I never knew exactly how long I was going to get an opportunity to play. I was not a top pick and essentially everything that ever came to me in the game of baseball I had to earn. There was a very real possibility that I would be out of a job the following year.

I arrived in Bristol not exactly knowing what to expect. I had always heard that ESPN was in the middle of nowhere, and it was like Planes, Trains, and Automobiles to get there, but when I finally did, I was pleasantly surprised. Connecticut is absolutely gorgeous and the ESPN "campus" was something that sports fans, including myself, literally drool over. What my actual role would be on the radio show was a mystery but I was fired up to be there.

For a week straight, I joined Freddie Coleman, John Seibel and Doug Gotlieb breaking down not only the World Series but other sports as well. The epic experience though was not just going on national radio but rather going on national radio for 5 straight hours! 5 non-stop hours of sports talk radio each night would probably seem like a little much to most people, but I loved every single minute of it. Breaking down the action on the field and then getting into fun-yet-intensely-heated discussions with Freddy, Seibel, or Gotlieb made the experience. All three of the guys, who are some of the best in the business, treated me as if I was a co-host and figured out I enjoyed confrontation early on in the week, making the 5 hours a night more enjoyable for everybody. I walked away from the week knowing exactly what I wanted to do when I was done playing baseball.

After I was released by the Orioles, I headed out to Baltimore with Sasson, who had against my advice broken off from Wichard to start his own agency. Because of my loyalty to Sasson, I stuck with him. The reality of the situation was that here I was as a 30-year-old journeyman outfielder without a job with a 32-year-old rookie agent. The prospects of finding a team looked relatively bleak. We packed up the condo I had rented and tried to figure out what the f*ck I was going to do next. As poorly as I hit down the stretch, we tried to figure out why a team would want me. I'll never forget when Sasson was delving into the numbers on his computer, then turned to me and said, "You kind of suck, bro."

He was right; I did suck, but that was for a half of a season over the course of playing for 2 different teams in 2 different leagues in barely 200 at bats. My response was, "F*ck off, get me a job or you are fired." Harsh words from both sides, but what you have to understand is the relationship between Sasson and myself went all the way back to UCLA. Sh*t-talking was and still is just part of how we communicated and probably one of the main reasons I stuck with him. Mike Sasson was never going to bullsh*t me, and I was not going bullsh*t him. There always is a bit of truth in everything the two of us say, but what I love about Sasson is that, ultimately, he is an eternal optimist. He has an incredible ability to address the reality of the situation and then figure out how to work to fix it. We had already addressed the reality. Now it was time to get to work.

Interestingly enough, the first phone call that we received after I was a free agent was from Dan O'Dowd. The Rockies wanted to bring me back and actually were going to pay me a million bucks guaranteed as well. I essentially told Sasson to jump on it before they changed their minds. We gave it a day to see if any other team would be interested, and we actually had some bites.

The next day Pittsburg and Cleveland both called and wanted to sign me as their 4th outfielder. The price Pittsburg offered was $2.25 million, the exact number that I had made the year before. It's not that I was dealing with any major confidence issues, but I didn't even feel like I was worth that number. Pittsburgh's belief in me despite my bad 2nd half of 2005 all of a sudden made me realize that I was a bad mother-f*cker before being traded from Oakland, and I will be an even badder mother f*cker after.

I then talked to the Indians and had an awesome conversation with Mark Shapiro, the longtime GM of the Tribe. Mark is one of the most respected men in all of baseball, and it was very easy to see why. Monetarily, Mark said he would match any offer that we got and then put $2.5 million on the table and said he needed an answer in 24 hours. This was getting ridiculous. Going into the process, I was wondering if I was going to be able to get an invitation to big league Spring Training and now I was looking at a raise. I was very excited about the opportunity in Cleveland, which believe it or not was always one of my favorite cities to play in. Besides the fact that "Major League" was one of my favorite movies of all time, my big-league debut at Jacobs Field endeared me to the city that always gave me a warm feeling. Yes, I am talking about Cleveland, Ohio, and no, I am not joking. Speaking with Mark, I loved everything the organization seemed to be about and him reaching out personally had a huge effect.

The 24-hour countdown was ON! I got together with my dad, Sasson, and my Uncle Terry, an absolute business shark in every sense of the word, and took the discussion to the golf course. We all agreed that the most important thing was me getting an opportunity to play and reestablish myself as an everyday starter at the big-league level. My dad and Uncle Terry both broke it down very simply. If Cleveland is willing to make the biggest financial investment, more likely than not, they would be the ones who would make the biggest investment in my playing time. Then I realized that I was playing out of a rental golf bag with an inscription across the entire bag that must have been sending me a message:

CLEVELAND.

On the 9th hole, I told Sasson to call Mark Shapiro after we got off the course and work out the details of the contract. I was going to be a Cleveland Indian.

Then something happened. On hole #16 I got a call from a 602 number. I did not answer but immediately checked the message. It was AJ Hinch, my recruiting host at Stanford and former teammate with the Sacramento Rivercats and Oakland A's. He was now the director of Minor League Operations with the Arizona Diamondbacks and wanted to talk. I almost did not even want to call him back for fear of them making an offer that might jade my thinking. Just out of curiosity though, I called and my fear became my reality. The Diamondbacks offered $1.75 million, but also something much more valuable, the starting centerfield job!

Ok, lets break this down: $2.5 million to play in Cleveland as a 4th outfielder or $1.75 million to play in Arizona as the starting centerfielder. I was at an interesting point in my career, 30 years old coming off the worst half season I could imagine, but I did have a good first half of 2005. The previous season I had hit .283 with 20 home runs and 17 stolen bases with an .814 OPS. If I was able to put up a solid year, I would be headed into my final year of arbitration followed by free agency. If I signed for $2.5 million with the Cleveland Indians and got 300 plate appearances that a 4th outfielder usually ends up with and hit .260 with 10 HR, I would be looking at a moderate raise for 2007: a salary probably in the $3 million range. Yet if I signed with Arizona, started in center field, and ended up with 600 plate appearances, more likely than not, my salary the following year would be in the range of well over 4 million dollars. So, the question then became: do I take a risk by leaving $750,000 on the table and bet on my ability to secure the starting job, and then play well enough to command a salary that would make up the difference of the $750,000 that I was walking away from?

At the last minute, we were able to get Arizona to come up to $2.2 million, so instead of leaving $750,000 out there, the final number was $300,000. Regardless, I was going to sign where I felt my opportunity for playing time was much better, and there was no doubt that was in Arizona.

Bottom line is: I was going to bet on myself. I was going to bet on my physical ability and my work ethic. I was going to bet on the strength of my will power and my ability to endure and overcome adversity. I was going to bet on me being the badass mother*cker I knew I had the potential to be.

Another attractive quality was that since 2000, I had owned a condo in old town Scottsdale just a few miles away from Chase Field in Phoenix. The Diamondbacks were also managed by Bob Melvin, a Bay Area guy I was very familiar with. Bob managed the Seattle Mariners who we played 19 times a year when I was with the A's. I also always had awesome conversations with "Bo-Mel" when we would play the M's; he no doubt seemed like a great dude, and I knew he would be fun guy to play for.

My dad made sure I personally called Mark Shapiro to thank him for the offer but tell him the Diamondbacks came in at the last minute and made me an offer I could not refuse. That was as difficult of a phone call that I have ever had to make. Mark and the Cleveland Indians took a chance and offered me a contract coming off a terrible half of a season. More importantly though, they did so because of their belief in my intangibles. When I talked to Mark he never even brought up numbers. Instead he talked about how much he appreciated the way I played the game and how he wished more of his guys put forth the same sort of effort.

Human Crash Test Dummy Life Lesson #73

Be grateful for opportunities in your life, especially when you do not see them coming. Analyze the opportunities, make sure to lean on your trusted resources, and take a broad view of the entire situation. Ultimately, so long as you believe in your ability, bet on yourself and don't be afraid to go ALL IN.

Chapter 74
Reality Check

*"The mentor-protégé relationship is
the most efficient and productive form of learning."*
-Robert Greene

As soon as I signed with the Diamondbacks, I got a call from Karl Kuehl, the co-author of *The Mental Game of Baseball* and legendary instructional league speech giver. He wanted to meet with me. Throughout my years in Oakland, Karl and I had developed a very good relationship. I had leaned on him over the course of my career at different times, always knowing I was going to get an honest assessment. This call I received was a little different than the occasional, "Hey, let's catch up." The message he left on my phone went something like this: "Eric, Karl Kuehl here. Give me a call, we need to speak." Straight to the point, no pleasantries, no bull sh*t. Very Karl!

We ended up meeting at CoCo's in Scottsdale for lunch a couple days later. "Eric, I root for your because you are good for the game of baseball. I hope you play this game for many more years to come because you are setting an example for future generations. But let me tell you something, you are not going to be around much longer if you keep up that horsesh*t I saw in the 2nd half of the season last year. What happened?"

I then proceeded to explain the two trades, Lee Mazzilli getting fired, and the once again overall lack of consistent playing time being an issue. Essentially, I began laying out every self-defense mechanism that I had to which Karl responded, "Are you done? You keep telling me about all of these outside things that you had no control over instead of telling me about the ones that you did. The only thing you can control is what happens between the lines and in the batter's box. What happened there?"

"I sucked."

"Why?"

"Because I kept focusing on the things that I had no control over."

"Exactly." At that point he had the waitress get me a pen and a cocktail napkin. We then went over all the things that were in my control and wrote them on one side of the napkin: work ethic, preparation, mechanics, thoughts, attitude, focus, approach, confidence, process. He then had me write on the other side of the napkin all of the things that are not in my control: weather, playing time, results, umpires, pitchers, pitches, fielder's positioning, great defensive plays.

Karl then proceeded to tell me that the reason why he believed I had been so hot and cold throughout my career is because I worried way too much about the things that were outside of my control. My biggest problem that made consistency very difficult for me was that I was a very emotional player. When things went well I would ride the wave, but when things were not going well, I would crash and crash hard. Karl by no means wanted me to change who I was, but he wanted me to channel my emotions instead of holding on to them and letting my frustrations compound and affect future performance. Oftentimes, I would swing and miss at a pitch, and I would let that swing and miss not only effect the rest of my at-bat, but the rest of my at-bats throughout the game and sometimes even beyond.

So Karl came up with the idea to pick a spot in the stadium that I could look at which would essentially act as my "release" of whatever had previously happened that I was upset about. It could be a bad swing; it could be a pitch that I took that I thought I should have swung at; it could be a bad call, or it could be that I just wasn't feeling good or seeing the ball well. It was my way to hit the reset button. I decided my release was going to be the top of the right field foul pole. I figured it would be easy to find, nothing really around it to distract me, and there was going to be one in every ballpark I played in. Karl and I made a commitment to one another to check in once a week throughout the course of the season regardless if things were going well or not.

I showed up in Spring Training 2006 as the starting center fielder in between two of the great players of my generation: Luis Gonzalez in left field and Shawn Green in right. I played well through the course of the spring, but another free agent sign, Jeff DaVanon, played even better. DaVanon had over a .500 OBP during cactus league play and then continued his hot run into the regular season. Bob Melvin called me into the office during an early season series in San Diego and essentially said, "You are my guy but what am I supposed to do?" My response: "Play DaVanon. He deserves it."

Thankfully for me, Bob would always make sure I played at least 1 game a series to stay fresh. He also would use me to pinch hit or double switch every chance that he had. When I was at UCLA, I actually had several opportunities to hang out with Shawn Greene during his offseason when he would come to visit one of his good friends, Mike Seal, who happened to be my roommate. Shawn always had an awesome opposite-field approach that allowed him to bomb away to all parts of the ballpark. I would pick his brain a bit when he would come to Westwood, but I always feared bothering him so I would never press the issue. Now that he was my teammate, I used every chance I got to unapologetically grind him. I wanted to learn how he hit opposite-field home runs at will.

Essentially, when Shawn was a youngster, his dad taught him the importance of staying inside the baseball and implemented several drills to make the approach habitual. In Toronto, Shawn and Carlos Delgado used to play "home run contest" on a daily basis, but this was like no other "home run contest" because balls hit out of the ballpark to the pull side did not count. Only home runs to center and to the opposite field would score you points. I loved it. I had no desire to learn how to slap the ball to the opposite field, but rather I wanted to figure out how to consistently drive the ball in that direction. I would watch him do his drills in the cage. I would watch how he approached each and every round of batting practice. I would then implement as much as I could without compromising who I was as a hitter. One of the things I noticed was how early he would get his weight on his back side, and then how much patience he had in letting the ball travel. I finally convinced Shawn and Tony Clark (now the head of the player's association) to play a similar "home run contest" that Shawn played in Toronto with Carlos Delgado. The way we worked the point system was 1 point for a pulled home run, 2 points for a homer to center, and 3 points to the opposite field. I got my ass kicked every single, freaking day. I would hit just as many home runs but the majority of them were still to the pull side. Shawn and Tony would go oppo at will. Soon enough, the direction of my home runs began to change, and I actually started to hit 1 or 2 out to right field per session. It was not that all of a sudden I was dropping one "oppo taco" after another, but the entire direction of my batting practice shifted away from left field. Left-center field to the right field foul pole became my sole focus.

DaVanon finally cooled off toward the end of April, which allowed me to get more regular at-bats. No doubt the results of my batting practices began to pay huge dividends in the game. It was a moment in my career where I was either going to be out of a job the following year, or I was going to grab the f*cking bull by the horns and wrestle it to the ground. I grabbed the horns and held on tight, finishing the season with 26 home runs and 25 stolen bases.

I spoke to Karl Kuehl every week of the 2006 season. When things were going well, we would keep our talks simple and sometimes not even talk about baseball. When things were not going so well, we would figure out a way to fix whatever the issue was. I will forever be indebted to Karl Kuehl. Ironically at the time, Karl was working as a special assistant to the Cleveland Indians, the team that I had planned on signing with until the Diamondbacks appeared out of nowhere at the last minute. He had nothing invested in me, never asked for a single thing, and for all I know, he never even told anyone he was working with me. He did not help me for any sort of reason other than he knew how badly I wanted to succeed and how much I loved the game.

In 2007, my best year as a Major Leaguer, we continued to talk every single week. In 2008, Karl Kuehl became very ill and our chats became limited. We continued to communicate through e-mail on a regular basis. On August 8, 2008, I lost a coach, a mentor, and most importantly a very close friend. Karl Kuehl died of pulmonary fibrosis; he was 70 years old.

Human Crash Test Dummy Life Lesson #74

Put your ego aside and realize you do not have all the answers. Everybody in life needs a mentor. Develop a relationship with somebody in your industry or somebody in life who has a lot more knowledge and experience than you do. Show your commitment to learn, earn their trust, then apply the knowledge attained within the confines of your strengths.

Chapter 75
Don't Force It, Live It

"A leader is one who knows the way, shows the way and goes the way."
-John C. Maxwell

After the 2006 season, I was tendered a contract by the Diamondbacks and went through the arbitration process, settling on a salary of $4.65 million. No telling exactly what would have happened had I taken the $300,000 more and chosen to play for Cleveland as opposed to AZ, but with over a 100% raise from 2006 to 2007, I am going to assume the gamble paid off.

Just a year removed from thinking my career could be coming to an end, I was now an "everyday" player on a good team with a great manager in a city that I absolutely loved.

In 2006, we were in contention for a NL West title until the last week of the season. Coming into spring training in 2007, there was a lot for us to be confident about as a team. The front of the rotation featured CY Young award winner Brandon Webb and future Hall-of-Famer Randy Johnson. Stephan Drew, Mark Reynolds, Justin Upton, Chris Young, Carlos Quentin, and Conor Jackson were all young studs that were considered the best young core group of position players in the game. Then there was Tony Clark. In 2007, Tony was our leader. He was ultimately the grounding force in the clubhouse on a team that needed some direction. Tony's presence also allowed Orlando Hudson and myself to not worry about any sort of over the top leadership role. I would like to think that Orlando and I best lead by example with our play on the field and kept things loose with our sh*t-talking in the clubhouse. We both had pretty good years in each category.

Scott Bordow of the East Valley Tribune depicted the leadership of the Arizona Diamondbacks perfectly:

"A first baseman, a left fielder and a second baseman walk into a bar. The first baseman walks behind the bar and begins to dispense advice. The left fielder turns up the volume on the jukebox, chugs a beer and heads out to the dance floor.

The second baseman starts up a conversation and doesn't stop talking until last call.

The punch line?

There isn't one.

Except for the fact that the Diamondbacks have had the last laugh on their skeptics, and the leadership provided by first baseman Tony Clark, left fielder Eric Byrnes and second baseman Orlando Hudson is a big reason why.

They're the soul, sweat and spirit of the team."

Human Crash Test Dummy Life Lesson #75

You can try to be a leader all you want, but the only way to authentically lead is by doing your job and doing it to the very best of your ability. People follow action, not words. Leaders don't force it; they live it.

Chapter 76
The Secret Truth

"Be grateful for what you have now. … You have to make a start, and then the law of attraction will receive those grateful thoughts and give you more just like them."
-Rhonda Byrne

Before the season, I knew I was coming into the biggest season of my career and was willing and ready to do anything to give me the best opportunity to have success. My mom introduced me to Tricia Garret, a hypnotist who had made positive affirmation tapes for several very successful Silicon Valley businessmen and women. I was beyond intrigued with the process. Knowing how much Kirk Gibson (I x V = R) and Karl Kuehl had helped my career, I realized how valuable the mental side of the game was. I figured I had absolutely nothing to lose. I also received a book called *The Secret* from one of my mom's best friends, Bonnie Black. Bonnie had a son, Erik Hanson, who was a few years older and was a stud baseball player at Gonzaga. He was my mentor and a guy I always looked up to growing up. Unfortunately, Erik had just recently died in an alcohol-related accident. Needless to say, everyone who knew Erik was heartbroken. He was always the person who would walk into the room and the entire mood would change for the better. Bonnie, always the baseball mom, knew how important the upcoming year was going to be for my career and knew how valuable *The Secret* could be in my life.

Ultimately, I combined the lessons learned from the Kirk Gibson I x V = R, Karl Kuehl, and *The Secret*. I then had Tricia put several specific positive affirmations on tape that I could listen to before I went to sleep at night.

Here is the list of my thoughts, commands, and affirmations that made up my hypnosis tape that led me to having the greatest year of my career:

General Affirmations:

- I am controlling my desire and my emotions.
- I am consistent in everything I do.
- There is nothing outside the lines. My only focus is on the task at hand.
- All self-talk comes from logical thinking.
- I am a great observer. I notice everything. I learn from others' failures and successes.
- I have a great perspective on life. Baseball is a fun game that I am very blessed to play.
- I am always learning.
- I am playing relaxed.
- I am establishing a routine that is making me a consistent player.
- I have studied and I am more prepared for the test than anyone on the field.
- I am always controlling my breathing.
- I am always playing with enthusiasm and joy.
- I am aggressive and under control.
- I am functioning with a modest amount of power and effort, and I am letting my skills and hard work do the work for me.
- I am always having fun, enjoying the moment.
- I am the most confident player on the field.
- I am always in my own zone; I am immune to external distractions, media, fans, manager, and coaches. Nobody has the ability to stop my inevitable success.
- My success is created by my God-given natural ability. I am trusting the Holy Spirit and letting it work through me.
- My success is also created by my ability to learn. I am improving each and every day, mentally and physically.
- I am relaxed and confident in all pressure situations.
- I am never afraid to fail. I have no fears. Success is imminent.
- I am healthy and strong. My body feels great each and every day.
- My physical and spiritual body is protected by angels.
- There are no limitations to my success.
- There is a reason and purpose for my success. This is not an accident.

Defensive Affirmations:

- I am always creating depth in the outfield and taking a perfect route to every ball.

- I am slowing the game down.
- I am simply seeing the ball and reading it.
- I am keeping my arms down until it is time to catch the ball.
- My wrists are loose and relaxed.
- My throws are easy and effortless.
- I am always picking up my target and throwing through it.
- The ball feels light and free in my hand.
- When I throw my body, elbow, arm and head are in perfect position.
- I am always getting my hand on top of the ball.
- I have the ability to get to balls nobody else can get to.
- My confidence shows in the way I run, throw, and catch.

Hitting Affirmations:

- I am hitting with my eyes, hips, and hands.
- I am always seeing the ball.
- I see the ball right out of the pitcher's hand.
- I am always standing straight up and balanced with my weight on the inside of my back knee.
- My arms are comfortable and loose.
- I am striding before the pitcher delivers the ball and putting all my energy into my eyes.
- I am creating all my power with my backside turn.
- My swing is free and easy; an effortless whip through the zone.
- I am always hitting against a firm front side.
- I am pulling my head back before contact. My head is always behind the ball.
- My head is behind my right butt cheek.
- I am rotating around my head which is still and never moving.
- 80 percent is all I need. 80 will get me 100.
- Stand tall, see it, turn, rake; hitting is easy.
- In batting practice, I am focusing on my head position, getting the barrel to the ball and controlling my effort level.
- On deck, I am controlling my breathing, controlling my heart rate and getting my timing.
- In the box, I am controlling my emotions, controlling my desire, remembering perspective.
- I am letting it flow, letting it happen.
- Hitting is easy. Hitting is fun.
- I am relaxed. I am confident.
- The pitcher and the ball seem as if they are in slow motion.

- I am constantly in the zone. The zone is natural for me.
- When I step into the box, I trust in all my hard work and preparation.
- I am the most prepared hitter on the field. Nothing surprises me.
- I put my weight slightly on my back foot. My posture is perfect, my arms and my hands are relaxed.
- I slightly lift my front leg and see the ball out of the pitcher's hand.
- Everything is slow and easy.
- I see the ball to my zone, and swing to my zone.
- My swing is effortless, easy and powerful.
- I am staying inside the baseball and driving the ball to all parts of the field.
- I am hitting all pitches in my zone: fastballs, curveballs, sliders, change-ups, and splits. It does not matter. If it is in my zone, I will crush it.
- If the ball is outside of my zone, I will not swing.
- My stride is even, easy and perfect every time. My head is always still. My swing is always effortless.
- I am relaxed, calm and confident...
- I am the F*CKING man.

Human Crash Test Dummy Life Lesson #76

The power of positive affirmations is real. VERY REAL.

Acquiring knowledge is useless unless you regularly reaffirm that knowledge and then put it to use. Our brains are just like our bodies in that we need to continue to train them in order to maintain and grow upon the strength that has been built.

Chapter 77
Break Barriers

"Limits like fear are often just an illusion."
-Michael Jordan

Towards the end of the 2006 season, Fox Sports Arizona (FSN) did a feature on me called, "In My Own Words." Essentially it was an abbreviated story of my life and baseball career. Todd Walsh did the interview, and they had cameras follow me around for a day in an effort to give the viewers an inside look of life off the field for a Major League Baseball player. It was a really well put together piece and I really enjoyed doing it. Before the season, FSN came to me with an idea for a TV show that would continue to give people a look into the life of a Major Leaguer away from the ballpark.

We began filming in the spring of '07 and it quickly became the highest-rated show on FSN Arizona. The show ran for almost 3 years, winning an Emmy award in the process. For me, it was a fun side project that in a lot of ways gave viewers "behind the scenes" access that they never really had before. The show took place right at the start of the social media generation and to no one's surprise proved to provide exactly what fans craved: more instant access and an in-depth look into a player's life. Throughout 3 seasons of the show, highlights included taking Kirk Gibson to get a pedicure, playing the "Dating Game" with Justin Upton, Conor Jackson and Micah Owings at a University of Arizona sorority, putting on a BBQ for Cody Bellinger and the Chandler Little League World Series team, and taking a tour of Half Moon Bay, which featured an in-depth look, by surf pioneer Jeff Clark, into Mavericks, one of the biggest, best, and deadliest big wave surf spots in the world. We would shoot one show a month, and it generally took no more than 4 hours to wrap.

One of my favorite episodes was "Daddy Day Care." We set the show up where I was going to give my wife, Tarah, the day off and send her to the spa while I was going to take care of our 7-month-old daughter,

Chloe, aka "Peanut." The day before, I talked the show out with Tarah, and we decided that the entertainment value of me feeding the baby, changing her diaper, and eventually giving her a swimming/surf lesson in the pool would provide more than enough content to fill the entire half hour. It then dawned on me that if I was to give her a swimming/surf lesson in the pool, I would have to take my shirt off. Baseball players spend hours in the sun and are infamous for their farmer's tans, and my white Irish ass was your picture-perfect example. I explained to Tarah that there was no way I was going to go on television with my shirt off unless I could instantly get a tan overnight, which I thought was virtually impossible. That's when Tarah introduced me to one of the newest, safest, and instantly gratifying trends going on at the time: the spray tan!

I was a bit apprehensive before I went in but immediately felt comfortable talking to the girl working the front desk. Judging by my complexion, she recommended a certain tint that would dial me in with the exact color I was looking for. I eventually stepped into the booth butt-ass naked and pushed a button. I lifted my arms above my head and thoroughly enjoyed the minute or two it took to complete the tanning process. When it was over, I walked in front of the mirror and marveled at what had just taken place. My white ass, literally, now had a nice tint to it. It wasn't over-the-top by any means, but it definitely had a fantastic glow that I needed to not embarrass myself on television the following day. When I walked into the clubhouse, I could not have felt more confident. I had a bronze going on that looked like Sylvester Stallone in Rocky IV. During batting practice, I had several teammates actually ask me if I had been laying out by the pool. "Yeah... Just catching a few rays. I am going to shoot the show tomorrow, and I am going to have to peel off my shirt for the 'pool scene.' Just making sure I have a little color." Meanwhile I am thinking to myself, if only they knew the truth!

I came in from batting practice and took off my uniform pants when I noticed that my white sliding shorts that I wore underneath my pants had turned orange! I quickly took them off and actually threw them away. I then went into the bathroom and checked on the overall color of my skin, which still looked okay. I figured that the sweat from

BP must have caused part of the sprayed-on tan to run. I started to get a little nervous, so I decided to take a shower to somehow try to neutralize the seemingly changing color. I was on the disabled list at the time with a broken hand, so I was not playing, but I needed to be in the dugout watching the game and supporting the team. By the time the game rolled around, I was standing on the top step leaning against the rail, speaking Spanish with Edgar Gonzalez and Augie Ojeda, a tradition I had begun in order to improve my fluency in the language and communicate better with my Latin teammates. As the game went on I began to become increasingly self-conscience when Augie kept giving me a weird look as if he was trying to figure out why I looked different to him. Finally, Augie goes, "Hey, dawg, why is your face orange?" "What are you talking about?" "Tu cada es NARANJA!" Panic then set in. I rushed inside the locker room to find a mirror, and sure as sh*t, I looked like a f*cking carrot!

I immediately called Tarah to tell her what had happened. She could not stop laughing. I realize why she thought it was funny, but I wasn't laughing one bit. I looked like some sort of alien cartoon character, and it was getting worse by the minute. I had Tarah get online and figure out how to get my skin color back to normal. I was no longer interested in having any sort of tan. I just wanted this bullsh*t body makeup OFF.

I watched the rest of the game from the corner of the dugout with my hat pulled down extremely low. As soon as the game was over, I bolted home where I was finally able to strip down and get a real good look at the spray tan remnants. However bad I thought it was, it was actually much worse. There was blotting all over my body. The one solution was to sit in scalding hot salt water and then scrub. Hours later, a layer of skin gone, and plenty of F-bombs dropped, I finally began to get my color back. By the time I went to bed and woke up in the morning, I was back to normal and good to go! Shockingly, the show went on as scheduled, and my epic shirtless pool scene probably lasted about 35 seconds!

Overall, the show was a blast, and it gave baseball fans a cool look into the life of big leaguers away from the field. One thing I obviously learned was to check my ego and vanity at the door. The reason the show had so much success was because it was real. It was the vulnerable positions that we put ourselves in that created the entire fabric of what that show was. I'm very grateful to Fox Sports AZ, my teammates, and the D Backs for allowing the show to take place.

Human Crash Test Dummy Life Lesson #77

Just because it has never been done before doesn't mean it is not possible. Think outside the box, eliminate ego, surround yourself with a supportive team, let your creativity work and break down barriers. Vulnerability is one of the greatest and most endearing traits somebody can possess. Lastly, if you need an overnight tan, go for the spray. You may end up with a story that will last a lifetime.

Chapter 78
Live Your Dash

"It is not the length of life, but the depth of life."
-Ralph Waldo Emerson

The show eventually took on an entirely new meaning when I received a letter from a kid by the name of Vaughn Davis. Vaughn's best friend, Saulo Morris, had just been diagnosed with leukemia and was part of the Make a Wish program. Instead of wishing for anything for himself, he wished to take all the money that would have been spent on him and donate it to Doctors Without Borders to help victims of the war in Sudan in which Saulo had learned about and studied. One of the most selfless things a teenager with a life-threatening illness could possibly do.

Vaughn also stated that Saulo was a big Diamondbacks fan and it would be great if I could send him a signed picture or something. I had the producers of the show reach out to Vaughn and see if he would be interested in us showing up at school and pulling him and Saulo out for the day and taking them to Chase Field for a tour, batting practice, and some lunch. Vaughn, the school, and Saulo's parents loved the idea, so we showed up a couple weeks later and literally barged into his class with the cameras rolling. To see the excitement and pure joy on Saulo's face throughout the course of that entire day made every hour that I had ever put into any one of those shows absolutely worth every last minute. It was one of the most rewarding experiences of my life on or off the baseball field. Saulo and I ended up forging an awesome relationship and even went to the Emmy awards together when the show and the program were nominated for several different awards.

When I met Saulo, he had just finished a round of chemotherapy, had no hair, and looked very frail. The only way you could have recognized him about 6 months later was by his infectious smile that was always there even through the darkest of times. Saulo now had a full head of curly locks and definitely looked like he hadn't missed a meal in a while. The leukemia was in complete remission and Saulo was now planning his attack to change the world. Saulo and I sat in the back of the event room with Tarah, who was pregnant with Chloe at the time, Saulo's dad, John, one of the head guys at FSNAZ, Mike Roth, and the producer of the show, Dan Omahan. Saulo and I actually heckled the bullsh*t show that somehow beat us out. I am not sure, but I have got to believe that heckling is not commonplace at an Emmy awards show? Regardless, we had a blast, and most importantly, Saulo's story had provided inspiration for so many people in so many different ways. Even now, years later, I will still have people approach me and talk about Saulo Morris. He was like the little brother I never had and the mentor that I still continue to strive to be. The overall selfless nature in which he lived his life was the blueprint to how every one of us should go about our daily activities.

Unfortunately, the leukemia came back and Saulo was once again in and out of the hospital going through several rounds of chemotherapy. In October of 2008, things got very serious. He was going to need to have a bone marrow transplant or he was going to die. In November, Saulo led a bone marrow drive that added nearly another 1000 people, including myself, to the bone marrow donor list. That day at Thunderbird High School, Saulo came out to personally thank everyone for showing up. It was tough to see him in the condition he was in, heartbreaking even. Then a month later I got news from John that they had found a bone marrow match! All he needed to do was get through one more round of chemotherapy, and they could perform the transplant that would very possibly eradicate the leukemia. Saulo never got through that last round. On December 2, 2008, Saulo Morris passed on to a better place.

That next year the D Backs and I had helped financially to build a baseball field near Thunderbird High School that was supposed to be named in my honor. Something about it did not seem right; that something was very obvious. The night before, I called John, Saulo's dad, and told him that instead of Eric Byrnes Field I wanted to name it Saulo Morris Field. When I arrived at the ribbon cutting ceremony the next day, John was there to accept the field in Saulo's honor. When I explained what I was doing and introduced John, I completely lost it.

Ironically, Saulo's best friend Vaughn played in the first official game ever on "Saulo Morris Field." Vaughn was a light-hitting second baseman that had never hit a home run in his life... Until that day.

Vaughn built on the momentum of his homer and has gone on to carry Saulo's spirit with him; he is now a part of the presidential press pool reporting for NBC.

Saulo's life was way too short. He was one of the greatest people I have ever come across in my life. His selfless nature was infectious on everybody he came into contact with, including me. Before I met Saulo, I was living a life that centered around ME. Saulo made me realize there is a lot more to life than our selfish desires. He opened my eyes to the opportunity to spread a message of awareness and love. He taught me that together we can make a difference if we are willing to go the extra mile to do something to benefit mankind. He was a leader in every sense of the word. I have no doubt that his spirit is alive and well, living through the people he touched throughout the course of his life.

Human Crash Test Dummy Life Lesson #78

Life is fragile and can be taken from us at any moment. When it's all said and done, it is not the amount of years that you live but rather what you decide to do with those years. Everybody is born and everybody dies, but how many of us truly live our lives? The dash between birth and death represents life.

LIVE YOUR DASH.

Chapter 79
Anybody Anytime

"I just love working hard. I love being part of a team;
I love working toward a common goal."
-Tom Brady

In 2007, we got off to a good start as a team, and you could just sense that this was going to be a special year. For me personally, I was in a spot that quite frankly I was not used to. I was in the lineup every day without the fear of losing my job after an 0-4 for the first time since I was in the Minor Leagues. People ask me all the time why I was such a streaky player, and I don't think there is any doubt that my successes and failures were directly related to my opportunities. That's not to say that there weren't times that my opportunities were limited and I had success, and there were also times that my opportunities were vast and I was sh*tty. Yet overall, with a larger sample size, it is way more likely that the true player will come out.

I have argued several times before, and will continue to argue, that there is no such thing as a "4A" player (a term put on a guy who had a ton of success in AAA yet would suck in the big leagues). Of course, there most likely will be some sort of drop off in numbers, but in my opinion, if given significant opportunities, there will be a significant amount of success that translates. Ask any player who has been in my situation of being a bench player and playing every day, and I promise they will tell you how much easier it is to play when the at-bats and repetitions are consistent. This isn't rocket science; simply look at the overall pinch-hitting numbers every year, and they dwarf in comparison to those of guys who started the game.

In 2,212 Minor League plate appearances that just about all came as an everyday player, I hit .307 with an .869 OPS with nearly a 1/1 strikeout to walk ratio. In 3,532 Major League plate appearances in which the majority came as a bench player, I hit .258 with a .759 OPS with a 2/1 strikeout to walk ratio. I mention the strikeout to walk ratio because I would say that it is a pretty good indication of how comfortable a player is. Walks generally come when a hitter is not trying to do too much and is able to hone in on his strike zone. This typically happens when that player is getting consistent at-bats. On the other hand, strikeouts usually happen when a player tries to do too much by expanding the strike zone. This often occurs with players who have limited opportunities and simply try too hard.

In 2007 from the first day of Spring Training, for the first time in my Major League career, there was no doubt I was going to be in the lineup on a daily basis. I responded by becoming just the 11th player in the history of Major League Baseball to hit 20 home runs and steal 50 bases. As the season went on, we continued to win games by dramatic fashion. Tony Clark started the slogan "Anybody Anytime," and that could not have been more of the truth. Each day there was a different guy who would contribute to the team's victory. Major League Baseball is an extremely selfish sport played by extremely selfish players. Just two times in my career did I get the feeling that guys were legitimately pulling for one another and that the overall greater good of the team was put in front of whatever individual goals that guys had: the first being in 2002 with the Oakland A's and the other being with the 2007 Arizona Diamondbacks.

Human Crash Test Dummy Life Lesson #79

In order to get the most out of a team of individuals, it is mandatory to make those individuals understand their roll and what it means to the overall success of the team. Keep everybody involved and make sure each person is comfortable with his or her roll. It is pertinent that everybody involved does not give a f*ck who gets the credit.

Chapter 80
Life's Not Fair; Your Response Is

"Don't worry when you are not recognized,
but strive to be worthy of recognition."
-Abraham Lincoln

Approaching the All-Star break, I was near the top of several offensive categories. I was no doubt having the best year of my career. I had come close to making the All-Star game in 2003 when I was one of the finalists on the extended ballot. I had good numbers in 2004 but missed out again. In 2006, I finished with 26 home runs and 25 stolen bases but once again was on the outside looking in on the mid-summer classic. Of course, I was a bit disappointed all 3 of those years but by no means did I ever expect to get selected. 2007 was a little different; our team was winning, I was playing the best baseball of my career, and the game was going to be played in San Francisco. To think about the nostalgia of playing in an All-Star game in the city where I grew up was bone chilling. The day the rosters were announced, we happened to be in San Francisco playing the Giants. Bob Melvin called me into his office for what I truly believed was to inform me that I had made the first All-Star game of my career. When I walked in, Bob had a very somber look on his face. In the back of my mind I was hoping he was just f*cking with me. "You didn't make it."

Despite having better numbers across the board than a couple of the other outfielders that were selected, I was not picked. Tony LaRussa was in charge of the final selections. I have to assume that he picked who he thought was going to help him win the game, and apparently, I was not one of those guys. Disappointment was an understatement; I was crushed.

Human Crash Test Dummy Life Lesson #80

Like anything else in life that you or I have no control over, we have no choice but to say, "F*ck it." Every single year, dudes get "snubbed" from an All-Star game, deserving people get passed over for a promotion at work, and your girlfriend may dump you so she can further explore her sexual freedoms. Go ahead and let out whatever natural emotions and frustrations you may have, but then get over it and get over yourself.

Life is not fair, but your response to life is.

Chapter 81
Make The Adjustment

*"We must let go of the life we have planned,
so as to accept the one that is waiting for us."*
-Joseph Campbell

Before the 2007 season, I signed a deal with FOX that contracted me to do 30 Best Damn Sports Show appearances, 6 in-season skits for FOX Saturday Baseball, and work the All-Star game and World Series, assuming I was not participating. I wasn't, so during the actual All-Star game, FOX naturally wanted me in a Kayak in McCovey Cove.

Originally, I was 100% against the idea. I then thought of a way that would possibly make it more entertaining for me and the telecast: bring my bulldog Bruin on the kayak with me. Of course, FOX, who typically likes to think outside the box, loved the idea and fully equipped the "Bruin Byrnes" (BB) kayak with microphones and cameras.

The theme of my Cove dwelling was that we were going to be waiting for a home run ball that Bruin could possibly retrieve. The idea was to capture the essence of the city, the ballpark, and the cove, which I believed was undoubtedly accomplished. I am just not sure if it was accomplished the way FOX or I had envisioned it. After a couple hours in the kayak, Bruin was becoming restless, and I had to take a leak. We ended up finagling our way on a boat with some SF locals who were BBQ'n and slugging down cold frosties. As Bruin was crushing a big pork sausage and I was pounding an adult beverage, I got the sound through the IFB in my ear from the producer, "We are coming to you in 30 seconds."

I slammed the remaining Anchor Steam and went to the rear of the boat where the camera up top in the stadium would be able to get a clean shot. Playing off the original concept that we were out there to catch a home run ball, I explained that Bruin was getting antsy and even though a home run had not yet reached the bay, I was not going to deprive my swimming bulldog of a chance to get into the water. I then chucked a ball into the bay. Bruin originally stood still and did not react at all.

Finally, after some high-pitched verbal encouragement, he flew into the water to retrieve the ball. The problem was that the ball had drifted off with the current, and Bruin couldn't find it! He started swimming in circles and eventually took a left turn and started heading out towards the Bay Bridge. Joe Buck then proceeded to chastise me for losing the dog right about the exact same time Ichiro hits a ball off the brick wall in right field. As Ichiro was scurrying around the bases, my ass was scurrying to the other side of the boat trying to make sure my dog didn't drown on national television. Just as I am about to launch myself into the freezing-ass water, I can hear Joe Buck's call of the first ever All-Star game inside the park homer. I then literally ripped my IFB and microphone off at about the exact same time two dudes on kayaks came flying out of nowhere to retrieve Bruin and bring him back to the boat. Ultimately, FOX and the millions of viewers at home were treated to a mildly entertaining, absolute debacle!

Of course, I was disappointed about not making the All-Star game, but I was fortunate to have FOX think enough of me to actually want me involved with the broadcast. It was also barely over a year from when I thought my career might be over. So what if I happened to be on a boat with my dog instead of in the outfield, F*CK IT!

Human Crash Test Dummy Life Lesson #81

We can try to plan all we want. We can have a vision of how we want life to turn out, but ultimately, it is our ability to react and adjust that determines our happiness. Oftentimes, it takes us stepping back, which allows us to gain perspective.

Chapter 82
Know When to Hold Them

"There will be time enough for counting when the dealing is done."
-Kenny Rogers

About three-fourths of the way through the season, things could not have been going better. We were winning, but most importantly, we were having fun doing it. I was playing as well as I could, hitting homers, stealing bases, and playing the best defense of my career. The TV show was a huge hit, and my celebrity status in the state of Arizona reached a point where Sen. John McCain referenced the great qualities about the state of Arizona, which included the Grand Canyon and Eric Byrnes (not a joke).

After the 2006 season, the Diamondbacks cut ties with the face of the franchise, Luis Gonzalez, who was a great friend and a great teammate. The D Backs took a ton of heat for letting Gonzo walk and I am sure lost some fans in the process.

When I was brought back for the 2007 season, a lot was made of me being the guy who was going to replace Gonzo in left field. I thought that was absolute bullsh*t. Gonzo was a fan favorite and will be forever immortalized by his incredible individual seasons, and of course, his game-winning base hit in Game 7 of the 2001 World Series. There was nothing that I could have done short of hitting a walk-off home run in Game 7 of the World Series that would have put me on the same level as Gonzo. It always bothered me to even hear my name mentioned with his. All of that said, I had become a popular face that was associated with the 2007 team, and it would have been another PR hit if I was to walk at the end of the season and enter the free agent market. Josh Byrnes, the D Backs general manager, contacted Sasson about a possible contract extension. The initial offer was 1 year and $8 million. The second offer was 2 years and $16 million. The final offer was 3 years and $24 million. Gary Matthews Jr. had just signed a 5-year $50 million deal, so without even counter-offering, we continued to point to the comparisons between the two of us. We politely declined.

Don't get me wrong; turning down 24 million dollars just a year and a half after I thought my career might be over was one of the most difficult things I ever had to do. As a player though, you need to remove yourself from becoming overwhelmed by the numbers and simply understand that future salaries, whether they are contrived through arbitration or free agency, are a byproduct of a structure that has been established through years of developing labor relations. The other thing that players and even fans need to remember is that a player's window for making money is relatively small. The average Major League career lasts less than 3 years. For many players, what they make on the field is every penny they will make in salary for the rest of their lives. Therefore, it is vitally important to maximize every last dollar to say the least.

2 weeks later, we just finished the last game of a home series against the Atlanta Braves when I was approached in the clubhouse by the president and CEO, Jeff Moorad. "Come see me in my office when you get a chance."

Jeff was a UCLA Bruin, so we always had a better relationship than most players and CEOs would. I showed up in his office and sat across his desk, which was an exact replica of the same desk that was in the White House's Oval Office. That should tell you a little bit about the man. Jeff got his start in the industry as an agent, so he no doubt understood the intricacies of a player/team negotiation. He is an easy-going, supremely confident guy who seems to have a passion for whatever he does in life. He is also a shrewd businessman and as cutthroat of a dude that I have ever been around. I knew exactly whose office I was walking in to.

"You have become a big part of what we are doing here, and we want you to stick around awhile. What's the number that will get that done?"

"Not sure, Jeff. I do know that Gary Matthews Jr. got 5 for 50. If you look at the numbers I feel as if I comp out pretty well."

"We can't do 5, but how bout 3, does that work for you?"

"3 with the same AAV? 3 for 30?"

"3 for 30," Jeff responded in his baritone voice.

I was then speechless, but I think my smile said it all. I was ecstatic. That was the amount of years and the exact number that Sasson and I had talked about in terms of what would get it done.

"Sounds pretty f*cking good to me. I need to talk to my agent and the guys over at the player's association, but I think I'm in." I then expressed my concern for a no-trade clause. Assuming I was on par with Matthews, which I was, there was a very realistic possibility if I waited just 2 months, I would potentially be looking at 5 years and probably over $50 million. So signing with the Diamondbacks for a hometown discount, so to speak, more likely than not was going to cost me money. Because of that, I wanted to make sure that I did not sign with the D Backs, and a year into my contract they trade me to another team. Bouncing around in '05 playing for 3 different teams, I no doubt understood and valued the importance of stability.

Jeff agreed and wrote up the deal on paper, offering a limited no-trade clause that included 10 teams I would be able to veto a trade to. I took the piece of paper and then called Sasson immediately when I got into the car. We both decided we needed to tame our excitement and call 2 people, the first being my dad and the second being Mike Seal, my college roommate, one of my best friends and a guy whose opinion I value above all others when it came to MLB contract negotiations.

My dad had his MBA and for years taught classes at San Francisco State about the art of business negotiations. At the time, he was also very successful in real estate, which obviously centers around negotiations on a daily basis. Both my dad and Seal agreed that a deal should not happen without a full no-trade clause, the main reason being that if I was playing well and the D Backs as a team happened to be struggling, there would be a very good chance that they would want to shed salary and trade me. So, in essence, I could be potentially playing for a team I had no desire to play for at a discounted rate. It's not that if the D Backs wanted to trade me I would not have obliged. I was not going to wear out my welcome on a team if they did not want me there, but what the no-trade clause would allow me to do is have the same flexibility to choose a team that I would have had if I had gone to free agency. It would have also potentially allowed me to renegotiate my contract before agreeing to a trade to get to a number more realistic of what I would have gotten had I entered free agency. We had a day off the next day, so I called Jeff, and we agreed to meet the following afternoon once Sasson arrived in town.

We walked into the office knowing exactly what we wanted, and we were not going to budge. We figured if they were unwilling to grant me a full no-trade clause, there was a very real possibility that I could be playing for another team at a discounted rate just months after giving up free agency. I realize you may be reading this and thinking to yourself, why does this knucklehead keep referring to this "discounted rate" bullsh*t? How is $30 million a discount? And who the F*CK does Byrnes think he is? Barry Bonds? The reality of the situation was that Aaron Rowand, who was a free agent the same year, was the most similar comp that I had not only in the 2007 season but throughout the course of my entire career as well. Rowand hit free agency that off-season and signed a 5-year, $60-million deal with the Giants.

I picked up Sasson from the airport, and he was surprisingly calm. In a lot of ways, this was Sasson's initiation into the agent world. He had worked for several agents ever since college, but he had never single-handedly negotiated any sort of big contract on his own. As a matter of fact, Sasson even interned for Moorad right after he graduated from UCLA. We walked into Jeff's office. Sasson explained to Moorad that he used to work for him. Everyone got some good laughs, and then we got to business.

Sasson very boldly told his former boss that we were good with the 3 years and $30 million, but we needed a full no-trade clause to complete the deal. He then went into a very detailed explanation of why the full no-trade clause was so important to us. At one point, I even jumped in, telling Jeff if they wanted to trade me I would undoubtedly go but needed to have some sort of leverage in the process. His response was that they were not willing to do a full no-trade and asked me if I was really ready to walk away from $30 million based on a no-trade clause. Sasson and I looked at each other; then very confidently, we simultaneously nodded in agreement. We had no problem leaving the deal on the plate. Jeff then went into a full-blown tirade about how asinine our decision was. Quite honestly, it was one of the most impressive and influencing negotiation monologues I had ever heard or experienced. Moorad then asked the same question one more time, "Are you guys really going to leave $30 million F*CKING dollars on the table?"

This time our head nods were not quite as convincing, but we did not budge. Jeff then left the room. We had no idea if the meeting was over; we both just sat there in silence not knowing what to do. 5 minutes passed. 10 minutes passed. At this point, we both assumed that was it. I commended Sasson for standing strong, and we began to walk out of the room. Just as we were about out the door, Jeff walked back in. "Sit down. 3 years, $30 million, and your full no-trade clause. Here are the papers. Nice work, I am proud of you, Mike, I must have taught you well!" The entire experience was one of the craziest and most intense moments I have ever witnessed in my life. Most importantly, I was going to continue to be able to play in an awesome city for a team and a manger that I absolutely loved.

Human Crash Test Dummy Life Lesson #82

Don't get overwhelmed by the numbers. Throughout the course of our life, we may find ourselves in positions we didn't necessarily expect. Educate yourself, know the market, and understand the values. Hold firm for what you believe is fair but always have an exit plan. The greatest thing you can have in a negotiation is leverage and the ability to walk away at any point and be content with that decision.

Chapter 83
Build Your Pyramid

*"Embrace your history because it's the stuff by which
legends are made and legacies are left."*
-Carmine Gallo

Late in the season in 2007, we were in LA playing the Dodgers. Jeff Moorad invited me to have breakfast with the guy I had drawn inspiration from my entire life, John Wooden! At the time, Wooden was in his late 90s, and although he had trouble hearing and he spoke very softly, he was sharp as a tack. I barely spoke the entire breakfast; all I wanted to do was listen. Coach Wooden went in-depth about the pyramid of success and how it took him 15 years to create. He also talked about how baseball was actually his favorite sport. He even recited several of his famous quotes fresh in his 97-year-old mind.

Tough to narrow down because there are so many great ones, but here are what I would consider my top 10 John Wooden teachings and inspirations:

Success is peace of mind, which is a direct result of self-satisfaction in knowing you made the effort to become the best of which you are capable.

Be more concerned with your character than your reputation because your character is what you really are, while your reputation is merely what others think you are.

If you don't have time to do it right, when will you have time to do it over?

Failure is not fatal, but failure to change might be.

Talent is God-given. Be humble. Fame is man-given. Be grateful. Conceit is self-given. Be careful.

Don't measure yourself by what you have accomplished, but by what you should have accomplished with your ability.

Success is never final; failure is never fatal. It's courage that counts.

It's the little details that are vital. Little things make big things happen.

Things turn out best for the people who make the best of the way things turn out.

Discipline yourself, and others won't need to.

Not surprisingly, a few years later when I was hosting my own radio show at KNBR, I would sign off with a different John Wooden quote on a nightly basis. The pyramid of success also just happens to be painted on the walls of each of my children's bedrooms.

Human Crash Test Dummy Life Lesson #83

Find somebody, past or present, that lives a lifestyle that speaks to you in your life. Utilize the inspiration drawn from that person and create your own pyramid. Learn from the legends; ask yourself why you were drawn to them, and what did they teach you by the way they lived their life? Legends and legacies are built through life experience.

Living it is building it.

Chapter 84
Let's Party

"The more you celebrate your life the more in life there is to celebrate."
-Oprah Winfrey

We ended up winning the division on the 2nd-to-last day of the 2007 season in Colorado. That same night, I stole my 50th base and became the 11th player in the history of baseball to hit 20 home runs and steal 50 bases in the same season.

The celebration was a little whacky because we were not sure if we had clinched until we were on the field shaking hands. Then Augie Ojeda comes running out of the dugout, "OYE OYE OYE. San Diego lost. We going to the playoffs, dog!!!" Chaos and champagne showers ensued.

A few days later, we opened the 5-game National League Division Series against the Cubs, who were heavy favorites. We won the first 2 games at home and then traveled to Chicago, only needing one more victory. Playoff baseball on the north side of Chicago might as well be some sort of national holiday. It had been 99 years since the Cubs last won a World Series and many believed they had the team to do it. The only other atmosphere that I can remember being as electric was Yankee Stadium in 2001 right after 9/11. The Cubs loaded the bases twice in the game, and both times I can remember speaking out loud to myself in left field trying to hear my voice, and I heard nothing. I finally understood what someone meant by saying, "Not being able to hear yourself think." Fortunately for us, Livan Hernandez induced double play balls in both situations.

As I have mentioned before, Will Clark was my favorite player growing up. One of my greatest childhood memories was watching Thrill hit a grand slam off Greg Maddux at Wrigley Field during the 1989 NLCS. I had the opportunity to meet and get to know Will when he worked as a special instructor for the Diamondbacks. Over a few beers one night, I had him tell me the entire story of the homer. Thrill actually read Maddox's lips on the mound when he said, "Fastball inside," just as a meeting was breaking up on the mound before Will came to the plate. The one thing that resonated with me though was when he said the Wrigley crowd became so quiet after he hit the grand slam that he could actually hear his feet hit the ground.

Fast-forward 18 years. In the top of the 7th inning, I came up against Carlos Marmol, the Cubs filthy right-handed reliever. He hung a first pitch slider that I jumped on and hit deep into the left-field bleachers. As I was rounding the bases, all I could think about was Will Clark in 1989, and ironically, I could hear my feet hit the ground with every step.

We swept the Cubs and then turned the visiting clubhouse into Chicago's best nightclub. Wrigley is notorious for having the worst visiting clubhouse in the big leagues, and we didn't help make it any better!

Human Crash Test Dummy Life Lesson #84

Celebrate when your hard work accomplishes a great feat. Don't take success for granted because there is definitely no guaranteed success in life, even when the necessary work is put in. Share in the celebration with your teammates and all the people who supported your great accomplishment. Be humble, be gracious, but be proud of your dedication to the process. POP BOTTLES.

Chapter 85

Truth Speaks

"Better to get hurt by the truth than comforted with a lie."
-Khaled Hosseini

The next series we faced the Colorado Rockies who were on a miraculous run. Colorado had to win 19 out of 20 games just to get into a one-game playoff with San Diego for the wildcard spot. They won that game and then went on to bust up the Phillies in the NLDS. The Rockies and the Diamondbacks were the only two teams with Spring Training complexes still in Tucson, so our season actually started off with scrimmages against each other even before official spring games started.

Not surprisingly, opening day of our season just so happened to be in Colorado. We played them 19 times through the course of the regular season. We were friends and foes at the same time. We would battle on the field and then go hang out at a bar or club together afterwards. No doubt we were sick of facing them, but who better to play a seven-game series against for a chance to go to the World Series than a team that you know better than any other?

Game 1 of the series started off well. Hitting 3rd, I came up in the bottom of the 1st inning against left-handed starter Jeff Francis. With Stephan Drew on 1st base, I drilled a fastball down the left field line for an RBI double. In the 7th inning, we had some action going when 19-year-old Justin Upton went hard into 2nd base with an awesome kick-ass slide to break up a double play. Upton was eventually called out for interference, resulting in a double play. Arizona fans went freaking nuts! For a Major League Baseball team that was not even a decade old, in a city of transplants, in which the Diamondbacks were essentially everybody's second favorite team, I was impressed with the passion. All year we were essentially begging for fans to come out to games and get excited about this team. Now here we were in Game 1 of the NLCS, and I would have thought I was back in the Dominican

Republic as fans started chucking anything they had within arm's reach onto the field. Normally, I would not condone such barbaric and childish activity, but I was so pumped up that Arizona fans actually cared enough to start chucking beer bottles, nachos, and bratwurst onto the field. The game was delayed for a good 10+ minutes.

As much as I loved playing in Arizona, one of my biggest issues was when the gates would open at Chase Field there would be elevator music going with a sign on the scoreboard that read "WELCOME TO AN EVENING OF DIAMONDBACKS BASEBALL." I tried to explain to anybody who would listen that this isn't the f*cking senior prom, this is a gosh damn Major League Baseball game in a sweet stadium with a team loaded with BAMFs (Bad Ass Mother F*ckers). Visiting teams would come in and it was like a country club for them. I can't tell you how many times over the course of my 4 years there that the D Backs fans were the minority.

Essentially, Chase Field would turn into Wrigley whenever the Cubs were in town. I always felt like I was back home in the Bay when the Giants would come to Phoenix, and when we played Boston, the Red Sox seemingly brought everything with them from Fenway Park except for the Green Monster. Not this time though, not Colorado, no way! It was time for die-hard Diamondbacks fans to stand up and let the world know that this was their house! This wasn't the Summer Gala or the Fall Formal; this was the "SNAKE PIT", and when your ass enters the building, look the f*ck out!

We lost Game 1, but Game 1 was not about us that night, it was about the oppressed Diamondbacks fans that had been held captive in their own ballpark since the organization's existence. The Arizona faithful finally rolled out to the front porch of their house with a 12-gauge shotgun and told the neighbors to get off their lawn! Chalk up the moral victory to the D Backs fans.

Unfortunately, Game 2 was more of the same BS. They were dinking balls all over the ballpark that were falling in, while we were hitting bullets that were getting caught. We fell behind 1-0 then came back to make it 1-1; Colorado then took a 2-1 lead. Then with a shot to break the game open in the 8th inning, we loaded the bases with 2 outs with my man Tony Clark (TC) coming to the dish. I was on 1st base, and TC absolutely unloaded on the baseball, drilling a line drive into the gap in right-center field. As I was rounding second and looking for third base, Coach Chip Hale swung his right arm as quickly as possible, waving for me to go home. I first heard a huge sigh from the crowd and then saw Chip with both hands on his knees and his head buried between his legs. Willy Tavares, the center fielder for the Rockies, chased down the ball in the gap and made an incredible diving catch to save the game. We still found a way to rebound and tie the game in the bottom of the 9th, but then lost in the 11th 3-2.

So there we were, down 2 games to none in a series that very easily could have been 2-0 the other way. We showed up in Colorado on the off day, and I was scheduled to speak to the media in the media tent right after our on-field workout. The mood in our locker room seemed to be down, knowing that we very easily could have and should have won both of the games in Arizona. When Mike McNally, our PR guy, came to get me to go to the media tent, I was sitting with Tony Clark in the dugout.

"What do you think, TC? Should I spice things up a bit?"

TC had a big smile on his face and nodded in approval. For me, getting a TC head nod with a little smirk on his face was like getting approval from the President of the United States. When I sat down to answer questions, I had no intention to speak anything but the truth. First reporter question: "What gives you guys confidence going into Game 3 down 2 games to 0?"

My response was simple. "We have out-played them. There was the controversial call in Game 1 that changed the entire dynamic of the game, then without Willy Tavares making the play of his life, we would have won game 2. The reality of the situation is that just about every ball that we hit hard has been right at somebody and every duck snort, squibber, and nubber that they hit is falling in. What gives us confidence you ask? I think we are the better baseball team. They have had a horseshoe up their ass."

The Latin players on the D Backs would call me "La Verdad," meaning "The Truth" in Spanish. I felt like I had a responsibility to live up to that name.

One of the things that I have learned in my life is that your words are forever creating your reality. The only reason why I ever had any regret about the words I spoke is because I gave more fuel to their LUCKY-ass fire. Sure as sh*t, I came up to boos from 50,000 people with runners on first and second and no outs in the first inning of Game 3. I drilled a ball off Josh Fogg that was headed up the middle for an RBI base hit that literally caught him on his follow through. He threw the ball to second for the 2nd out, and then they just missed getting Stephan Drew at first for a triple play. The horseshoe had already been there, and I just helped shove it in their even further.

We lost 4-1. Then the next night, I came up down 6-4 in the top of the 9th inning with 2 outs. I was looking for a Manny Corpus sinker on the inside part of the plate to hit into the left field bleachers to tie the game. That's exactly what I got. I started to swing then realized it was going to be too far inside. I tried to pull the bat back but was not quick enough. The result: a bullsh*t check-swing ground ball to Troy Tulowitzky. I busted my ass as hard as I could down the line with hopes of beating the throw to first. I dove into the bag, but the throw beat me by plenty and the Rockies were going to the World Series. There is an iconic photo of Todd Helton with his hands raised as I am eating dirt at first. The shot is by no means hanging in my office, but to be honest, it is a pretty sweet pic!

Human Crash Test Dummy Life Lesson #85

There is no doubt that truth speaks. Truth resonates with everybody involved, and although it may be painful at times, it can provide much needed perspective to a difficult situation. Be truthful but use your words with great awareness. Your thoughts and your words are forever manifesting your reality, so be conscious of both. Speak your truthful words wisely!

Chapter 86
Get Cozy

"We will not tire, we will not falter, we will not fail."
-George W. Bush

While on my honeymoon on the North Shore of Oahu, I got a message from Jeff Moorad telling me that George Will, the great political and baseball historian, was going to be calling me. I had read several of George Will's books including *Men at Work*, which was all about the development of baseball labor relations and anti-trust laws. When I received the call the following day, I was like a giddy little school kid.

"Eric, George Will here."

"George, what's up, my man? I am a big fan of yours!"

"Thank you! I am actually calling to invite you to the White House to have dinner with the President of the United States on January 29th."

"Wow! Sweet, dude."

"Will you be able to join us?"

"Not sure if I can make it, George. Let me take a look at my schedule and see if I can pencil you and President Bush in." Awkward pause. "George!!! I am messing with you. Of course I will be there. I am humbled and honored, sir!"

The dinner was something that Mr. Will had orchestrated every year George W. Bush was in office. Five people and a guest within the baseball world were invited to the White House to have dinner with the President and First Lady to discuss the current state of the game.

On January 29, 2008, my wife Tarah and I arrived in Washington DC. We then hopped into a cab and dropped, "1600 Pennsylvania Ave. PLEASE."

I long had this incredible infatuation with American history, and in particular the White House, and to that point, the 43 Presidents who had served in office. We were dropped off at a security gate and first had to get past the armed guards on the street just to get onto the premises. We then had to walk through a security booth, where we were screened pretty much the same way as if you were about to board a flight. In the booth, we ran into the Tigers All-Star outfielder Curtis Granderson and his father, as well as Red Sox manager Terry Francona, fresh off Boston's 2nd World Series championship in 4 years. Also attending were San Diego Padres pitcher and Princeton graduate Chris Young, his wife, and 48-year-old Dominican sensation Julio Franco and his wife. Julio had just completed his 23rd season in the big leagues. NL MVP Jimmy Rollins and his wife rounded out the eclectic crew.

When we walked inside, we were escorted to the "Green Room," where the President was standing with the First Lady and engaged in casual conversation with Chris Young, Julio Franco, and their spouses. The President then greeted George Will and his wife, and then Mr. Will introduced Tarah and I to the President and First Lady. I can't remember the exact formality, but I do remember thinking how extremely comfortable the entire situation was. Within minutes, it almost seemed as if we were at a good friend's house for a dinner party.

The conversation was lighthearted and all encompassing. The President and the First Lady had obviously been well versed on who everybody was and knew everybody's names and backgrounds. President Bush even joked about the San Francisco Bay Area: "Not a lot of red in that part of the state!" The First Lady then took the lead and walked everyone into the ballroom, where she told a riveting story about the War of 1812 and how the British Army completely destroyed the interior and nearly burnt down the entire White House. Apparently, the only thing White House workers were able to save was a painting of George Washington, which was proudly hung on the south wall of the ballroom, essentially the only wall that withstood the fire's wrath.

After the ballroom, we were escorted into the "Blue Room," where we were going to pose for a picture with the President and First Lady. I had a little bit of a problem though; my stomach was churning a bit and I needed to take a leak, badly!

"Excuse me, Mr. President. Where's the restroom?"

"Downstairs and to the left towards where you first walked in, Eric. Would you like me to show you?"

"Ha! I don't imagine I'll ever get another opportunity for the President of the United States to escort me to the restroom, but I am good. I have a feeling if I get lost, I won't get very far." I headed downstairs and after a few wrong turns and peaking my head around areas I probably shouldn't have, a dude popped out of nowhere and led me to the can. As I was relieving myself, the gastric build-up began to intensify. I was now regretting the double chicken burrito with rice, beans, extra guacamole, corn salsa, and hot sauce I scarfed down a few hours prior at Chipotle. I then figured it wasn't every day that I would get an opportunity to take a dump in the White House, so I went for it.

Overall, it wasn't a quick bathroom break, but all considering, I felt like it wasn't that long either. When I returned up to the Blue Room where the President and First Lady were taking pictures with all the guests, my wife Tarah and the Bush's were the last ones left. Waiting for me!

We snapped a quick photo and then headed to the "Family Dining Room," where the other guests had already sat down. I just assumed there would have been a couple seats left and Tarah and I would sit together, but that was not the case. There was one seat on one side of the table and then another seat completely on the other end that was barely within an earshot of conversation. I then noticed that each place setting had a nametag in the middle, and mine was in between Julio Franco's and Chris Young's wives. To the left of Julio Franco's wife was the President, and the First Lady sat directly across from the President. Tarah's spot was the open seat situated on the far end of the table.

I quickly realized the male/female dynamic of the seating arrangement. Dude, chick, dude, chick, dude, chick, President (can't refer to him as "dude"), chick, dude, chick, dude, chick, dude, First Lady (can't refer to the First Lady as "chick").

Once we were all seated, the conversation turned rather serious right away. Congress had just spent months investigating performance-enhancing drug use in baseball, and guys such as Roger Clemens, Sammy Sosa, Rafael Palmeiro, Mark McGwire, and Jose Canseco were all called to testify in front of Congress regarding their knowledge and individual use. The President wanted to gauge how we felt about the investigation. After a few answers from some of the other guys that included the standard, "I am glad they are helping clean up the game," I weighed in.

"Mr. President, as much as I agree with the guys here about cleaning up the game, can you tell me what Congress is trying to accomplish by conducting these hearings? Major League Baseball already has the most stringent drug-testing program out of all the major sports. The game is not perfectly clean, but at least I feel that we as a sport are making progress towards one day hopefully accomplishing that goal. No disrespect, sir, but the last time I checked, we were involved in two major wars, the stock market is falling, the dollar is weakening, the unemployment rate is rising, the welfare system is a mess, and major reforms in education and healthcare are looming. In my opinion, Congress is wasting their time and my tax paying dollars trying to figure out what? Who was taking steroids during the 1990s? What exactly is Congress trying to prove?"

The President, with a big smile on his face then responded. "Well Eric, I have been asking that same question for years!"

After dinner, the President led us through the halls of the White House. As we passed paintings of the different presidents, President Bush would drop a nugget about each one as if he was a tour guide for a 7th grade field trip. As I mentioned, going all the way back to my childhood, I have had a fascination with United States history and presidential history in particular. I was also a History major at UCLA. The entire White House night was quite possibly the coolest thing I had ever experienced in my life. Throughout the tour I felt inclined to drop a few presidential nuggets of my own.

Grover Cleveland, our 22nd and 24th president, was the only president to serve two non-consecutive terms. I spoke about our 23rd president, Benjamin Harrison, who was the grandson of our 9th president, William Henry Harrison, who just so happened to be the first president to die while in office just 32 days into his term after contracting pneumonia during his inauguration speech. Then there was William McKinley, our 25th president, who is one of our most underrated presidents. McKinley brought economic stability to the U.S. by laying down the law and implementing huge tariffs to help promote and sell goods MADE in the USA. He also took care of business quickly in the Spanish American War of 1898. What did we as a country get from that? Well, not Cuba, but how do Puerto Rico, Guam, and Hawaii sound? Unfortunately, McKinley was assassinated but obviously not before leaving a storied legacy.

As we were walking, I never bothered to ask where we were going; I was just simply enjoying the ride. The President escorted us outside and then all of a sudden, I realized where we were: the West Wing headed toward the Oval Office. I felt as if I was floating. This was like going to the Super Bowl, World Series, Masters, and Kentucky Derby rolled into one. I felt like I was 32 going on 6. We walked in and it was as if I had been there a hundred times before.

It was exactly how it looked in the textbooks and movies. The first thing I noticed was the presidential desk and the red button that I always thought was fictional. I couldn't help myself. "Mr. President, what is the red button for?" Embarrassed that I would be so blunt and ask the question we were all wondering, my wife pinched me. The room then became silent as we all awaited his response.

"I shouldn't be telling you guys this, but that button is for when I need a cup of coffee."

He then went on to explain that the red button was a direct line to one of his assistants, and although it could be pressed to communicate something major, more often than not it was so he could get a turkey sandwich. The President then turned our attention to the large area rug and talked about how he believes all great leaders have the ability to delegate their power, and that was exactly what he did when it came to decorating the Oval Office. Like many husbands, he bowed to his better half to make the decorative decisions.

One decision that the President made himself was to bring with him a painting that he had in his governor's office in Texas. It was a 1918 painting by W.H.D Koerner, based on a Charles Wesely hymn that resonated with the president, called "A Charge to Keep." The President also paid homage to his Texas and western roots with a super-cool Remington iron statue. Each president got to choose a painting of the president that he most admired, and that painting serves as the centerpiece in the Oval Office.

Not surprisingly, Abraham Lincoln was President Bush's choice. The President talked about how during Lincoln's time in office, and even for several years after his death, his tenure was looked upon by many as a colossal failure. Then, as time went on, people began to realize the injustices that Lincoln had fought to correct and how influential President Lincoln was in shaping modern America. At this point, I believe many people look at Bush's presidency much like people looked at Lincoln's during his term in office. Both presidents acted the way they felt was appropriate for the safety and future well-being of our country. Without turning this book into any sort of political propaganda bullsh*t, one way or another, in my opinion, his overall harsh stance on terrorism, and the ultimate war on terror that we still continue to fight today is the stance this country must take. In our current political situation, all of a sudden President Bush is looking a lot better in everybody's eyes. He will go down as the President who declared the war on terror and is already looked upon as one of the most influential presidents in U.S. history.

Human Crash Test Dummy Life Lesson #86

Don't be intimidated by a grand meeting. Being excited and even anxious are normal emotions leading up to such an event. Focus on being as natural as possible in any social situation. It's okay to let your opinion be known, so long as you are not forcing it or being disrespectful. Do your homework on the other people at the event and ask them about their interests. Get cozy, ask questions, listen, learn and don't ever be afraid to share.

Chapter 87
Embrace The Suck

*"Let me embrace thee, sour adversity,
for wise men say it is the wisest course."*
-William Shakespeare

I showed up in Tucson for Spring Training two weeks early. After a crazy off-season, I couldn't wait to get back to playing. There was a small group of guys in camp the first week, and as we got closer to the actual report date, most everyone was there. 2 days before camp officially started, we had a group of at least 12 guys take batting practice, and then it was left up to me to decide what running we were going to do. Twelve poles sounded like a good challenge to me. Essentially, we ran from one foul pole to the other foul pole along the warning track. We would jog until we got to the middle section, then we would sprint from the left centerfield gap to the right centerfield gap, then finish by walking to the foul line where we would immediately start the next one once we reached.

We were all running hard, pushing each other, and talking sh*t during each one. When we got to the final one, the dudes were gassed. I jokingly called out our speedy center fielder Chris Young (CY) for "dragging ass." He took the challenge and lined up next to me for the final one. We started off the jog portion at a good pace, bumping shoulders and playfully running our traps. We got close to the 375' sign in left centerfield and it was on. We both went into a full sprint, running stride-for-stride the entire time. Just as we were approaching the 375 sign in right-center field, I felt a twinge in my upper-left hamstring. I didn't think much of it until I laid in bed that night and felt a throbbing sensation where the top of the hamstring meets the butt.

I showed up the next day, and although the pain had not subsided, I did not tell the trainers and went about my work as scheduled. The way I came up in the A's organization, it was looked upon as a bad thing to ever be in the training room, so unless I absolutely had to be in there, I avoided it at all cost. I also felt that I was now a legitimate leader on the team and did not want to sit out any games because of a "twinge." I wanted to set an example that you don't have to be at 100% to play, even if it was just Spring Training.

Dumbass move. Possibly the stupidest decision of my life.

The twinge just got worse and worse through the course of Spring Training, and by the time the season started, I was practically playing on one leg. By the time we reached the end of the first month of the season, I could barely run. The only thing I had going for me was that I had a hit in 10 consecutive games and had a 10-day mustache to go with it. Right before the season, I went to a "mustache party" and felt like it would be a fun idea to bring back the art of the Furry Murray. Once the season started, I decided that I was going to grow out my 'stache so long as I got a hit, then would shave after any game in which I did not get a hit. As a complete joke, I declared 2008 the "year of the 'stache."

Shockingly, there was actually a trend of mustaches around baseball that season popping up everywhere, with Jason Giambi's lip lettuce getting a ton of attention in New York. By no means was it any sort of impressive streak, but I did hit in 14 consecutive games, and the mustache was flowing! Once the hitting streak ended on a bullsh*t call at first base on a play in which I was safe, the DL was inevitable. At this point both hamstrings were actually killing me. I had favored my right hamstring so much and for so long that I partially tore that one as well.

When the pictures came back from an MRI, the doctor said he had never seen anything like what I had going on. I was a mess. The decision was made to put me on the disabled list for the first time in my career. I spent my time rehabbing with Ken Krenshaw, the head athletic trainer, and Nate Shaw, the strength and conditioning coach. Within 3 weeks of busting my ass every day, these dudes had me dialed in. I took off on a rehab assignment to Visalia then rejoined the team in Boston. A few days later back in Arizona, I hit a double and decided to give my rehabbed hamstrings their first real test. I took off on the first pitch in an attempt to steal 3rd base. I got three-quarters of the way down the line, and then all of a sudden, it was as if somebody shot me in the left leg.

I heard a huge pop; my season was done.

As I hobbled toward the dugout, I will never forget the reaction of Diamondbacks fans showering me with boos. It was one thing getting booed when I would strike out, but knowing my season was done and this was the last time walking off the field for the 2008 season, this one hurt both physically and emotionally. There was one guy in particular sitting right above the dugout that stood up and leaned over the rail and began waving his finger and passionately screaming, "You suck, Byrnes, f*ck you, Byrnes."

I was hitting .209 with 6 homers in 206 sporadic, injury-filled at-bats. I had played parts of 5 seasons with the Oakland A's in front of their incredibly emotional fan base and sucked balls plenty along the way. At one point, I endured a historically epic 9-95 slump. I never got booed. I went to Colorado and Baltimore where I didn't even hit .200. I never got booed. I played all of 2006 and 2007 with the Diamondbacks and had plenty of ups and downs. I never got booed. There is no doubt that as soon as I signed the 3-year $30-million contract extension, fans no longer looked at me as a fun-loving underdog sort of dude. Their expectations changed, and they had no problem expressing their disappointment.

I understand the fans' sentiments, but as far as I was concerned, I am not sure what I could have done differently other than sitting out Spring Training. It's pretty simple; my horrific season was a result of trying too hard. If I had used better judgment in Spring Training, I could have been 100% by opening day and potentially not had to deal with the lingering hamstring issues and overall lack of production. As a fan myself, I appreciate passion, energy, and a fan base that cares about their players and their team. Personally, I was taught by my father never to boo performance, only a lack of effort. So, through all of this, the one thing that I was able to be proud of was that I was able to look myself in the mirror at night and know that my effort was always there, every f*cking day. No matter how much I got booed, there was not a fan that wanted me to play better and be 100% healthy more than I did myself.

The next day I underwent another MRI that revealed my left hamstring had just about ripped off the bone where it attaches to my ass. Essentially, it was hanging by a thread. The doctor in Arizona recommended that I have it surgically reattached. The recovery time was about a year. I decided to get a second opinion. My dad was able to get me in right away with Dr. Gary Fanton, the 49ers' team doctor who had a long history of dealing with hamstring injuries. Dr. Fanton's general philosophy cautioned against surgery unless there was no other alternative. One look at the MRI and Dr. Fanton immediately advised against any form of surgical repair. He felt that so long as it was not completely torn off the bone, the hamstring was going to have no problem healing itself. The recovery time was essentially the same either way but being able to avoid surgery was a definite bonus.

Fortunately for me, the Diamondbacks training staff, which I believe was one of the very best in all of baseball, decided to take on my extended rehab themselves. That meant that instead of being away from the team and not going on any road trips, I was able to travel with the guys and do my rehab with the training staff that I liked and trusted. As much as I was happy to still be around the team, I was also miserable being so close to the action and not being able to contribute in any way.

I had always heard from other guys who were injured about how difficult it was for them. Guys would talk about how other players and the coaching staff would ignore them. I never realized it because I felt like I always treated everybody the same way, regardless if they were healthy or injured, superstars or the last guy on the end of the bench, playing well or playing sh*tty. I ultimately judged my teammates on their character, not by what they were doing on a baseball field.

It was an eye-opening experience for me. Some dudes that I thought were friends above all else ended up being pieces of sh*t. I realize that it was a sensitive time for me, but several instances of blatant disrespect had me so disgusted it became very difficult to head to the ballpark on a daily basis. Toward the very end of the year, when I was finally cleared to hit in a batting practice group, one player asked, "Byrnes, why are you even here?"

Ultimately, I decided to take control of my emotions. It hurt badly, but I couldn't control another coach's, teammate's, or fan's perspective of me. I could only control doing my work and getting healthy, so that's what I did.

The 2008 off-season was one of the most grueling of my career. On top of the normal workout routine that would generally take up almost the entire day, I was vigorously rehabbing my hamstring and trying to get it back to normal. When I finally got to spring training, it still wasn't right. I could run in a straight line no problem, but it essentially took the entire spring until I was semi-comfortable turning around the bases. I was healthy enough to break camp with the team, but it was still very much a struggle to get back to the player I was before I had gotten hurt. Not to mention, my opportunities were nowhere near what they were pre-hamstring. The Diamondbacks had moved on, and I rightfully had to earn back any playing time I was going to get.

Whoever came up with the theory that you can't lose your job because of an injury is full of sh*t. Professional sports, like any other industry, is about producing, and if you are not producing for whatever reason, the team or business will go out and find somebody who will. One reason why I felt like I always was able to get along well with other outfielders that were considered my competition was because I figured if I did my job, my playing time would take care of itself, and it usually did. I also figured that if I sucked enough, the team would have no problem finding somebody else to come take my spot, and they didn't have any issues finding replacements.

That said, there is no reason to make it personal or hold any resentment against another guy trying to take your job. I promise you that once he or she is gone or eventually takes your job, there will be plenty more capable people waiting in line to do the exact same thing. Don't take it personal.

Human Crash Test Dummy Life Lesson #87

When you have a small problem, make sure to take preventative measures before it becomes a big problem. Treat people with respect, regardless of their position at work or in life. Embrace your competition because there will always be more out there. Even take it a step further and go out of your way to help your competition; the good vibes that will be added to the relationship and the rest of the team will be invaluable. Ultimately, we have no choice but to embrace the suck and everything that comes with it.

Chapter 88
Let Go, Let Life

"Incredible change happens in your life when you decide to take control of what you do have power over instead of craving control over what you don't."
-Steve Maraboli

I started the '09 season playing sporadically and struggled to find any sort of rhythm at the plate. I was also still only 8 months out of tearing my hamstring, which was supposed to have a healing time of at least 12 months. By June, I was finally starting to feel close to 100% and was taking much better at-bats. Just when things finally were starting to return to normal, Scott Feldman, a Bay Area native and pitcher for the Texas Rangers at the time, threw a 2-seam fastball that ran up and in, hitting me square in my left hand.

It wasn't good. I immediately took off my batting glove as I walked to first base, and my hand looked as if somebody had taken a sledgehammer to it. It was completely concaved. When Ken Crenshaw, our head athletic trainer, came out to check on me, I took one look at his face, and I knew it was broken. I didn't care; I refused to come out of the game. I had endured too much over the past year and a half, and I wanted to try to pretend as if it did not happen. I ran the bases and then after the inning headed out to left field to take my position. I caught one warm-up toss in between innings and then walked off the field. It quite possibly could have been the most excruciating pain I had ever felt, which essentially caused my entire arm to become numb. Two days later, I had surgery to put a plate and 8 screws into my hand. I was out for at least another 2 months.

I had dealt with a lot over the past year, and for the most part, I felt as if I had handled everything professionally and with pretty good perspective. After the X-rays confirmed that my hand was broken, I calmly showered up, got into my car, and began sobbing like a 3 year old. This was the first time that I had emotionally combusted in years.

On the ride home, I was reflecting on the past 12 months and thinking how things could not have possibly gone worse. Then, right in the middle of my self-pity party, driving 70 mph on the I-17 freeway, "BOOM!" The "Shaggin Wagon" loses control then comes up on 2 wheels, does a full 180 that leaves me facing head-on into oncoming traffic in the slow lane. My life literally flashed before me; I thought that was it.

Several cars swerved just missing me as I sat there seemingly in the middle of a war zone. I quickly turned the van around and realized I had completely blown at least one tire as I drove on the rim into the emergency lane. What probably would have freaked most people out actually had an opposite sort of effect on me. I felt this overwhelming comfort and peace. I then began hysterically laughing. As bad as I felt things were going in my life, I all of a sudden realized how many things in my life that I was grateful for, including life itself.

Most professional athletes are selfish pricks, and to this point in my life, I wasn't much different. You need to have an edge to excel at the highest level, and in order to have that edge, it generally starts with a "ME first" sort of attitude. For whatever reason, it took until that night for me to realize that my life had become much more than me, much more than baseball. 5 months earlier, I had become a father to a baby girl, and I don't even think I paused to understand the magnitude of what that meant. In a lot of ways, I feel like the series of events was God's way of telling me to slow down and instead of dwelling on all of the things that were not going well in my life at that point, appreciate all of the things that were.

When my wife Tarah arrived to pick me up on the side of the highway, the van was on a flatbed tow truck nearly totaled, and my broken hand was beginning to throb beneath the ace bandage. I realize this sounds corny but I needed a hug, and I am not sure if I ever received a bigger one in my life. Of all of the people in my life, she no doubt understood better than anyone how hard I had worked to get back onto the field and how much baseball meant to me. She was as emotionally rock-solid as anyone I had met in my life, so to now see her crying, I lost it once again. But this one was crying backed with laughter.

I spent the next 8 weeks focusing on learning what it meant to be a great dad and a great husband. I also realized there were other people that I had neglected in my life, including my own mom and dad, sister, and many other life-long friends who had always been there for me. I began to appreciate all the luxuries that I had always either taken for granted or ignored. I went from being selfish and miserable to selfless and exuberant. Very few professional athletes ever take the time to understand how fortunate they are to be playing a game for a living. I was not any different. I believe the constant battle to get to the top and then the constant battle to stay there takes away almost all of the time for reflection and appreciation. Sure, athletes will say all the right things, just as I did, about enjoying the experience, but I truly believe you don't fully appreciate something until either there is a major eye-opening experience or that something is gone. I experienced both. I began to truly appreciate the fact that I had been able to play professional baseball for over a decade and make a great living doing it. More importantly though, I began to realize what is the most important thing in the world.

"Nothing else than family." That is the response that I get each and every morning when I ask my 3 kids that very same question. When I was young, my parents were huge into positive affirmations. Whenever my sister or I would say, "I can't," we would have to follow that up with 10 "I know I can's."

Somewhere along the way, "Today is going to be a great day" became a mantra I would say before I got out of bed in the morning. So now, with my kids and the guide of a few Harbaugh family traditions, the routine has been expanded to, "Today is going to be a great day; attack each day with an enthusiasm unknown to mankind. What's the most important thing in the world? Nothing else than family. Who's got it better than us? NOOOOOOBODY!!!!!!"

Attitude and effort are the only two things in our direct control. Control your attitude and effort by reminding yourself of the most important things in your life.

As the hand healed, so did my life. I was no longer dependent on baseball as the ultimate reflection of my self-worth. I still loved the game, but I now realized that baseball was not life. In a lot of ways, I learned to let go. I let go of things that were out of my control, and I let go of worry and stresses that had plagued me ever since I began playing baseball professionally. I let go of all outside opinions and animosity toward me. I let go of the idea that baseball defined who I was in life. I focused on being in the moment. I focused on what it meant to be a great husband, father, son, brother and friend, all things that I had often failed miserably at before this time.

Human Crash Test Dummy Life Lesson #88

Life can be a bitch, and we will be constantly challenged. But until you learn to "let go" and "let life," you will be in a battle you cannot win.

Chapter 89
Free and Easy

*"Not giving a f*ck does not mean being indifferent; it means being comfortable with being different."*
-Mark Manson

When I finally got back onto the field in the middle of August, I was sent out on a 20-game rehab assignment with AAA Reno. Normally, somebody in my situation would play 3-10 games max, and so long as they were healthy, would be called back up to the big leagues. I had an extended conversation with general manager Josh Byrnes, and we both agreed that since it had been nearly 2 years since I last played healthy baseball, the best thing for me to do was get as many at-bats as possible in AAA, most likely using up the entire 20 days.

Brett Butler, the manager of Reno was an absolute hard-ass, and I absolutely loved it. It reminded me of my early days in the Minor Leagues when coaches truly coached and were not afraid to give advice to players in fear of stepping on another coach's toes. We actually stretched as a team and took infield, which essentially has become a lost art. We had a strict dress code on the road and running drills were done how they should be done, at 100%.

The guys on the team were awesome. It was like most AAA teams, an eclectic group of your budding prospects and aging veterans just trying to hang on. It reminded me of how and why baseball used to be fun. During the 20-day stretch, we had a 5-game series in Las Vegas. Let me repeat myself: a 5-game series in Vegas! I approached it as any veteran coming off two blown hamstrings and a broken hand, staring the end of his career in the face should: play hard, party hard, sleep little, do it all over again the next day. Throughout the course of my entire career, I was always the guy who would arrive hours before game time and make sure I got my workout in, extra batting practice, and anything else done to make sure I was 100% ready for the game. Rarely would another player ever beat me to the yard. This road trip was different. By no means was I going to go into the game unprepared, but to say I approached the series with an "I don't give a f*ck" attitude would be very accurate.

Ironically, it was the best baseball I had played in 2 years. I went 5 days of squaring up the baseball in just about every single at-bat. I also took the opportunity to show my AAA teammates the town and let them experience a little bit of the "big league" lifestyle. In 12 years of professional baseball, it was the most fun road trip on and off the field that I ever had.

When I read Mark Manson's book, *The Subtle Art of Not Giving A F*ck*, I couldn't help but think of that Las Vegas road trip and the success and joy I was able to experience because I truly didn't give a f*ck. I had accepted that my career could be coming to an end, which liberated any physical and mental reservations I or anybody else could have imposed on me.

Human Crash Test Dummy Life Lesson #89

It's okay to want something badly, and it's okay to work for something and to try hard. But oftentimes we care too much, and it actually restrains us from our full potential. Think of life like swinging a golf club or a baseball bat. It's been proven that tense, restrictive swings are a lot less powerful than free and easy swings. The harder we swing the club or the bat past a certain threshold, the worse results we get. Swing free and easy, live free and easy, and you will get incredibly powerful results.

Chapter 90
No Love

*"I focus on one thing.
Forgetting the past and looking forward to what lies ahead."*
-Philippians 3:13

Shortly after the Vegas series, I was back in the big leagues. Josh Byrnes, the General Manager of the Diamondbacks, made it a point to tell me that the team had already moved into a different direction and the probability of any sort of significant playing time was very unlikely. That September, I hit 3 home runs, stole 2 bases without getting caught, and had a .533 slugging percentage with an .846 OPS in 48 plate appearances in only 9 starts. All good numbers but more importantly, I was playing the type of baseball I played before tearing both hamstrings and shattering my hand. Even more importantly was that I was finally having fun again. I went into the off-season unbelievably optimistic about the upcoming year. I even went to the Dominican Republic for a few weeks to get some more at-bats and build upon the good feelings I had while rehabbing in AAA and playing the last month of the season.

When I returned home after the New Year, I got a call from a reporter saying that the Diamondbacks were going to release me. Release me? Didn't make a ton of sense. I was finally healthy, just finished a 2-month stretch of playing great baseball, and oh yeah, I was still owed $11 million. Even if Josh and AJ had no plans of using me as a regular guy, I still felt as if I had value off the bench and against left-handed pitching. For the most part, dudes that get released when they are owed a lot of money are either hurt, completely incompetent, or the worst teammate in the world. I wasn't hurt anymore, I just proved I was not completely incompetent, and I always prided myself on being not just a good teammate but a great teammate. Why in the f*ck would they release me?

2 hours later I got a call from Josh. They released me.

To say that I was heartbroken would be an understatement. I literally had put my heart, soul, blood, sweat, and tears into coming back from 2 years of devastating injuries. The Diamondbacks organization, who I was so grateful to for every opportunity they ever gave me, had essentially spit into my face and told me to go f*ck myself. Imagine getting married. First few years are awesome, and then the "honeymoon" period ends and many everyday-life realities kick in, making things difficult. You guys start arguing and even questioning the commitment that the two of you made to each other. Then, you decide to seek counseling and start to mend a relationship that appeared to be broken. Things are finally getting back to normal when you come home one day and all your sh*t is left out on the doorstep with the divorce papers and a pen.

Or you can just imagine one big fat kick in the nuts; that's how it felt.

As badly as it hurt, I had no choice but to quickly put my emotions in check and focus my energy on finding a job. I wanted to prove I was healthy; I wanted to prove I could still play. I had absolutely no time or energy to dwell on an organization's decision that I had absolutely no control over.

Human Crash Test Dummy Life Lesson #90

We could do all the right things, say all the right things, and have a perfect vision of the path in front of us, but then that path can become blocked. The path is closed. You have no choice but to find a new route. Get your ass moving, don't look back, and go carve out a new path. Regardless of what has happened in the past, the central focus needs to be on the moment and what lies ahead. Becoming consumed with anger or bad feelings when you feel like you have been wronged will only hold you back.

Chapter 91
Face It

"No legacy is so rich as honesty."
-William Shakespeare

One good thing from being sent down to the Minor Leagues 9 times, getting traded twice, and now released twice, was that I was getting used to rejection. It also meant that I was used to figuring out WHAT's NEXT?

I immediately got onto the computer and started to figure out what outfield situations looked like with the other 29 teams around baseball. The one team I kept coming back to was the Seattle Mariners. They had Ichiro in RF, a young stud Franklin Gutierez in CF, and Milton Bradley in LF. Ichiro was a lock to play every day, but Gutierez would probably get some days off in CF, and Milton Bradley was as injury-prone and volatile as any player in MLB. I figured he could combust at any time, and there could potentially be a significant amount of playing time in LF.

The first day teams could call, I heard from the Cardinals, Twins, and Mariners. The Cardinals and Twins showed interest, but the Mariners went all out. Jack Zduriencik, the Mariners general manager, insisted on personally calling me. Jack essentially laid out the same sort of situation that I had figured out on my own when researching the M's outfield. There was not a doubt in my mind that the Mariners were going to be the best opportunity for playing time, which was exactly what I needed.

This was the second time in my career that I had been a free agent, and I approached it nearly the exact same way as the first when choosing a team. There are 4 major criteria to consider: individual situation (potential playing time), team situation (how good are they going to be, other players on the team), geography (city the team plays in and Spring Training location), and money (multiple dollar bills with Benjamin Franklin's head on it).

The Mariners seemed to no doubt be the best "individual situation." They traded for Cliff Lee and had other quality off-season signs, so the "team situation" looked good. Seattle has always been one of my favorite cities, and their Spring Training facility in Arizona was 5 minutes from my house. The "money" was all taken care of courtesy of the Arizona Diamondbacks, who were responsible for paying nearly all of my $11 million salary. Seattle would only need to pay the minimum salary portion of my contract, which was around $300,000 or $400,000 at the time.

Just a few days later, I was a proud Seattle Mariner.

I went to Spring Training and it really could not have gone much better. I loved the organization and everything about the way they conducted business. I was getting all sorts of opportunities to play and was playing very well. A few weeks into the spring, I got my first and only chance at redemption against the team that had paid me to go away. Before the game was the first time I had talked to the Arizona media since being released. As badly as I wanted to reveal how I truly felt, I gave all the politically correct answers. I realize it was just a meaningless Spring Training game, but to be honest, it might as well have been Game 7 of the World Series. I had something to prove and wanted so badly to make a statement to the Diamondbacks that they f*cked up. Irony, fate, whatever you want to call it, Stephen Drew, the very first batter of the game for Arizona, hit a ball that was slicing down the left-field line. Playing left field, I sprinted toward the foul line at full speed, covering ground as if it was 2007 again, pre-hamstring injury. I then laid out in a Superman fashion, flying several feet through the air and made one of the best catches of my career. "Wooooooooooooooo!" In all my years playing baseball, I had never screamed so loudly.

I absolutely loved the guys on the Seattle team, and I had a feeling that we were going to win a lot of games. The rotation included Cliff Lee, Jason Vargas, and Doug Fister. Bullpen had two flame-throwers:

David Aardsma and Brandon League at the back end. The lineup featured Ichiro and Chone Figgins at the top and Ken Griffey Jr. in the middle. There seemed to be a perfect balance between young players and veterans. The bench, or "goon squad" as we liked to refer to ourselves, was led by Mike Sweeney, one of my favorite teammates and one of the best people I ever met in baseball. Every day, Sweeney and I would hit in the same batting practice group and play the game where we would try to hit opposite field homers. Sweeney coined them as "oppo tacos," and the legend was born from there. The talent on the team was legit, and the vibe around camp was even better. Overall, this team had all the makings of a winner, right up until the point the season started.

We scuffled badly as a team through the first month of the season, and individually, I sucked ass in my limited roll. Throughout the course of my career, I generally struggled whenever I did not get consistent playing time, and this was not any different. I went from playing at least every other day in Spring Training to playing once a week, and the results were atrocious. Late in the spring, I had an at-bat against Rafael Betancourt in an exhibition game in New Mexico that completely baffled me. Dude kept throwing straight fastballs right down the middle, and I kept fouling them off until I finally struck out swinging through another cock shot. Instead of writing it off to facing a guy who throws a great 4 seam fastball, a rarity in the game these days, I completely mind-f*cked myself by thinking I needed to make some sort of major change. Years later, with the invention of stat cast, it was no surprise when I found out that Rafael Betancourt had the highest spin rate in baseball.

I made my first start of the regular season a few days after the Betancourt debacle and struggled. A couple weeks into the season, I could not buy a hit. The few good at-bats that I did have resulted in hard hit balls that found a way into a fielder's glove. I got a start in Chicago against the White Sox and was hoping sh*t was going to turn in my favor. The result: 5 pretty good at bats and 0 hits. I also scaled the left-field wall to rob a homer, a play that you would still be seeing highlights of today if it had not come out of my glove while I was bringing it back. The ball actually flung so far back into the field that the shortstop picked it up!

I had endured failure in baseball since I was 9 years old, but for whatever reason, maybe 2 years of being hurt, the D Backs releasing me, the promising Spring Training and the untimely extremely-disappointing perfect storm start to the season, I was mentally beat down. I needed a break. I needed air.

When I finally left the stadium, I began walking the streets of the south side Chicago, wearing checkered Vans and an OP shirt. I was not in a safe place, but at that point, I did not give a f*ck. I was in such a rage that I would have invited any sort of altercation had one happened to present itself. Looking back, I was in a relatively unstable state of mind. The people who were on the streets were looking at me as if I just got dropped out of a space ship from Mars. I had no problem staring back.

After walking aimlessly for almost an hour, I finally realized I better get my ass back to the city. My compass then became the tall buildings of downtown Chicago several miles off in the distance as nightfall began to set in. Even today, the entire walk still seems like some sort of daze. I remember run-down apartment buildings, liquor stores, and sirens the entire way. By the time I got back into the city, 3 hours had gone by and it was completely dark. Sweeney called because he was worried about me and actually came and met me at a restaurant on the outskirts of the city. I would have never asked anybody, but I needed somebody to lean on. I am forever grateful for him being there.

A few days later, back in Seattle, I came into the game in the 9th inning with 0 outs in a tie game as a pinch runner for Ken Griffey Jr. I ended up on 3rd base with 0 outs, and somehow, we managed not to score. I came up to bat the next inning with a runner on 3rd base and 1 out. Mike Brumley, our 3rd base coach, began flashing signs. I thought I got the squeeze sign, but I was not positive and figured if I asked for the sign again it would give away that something was up. I decided that I was going to wait to see if Ichiro was coming home, at which point I would bunt.

Dumb idea. Ichiro was coming but I obviously squared around late, and then when I saw that the pitch was way outside I instinctually pulled my bat back. The catcher made a nice backhanded play and tagged Ichiro out at home plate. I had never been more embarrassed on a baseball field. I completely hung Ichiro out to dry. Why did I not at least toss the bat at the ball? I had always been a horsesh*t bunter and had never attempted a squeeze in my life. Pair that up with Rangers rookie closer Neftali Feliz on the mound, a flame throwing right-hander with all sorts of movement on his ball, and I guess it was just the perfect recipe for disaster, much like the season itself.

We went on to lose the game, and of course, as soon as I felt like there was no way things could get any worse, they did. I was so upset after the game I didn't even shower. I changed into my street clothes, grabbed my beach cruiser, which was my means of transportation around Seattle, and steamed out of the clubhouse. As I flung the doors open, there was a throng of media waiting for the locker room to open. Apparently, also standing there was General Manager Jack Zduriencik.

I put my head down, hopped on my bike, and rode out. I did not think anything of it at the time. I bolted through the streets of Seattle until I got back to our condo on the other side of City. Tarah was waiting at the door, holding our daughter, anticipating my arrival. She didn't say anything and neither did I. She handed me "Peanut" and there was no more comforting feeling in the world than my 1 year old latching on to me as tightly as she could. Tarah was 8-months pregnant at the time, just found out that her mom had terminal breast cancer, and had to deal with her husband going through a major crossroads in his career. Life was not easy for any of us at that point.

I then went to the room and laid on the bed. Peanut snuggled into her normal spot underneath my left arm and quickly fell asleep. I spent the next hour or so staring out the window at the Seattle skyline. I thought about my life, which had now become our life. For years, I lived for one person, myself. I now was living for much more. Life was no longer about just me. I was 34 years old; I had made more money than I could have ever dreamed of playing a sport that I loved more than anything in the world. I had a beautiful wife, a gorgeous 1-year-old daughter and another baby due any day.

Yet, baseball was psychologically beating me up on a daily basis. The injuries, the struggles, and the overall baseball experience of the last 2+ years were eating me up inside. For the first time in my life, I no longer looked forward to going to the ballpark. Baseball was no longer fun. That's when I knew.

I turned to Tarah as she got into bed next to me..."It's time to go home. I am done."

I had never quit anything in my life, and I was not about to start, but if I knew that was it so did the Mariners.

Human Crash Test Dummy Life Lesson #91

Face the realities of life head-on. Don't hide from your emotions; don't deny their existence. Address the truth within yourself and do your best to objectively look at your situation. At that point, figure out what is in your control, and then make a decision on how you plan to move forward.

Chapter 92
Balance Your Act

"Life is like riding a bicycle. To keep your balance, you must keep moving."
-Albert Einstein

Two days later Jack Z called me into Don Wakamatsu's office. I made it easy for both of them. "This will be the easiest release you guys have ever had to do. Thank you so much for the opportunity to revitalize my career. I can't tell you how thankful I am for you guys believing in me. I am sorry I did not play to my potential."

Jack and Don both sat there, silent. I am pretty sure there are not too many cases where somebody's instinctual reaction is to thank the team that is about to fire him or her, but I could not help myself. I truly was grateful. Jack then broke the silence by saying that if there is any team I wanted him to call, he would be more than willing. He told me he was inspired by the Spring Training that I had and knew that I still had plenty of great baseball left in me.

"Thanks Jack, but this is it. I am ready to move on with my life. I am ready to figure out what's next. I'm done."

Don Wakamatsu then chimed in... "Byrnesie, in all my years coaching, I have never had anybody play as hard as you."

That's when I knew it was okay to walk away, knowing I left absolutely everything I had out on the field.

I went back to my locker, packed up my stuff and walked out of a Major League clubhouse for the final time as a big league player. Tarah was waiting for me, and when she saw me with two duffel bags draped over each shoulder, I didn't have to say anything. She knew. "Half Moon Bay?"

"Yup."

We didn't dwell on sh*t. That's not who my wife is and sure as f*ck is not who I am. Immediately, the logistics of packing up and moving out of our Seattle condo became the only concern. Within hours, we were on the road driving through the middle of the night. I had a morning surf session and afternoon golf round lined up, so I wanted to get home. For the first time in 12 years, I felt liberated.

At the time, the only thing I knew was that there was a major imbalance in my life. As I mentioned, physically I was in great shape, but physical wellness is just 1/6th of what makes us happy, according to a sign I read above the urinal at MLB Network. Emotional wellness, occupational wellness, intellectual wellness, social wellness, and spiritual wellness are all factors that complete who we are as humans. It is vital for us to be in touch with all 6. At that time, I was not even close. As a matter of fact, when I read about these different forms of wellness, it started to make a lot of sense. Thinking back to some of the most difficult times in my life, I was severely lacking in at least one if not more of the categories.

I loved and appreciated every single day I spent as a professional baseball player, but there was no doubt that baseball was an all-encompassing element that controlled my entire life for a better part of two decades. Thankfully, the best thing I ever did was refuse to let the game define me as a person. There are way too many ups and downs within the game to put your self-worth into it. More importantly, the game is going to end at some point for everybody. I don't care if you are the last dude on the bench struggling year in and year out to make a team or a sure-fire Hall-of-Famer. It will end. I was always ready for that day. I always looked forward to that day. An entire new chapter of my life began on the drive home.

Human Crash Test Dummy Life Lesson #92

Think about the balances in your life and reflect upon which areas you may need to work on. Decide what changes you need to make to find your inner peace. Oftentimes the adjustments will be small, and at other periods of your life, the changes will be monumental. Ultimately, life is constantly changing which means we must be changing with it in order to maintain balance. So long as you are willing to embrace change, you will begin living your life on a different level.

Chapter 93
Cover the Bases

"It's time to say goodbye, but I think goodbyes are sad and I'd much rather say hello. Hello to a new adventure."
-Ernie Harwell

My first few days home were a trip. I kept feeling like I needed to be somewhere. The very first day, I played golf with Brendan Royer, John Gall, and Matt Doyle. I grew up playing little league with all 3 guys, and they all happened to now be playing softball for the Dutch Goose, a legendary local burger and beer joint, every Wednesday night. They did their best to talk me into coming out and playing. What seemed like a joke at first actually started to sound pretty fun. By the time the 18 holes were over, I was in.

That was on Monday. On Tuesday, I was contacted by a couple more teams in addition to the Dutch Goose. The offers from both organizations were essentially the same: go to AAA on a 1-month contract, get into a comfortable groove of playing every day again, and if I was not in the big leagues by the end of the month, I would be a free agent again. That was no doubt the best and most ideal scenario I could ask for. The most fun I had playing baseball in the past 3 seasons was the time I spent rehabbing with the Reno Aces. I also needed consistent playing time and that was not going to happen at the big-league level at that point. It would have been a very realistic scenario for me to sign, go to AAA and play well, then find myself contributing on a contending team down the stretch. I was 34 years old at the time. There was no doubt in my mind I could continue to keep myself in good enough shape to play into my 40s. The biggest issue with age in baseball though is opportunity. Opportunities for somebody at 34 compared to 24 are limited and typically short-lived.

I also thought about what my career and life would be like at 40 years old if I did continue to play. Let's say I signed with St. Louis, played well, got called up, and continued to play well; what sort of job security would that mean? Most likely none, I would be right back in the same spot the next spring, fighting to make a 25-man roster and scratching and clawing for every at-bat. I have mentioned before that I had sucked as a part-time player in the past, but most importantly, it wasn't fun for me.

At 24, I had no problem grinding through part-time opportunities because the thought and idea of one day playing every day far outweighed whatever issues I incurred while sitting on the bench. As a 34-year-old husband and father, I had a much different mindset. So what if I played another 5-7 years bouncing around from team to team doing the same bullsh*t routine, heading to Spring Training every February with no idea if that would be the team I would be with in April? I essentially would be playing on a day-to-day contract in a sport with very little loyalty. At 24, I was single with one person to worry about.

At 34, I had a wife, a daughter, and another one just a few weeks away from being born. I wasn't living for one; I was living for three and soon to be four. The idea of being away from them for 6 months was heart breaking, and for what? Financially, I had made enough money to comfortably live the rest of my life. Baseball-wise, I loved playing the game more than anything, yet the issue was that I was no longer looked at as an everyday player, meaning more likely than not, I was going to be spending the majority of my career from that point on watching more baseball than I would be playing. I had already fought the baseball fight and won; I had already fought the baseball fight and lost. I was psychologically drained from fighting the same fight for 12 years in a row. I needed a new fight. I needed a new challenge.

Wednesday afternoon rolled around and I had long conversation with my dad. He felt like I had a responsibility to tie up some loose ends in Seattle. I had been perceived as very flakey and somebody who didn't care, which was the furthest thing from the truth. Since I had been released, my phone was blowing up from several different media outlets. I had ignored all calls since Sunday, and I had no problem leaving it that way.

After talking to my dad, I decided that I was going to make two phone calls, the first being to a Seattle radio station who has a producer named Jessamine Macintyre that I had known since her days at ESPN. I needed to explain my side of the botched squeeze and bike ride out of town. I wanted to convey how much I loved the Mariners organization and everything Jack Z and WAK were doing. I wanted to make sure everybody in Seattle knew that I did not give up on them. I wanted them to know how badly I wished I had hit better and how badly I wished our entire team had played to our potential. It really was a talented group of guys and a bunch of good dudes.

The other phone call was to MLB.com writer Steve Gilbert. Gilbert was MLB.com's beat writer for the Arizona Diamondbacks and I always felt like he treated me fairly. I explained my story to him. I explained how much I still loved the game and how fortunate I was to play baseball at the highest level for parts of 11 Major League seasons. I expressed my gratitude to the Diamondbacks organization for giving me a shot to play and revitalize my career there. I also explained that I was done. I was ready to move on with my life and figure out WHAT'S NEXT? Very casually at the end of the phone call, in response to Steve's final question, "are you really done?" I told him I was on my way to play in a Wednesday beer league softball game with a bunch of dudes I grew up with. "Trust me, I am done."

Human Crash Test Dummy Life Lesson #93

Trust your instincts, but make sure to step back and look at your situation from a much broader perspective. Listen to your emotions but do not let your emotions make your decisions for you. Lean on those closest to you and always hear what they have to say. Ultimately, it is your life; you are the one who will have to make the decision. When the right moment of opportunity arises to move on, there is no need to look in the rearview mirror. There will be an entire new life right in front of you.

Chapter 94
Authenticity Plays

"I try to make music with emotion and integrity. And authenticity. You can feel when something's authentic, and you can feel when it's not: you know when someone's trying to make the club record, or trying to make the girl record, or trying to make the thug record. It's none of that. It's just my emotions."
-Jay Z

The same night I talked to the Seattle radio station and Steve Gilbert, I also played in my first game for the "Dutch Goose" in the Menlo Park Recreational Softball League. I absolutely got my dick handed to me. The softball swing is much different than the baseball swing, and I kept beating everything into the ground. In 4 at-bats I had 3 groundouts and 1 seeing eye, ground ball single up the middle. Regardless of the results, I had a blast. I pounded a few Coors Lights throughout the course of the game and talked sh*t to and with all my boys that I literally used to play little league baseball with. It was as if I was in some sort of time warp, and I absolutely loved it. The game was once again pure. In a lot of ways my entire athletic career had come full-circle.

The next day when Steve Gilbert's MLB.com article came out, it explained my decision to move on from playing baseball. Just as our conversation had gone, he mentioned towards the very end of the article that I was on my way to play in a beer league softball game. Even when I read it, I had no idea that the one blurb about softball at the end of the article would cause so much noise. By the end of the week I had media requests from every major outlet across the nation. To be honest, for the first time in my life I was overwhelmed with the attention. The next Wednesday I showed up at the game and every major news station from the Bay Area was there with cameras. Scott Ostler, the legendary San Francisco Chronicle columnist, and Dan Brown, a very well-respected writer for the San Jose Mercury, were both there to do stories. All I could think is "F*CK, I started playing softball so I could relax with my boys, down some beers and try to hit bombs. If I did hit bombs, great. If I didn't, I wouldn't give a f*ck, so long as the beer was cold, and the burgers were good, I didn't give two sh*ts."

Now I had a contingency of media members there to document my every move on the softball field. I had no choice but to laugh. That night we were facing the "Barnes Brawlers" who had gone over two seasons without losing a game. The pitcher was Bill Lopez, a legendary bay area softball player and former little league coach. As a matter of fact, although Bill will try to disagree, he passed over me in the little league draft when I was 9 years old. I had redemption on my mind; I had a score to settle.

What makes hitting a softball difficult is when the pitcher puts a huge arc on the ball. The best pitchers have the ability to toss the ball to the extent of the legal limit every time, occasionally getting called for exceeding the arch limit, in which the pitch does not count in that case. Apparently, Bill was unimpressed with all the media attention and was out to do what he does best: get dudes out. He hit that arc limit with the first two pitches. The third pitch did not have quite the same difficult arc and I absolutely unloaded on it. In 2007 against the Philadelphia Phillies, I hit a ball into some dude's french fries sitting in the TGI Friday's above left field. The ball was estimated to have traveled 473 feet. The ball I hit against Bill Lopez and the Barnes Brawlers very easily could have been further. A video of the home run went viral and got more than 100,000 YouTube hits within the first couple days.

The next week the Jim Rome Show came out to do a piece. The Stanford Marching Band came out to show their support for the Goose and took over both sets of bleachers! They razed the other team and came up with several different chants throughout the course of the entire game. The Dutch Goose is of course famous for their burgers and beer, but the true locals know it is their deviled eggs that set them apart from their competition. So on cue, one set of bleachers would shout "DEVILED" then the other set of bleachers screamed "EGGS!" The only other place I played where the atmosphere came close to resembling Nelon Park during a recreational league softball game was in the Dominican Republic when Licey and Aguillas squared off.

Quite honestly, for that short period of time during the summer of 2010, I am not sure the recreational softball world had ever seen anything like it. The media attention eventually died down and the band stopped coming to games. Yet for the people who were there and got to experience the Dutch Goose playing softball on Wednesday nights and the circus act that came with it, they were treated to a lifetime of epic and comical memories. It was pretty f*cking cool!

Human Crash Test Dummy Life Lesson #94

When you do something authentically, it will always resonate with people way more than anything that is choreographed. The power of authenticity is as great as or better than any other characteristic you can possess. Your authentic character will have an incredible influence on anybody you come into contact with and ideally will serve as an inspiration to others. Also, there is nothing better than connecting with old friends. Old friends give us a humbling connection to our past and a beautiful and AUTHENTIC perspective going forward.

Chapter 95
Yes, Yes, Yes

"If somebody offers you an amazing opportunity but you are not sure you can do it, say yes - then learn how to do it later!"
-Richard Branson

Throughout my entire career, I was never considered a top prospect or any sort of superstar, and I am incredibly thankful for it. The game continued to humble me to the point where I was not sure exactly how long I was going to be able to play. This allowed me to continue to think about WHAT'S NEXT. A couple weeks after I got done playing, I got a call from Kyle Peterson, the same Kyle Peterson who purposely drilled me in the ass and caused me to charge the 2nd baseman when we were freshman in college. Kyle was the lead color analyst for ESPN's college baseball coverage and wanted to know if I had any interest in joining him in the booth for the regionals in Miami.

At this point, I had completely disassociated myself from baseball. I wasn't following MLB let alone college baseball. On the surface, it didn't make a ton of sense to head to Miami to call 7 games in 4 days for teams and players I knew nothing about.

I called Kyle back. "F*ck it, I'm in."

I felt like this would be the perfect opportunity to slowly get back into the game. I headed down to Miami, not having any idea what to expect. I had never been in the booth and I obviously knew very little about the current college game. In 4 days I called 7 games, riding the coat tails of one of the most underrated play-by-play guys in the business, Clay Matvick, and one of the best color commentators at any level, Kyle Peterson. I learned a lot about the timing of calling a game, when to talk, when to shut up, and when to tell a story about European dudes and mankinis. That was also where the term "oppo taco" had its coming out party and became known in households across the country. I had an absolute blast talking to coaches and players and doing my best to learn about the fabric of the teams.

Human Crash Test Dummy Life Lesson #95

Sometimes you won't think you are ready to move on to a new phase of your life, and then an opportunity may arise that just speaks to you. Don't pass up on that opportunity, even if it is not the exact thing you may envision. Taking advantage of every little opportunity for growth is the key to successfully moving forward. Little opportunities and little things make big opportunities and big things happen. It's all universally connected.

Chapter 96
Ace is Wild

"Can you pull the flag please?"
-Phil Mickelson

Ironically, just a few weeks later I got a call from Todd LaRocca, my old recruiting host at Stanford and my current financial advisor. I was in San Diego visiting for a week with the family, and he invited me to play golf at Santa Luz, a very nice track just north of Rancho Santa Fe. I was primarily there to surf, so I politely declined. He then proceeded to tell me that there was not a wave in San Diego that would match the experience that I would have if I golfed with him and his mystery guest. Jokingly I responded, "Dude, I was just hanging with Tiger Woods on the driving range at Isleworth, so unless it's Tiger or "Lefty" (Phil Mickelson), I am not interested."

Rock adamantly responded, "Just show up!"

When I arrived at the course at 7 am the next morning, I headed to the range to whack some balls while I waited for Rock to arrive. There was one other dude hitting balls on the other end of the range that just so happened to resemble "Lefty". Soon after, LaRocca walked up. "Byrnesie!!! Have you met Phil?"

Fact of the matter was that LaRocca had befriended a guy by the name of Harry Rudolph, who at one time was one of the greatest amateur golfers in the world and Phil Mickelson's arch rival growing up in the San Diego area. Rudolph had just begun playing competitively again and he and Mickelson had been playing a bunch of golf together. Rock brought me along as his partner as we took on the former amateur star and arguably the world's best golfer. We were f*cked from the get-go, but did it really matter?

Word on the street was that Phil liked to gamble, and in this case, the street's word was gold. We settled on an 18-hole team Nassau game where Rock and I would take on Phil and Harry. My index at the time was an 11, Rock was a 3, Harry's was a +2, and somebody tell me how you are actually supposed to handicap the 2nd best golfer in the world? Phil played at a +4; this is where we got screwed. I got 15 strokes from Phil and 13 from Harry. I also agreed to play Phil head to head in another 18-hole Nassau game. My individual game with Phil was done by the 12th hole. I got SMOKED. Rock played well so we hung tight on the team game before butchering the 18th hole. Nonetheless, the lost dollars were well worth the experience.

Regardless of the sandbagging and trash talking, Phil and Harry are both very likable dudes. We hit the clubhouse for lunch, and then Phil wanted to go Round 2. Even if it ended up costing me my kids' college fund, I was in. We had the same team game, and even though I got thumped, I went with the same Indy game against Phil as well. The second round I played well and somehow managed to not lose money. Before it even settled in that we just played 2 rounds with one of the best golfers of all time, Phil invited us to play with him and his brother the next day at the Grand in San Diego. Either he enjoyed our company or thought we were easy money; I am guessing probably a little bit of both.

The next day, Rock and I showed up at the Grand and met Phil and his brother Tim for breakfast. At the time, Tim was the head golf coach at the University of San Diego and you could tell he was very passionate about teaching the game. Tim also loved racehorses and had owned a few ponies in the past. Ironically, I had gotten into the horse racing game with Luis Gonzalez and Craig Counsell, and we had just sold off our last horse. Over breakfast the four of us basically formed a new horse racing partnership that got us back in the game. Because I had pushed my bets with Phil in the second round the day before, we played the first round at the Grand with me getting the same amount of strokes (15). I had no chance.

Late in the second round at Santa Luz the day before, I had hit a nice shot and had about a 10-foot birdie putt. Phil's drive had drifted to the right, so his only play was to an area about 30 yards in front of the green. I had a 10-foot birdie putt and was getting a stroke; he was

30 yards away from the green and had a ridiculously difficult shot for birdie. The pin was in the front and I was walking by to get an early read on my putt when Phil shouted out for me to pull the flag.

"Pull the flag? Come on, dude, you can't even see the hole!"

"Just pull the flag!"

I yanked it, and then he pulled out one of his famous flop shots that landed just on the front edge of the green, then rolled towards the hole as if he had putted it. It dropped into the center cup; birdie! I missed my putt so with my stroke we pushed the hole. It was the most incredible shot I had ever seen on a golf course.

On the first hole the next day, I was again on the green with a birdie putt and getting a stroke. As I drove toward the green, I shouted to Phil, who had yet to hit his approach shot from about 100 yards. "Hey, you want me to pull the flag again?"

Without hesitation Phil fired back, "No, but grab it out of the hole for me, I'll make it anyway."

He then proceeded to hit a shot that seemed to be a bit left of the hole. When the ball hit the green, it immediately started rolling to the right and tracking the flag. The ball then hit the flag and dropped in. This is the type of story that you hear second-hand that sounds cool but seems so ridiculous you have a hard time believing it. Two days in a row, he called his shot, one from 30 yards and another from 100. I played four rounds with Phil and those were the only two shots he told me he was going to make the entire time, and he drilled them both. Like I told him immediately after, "F*ck the PGA, dude, this is straight up magician sh*t. You are in the wrong profession."

The first round at the Grand I got throttled again. We had lunch afterwards with Doug Manchester Jr., the owner of the Grand. The Manchester family is an iconic San Diego family, very instrumental in the development of the greater San Diego area. Doug was a smooth and good-looking guy that dabbled in the professional golf world himself. He seemed like a very good dude, especially when you could imagine the privileged upbringing that he had. After lunch, we headed back out for a second round, this time in a five-some with Doug joining us. To Phil's credit, he now gave me a stroke a hole to give me a chance to even the bets. When we got to the 11th hole, despite the extra Mickelson generosity, I was once again getting bamboozled.

The 11th hole at the Grand is a downhill, 212-yard Par 3. Phil stuck it within 10 feet. The 3 other guys were on the green as well. I then stepped up to the tee and began talking to my 6 iron out loud. "One time, Mr. 6 Iron, get inside Phil's ball; he has been talking trash and pulling rabbits out of his ass for 4 rounds now. F*ck him and his sandbagging +4 ass. Nice and easy, dude. Let's do this."

I then proceeded to take a whack and absolutely nutted it. The ball started over the left sand trap and then began slightly cutting back towards the green. It then hit the fringe just right of the trap and began slowly tracking toward the hole. The green was cluttered with the 4 other balls so it was tough to follow exactly where my ball went, but it seemed to have disappeared. Tim Mickelson then blurted out, "Holy sh*t, I think that went in!!!" He grabbed his range finder and looked through the mini telescope. "I don't see it, dude."

I did my best to try to play it cool, but the thought of hitting my first hole in one while playing with the Mickelson brothers, the owner of the golf course, and one of my very best friends was beyond surreal. When we got to the green, there were still only 4 balls in sight. I jumped out of the cart when it was still moving at probably at least 15 mph. I barely caught my feet and immediately broke into a full sprint toward the hole, stopped just short, took a deep breath, and looked down. I then looked back up at the guys, shaking my head and letting out a huge sigh. Rock then chimes in, "Where did the ball possibly go then?"...

I delayed a few more seconds, reached down into the hole and grabbed the ball.

"Right f*cking here, dude!!! WOOOOOOOOOO HOOOOOOOOOOOO!!!!!

Rock then came jamming in from about 10 yards away, launching himself into our signature celebration move, the flying chest bump. He was obviously the most excited, figuring he was my partner in our money game, but this is something you can't put any sort of price on. The Mickelson brothers seemed stoked as I posed for a few pics with Phil by the flagstick and with the ball. Phil then grabbed his cell phone and called the clubhouse. "Hey, this is Phil Mickelson, we just had a hole-in-one on number 11, can you please bring out your two most expensive bottles of wine and put them on Mr. Byrnes' tab. Thanks!" By far and away, the most f*cked-up rule in golf: a dude hits a hole in one and he is the one who has to pay. Manchester insisted on taking care of the wine, but Phil, the hardcore golf traditionalist, made sure that didn't happen. Overall, between the wine and the bets it was a very expensive two days, but worth every last penny!!!

Human Crash Test Dummy Life Lesson #96

When it comes to getting along with people in life, find out what somebody likes and ask them about it with genuine interest. Play their game and do what you can to pique their interest. Life and opportunities come at you hard and fast. Don't pass up either. Life is meant to be lived and opportunities are meant to be taken advantage of. When you act, you never know what sort of extraordinary things will happen.

Chapter 97
Conform Consciously

"Individual commitment to a group effort - that is what makes a team work,
a company work, a society work, a civilization work."
-Vince Lombardi

After broadcasting the Super Regional, I made a trip to ESPN in Bristol, Connecticut to meet with a couple of top executives in charge of hiring talent. Immediately after, I made my first trip to Major League Baseball Network in Secaucus, New Jersey. I wasn't exactly sure what I wanted to do, but I knew I loved live TV. MLB Network had me go on the air during their flagship show "MLB Tonight" and I absolutely fell in love. I was on the air for 4 hours straight with MLBN's up and coming superstar host Greg Amsinger, and two of my favorite people I ever came across in baseball, Harold Reynolds and Sean Casey. We moved in and out of the best parts of each game, commenting as if we were sitting on a couch at home.

Because MLBN is owned by Major League Baseball, they have the ability to go to live look-ins at every one of the games and often at the most critical times. For example, it could be 10 pm in New York and Aaron Judge is up with a runner on 2nd base with 2 outs in the 9th inning. Immediately after Judge wins the game with a 500-foot homer, we now go to Houston where it is 9:05 pm and Dallas Keuchel has a perfect game going into the 7th inning. Keuchel gets through the 7th so we go out to San Francisco where it is 7:10 pm local time in the 1st inning, and the Giants already have the bases loaded against Clayton Kershaw and the Dodgers with Buster Posey at the plate. Essentially, it is next-generation baseball, or as I like to describe it, baseball for people with ADD. We go into the best games at the best times and get to naturally react to real time action. I couldn't have asked for a more entertaining job in the world, so when they offered me a contract to come and work with them, I was in.

The reason why MLBN has had so much success in the early going is because of the man that ran it, Tony Petitti. For years, Tony ran CBS Sports and is known for putting together a very clean product that can be looked at as extremely efficient and relatively conservative. John Entz, who I met at Best Damn Sports Show when he was with FOX Sports, was second in command when it came to hiring and managing talent. I am going to assume because I did not fit Tony's prototypical mold of a broadcaster that it was Entz who in many ways had to vouch for me.

The first year working at MLBN, I learned a ton through personal on-air experience but mainly from John Entz riding my ass every single day. It actually became a goal of mine to try to make it through a show without an email or phone call from Entz afterwards. He was determined to turn me into a legitimate broadcaster, and although it was frustrating at times, he helped bring me to the next level. With my goofy personality and long-haired surfer look, I had an image that, no matter what I said as a broadcaster, was going to be difficult for some people to overcome. I don't care one bit if people criticize my look or the way I talk. They can call me "Spicoli," make fun of my California lingo, or disagree with everything that comes out of my mouth, yet the one thing that nobody will ever be able to say with any sort of validity is that I am unprepared.

Much like baseball, I was never the best player and by no means am I the best broadcaster, but I promise you that each and every single day, I did and will continue to do everything in my power to be the best that I am capable of becoming. Yes, I do realize I am channeling my inner John Wooden. The best advice that Entz gave me, which I also heard from legendary Giants broadcaster Duane Kuiper as well, "Make sure you are good before being funny."

In the early going, I would be up on the set joking around with the guys almost to the point where I didn't even feel like I was on TV, and at times, I would pass over opportunities for legitimate and quality baseball analysis. It finally reached a boiling point one night when I started off the broadcast wearing a Jerry Garcia psychedelic tie and promptly recognized that it was "Grateful Dead" night in San

Francisco. I then closed the show paying homage once again to "The Dead" by busting out my iPhone and playing "Uncle John's Band" into the microphone attached to my shirt. What I perceived as TV gold turned to pure pandemonium on the set and in the control room. Something about MLBN not having the licensing rights to play the song set off mass chaos. After talking to the producers after the show, I figured I had officially sealed my fate at the Network. As a matter of fact, when I got the phone call from Entz the next morning, I answered the call with, "Am I fired?"

"Not yet, but you are getting very close, this isn't the f*cking Eric Byrnes show!"

I apologized and recognized that I needed to tighten up my game and was willing to continue to make adjustments.

Through the course of the entire next year, I made sure I played within the rules without compromising who I was as a person or a broadcaster. All was going well and I was on my best behavior until Harold Reynolds came to me just minutes before we went on MLB Tonight and told me he wanted to reenact a play he saw in Chicago, where Koyie Hill, the Cubs back-up catcher, was sitting in the bullpen and refused to move as the left fielder came into the bullpen to make the play. Harold asked what I would have done had I been in left field and I told him I would have ran right over Hill and hoped for some sort of interference call.

"Alright, I'll be Hill and show me what you would have done. I'll set it up as soon as we come on camera."

I responded, "Hold on, dude, you want me to blow you up?"

"Do what you would do if you were on the field."

The next thing I know we are on live TV and Harold is describing the play and then says, "Hey, Byrnesie, what would you have done?"

Without hesitation, I came running over to where Harold was sitting on a big water jug and absolutely lit his ass up. To be honest, I thought I might have really jacked him up. Once I knew he was okay we both got a good laugh. I am biased but it was definitely one of the finer moments in MLB Network's history.

Human Crash Test Dummy Life Lesson #97

Do your job but don't ever compromise who you are as a person just to appease somebody else. Be willing to learn and make adjustments, but also share your perspective as to what you believe is the best way to go about doing your job.

First and foremost, be a team player. The best teams are made up of individuals that are striving toward a common goal while maintaining their individual identity. A person's freedom of expression is necessary to get the most out of their talents.

Chapter 98
Tebow Time

"We have to humble ourselves and the way you do that is by serving other people."
-Tim Tebow

Working with MLB Network has put me in New York City around 120 nights a year. As my kids are getting older, it has been fun for the family to travel back with me at times and experience a culture much different than Half Moon Bay or Truckee. The studios are located in Secaucus, New Jersey, where most of the other guys stay when they come into the area to work at the Network. From the get-go, I figured if I was going to travel 3000 miles away from home to work, I could travel a few more miles across a river so I could stay in and experience what many would refer to as the greatest city in the world. I originally stayed at various hotels in the Meatpacking/Chelsea area until I recently bought a condo. Not surprising, there are several celebrities that either live in or frequent that area of the city.

There is a restaurant named "Catch" in the heart of the Meatpacking area that I will usually go to, post up at the bar, crush a few drinks, sushi, and get some solid people watching in. I was randomly there sucking down a couple Tito's and sodas, waiting for my fish when I ran into Jim Ornstein, my broadcasting agent from William Morris, who was there with another William Morris agent entertaining clients. Ornstein then invited me to the table to meet his crew, which consisted of Heisman Trophy-winning quarterback, Tim Tebow, actress Hayden Panettiere and her boyfriend at the time, and Jets wide receiver Scotty McKnight, a former Colorado stud receiver and skier. After a couple minutes of basic introductory conversation, they invited me to sit down and eat with them.

Hayden, Scotty, and Tebow all seemed like very nice people. We talked about New York City, Southern California where Scotty is from, and the prospects for the Jets for the upcoming season. I explained to them all about working for MLB Network, essentially describing it as the "Red Zone" for football with much more analysis and actual demos on our make-shift field in Studio 42. Ornstein then brought up that I had just completed my first Ironman. That was probably the only part of the conversation where Tebow actually seemed very interested. Looking back, the whole chance meeting seems a bit ironic because just a few years later, Tebow became a professional baseball player and I was analyzing his swing and outfield play on MLB Network.

After dinner, we walked to the elevator and I noticed a very familiar-looking guy standing in line behind us, who happened to be Eli Manning. In the baseball world, if there was a situation like that with two players, generally there would be a simple exchange of pleasantries out of courtesy. I was shocked that both guys just completely ignored each other. When we got downstairs, I said goodbye and thanked them for dinner, which both Ornstein and the other William Morris agent picked up. As they were getting in the SUV that was waiting for them downstairs, they asked if I wanted to join for some karaoke! I was not the least bit interested in going to karaoke, but again, the situation was way too humorously awkward to pass up. On the way there, Journey was playing and the karaoke session started early. I could not stop laughing with Ornstein who was sitting next to me. A couple hours earlier, I went to grab a bite to eat and a couple cocktails by myself and I was now in a town car singing "Don't Stop Believin'" in unison with Tim Tebow, Hayden Pannetiere, and Scotty McKnight, trying to figure out what the f*ck was going on.

When we got to the karaoke place, the people up front immediately took us to a private room where the three of them grabbed the mic and went nuts. It seemed like they hit every genre possible: 70s, 80s, 90s, hip-hop, country. If you can name it, Tim Tebow sang it! Maybe it was because I had now sucked down several vodka and sodas, but the three of them actually sounded pretty good.

When a small group of other people joined I figured it was a good time for an Irish goodbye. I headed out the front of the place, which was on the lower east side and tried to hail a cab, but there was absolutely nothing in the area. The driver of the SUV that dropped us off pulled up and asked me if I would like a ride. "No thanks, dude, I am not sure how much longer the rest of the crew will be here for. I already stole a dinner from them tonight so I prefer not to steal their car." The driver insisted that they told him they were going to be awhile and it should not be a problem, so I hopped in.

We were half way across the city when the driver's cell phone starts blowing up. It was the other William Morris agent, and she was pissed! I don't blame her. From the time the driver received the phone call to the time he would drop me off and then return to pick them up it would be at least another 20 minutes. I gave the driver a $100 and told him to make sure to thank the Tebow clan for dinner, karaoke entertainment, and the car. I guess it's pretty easy to figure out why I haven't gotten another invite.

Human Crash Test Dummy Life Lesson #98

Always be open to meeting new people and making new friends. It can be an incredible life experience and chance for major growth when you throw yourself into an awkward situation. But whatever you do, DON'T steal their ride home.

Chapter 99
Become Comfortable With The Uncomfortable

"My life was going to be different. I felt my life changing. I made a deal with myself. A deal was struck. And I don't care if it hurts, I don't care if it's messy, I don't care how it looks, but I would finish. I would finish."
-Julie Moss

As much as I loved my new job and was having a blast golfing, surfing, and playing slow-pitch softball, there was still definitely some sort of void in my life. I took the infamous beach cruiser for a spin one day in Half Moon Bay and ended up running into some grade school friends of mine over at States Beach that I had not seen in years: Kevin "Chops" Quellmalz and the Wray sisters, Erica and Lauren. They were telling me about a triathlon that they were going to be doing in a few weeks. I had always been intrigued by triathlons ever since I was a 6-year-old kid sitting on the couch with my dad, watching the Ironman World Championships and Julie Moss collapse at the finish line in Kona in 1982.

I always wondered what kind of event could possibly push somebody to the point of complete and total exhaustion, and what sort of person would put themselves through such extreme agonizing pain. Every year from that point on, I would watch the Ironman World Championships with my dad and we would marvel at the athletes that would put themselves through the challenge. All three of my friends were experienced triathletes and began trying to convince me to join them for the sprint distance triathlon.

The problem was, like most of the people who get into the sport, I didn't really know how to swim. I surfed a ton growing up, but I was always attached to the board, which essentially serves as a flotation device. Swimming without a pool wall to stop and hold onto seemed daunting. Nonetheless, I took the challenge and had about 2 weeks to get ready. The race was the Pacific Grove Triathlon that took place in gorgeous Pacific Grove, California, right next to Pebble Beach and Carmel. The distances consisted of a 750-yard swim, a 12-mile bike, and a 2-mile run. Immediately, I headed to the swimming pool to figure out what I was working with. I started off swimming the first 25 yards freestyle. When I got to the other side of the pool, I was completely gassed. There was absolutely no way I could swim 50 yards, let alone 750. I needed a new plan. I then swam the next 25 yards breaststroke; albeit I was extremely slow, I actually felt okay when I got to the other end. That first day I swam two more lengths of the pool to finish up my first ever 100-yard swim workout! That was it; I was going to have to swim breaststroke so I could become confident that I wasn't going to drown. I did 150 yards the next time, then 200, 250 and so on, celebrating my miniature "50 yards more" victory every step of the way. I went to the pool just about every day leading up to the race and slowly built up to the 750-yard distance I was going to have to cover in the competition.

Race day arrived a lot quicker than I would have liked, but I felt like for 2 weeks of preparation I had done all I could do. The morning of the race I was running late so I had Tarah drop me off as close to where the race started as possible. I hopped out of the car with my 5mm surfing wetsuit, my beach cruiser, and some board shorts to ride and run in after I got out of the water. When I got to the expo area, the place was absolutely booming with energy. Music was bumping and it seemed to me like everybody was good-looking, in shape, and genuinely very motivated and happy. The workers handed me a packet with a timing chip inside and all sorts of numbers that I had no clue what to do with.

I met up with "Chops" and the Wray sisters in the transition area where the three of them quickly dialed me in, putting the appropriate stickers where they needed to go. We then scurried down to the start and before I knew it we were off. I headed into the water towards the back of the pack, figuring just about everyone there was going to kick my ass in the water. I was right.

I started swimming breaststroke but kept getting tangled up in the overwhelming amount of kelp in the water. Apparently, I came to find out that the swim portion of the race was notorious for the kelp, so much so, it is actually publicly referred to, and even advertised, as the Kelp Crawl. All I could think was, "I may die today."

With only a couple weeks to prepare, I was just worried about being able to swim the distance and never really gave the kelp any sort of thought. Bad idea. However hard I thought the swim was going to be, and I thought it was going to be bad, it was 10 times worse. At one point, I thought I was drowning; I thought that was it. I then went into a doggie paddle, straight survival mode, and somehow made it through the kelp-entangled water and literally came stumbling onto the beach, where I laid down as if I was some sort of beached whale or a sailor who finally made it to shore after days stranded out at sea. After a few minutes of laying on the beach, watching hundreds of people who started after me fly by, my heart rate began to slow down and I once again began to breath normally. I was ecstatic that I was still alive. Realizing that the worst was over, it was time to move on to the bike.

I began the trek up some stairs that took us to the transition area where my beach cruiser was parked amongst a bunch of high tech triathlon bikes. By the time I got my surfing wetsuit off and towel-changed it into my board shorts, the only other people in transition were women, who started a good 10 minutes behind me and already had caught up. Just thankful I was still alive, I hopped on the bike with a big smile on my face and started pedaling away.

I felt okay at first, and then as I got through the first few miles, I actually started to feel pretty good. One chick after another continued to pass me as I "cruised" along. Finally, a 14-year-old girl went flying by and my competitive spirit took over. It was on!

I started cranking the pedals, and pretty soon, not only were people not passing me anymore, but I started actually passing people. As we made our way into downtown Pacific Grove, people on the streets were going nuts, "Look at the guy on the beach cruiser. Go Beach

Cruiser Dude!" All of a sudden, I became the sentimental fan favorite and I was loving every minute of it. I finished the 12-mile bike ride in a very respectable 44 minutes. I couldn't feel my feet, but I started running and hammered out a couple 6-minute miles and crossed the finish line with a high I had not felt since 2007 when I hit a home run in the playoffs at Wrigley Field.

The Wray sisters and "Chops" were all waiting for me at the finish, and I immediately gave them hugs and thanked them for introducing me to the triathlon world. I then told them that was going to be the last time any of them would ever beat me. I was hooked. Tarah was there with Chloe and Cali in the stroller, took one look into my eyes, and knew I had found WHAT'S NEXT. We all went back to the hotel, rehashed the day over BBQ and cold beers, scoured the internet, and immediately found our next race in Arizona a month later.

Human Crash Test Dummy Life Lesson #99

Push yourself into the unknown. Try everything and always be prepared and open to what may come your way. Understand the situation and the dynamics involved, and then realize it is going to be difficult and uncomfortable. Becoming comfortable with the uncomfortable is the key to life and will push you beyond limits you never thought possible. When you do the work that allows you to complete a new and challenging task, your sense of accomplishment will be a direct result of immersing yourself in the process and will help redefine what you believe is possible.

Chapter 100
Head First

"Until you face your fears you don't move to the other side, where you find your powers."
-Mark Allen

The first thing I did the next day after the Pac Grove Triathlon was head to Front of the Pack, a triathlon shop in Palo Alto. That's where I met my man Darrell Eng, who gave me a tutorial introduction into all things triathlon, including the difference between a road bike, a triathlon bike, and a beach cruiser. He helped explain all the nuances of the sport and the bare necessities I would need.

First things first: I spent 10 minutes sitting on a bike learning how to clip my shoes in and out of the pedals. I am not sure how it was possible because the bike inside was attached to a trainer keeping it stable and upright, but I somehow managed my first fall right in the middle of the store. I had absolutely no clue whatsoever as to what I was getting into. Darrell started talking about carbon vs. aluminum frames, components, cassettes, de-railers, automatic shifting, aero bars, 404's, and 808's. My head was spinning. Trying to be the responsible store owner, Darrell recommended that I start out with a lower-end road bike which he felt would be more comfortable, easier to ride, and relatively cost efficient. The problem was that I know myself all too well. I have never eased into anything in my life. When I make a commitment to something, I am all in. No point to start my meal with a hamburger if I am going to eat a filet.

"Give me the best, fastest, and most aggressive triathlon bike and gear that you have. I have a score to settle with some old friends!"

I continued to go to the pool and work on swimming freestyle, and I now had my runs up to 4 miles. The other thing I did, and probably was one of the best moves I have made since I got into the sport, was get Tarah involved. We began swimming and running together, and I eventually got her to sign up for the races. A month later, the showdown in Arizona was on. Once again, I scuffled through another terrible swim, this time in super windy and rough water conditions. I eventually made it out of the water and then the chase was on. One by one, I picked off Lauren, "Chops," and then my arch nemesis since grade school, the other part of the Wray Sister Mafia, Erica! The new bike immediately paid dividends and became worth every penny. I had a good run and ended up winning the "Clydesdale" division (over 200 lbs.) and got my first taste of triathlon success; I wanted more.

I signed up for the "Pumpkin Man" race a month later in Las Vegas and began realizing I can make this a perfect excuse to travel to all sorts of vacation destinations around the world. This time, the swim would be in a calm lake but it was still an issue. I had another good bike, run, and "Clydesdale" medal to go celebrate on the strip that night with my boy Artie Baxter, who I convinced to do the race with me. It was a perfect excuse for the two of us to hit Vegas for the weekend.

There was one more Thanksgiving Triathlon that I wanted to get in before the season was over. Another sprint tri but this was actually a reverse triathlon. We ran 2 miles to start the race, then rode 12 miles and finished with a 400-meter swim in the YMCA pool. The run and bike went great again, but even though the swim was in a pool, it pretty much reached an all-time low for me. I got off the bike and hopped into the pool determined to finally swim freestyle the entire way. After two strokes, I not only could not swim freestyle, but I could barely stay afloat at all. My entire body was cramping up and I quickly realized why the swim is generally always the first part of the triathlon. I eventually made it through, but it had now reached a point where I no doubt needed help before I found myself at the bottom of some ocean, lake, or pool. I needed a coach.

Right after the race, I called over to Lifetime Fitness in North Scottsdale and left a message. "Hi, my name is Eric Byrnes I am just getting into triathlons and have almost drowned in each of the four sprints that I have done. I am looking for any sort of swim coach that can give me some swimming lessons that will hopefully save my life.

Thanks." Soon after, I got a phone call back from a guy by the name of Frank Sole. Not only was he a swim coach but he was a triathlon coach as well. This guy was right up my ally; he was a fast-talking New Yorker that had an extreme passion and energy not only for triathlons but for life in general. Frank, who was in his 50s, had just completed his second Ironman. After the very first session of watching me hack up the water, he asked me where I wanted to go with triathlons. I thought about it and somewhat embarrassingly told him that I wanted to do an Ironman one day but figured I was years away. He then proceeded to tell me that he could get me ready for Ironman Arizona by next November.

"Let me get this straight. After watching me swim, you think you can get me ready to swim 2.4 miles in 11 months? That's not even considering the fact that I would have to ride 112 miles and then run a marathon after. You seem like a very nice guy, Frank, and I love your optimistic outlook on this, but do you realize that you are absolutely nuts?"

Frank then went on to say that not only could he get me ready to swim 2.4 miles, but he guaranteed me I would be out of the water in under 1 hour and 18 minutes. "Ha! Now I think you are certifiably insane. I absolutely love it, where do I sign up?" I went home that night and signed up for my first Ironman triathlon, never having swam more than 750 yards, biked more than 12 miles, and ran more than 4. The next 11 months of my life would forever change me as an athlete and as a person.

Human Crash Test Dummy Life Lesson #100

Don't be afraid to dive in headfirst. Too often we pussy-foot our way around and waste a boatload of time before making a commitment that we know we are ready for but are too scared to commit to. Time is the most valuable resource on earth; don't waste it. Face your fears and get your ass to work.

Chapter 101
Enjoy the Suffering

"Success in the sport, above all else, is about enduring suffering."
-Chris McCormick

The first person I called after I signed up for Ironman Arizona was my dad. "Yo, Dad, remember when we watched Julie Moss completely collapse at the Ironman finish line and I told you one day I wanted to do that?"

"Of course."

"November 20th is going to be that day."

"HAHA!!! Awesome E. I will be there with you."

Frank immediately put me on a plan that had me gradually increasing my mileage on the bike and run. For example, I would run 4 miles one day, then 4.5 the next session, then back to 4 then up to 5, back to 4.5 then back to 5, then to 5.5 and so forth. By mid-January I had gotten all the way up to 13 miles and I was officially creating an Ironman base. Same sort of thing on the bike: 20 miles became 25 then 35 and so on.

In the water, Frank had me doing drills for the first 8 weeks and that was it. Catch-up drill, fingertip drill, one-arm drill, kicking drills, whatever drill you could think of, I was doing it. He wanted to make sure I had the proper form before I even thought about accumulating any sort of distance.

The next thing I needed if I was going to be putting in these ridiculous hours training was a good training partner. The Wray sisters and "Chops" had no interest in the Iron distance so that ruled them out. A lot of my friends were still playing baseball, so obviously, they were not an option, and most of my high school and college buddies worked full time so training 20 hours a week was unrealistic. Other than my dad, who was actually considering doing it at 65 years old, there was only one guy that I knew had that same sort of passion about endurance sports that I had.

My college roommate, my "unofficial" agent, one of my best friends, and a dude that was a 7-time marathoner: Mike Seal.

I was able to convince Seal, who already was a great swimmer and runner, to sign up for this Ironman training camp with me in Tucson. Seal had never ridden a road bike and obviously my experience was limited, so the week ahead was eye opening to say the least. Two professional triathletes, Brendan Halpin and top female pro Linsey Corbin, led the camp that included swimming every morning followed by a 50-100-mile ride and some sort of transition run to follow. By the end of the week, what seemed like an impossible feat of completing an Ironman all of a sudden started to seem very realistic. It was not going to be easy but I was starting to see how it would be attainable. The week also furthered my love of the triathlon culture that seemed to attract very driven and successful people with very intriguing backgrounds: Doctors, lawyers, venture capitalists, tech geeks, teachers, firefighters, you name it. I felt like of the 12-15 people at the camp, we had almost every industry covered. Not to mention, the athletic background of the campers ranged from former college swimmers, runners, tennis, football, basketball, and even baseball players. The most rewarding part was meeting all of the different people and hearing everybody's story as to what drove them into the endurance world.

When I arrived home after the week in Tucson, I had full blown shin splints caused by the massive volume of training I was not accustomed to. Unfortunately, I made the mistake of getting in every workout the entire week, including a 15-mile run the last day. I was the only one that did not sit out at least one swim, bike, or run session. I got to learn all about the importance of rest, recovery, and overtraining. After a couple weeks of not running, I was good to go and officially had a decent Ironman base.

Human Crash Test Dummy Life Lesson #101

Study your craft and immerse yourself in the culture. Learn through experience. Spend time in the saddle of the bike and in the saddle of life. What may seem extraordinary and not possible without experience becomes very possible and very ordinary when you focus on the details of the process. The process will not be easy and suffering is part of the blue print. You might as well enjoy it.

Chapter 102
Momento Mori

"You could leave life right now.
Let that determine what you see, think and say."
-Marcus Aurelius

Back in the Bay Area, my dad had become mesmerized by the entire process. We went to lunch at Harry's Hofbrau, and after I rambled on for an hour about the new triathlon world I was now living in, I had him convinced to test the waters of a new challenge but it was going to have to wait.

My dad then explained that he was going in for heart surgery in 2 weeks. In one sense, I was shocked. If you looked at my dad, he was 65 going on 45. He was a 4th degree black belt in Kenpo Karate, a class A tennis player, an expert skier, and he actively participated in all three.

In another sense, I wasn't surprised at all. He had a long history of health problems including beating melanoma and prostate cancer throughout the course of his life. At times, he drank too much and for the most part did not eat great. He also worked his ass off and would rarely ever take a day off. We would joke around and call him the Dad with 9 lives. He drove his car off a 100-foot cliff on Skyline Boulevard near our home in Woodside and walked away without a scratch, beat two forms of serious cancer, and once got mugged by 3 guys walking back to his car after having lunch in San Francisco. He sent all three to the hospital. As the police were arriving, based on the condition of the 3 guys, they actually thought my dad was the assailant and put him in handcuffs. Like most sons that look up to their fathers, he seemed to be bullet proof to me, even at 65. So to hear that he was going in for heart surgery, I really did not think much of it. This was simply going to be another hurdle he would fly right over.

I wish I would have looked at it differently.

Stoic philosophers past and present live by a term called Momento Mori. Today, on the Daily Stoic website, they even sell a Momento Mori coin that serves as a constant reminder that life can be taken from us or somebody we love at any moment. Don't fret over trivial things in your life or relationships because our time is limited on this earth; why waste it on worry? We need to use our own mortality as a constant reminder to LIVE our lives.

Human Crash Test Dummy Life Lesson #102

Let Momento Mori be a constant reminder to NEVER take for granted the people you love in your life. Let Momento Mori be a constant reminder to be thankful for the health we and our loved ones are blessed with each day. Let Momento Mori be a constant reminder to live your life for the moment because we have no idea when that moment will be taken away.

Chapter 103
Trust but Verify

"The trust of the innocent is the liar's most useful tool."
-Stephen King

A couple weeks later just before my dad's surgery, I decided to have a retirement party, mainly as a gag and an excuse to get together and hang with family and friends who supported me through the course of my entire baseball career. Dad was in rare form. He gave a speech that involved some Captain America under-roos referencing my Dominican days and gave me an AARP card gloating that I had officially retired before he did. A couple of days later on February 16, 2011, my 35th birthday, my dad underwent bypass surgery. He came out with flying colors and the doctor said everything went as perfectly planned. I went to see him as soon as I could the next day.

I have always hated hospitals, so when I walked into the intensive care unit, it was one of the most depressing sights I had ever seen. Half the people looked as if they were already dead. I finally got to my dad's room where I walked in but his bed was empty. As you could imagine, panic set in. Where was he? He was about 12 hours removed from major heart surgery, so I couldn't imagine he was up taking laps around the hospital.

Next thing you know he flies up from behind me. "E!!!!!!" He absolutely scared the crap out of me.

"What are you doing out of bed?"

"I had to get up and move around. What a depressing sight out there. I had to get out of the ICU; I couldn't tell if these people were dead or alive." We both busted up laughing. Not only was my dad still alive, but he looked as if he had just gotten a massage as opposed to heart surgery. The man with 9 lives just used up another one.

All seemed to be good and after the third day the doctors were ready to release him from the hospital. Then out of nowhere, the night before he was to be released, his heart went into A-Fib. Essentially his heart was beating at nearly 170-180 beats per minute. Apparently, this was relatively normal after heart surgery. The basic protocol was to give my dad medication to slow the heart rate and also to put him on Coumadin, which is a blood thinner that would help prevent any sort of blood clots or stroke. He was also going to have to stay in the hospital for at least another few days. When I went to visit him at Sequoia Hospital, which was supposed to be known as having a world-class cardiology department, my dad explained to me that because he is a "bleeder," he had major concerns about taking Coumadin, which he had avoided in the past.

We talked about the other alternatives, but apparently, the doctors assured him that so long as he is closely monitored, there would not be any issues. Hearing that, I made it very clear to him that he needed to keep his ass in the hospital as long as possible. I am not a doctor but the most important thing for me was that they continued to monitor his heart rate and make sure the Coumadin wasn't causing any sort of internal bleeding. I imagined he would be in the hospital for at least another week. A day later he was released. I called my sister, livid.

"Why the f*ck is Dad out of the hospital!!!"

She didn't really have an answer other than they released him. He went to stay at his girlfriend's, where she was going to watch him and a nurse was going to come in once a day. It didn't make any sense to me and my sister questioned it as well, but who are we to question a hospital and doctors who deal with this sort of situation all of the time?

A couple of days later, I took the family up to my dad's place at Northstar in the mountains above Lake Tahoe. All my years playing baseball, I never really got an opportunity to stay at the "ski up" condo which is perfectly situated right on the slopes.

Looking back, I am not sure how many times in my life I ever really complimented my dad. How many times I said "good job" or "nice work" or really praised him for all of the accomplishments in his life. I spent my whole life saying, "thank you," but I never stopped to really recognize how hard he had worked for our family over the years. When I called him, I wanted him to know how much I appreciated how well he had provided for us and how thankful I was for every opportunity he helped provide for me in my life. I then went on to rant and rave about the kick-ass set up in Tahoe. There was almost this awkward long pause after I finished. He then broke the silence with a crack in his voice that I hadn't ever heard from him my entire life. At first I thought it might have been because of the surgery, but I quickly realized he was actually choked up by my words.

"That's why I built it, E. I built it for the family. I built it for you. It's yours whenever you want it. It has been, always will be."

For my dad's entire life, all he wanted was approval from his father. One of the reasons how and why he was so successful was that he was constantly trying to earn his dad's approval. Unfortunately, he never really got it. After 35 years though, he finally got it from his son. I am not even sure if he knew that's what he was looking for or that's what he wanted, but I had never heard him react like that. It all began to make sense.

Monday, March 1, 2011, I woke up on a gorgeous Lake Tahoe morning and headed to the pool to swim some laps. I got a call from an unknown number on my cell phone just as I had walked into the facility. I generally never would answer an unknown number, but for whatever reason, I did. It was my dad.

"Hey, E, just want to tell you that I am about to go to a luncheon and receive an award for being one of the top-selling real estate agents in the world. Not the Bay Area, not the state of California, not the United States, the world!"

"Nice work, old man. Nice work."

I asked how he was feeling and he said he felt great but had tingling in one of his arms and he wasn't sure what it was. He had called and emailed the doctor and he told him to come in the next day. "The next day? Dad you need to get your ass in and see somebody today." He assured me that the doctor seemed to think everything was okay and he would go in first thing the next morning. "Again, I am not a doctor, but your ass just had bypass surgery, went into A-Fib, and you are on Coumadin and you are not in the hospital. Your arm is tingling and you are telling me it almost feels numb. What kind of doctor would say it is okay to come in tomorrow?" He insisted that he felt as if everything was fine. "Alright, Dad, congratulations on the award. I am proud of you."

"Thanks, E, I love you, buddy."

That was the last time I ever talked to my dad.

Human Crash Test Dummy Life Lesson #103

Don't ever assume anything in life. "Trust but verify" is a Russian proverb that needs to be adhered to. President Reagan used it to better communicate with the Russians during the Cold War. Trust people and their opinions but verify if that is the right information or truly the right way to go about doing something.

Chapter 104
Dad's Dead

"The fear of death follows from the fear of life. A man who lives fully is prepared to die at any time."
-Mark Twain

The next morning, I woke up early with this incredible calm over me. I grabbed a cup of coffee and opened the back patio door. It was dumping snow. I am not sure if there is a more peaceful sound then fresh snow falling from the sky and hitting the ground. I thought about my life, my career, my family. I thought about my dad. I thought about how thankful I was that he never pushed me into anything and always encouraged me to walk to the beat of my own drum. I thought about baseball and all those years when no matter what the result, he was there to pat me on the back and tell me how proud he was. I thought about his work ethic and encouragement and how it shaped who I had become as a man. I also had this realization that he was not going to live forever, and for the first time, I thought about what life would be like without him. I thought about the past couple conversations I had with him. I thought about how grateful I was that I finally got the balls to tell him how thankful I was and how proud I was to call him my dad.

I headed to the gym right next door and got on the spin bike. The plan was to ride an hour at Ironman race pace. 47 minutes into the ride, I got a phone call from my sister, Shea. I hit ignore and continued pedaling. I got another phone call immediately after the first one. I answered the phone but I didn't even have to. I knew what had happened. I had already felt it that morning.

"Dad is dead, Dad is dead, Dad is dead." She was frantic.

I got off the bike and tried to calm Shea down so I could figure out what had happened. She told me that apparently Dad had woken up around 6 am and immediately called 911. He was having difficulty breathing. When paramedics arrived 10 minutes later, he was dead.

When I finally got off the phone, I hopped right back on the spin bike and peddled as hard as I could until I literally collapsed off of the side of the bike. I felt as if somebody had punched me in the stomach and then kicked me in the balls. It was the most painful feeling that I had ever had in my life. I picked myself up off the ground. I needed air.

I walked outside. The snow was now coming down so hard that it was actually tough to see beyond just a few feet in front of me. There was a jacuzzi with steam coming off it and I just stood there and stared, alone with my thoughts. I thought about the yellow banana motorcycle my dad taught me to ride when I was a kid, the karate tournaments we used to travel to, the epic battles we had on the tennis court, the batting practice he used to throw me at the Portola Valley Town Center, the runs we would go on, and the super power jet speed he would always dial up at the end. I thought about the unconditional love and support he had for me in whatever endeavor I pursued in my life. I thought about our recent relationship and the friendship that had just grown to an entirely new level. I thought about my two daughters and how they would never get to know their Great Pa. I thought about my unborn child who would never have an opportunity to meet him. As the snow continued to fall harder the reality that he was gone slowly began to sink in.

I stood out in the snow for nearly an hour, waiting for the pain to go away. It didn't. When the cold became physically unbearable, I made the walk back to the condo to tell Tarah and the girls. I walked in shivering with borderline hypothermia and could barely speak. Tarah was still lying in bed and the girls were watching cartoons.

"Great Pa had to go to heaven."

My 3 year old immediately chimes in. "It's okay, Daddy, we can go visit him in heaven, and I'll bet you he will have a prize for us in heaven too."

Tarah just gasped and grabbed onto me.

My wife is one of the strongest people I have ever met in my life. She immediately started to deal with all the logistics. The hardest thing for me was having to tell those close to my dad that he was gone. I didn't want to talk to anybody. I needed time. I couldn't even take my mom's call.

Tarah also dealt with my sister, who was communicating with the hospital where he was pronounced dead, the hospital where he had surgery, and the doctors and nurses who obviously either screwed up the surgery, the handling process post-surgery, or both. I was in the process of quitting chewing Copenhagen and I must have gone through an entire can, within hours. I just kept reloading one dip after another trying to figure out what to do next.

Human Crash Test Dummy Life Lesson #104

Death is real and it is going to happen to all of us. Nobody has gotten out of here alive. Be aware of the mortality of everybody around you, and if there is an opportunity to help them live a healthier and happier lifestyle, make sure you do so. Little bits of encouragement can change a person's life. Compliment those around you and express your feelings because you may not have the opportunity to do it tomorrow.

Chapter 105
Let Go

*"Some of us think holding on makes us strong
but sometimes it is letting go."*
-Herman Hesse

As the day and then week went on, I did my best to learn about the details of my dad's condition: Why they decided to do surgery in the first place, who was calling the shots on his post-surgery care, and most importantly, how did he die?

When I talked to my dad before the surgery, he told me that the surgery was a preventive measure. I questioned the surgery from the get-go. I obviously don't know much about cardiology, but from stories I have heard, I am very skeptical of doctors and their ability to jump the gun on bringing the scalpel out. In most all cases, surgery means more money for doctors, so many have been accused of performing surgeries that didn't necessarily warrant it. As far as my dad's care after the surgery, there actually were two doctors that performed the surgery, so you would think the care would have been very detailed to say the least. Not the case.

The original hospital that did the surgery demanded that the autopsy be done at their hospital. So, without the family's permission, they moved the body back to the hospital that did the surgery and performed the autopsy. They said that the cause of death was cardiac arrest brought on by his inability to breath because his lungs had filled up with blood. Essentially, the scar tissue around the heart began bleeding because of the blood thinner Coumadin. Because it was not properly monitored, my dad drowned in his own blood.

I got on the phone and called the doctor. To the doctor's credit, he took my call immediately and was overly apologetic about what had happened. He kept saying that this had never happened to any of his patients before. I bombarded him with questions; the main one being why when my dad contacted him about a tingling sensation in his arm did he dismiss it as something minor?

"I didn't think it was a big deal. I deal with complaints like these all the time. In hindsight, I should have told him to come in. This is something I will live with for the rest of my life."

I was surprised at how the doctor seemed to hold himself accountable. He admitted that had my dad come in on Monday, he would have figured out immediately with a stethoscope that he had fluid (blood) in his lungs. I then hired an independent pathologist to do our own autopsy before we had the body cremated. The conclusions were essentially the same and did not teach us anything new, but the way they rushed the body back to the original hospital and the doctor admitting that there was an error with his monitoring process, I did not want to leave a stone unturned. I talked to several lawyers about what had happened, and although my family had a very formidable case, we ultimately decided not to pursue any sort of lawsuit. My sister Shea was the one who had been dealing with everything and it was becoming too much for her. She wanted closure. I wanted to absolutely bury the hospital and both doctors and it had absolutely nothing to do with money. I wanted to make sure this blatant ignorance and bullsh*t care didn't cost somebody else their life. Yet unless we were all in it together, I was okay with moving on.

Human Crash Test Dummy Life Lesson #105

Ask yourself what you are looking to achieve. What message are you trying to send, and what are you ultimately trying to accomplish? From that point, think about what appropriate action to take but also be sensitive to how it will affect those close to you. In order to let go you have no choice but to give up the fight. In order to move on you have no choice but to truly LET GO.

Chapter 106
Read, Learn, Apply

"Let your behavior reflect your commitment."
-Jim Byrnes

While in the hospital, my dad had begun writing. I am not sure exactly what you would call it, but essentially, he put down many of his theories on life. He wrote about life lessons and certain things that influenced him in both positive and negative ways. He wrote about his readings and how he applied the lessons and messages to his life. It was almost as if he wanted to get everything out and share his life experiences that ultimately shaped who he had become as a person.

My dad wasn't perfect; he wasn't even close, yet it was his ability to always keep this eternally optimistic view on life no matter what the circumstance that made him who he was. Most importantly, it was the blueprint for his life that he laid out for my sister and me. One day, I will have an opportunity to pass it on to my children. Here, are a few of the excerpts from the email he wrote on his iPad while in the hospital just days before he passed...

Subject: Magical Thoughts from myself and Messages from others that help me be the best I can be for myself and for others.

Feb 19, 2011
Hi Shea and Eric, I want to share some summary thoughts from myself and messages from others that have helped me become a better, more joyful and appreciative person. These messages have given me perspective and peacefulness of who I am and how I can be a better person, for myself and others. Enjoy and apply those thoughts that resonate in your mind, body and spirit into action, with passion, purpose and performance! Love You, DAD

First and foremost, We are a fragment, a segment, a piece of GOD. NAME A PLACE WHERE GOD ISN'T, THEREFORE IT HAS TO ALSO BE IN YOU AND EVERYONE ELSE.

CHANGE THE CONCEPT OF YOURSELF

1. Elevate your life by helicopter vision of going outside yourself, be the observer, come back within yourself with better perspective, better behavior.

2. Your "truth" is where you are now from the thoughts and experiences that you have used and paid attention to in the forms of habits, based on the thoughts and limiting beliefs of the unreflecting herd.

3. To go from conscious to super conscious creates a renewal of your pure divinity, pure light. There is no subconscious of your thoughts. YOUR THOUGHTS DON'T COME FROM YOU, THEY COME THRU YOU FROM GOD. Over 60,000 separate thoughts per day. The good news is that you get to accept or reject these thoughts! You can choose, pursue and live your thoughts. PAY ATTENTION, ATTRACTION, ALIGNMENT TO THE THOUGHTS AND OPPORTUNITIES THAT GOD PRESENTS TO YOU. AS YOU PLAN YOUR LIFE PAY ATTENTION TO GOD'S PLAN, GOALS, OPPORTUNITIES ALONG YOUR "WAY"

4. Surrender, trust and use your experience not your intellect. Practice Radical Humility and Forgiveness to yourself and others and pursue those thoughts, passions, purposes.

5. YOU ALWAYS GET WHAT YOU THINK ABOUT AND IF YOU THINK ABOUT WHAT YOU DON'T WANT, YOU WILL NEVER GET ENOUGH OF WHAT YOU DO WANT!!!

6. "WHEN WE ARE NO LONGER ABLE TO CHANGE A SITUATION, WE ARE CHALLENGED TO CHANGE OURSELVES." Victor Frankel - Always be prepared to change yourself.

7. People overestimate how they can change others and underestimate how much they can change themselves.

8. WE DON'T SOLVE OUR PROBLEMS, WE learn to GROW OUT OF THEM!

9. EGO - Edge God Out - The ego says you are what you do, the things you have, your reputation, who you know, you are separate.
The ego is a tiny fragment of your mind that thinks it is everything in you. It is the ripple in the water that thinks it's the ocean. It is the tiny sunbeam that thinks it's the sun.

10. "Don't die with your music still inside you." Wayne Dyer - Live your dreams.

11. Don't ever regret what you do, only what you don't do.

12. It's the space between the notes that make the music. Take time for yourself, don't over schedule.

SUCCESS AND FAILURE:

1. DON'T TAKE YOUR FEELINGS SO PERSONAL!!!

2. You only fail if you don't try.

3. You don't fail or pass, it's what you do with the results.

4. Failure is not fatal it is directional.

5. Life is not linear or compartmentalized. Life is the culmination of synchronistic forces that create an elliptical pattern of past, present and future experiences.

6. Stay in the present. If your attention is in the present, you are in the presence of God.

7. There is no good or bad, right or wrong. When we were growing up (and still are) Remember what you thought was good for you? Bad for you? What you thought was right or wrong? These words are

temporary value judgments from the ego. NO JUDGEMENTS ON YOU OR OTHERS.

RELIGION VS SPIRITUALITY

1. Any entity that includes some and excludes other is not from GOD.

2. "When you label me, you negate me." Søren Kierkegaard Danish Philosopher

3. "I love your Christ but I'm not sure about your Christians. They don't seem to know their Christ very well." Ghandi

4. The truth is the truth until you organize it.

STREET SPIRITUALITY

What makes sense to you? What you want to be you already are. It has arrived with your perception, permission, passion, purpose, performance.

CHILD REARING

Before children, I had 1 child rearing theory. After 2 children I had 2 different theories on how to raise children. Now, after 2 children, I have no theories, just 2 different children. Yet I know to:

1. Love them with open arms (wide but defined boundaries).
2. Catch them doing things right.
3. Give them opportunities but make them accountable and responsible for their choices.
4. Let them make choices.

This is just a small amount of the Jim Byrnes' life lessons. He shared much more and included references, suggested readings and specific lifestyle optimization activities to apply. He also shared his personal experiences that led him to his philosophies and spiritual convictions.

Human Crash Test Dummy Life Lesson #106

Never stop learning and challenging your views on life. As we evolve, so do our attitudes and theories. Read, learn and apply all of your life lessons, and then create your own manual as if you were going to pass it on to your own children. What messages will you leave?

Chapter 107
Deal With It

"Facing it, always facing it, that's the way to get through. Face it."
-Joseph Conrad

Everybody deals with the loss of a loved one in a different way. My sister was overly dramatic and then became very business-like and proactive in dealing with all the logistics after my dad died. She also wanted to be around people. I was the opposite. I dealt with the original news almost without shedding a tear. It then hit me once I got off the phone and back on the spin bike. After telling my wife and girls, I didn't want to talk to anybody. Nobody. I wanted to crawl into a hole and then come out 3 weeks later. I couldn't get through an hour without thinking about something or seeing something that caused me to melt down. The thought of never again being able to see or talk to my dad hit me way harder than I could have ever imagined. I was a 35-year-old, grown-ass man that had gone through my fair share of tragedy in life. My best friend when I was 11, Todd Wilbanks, was killed when he was hit by a car while riding his bike. I was too young to truly conceptualize the magnitude of what had actually happened. Amanda MacDonald, my first love, died in a car accident her freshman year of college in Boulder, Colorado. I had lost every one of my grandparents and my Mom's sister, "Crazy" Aunt Pattie, who I used to stay with every summer for 2 weeks in Los Angeles. My high school lab partner and super-close friend Erica Reynolds was killed in a car accident while at UC Santa Barbara. More recently, the death of Erik Hanson, Karl Kuehl, and then Saulo Morris hit me like a ton of bricks. Like everyone else in life, I was not immune to the loss of loved ones. Much different from friends that passed away way too young, my dad lived a full life and I definitely took solace in that, yet the thought of my kids never getting to know their "Great Pa" hurt, badly.

March 17, 2011, on St. Patrick's Day, we held a service for my Dad at Menlo Park Presbyterian Church. I knew my dad was a popular guy and had all kinds of friends not only in the Bay Area but from all different parts of the country as well. I was still SHOCKED when 2,000 people showed up to say goodbye. My sister gave an awesome, very well prepared speech about everything our dad meant in her life. I had never seen my sister speak in public and I could not have been prouder of her. I then followed it up with a completely unscripted, off-the-cuff recount of my relationship with my dad. I spoke about my superhero-like perception of him when I was a child. I talked about how grateful I was that he gave me the liberty to pursue my own passions. I spoke about how our relationship deteriorated when he left my mom and how I wouldn't speak to him for months. I spoke about his strengths, like putting himself through college and earning his MBA while working two jobs and serving as a teacher's assistant at the same time. I spoke about his weaknesses: too much alcohol, a questionable diet, and his love for women, too many women. He coined the phrase "serial monogamist." Ultimately, he was a pleaser, he was a giver, and he was a lover. I spoke about the very "real" friendship we had recently developed and how much it hurt that my new best friend was gone.

I urged the overflowing church to appreciate each day that they have with their loved ones. I encouraged fathers and sons to not let a single day go by taking for granted their relationship. I then reminded them that at some point they will wake up, similar to the exact same way I did, and their dad, mom, brother, sister, and/or spouse will not be there. Appreciate the moment, appreciate the now, appreciate the relationship, appreciate the love, and realize that one day that moment, that now, that relationship, that love, in the flesh at least, won't be there anymore.

I spoke about how I wish I had developed my adult relationship with my dad much sooner. I spoke about how I wish I told him how much he meant to me in my life and how incredibly influential he was in who I had become as a man.

I also made a commitment to quit being such a selfish prick. My Dad laid an incredible foundation of "giving," and it was now my job to integrate that same sort of attitude and action into my life. "Let your behavior reflect your commitment." He gave financially, physically, and emotionally. Whether it was supporting the Melanoma Research Foundation, handing out turkeys in East Palo Alto on Thanksgiving with Coach Parks, or just spending time and lending an ear and advice to a friend or family member in need, he was there with a smile on his face with the same energy and enthusiasm that he had ingrained in me as a little boy. I always wanted to be more like him.

I now need to be more like him. It is my responsibility as a son and as a father to carry on the core values of the Byrnes family. I then will pass on those same lessons and values to my three children in hopes that they will have an opportunity to one day do the exact same thing.

Human Crash Test Dummy Life Lesson #107

We all cope in different ways. Understand that there is no easy way. It HURTS. Ultimately you have to face the reality of what happened and who is gone. Learn from the person you lost and let their spirit live through you. It's their spirit that never dies.

Chapter 108
Be The Moment

"Listen if you want to be heard."
-John Wooden

I started working at KNBR 680 in San Francisco soon after my dad's service. I was embarking on a new life and a new journey without any sort of real expectations. I knew that running a 3-hour night time radio show was going to be one of the biggest challenges of my life. Imagine sitting in a room by yourself with a microphone and having to talk for 3 straight hours. Daunting to say the least. It did not take long for me to realize how much I loved that challenge and how much work went into it as well. I don't care what I do for the rest of my life in the media world, there won't be anything close to as demandingly difficult as the year I spent hosting "Sportsphone 680."

That was the exact reason why I signed up. I got settled into a very nice routine. For about 3 weeks out of the month, I was in San Francisco and would host the radio show, do my best Mr. Mom impression, and train and race my ass off in my remaining free time. The other days, generally 5-10 each month, I would be in NYC working at MLB Network and training any way I could. There was not an hour of my day that I spent awake that I did not have planned out. Much different from when I played baseball.

Playing ball, that was my number one priority and that was it. Whenever I would get free time, I would then figure out what to do. I was now extremely regimented. Not a single minute went to waste. It was the only way I was going to be able to maintain a happy family, two jobs, and an Ironman training schedule. It also helped me cope with the loss of my dad and adjust to my first season not playing baseball in 25 years. My life was and still is the definition of organized chaos. The only way I am able to maintain this lifestyle is to be present at all times.

Human Crash Test Dummy Life Lesson #108

Too often we try to juggle ten balls at once and it becomes impossible even holding onto one. Focus on where you are at the moment and slow life down. Whenever I would get in big situations playing baseball, I would do everything I could to slow the game down. When I first started in the radio and TV world, I would do the exact same thing. "Listen if you want to be heard" is one of the many John Wooden life mantras. This just doesn't apply to listening to other people but to life situations as well. Listen to your situation, the people around you, and most importantly, yourself. Listening will give you clarity, allow you to stay in the moment, and give you the direction you need to move forward.

Chapter 109
The Other Half is Better

"I no longer believed in the idea of soul mates, or love at first sight. But I was beginning to believe that a very few times in your life, if you were lucky, you might meet someone who was exactly right for you. Not because he was perfect, or because you were, but because your combined flaws were arranged in a way that allowed two separate beings to hinge together."
-Lisa Kleypas

Tarah Peters grew up in Alpine, East County San Diego. Her father, Terry, was a carpenter by trade and a pilot. Tarah's mom, Toni, was a genius hippie that could pick up a crossword puzzle and finish it before I could pour her a cup of coffee. A lot of who Tarah is was obviously shaped by her father and mother, but in a much different way than you might think. When Tarah was 8 and her younger sister Tawny was 5, her dad took off on a weekend trip with some buddies to Mexico. They never saw him again. The only thing they could assume was that the plane her father was piloting had crashed. Months went by, and finally after almost a year, they found the plane in the middle of the Borrego Desert. The odd thing was that the plane had not crashed; it appeared to have landed and had been completely charred. There were no bodies discovered.

Go ahead a come up with your own conspiracy theory. Any way you cut it, Tarah and her sister were without a dad and Toni was without a husband. To make matters worse, the life insurance policy they were finally able to collect on after 12 months of her father being gone was stolen in a Ponzi scheme. So there they were; Toni had no job and no money, trying to raise two kids while still dealing with major emotional breakdowns over the loss of her husband and finances.

Tarah had no choice but to grow up in a hurry. She would help her mom fill out job applications and help prepare 3 meals a day for the family. Essentially, she became the leader of the household at 8 years old. When she was young, given the family's financial trouble, she wanted to figure out a way she would be able to go to college. Earning a scholarship seemed like her only option at that point. She read about a local pageant in which the winner would receive a scholarship. At that point, she decided that could be the way that would allow her to go to college and pay for it herself. She was officially all in. She won several crowns including Miss Teen Alpine, Miss El Cajon, Queen of the Del Mar Fair, and then Miss Greater San Diego. Eventually, she earned a scholarship to attend UC San Diego.

I was playing for the Oakland A's in 2001, and I basically was caught on the Sacramento to Oakland shuttle. I was the 26th guy on the roster, and depending on the A's need for a pitcher or an extra position player, I was either living the big league life or hacking it around in the bushes. In the middle of that season, I happened to be with the A's when they traveled to San Diego's Jack Murphy Stadium to play the Padres. The first day in, I noticed a gorgeous girl entertaining a group of people on the field during batting practice. She was working for the Pad Squad. The Pad Squad was a group of girls that were involved with the Padres' fan and community relations. For whatever reason, I became absolutely mesmerized with this girl; I could not take my eyes off her. It got to the point where I gave Mark Bellhorn a $100 bill and told him to keep it if I did not get the balls to talk to the Pad Squad chick before the series was over. If I did, the only thing I wanted was my money back. Bellhorn, doing his best to encourage me, offered to give me back $200 if I made the move. So after batting practice on the 2nd day, I got a glimpse of her on the field behind home plate entertaining a group of fans.

I sat on our dugout bench and tried to figure out how I was going to get the job done. Finally, there was a man who had walked over from her direction, and I stopped to ask him if he could please have the Pad Squad girl come over to the dugout. He obliged. She had somewhat of a bewildered look on her face as she walked over. "Hi, can I help you?"

For the first time in my life I was f*cking tongue-tied. "Um, ugh, Hi, I'm Eric." I then looked to my right and there was this cute kid sitting on the end of the bench. "This is my little buddy and he wanted to meet you." The little kid played the part perfectly, looking up at the girl with a huge smile on his face. I thought my move was brilliant! Then the girl looks at this cute 6-year-old kid with the same big smile and says, "Hi, Caden."

"Hi, Tarah."

Oh sh*t! They already knew each other! I began laughing and then stood up and said, "I am caught, I am Eric, I wanted to meet you."

Tarah was a good sport. I ended up having some basic casual conversation: where are you from, what school did you go to, and when do I get to see you again? Apparently every Wednesday night, the Pad Squad went to this country bar right by the stadium and she said there was a chance she would head there after the game. I got the $200 from Bellhorn and told him drinks were on me, let's go!

When we showed up, I didn't see her for a good half hour and just about when I had figured she had not showed up, I took a peek at the dance floor and there was this chick front and center, leading the line dance; it was her. I was originally mesmerized, I was in lust beforehand, and now I was in love. I usually don't dance unless I have had way too many cocktails but I didn't hesitate firing out there. I had no idea what I was doing. I was practically tripping over myself but I gave it my best effort, and I got the sense that she appreciated the attempt. At the end of the night, she was very clear about how far I was going to get. "There is no chance I am going back to your hotel but here is my number, call me."

I walked out of that bar so fired up; it was tough to think clearly. So much so I actually forgot her name! The next day I had to have my agent call the number and pull the, "Hi, this is Mike, who's this?"

"Tarah."

Ironically, I got sent back down to AAA that day, so I figured it was a good time to play the sympathy card. I also figured it would be a pretty good test to see if she would still talk to me now that I was no longer in the big leagues. I got no answer, so I left a message telling her I had been sent back to Sacramento and to give me a call back if she was a Rivercats fan and wanted to come to a game sometime. She had never heard of the Rivercats but she did call back. She actually was going to be heading up to Berkley the next weekend to stay with a friend, so I convinced her to stop in Sacramento for a game on the way up. She showed up with her best friend Amanda "Panda Can of Worms" Agajanian, and we had an absolute blast. Don't take this the wrong way but it was like hanging out with dudes. They were two of the most real girls I had ever met. A bit ironic, I'd say, because of Tarah's pageant background and the typical stereotypes that go with it.

I had no clue about Tarah and her pageant exploits until Amanda brought it up that night in Sacramento. The two of them explained to me the details of the entire pageant world and talked about how Tarah was getting ready for the Miss California pageant coming up in a few weeks. Essentially, there were 100 of the hottest girls in California vying for Miss California USA. Although Tarah was beautiful with a personality to match, I was very doubtful she had any sort of chance. As a matter of fact, I was not even sure I wanted her to win. I figured the hoopla and obligations surrounding Miss California would make it nearly impossible to develop any sort of REAL relationship. Two weeks later, she WINS!

Even with both of our ridiculous travel schedules, we found a way to make it work. Tarah had numerous obligations for her role as Miss California but came out and spent a lot of the winter with me in the Dominican Republic. Essentially, this was when I realized I would one day marry this woman. A pageant chick from San Diego who happened to be the reigning Miss California embraced the entire Dominican culture. Often against my advice, she came to every game traveling on crazy-ass roads with crazy-ass drivers. She had no complaints about the food, absolutely loved the coffee, and the classic Dominican beer, Presidente, became her staple. Most importantly, she loved the people who in a lot of ways had become my people.

A few months later, Tarah represented Miss California at the Miss USA contest. I had just faced Mariano Rivera in Yankee Stadium with 2 outs in the 9th inning with the playoffs on the line, and whatever nerves I felt then did not even come close to how I felt watching the Miss USA pageant on TV with all my boys from Spring Training. My biggest fear was her tripping over her dress or butchering a response to a question. Thankfully, she did not do either! She absolutely nailed it and ended up finishing in the top 10! As soon as she gave up her Miss California crown, she had all sorts of opportunities in the television and entertainment industry. Yet her main goal was to get married and be a mom. As I continued working to try to establish myself at the big league level over the next few years, she was incredibly supportive and understanding of how important baseball was to me. Somehow, I got her to stick with me for six years before I showed up to her mom's condo in San Diego with her Christmas gift: a new Cadillac CTS. That's when I told her to check how cool the cup holders are. Inside, a 2-karat diamond ring. She thought it was fake or some kind of joke then realized what was going on. Tarah, who always has her emotions in check, broke down and began uncontrollably crying.

I've pondered whether or not I believe in soul mates since I was a kid. I would have told you yes at 16, and then no at 26, then yes again at 36, all the while changing my opinion 9,000 times in between. Then I realized that my belief in soul mates never changed. My definition did.

When we are young, a soul mate is the ultimate form of pure puppy love. Perhaps the truest definition of a soul mate, but we are so young and ignorant to the process of life that we all will phase out of it at some point. When we get into our mid 20's, we have a vision of what our ideal spouse would look like and be like, and thus we create a new, more specific version of a soul mate. Our expectations become nearly impossible to meet and we ponder if it is possible a true soul mate was put on this earth just for us. Then, as we get older and the honeymoon phase of all relationships end, we realize like everything else in life, a soul mate is developed through a process.

Human Crash Test Dummy Life Lesson #109

A soul mate is developed over time and trials. A soul mate should be the most influential person in your life; the person you can rely on for anything and everything. Being a soul mate is being a partner, and the key to a successful partnership is reciprocation and understanding that person. Roles need not be defined by gender but rather love and passion. How can you guys best operate and utilize your individual strengths to benefit your family, the people around you, and your relationship?

If you both do something you love and work for the common good of each other and the family, you will give yourselves the best chance for a happy and successful relationship. Soul mates are able to anticipate the storms and then wink at each other through the eye of it. Accept each other because of every one of their flaws just as much as their strengths.

Chapter 110
Create Your Legacy

"The greatest legacy one can pass on to one's children and grandchildren is not money or other material things accumulated in one's life, but rather a legacy of character and faith."
-Billy Graham

Tarah and I got married at the Ritz Carlton in Half Moon Bay on December 1, 2007. We both knew we wanted to have kids but I don't think either of us had an exact timetable of when we wanted to get started. I can definitely say that the plan was not to knock her up within the first few months of marriage. I was still so incredibly immersed into baseball that it was difficult to think about embarking on anything that would take precedent over my profession. A baby at that point in my life certainly was not in the plans. In late March, Tarah was having severe abdominal pain that landed her in the hospital. She felt as if her appendix had ruptured and she was going to need an appendectomy. Turned out she was going to have a baby instead! People talked about how getting married was going to change my life. I couldn't disagree more. Getting married was a very cool ceremony and celebration followed by life as I knew it. Having kids was an entirely different story.

Throughout the pregnancy, I was like most other men. The first thing I was obviously rooting for was a healthy and happy baby. The second thing I was openly rooting for was the little baby to come out with a penis attached. I wanted a boy and I wanted a boy badly. The main reason being that I was scared I was going to have smoking hot daughters and all my karma was going to come back and haunt me.

People talk about how watching the birth of your own child is one of the most beautiful things that you will ever witness in your life. I would have to respectfully disagree. It was one of the most disturbing things that I ever watched. My wife was in excruciating pain for hours, all leading up to a bloody alien-looking creature coming out of her followed by one of the gnarliest things in the universe: the placenta. Yes, of course I understand the placenta is what keeps the baby alive in the mom's belly, and in that sense, it is no doubt a magical thing, but by no means is it in any way aesthetically beautiful.

The doctor then asked me if I wanted to cut the umbilical cord, to which I politely declined. I then watched him clip it off. As the doctor was putting the clamp on, he somehow lost control. The umbilical cord became a loose fire hose spraying blood in every direction. It looked like a bloody crime scene of a mass murder.

After I wiped the blood from my face, I headed over to meet my new child. As soon as the nurse was done sucking fluid out of the kid's mouth with a turkey baster, I finally had a chance to have my moment. No penis, but it did not matter; this was the most beautiful looking alien creature I had ever laid eyes on. Shockingly, she did not cry one bit; she was totally calm, cool, and collected. She did, however, stare right at me. I immediately fell in love. My entire life was forever changed on the 16th of December 2008, when Chloe Laine "Peanut" Byrnes entered this world.

After Peanut, we figured we might as well start firing them out. One thing that Tarah and I did discuss was that we wanted to have all our children close together, giving them an opportunity to be friends and look out for one another as well. When we found out that Tarah was pregnant again, as much as I would not have traded Peanut for any swinging dick in the world, I could not help but root once again for a boy. May 25, 2010, Tarah gave birth to our second child, another baby girl: Cali Annette "Sissy Small Fry Fancy Pants Strawberry Shortcake" Byrnes. Thankfully for her, she has every one of my wife's best physical features, so it is not surprising that she is absolutely gorgeous. Even better is that she has an attitude to go with it.

By the time we found out that Tarah was pregnant for a third time, I had become so mesmerized with my daughters that I finally stopped rooting for a boy. As a matter of fact, I wanted another girl. September 1, 2011, exactly 6 months after the death of my dad, Tarah gave birth to our third child, a baby boy named after his "Great Pa," Colton James Byrnes.

In our now 17 years together, I have been far from perfect, yet Tarah has still accepted me for all my shortcomings as a husband and as a father. Daily, she continues to help me grow spiritually, personally, and professionally. She is the stabilizing force in my chaotic life, and I thank God every day for everything she is as a person and everything she does as a matriarch to maintain our family.

Toni, Tarah's mother, was diagnosed with breast cancer, and when Tarah felt like she wasn't getting the proper care back east, she went out to Baltimore where Toni was living, packed her up, and brought her home to live with us for the next two years. Tarah micro-managed the entire treatment process until Toni eventually lost her battle and passed away in September of 2012. The patience and heart that she displayed was one of the most remarkable things that I have ever seen out of anyone in any situation. I can only pray that my children would show me that same sort of unwavering commitment and love.

Human Crash Test Dummy Life Lesson #110

Children are the greatest gift of life. To have an opportunity to bring a child into the world is something that trumps all else you will ever experience. Then, the process to help mold your children into loving, kind, caring, and productive members of society can be the most challenging-yet-rewarding experience you will ever encounter. Embrace the process for everything it has to offer. You can create your legacy through knowledge and experience but you must be able to pass it on; otherwise, the legacy you worked so hard to create will die with you. Spread the love.

Chapter 111
Smile in the Face of Death

*"The real man smiles in trouble, gathers strength from distress,
and grows brave by reflection."*
-Thomas Paine

Toni became very much a part of our everyday life. For two years, "Nina," as my kids called her, never once complained about anything, including the obvious pain she was in. She was terminally ill and faced death on a daily basis, yet I truly believe that is what allowed her to fully live her life. She became so unconcerned with trivial bullsh*t that she constantly had a smile on her face and enjoyed each day to a level most of us could only dream of. She was given two months to live when she first moved in with us, but her attitude, faith, and spirit kept her alive for another two years.

Toni taught me that no matter what the circumstance, wake up with a smile on your face, be thankful for all of the gifts in your life, and enjoy every moment. Till the day Toni died, she did exactly that.

Human Crash Test Dummy Life Lesson #111

No matter what the circumstance, good or bad, the only thing that matters is your reaction to it. If you can find a way to find peace in the face of perceived adversity, you will maximize the potential of your life. Ultimately, that is all any of us can ever ask for.

Chapter 112
Find an Outlet

*"I always channeled what I felt emotionally into skiing - my insecurities, my
anger, my disappointment. Skiing was always my outlet, and it worked."*
-Lindsey Vonn

Within the first few years of their life, my kids experienced the loss
of their Great Pa and then their Nina. Shortly after Nina passed away,
Bruin, our first bulldog, had to go to doggie heaven.

Enough was enough with death in all of our lives in such a short
period of time. It was time to bring in some LIFE. It was time to start
looking for a bulldog puppy!

We already had two other bulldogs, Bella and Mr. Hitch, and they
were both getting up there in age. The idea of having a puppy to
stimulate any sort of activity from the two other dogs would be huge.
The other thing I knew was that I wanted to name my next puppy
"Porkchop."

When I began looking for dogs, I was completely overwhelmed with
the process. The last time I actively searched for a bulldog was Bruin,
and I found him in the advertisement section of the San Francisco
Chronicle. We got Bella from a pet store in Scottsdale and we took
Mr. Hitch in when Tarah's grandmother got sick. She originally had
gotten Mr. Hitch because she loved Bruin so much.

There were hundreds if not thousands of bulldogs online for sale. I
had no idea where to start, but I definitely had a clear vision of what
I wanted: championship blood lines, big head, big paws, stout body,
white with brown spots, and a patch on his eye, and had to be no
older than 8 weeks. Simple requests, right?

I looked at nearly 1,000 bulldogs from all over the world and nothing
came close to meeting my ridiculous demands. Just as I was giving up

and figured it was a lost cause, BOOM! Quite frankly, it was the cutest puppy I had ever seen in my life. Of all the dogs that I looked at, it seemed that about 50% of them were named while the others just had basic statistical information. I was in such amazement that the dog had every characteristic that I was looking for that I didn't even bother to look if he had a name or not. Then, as I was closing my computer I looked below the dog's pictures and noticed that he was already named... Porkchop!!!

Once I found out his name was "Porkchop," there was no way I was not going to get him. Call me crazy but I believe it was Bruin's way of talking to me. Okay, maybe I am crazy, but you bet your ass "Porkchop" arrived to the Byrnes family home a week later.

From that point on, "Porkchop" and I became inseparable. If I went to the coffee shop, Porkchop was with me; if I went to the grocery store, Porkchop was with me; if I went to take a dump, Porkchop was with me. He was my little buddy and I was showing him the way of the world. I even spent 15 days in Arizona working for MLB Network traveling from one Major League camp to another, with Porkchop in tow. He was the hit of every camp.

While in Arizona, Porkchop developed "cherry eye." Cherry eye is essentially when part of the eyelid becomes so inflamed at times that it looks like some sort of large red growth that can literally cover the entire eye. Porkchop would wake up some mornings and it looked like he had an eyeball popping out of the socket. Other mornings it was completely normal. When we got back to Half Moon Bay, I took him into the local vet that we had an extensive history with. The solution was to do a minor procedure that would tuck and sew the eyelid that continued to flare up. The morning that I was scheduled to drop Porkchop off, I could just feel that something wasn't right. I don't have any rhyme or reason as to why I felt that way, but as I dropped him off, the vet literally had to rip him out of my hands. I got one last big wet smooch on the lips.

When I got home that night from work, as soon as I walked into the door, Chloe and Cali were there to greet me. "Porkchoppy had to go to heaven, Daddy."

I immediately looked up and saw Tarah standing over the kids with tears falling down her face. I turned around and punched a hole in the door. "Don't worry, Daddy, Porkchoppy can play with Great Pa, Nina, and Bruin; they are all in heaven together."

When somebody deals with a traumatic event in their life, they usually will originally respond with great sadness and grief. Many times, this is followed by some sort of remorse, regret, or reasoning. Ultimately, anger will typically set in. Within a very short period of time, my family had dealt with the death of my dad, Tarah's mom, and Bruin. Emotionally, I didn't have it in me to get sad. I was spent. I was completely grieved out. So, I just got pissed, really f*cking pissed.

How could the vet botch such a basic surgery? Apparently, they put Porkchop under anesthesia, and after the surgery was complete, while he was slowly regaining consciousness, he stopped breathing and went into cardiac arrest. I had heard stories of that happening to other dogs but I didn't give a f*ck. As far as I was concerned, I had officially lost all faith in the medical industry. Between what had happened to my dad, Tarah's mom, and now Porkchop, forgive me if I have reservations about the competency of the people who are supposedly qualified to take care of us.

Tarah was there once again to be the stabilizing force to keep our family, specifically me, sane. That task was obviously growing increasingly difficult. My children were becoming immune to death. Going to heaven to them seemed like going to the grocery store or going to the park. For several weeks after we lost Porkchop, Cali kept telling me that she wanted to go to heaven to play with Porkchoppy and Bruin. She couldn't understand why Great Pa and Nina got to go and play with the doggies but she didn't. Chloe understood a little bit more and would say that she wanted to go to heaven to see everybody, but not yet. Baby Colton, who used to jump on Porkchop's back, was much too young to comprehend any of this. Although the little dude did ask, "Where my horsey go?"

With all of the events and happenings in my life, triathlons were and still are my release. At times, it has served as my escape from reality. The long training hours have been extremely therapeutic and in many ways have helped organize my chaotic life. From the time I wake up in the morning to the time I put my head on my pillow at night, I make sure there is not a wasted minute in the day. Being a good father and husband will always take precedent over any sort of endurance training or work schedule. Yet, in order for me to best function as a father, a husband, or even a broadcaster, I am generally much better off AFTER I get my workouts in. There have been several days when Tarah has actually told me to get out of the house and go on a run, bike, or swim.

The best thing I could have ever done to maintain a solid home life and manage a chaotic work and training schedule was to integrate the family into my travel schedule and endurance world. Both Tarah and my sister Shea have completed several Olympic distance triathlons and half marathons. My sister's husband, Justin, has taken up triathlon as well and recently completed his first Ironman. As far as my children, Chloe at 5, Cali at 4, and Colton at the ripe age of 2, all finished their first triathlon and have participated in every "Iron Kids" race before each event that Tarah or I have competed in.

Human Crash Test Dummy Life Lesson #112

Just when you think that things can't get any more difficult, understand that they can. Use each of these incredibly difficult situations as a learning experience. There is no doubt that life can be incredibly overwhelming. Find a release. Find an outlet to let go of your hurt, tensions, and anxieties. Then don't be afraid to share that outlet with the people you love and the people you want to spend your time with. Life is lived better as a team.

Chapter 113
Ready, Set, BOOM!

"The most difficult thing is the decision to act, the rest is merely tenacity. The fears are paper tigers. You can do anything you decide to do. You can act to change and control your life; and the procedure, the process is its own reward."
-Amelia Earhart

When I finally got to the start line of Ironman Arizona 2011, I had raced 13 times in an 11-month period. If there was a race in California, Arizona, or Nevada and I wasn't working at MLB Network, I was going to race. I figured the more races that I got to participate in and gain experience, the better chance I would have to complete the Ironman. Even as a kid, I always had a fear of being unprepared for any sort of test in school or game in any sport. The thought of not being prepared absolutely freaked me out. So, when I found myself amongst 3,000 people treading water waiting for the famous Ironman cannon to sound, I was amazingly confident. I was ready.

When the swim began, absolute chaos immediately set in. I couldn't take a single stroke without bumping into the person in front of me, and I couldn't get away from the dickhead grabbing my ankles and calves from behind. I had done some gnarly swim starts including Escape from Alcatraz, where you jump off a perfectly good boat with 2,000 other people and do what was thought to be impossible just 50 years earlier: swim to San Francisco. As daunting as that swim was because of the water temperature, current, and chop, it did not compare to what I was experiencing in my first Ironman. 3,000 Type-A personalities fighting for swimming room in a confined space was a complete and utter debacle. Just as I thought it had cleared up about 10 minutes into the swim, I got kicked in the mouth and began profusely bleeding. The reason I knew I was bleeding was not because I could see the blood in the water, but rather with every breath I would take I could taste the blood gargling in my mouth.

By the time I got to the turnaround point 1.2 miles into the swim, I had spent so much time in a horizontal position trying to kick the dude off of me that my legs had begun to cramp. I had no choice but to swim the entire second half as if my legs were dead. By the time I got out of the water 1 hour and 15 minutes later (3 minutes under what Frank had predicted), it was a huge relief! To think how far I had come as a swimmer in such a short period of time was nothing short of a small miracle. When I said that I could not swim 25 yards without stopping 11 months earlier, it was not a joke. If anything, I am overestimating where I was as a swimmer because several times I remember stopping before I reached the end of the 25-yard pool.

When I got out of the water and into the transition area, my legs continued to cramp and go into spasms as I struggled to put on my bike gear. Eventually, 10 minutes later, I rolled out of transition ready to attempt to bike 112 miles. Not surprisingly, I had a huge urge to eat bananas at every aid station. The first 80 miles of the bike went exactly as planned; I was very comfortable and felt like I was managing my effort level very well. I did my best to not think about the marathon that lied ahead; I just tried to enjoy the moment and focus on each pedal stroke. By the time I got to around to mile 90, I was toast; the marathon I tried to ignore now seemed to hang over my head like the darkest of clouds. I was in a bad place trying to figure out how the f*ck I was going to finish the race. I was holding around 230 watts of power output the entire ride, and then all of a sudden, I could not touch 200 watts. The drop-off was absurdly ridiculous and no doubt was attributed to my limited endurance base. Most people who do their first Ironman spend several years building up to that distance, not months.

By the time I got off the bike, my legs were so shot I felt like there was no way I would be able to run a single mile, let alone 26.2. I took off on the run course with limited expectations and just continued to put one foot in front of another. Surprisingly, my legs actually started to feel better as the miles began to pile up. Eventually, I hit the 20-mile mark that everybody had warned me so much about, and I flew right past it, feeling sexy as could be. Yet 2 miles later when I reached mile 22, and had only 4 miles to go, I all of a sudden felt like I couldn't take another step. The one goal I had going into the race was to not walk at all during the marathon. At this point I didn't want to walk; I wanted to lay my ass down on the pavement. I knew the only way I was going to be able to continue to run the last 4 miles was by doing the same thing that got me through the 6-hour training rides and 3-hour training runs: long conversations with my dad.

I came down the final stretch along Tempe Town Lake. The sun was setting and spectators were going nuts. I had always tried to not think about what it would be like to cross the finish line of an Ironman because I knew in order to get there I was going to need to focus on the process and not the end result. Probably because I was talking to him not only as if he were still alive, but essentially as if he was running right next to me, there was no surprise the same visual images of my dad from the beginning of the race came back. The comical element was that he was running in his short-ass 1970s dolphin shorts and a cut-off Kenpo Karate T-shirt; the exact same get-up that he used to wear when I would go on runs with him as a kid. Don't get me wrong, I was coherent enough to realize he wasn't really there, yet after 10 hours of exerting my body to the limit, I was ready to roll with whatever delusional tricks my mind wanted to play. The feeling in my body eventually became numb. No way for me to really explain what was happening; maybe I was just getting excited that the finish line was finally near, but all of a sudden, I was f*cking MOVING!

My dad had this thing at the end of runs he would call "super jet speed." He would take off sprinting and I would do everything to try to keep up but always ended up getting smoked. I felt as if he called for "super jet speed" and then let me hop on his back. The way I felt just a few minutes prior, there was no chance I should have been capable of running that fast.

As part of the Ironman Foundation fundraising efforts toward local charities, I had raised several thousand dollars for the Pat Tillman Foundation and found it appropriate to cross the finish line holding Pat's jersey. My intent was and still is to remind people of who Pat was and the ultimate sacrifice he paid while fighting for our country after passing up a multi-million-dollar NFL contract post 9/11. I had asked my sister to handoff the jersey right before the spectator stands started. So, there she was, jumping up and down right in the middle of the racecourse holding Pat Tillman's Arizona Cardinals #40 jersey. Apparently, she saw no reason to stay behind the barricades and I absolutely loved it. I couldn't help but break out in laughter as she handed it over.

Just like my dad, my sister has always created her own boundaries.

I made the final turn into the finishing chute with Pat's jersey proudly elevated above my head. I am not sure how many people the grand stands of an Ironman hold, but I assume there is no way it could be much more than a couple thousand. I have played baseball in front of 65,000 people before and very rarely have I ever heard an instantaneous roar like I did when I came around the corner flying Pat's jersey above my head. After 140.5 miles and just one tenth of a mile to go, I stopped to enjoy the moment. I knew exactly why people were cheering, and I wanted to give parents a chance to explain to their children who Pat Tillman was.

With my head down, I turned the front of the jersey to the stands on the left, then to the stands on the right. I then proceeded to cross the finish line 10 hours and 46 minutes after the day had begun. I was so incredibly overwhelmed with emotion that there are really no words to describe exactly how I felt at that moment. Legendary announcer Mike Riley shouted in his famously enthusiastic voice, "Eric Byrnes, you are an Ironman."

Thanks to the Ironman Foundation, who granted access to my family just beyond the finish line. My mom, sister, wife, and 3 kids were all right there waiting as soon as I crossed. We hugged, we cried, we hugged again, and cried some more.

I realize this is starting to sound a bit over the top. In the grand scheme of things, by no means was me doing an Ironman any sort of monumental feat, but for me, considering the circumstances, it was the greatest accomplishment of my life. First day of school, first day in the big leagues, first home run, you can roll all of them into one and they don't come close to the emotion I experienced after finishing my first Ironman. Not exactly sure why but I have to figure it was the culmination of the long physical and emotional investment, my dad's passing, an overwhelming pride of being able to represent the Pat Tillman foundation, and sharing all of this with my wife, kids, mom, and sister after the very difficult year that we all endured together.

Human Crash Test Dummy Life Lesson #113

The only way to conquer an incredibly difficult challenge is by completely going ALL IN on the process. There are different ways of training, but there is no such thing as a short cut. A short cut is simply a route to underachievement. The route to success involves making the ultimate commitment to becoming your best. If you want to become your best, you must have the support and involvement of those closest to you. Their backing will touch you spiritually and elevate you to an entirely new level.

Chapter 114
You Don't Do This Sh*t Because It's Easy

"Accept the challenges so that you can feel the exhilaration of victory."
-George S. Patton

There are typically two reactions after people complete their first Ironman:

#1: "Great experience! I am DONE."

#2: "When can I sign up for the next one?"

I chose door #2 and immediately signed up for the inaugural NYC Ironman, which ended up being an absolute ball-buster in 100-degree heat. I then did Ironman Arizona again in November of 2012, setting the stage for what I would consider the toughest and gnarliest Ironman on record: Ironman Lake Tahoe in 2013.

September 22, 2013, a day after a freak early season blizzard hit Lake Tahoe, I completed Lake Tahoe's inaugural Ironman despite a 40% DNF (Did Not Finish) rate. It has now become known by many as the most challenging Ironman in the world. IMLT was my 4th Ironman. Below is the race recap I wrote the day after the race:

"The World's Toughest Ironman? Ironman Lake Tahoe Race Recap"

Over 2700 people signed up for the inaugural Ironman Lake Tahoe with hopes and dreams of crossing the finish line at Squaw Valley with legendary announcer Mike Riley calling their name followed by the declaration, "YOU ARE AN IRONMAN!" Unfortunately for just about 40% of the original entrants, that never happened. Many never made it to the start line because of below freezing temperatures, while others made an attempt but simply just couldn't pull it off for a variety of reasons. Several athletes were actually pulled out of the water or decided to shut it down after the first loop of the swim course. Visibility was an issue because of steam coming off of the water and chop left over from the storm the day before, making swim conditions rough toward the middle of the lake. On the bike, there were actually busses that needed to be sent out to pick up athletes because so many people met their Ironman fate on the brutally hilly course. Many participants who were lucky enough to make it to the marathon eventually fell victim to nightfall, rapidly decreasing temperatures, and/or the eventual 17-hour cut off.

Growing up in the San Francisco Bay Area, I spent many summer and winter days with the family in Lake Tahoe. I grew up on the slopes skiing in between my Dad's legs when I was 2 years old. During the summer, water skiing, jet skiing and cliff diving were family rituals. I actually even learned to surf on the lake with my feet locked in by two wind surfing straps Dad had drilled into the board, years before wake boarding ever existed.

No doubt Lake Tahoe has always been somewhat of a sacred place for me, so when I heard Ironman was going to be coming it was a no brainer. I was in! Apparently 2700 other people had similar feelings because within 20 minutes of opening online registration, the race sold out.

The course included two 1.2-mile swim loops at Kings Beach in Lake Tahoe, followed by a two-and-a-half loop bike course through Tahoe City, Truckee, Martis Camp, and Northstar, and then up over the 267 "Brockway" summit, back to Kings Beach and eventually ending at Squaw Valley 112 miles later. The run took us from Squaw Valley to Tahoe City then back to Squaw for a fly-by-the-finish-line tease, only to head back out for another 8 miles, completing the marathon and 140.6-mile day back at Squaw Village. The official elevation profile on the Ironman website for the bike was 6,550 feet of elevation gain and 653 feet for the run. Although, several people (including myself) measured the gains at well over 8,000 feet for the bike course and 1000 feet for the run. Ultimately, does it really matter? Ironman races were not meant to be easy.

On Saturday, the day before the race, I got up at 5 am and headed to the swim start at Kings Beach thinking I was going to jump into the water for a short swim session. By the time the sun came up, a storm was in the process of moving in and by 6:40 am, exactly 24 hours before the race, there were 3-foot waves in the lake. I then headed to Squaw to meet my 3 munchkins for the Iron Kids race, which was a very cool event; the kids absolutely ate it up! Not long after the race was over, the torrential wind and rain officially shut down the expo. By the time I got back to my house, which is literally located on the bike course, it looked like a very standard Lake Tahoe Christmas. My kids were in the backyard building Frosty, having snowball fights, and asking Daddy where their sled was. Not surprisingly, talks of Ironman canceling the race spread quickly. When I went to bed at 9 pm Saturday night, I had no idea whether or not we were going to race. The below-freezing temperatures and potential ice on the roads became a major concern. I got up at 4:30 am, fired down a banana and two packets of instant oatmeal, then filled up my coffee cup and headed to my early morning "office" with my cup of Joe and the open package of coffee grinds that I held under my nose. The coffee was helping build up the explosion that was about to take place in the toilet. I followed up the session with a race day trick that has yet to fail me: two Imodium tablets to clog the pipes for the rest of the day.

When I got into the family conversion van at 5:30 am the temperature read 27 degrees. I picked up my race/training compadre, Team Firefighter Captain Kyle Hamilton, on the way down to Kings Beach, still not knowing our racing fate. When we got out at about 6 am to drop off our water bottles on the bike, we got word everything was on as scheduled, meaning a 6:40 am rolling start for the age-groupers. It was on! Now the question was, how was I going to stay warm?

I reverted back to my baseball days. Whenever I would play a game in cold weather, I would lather up my ENTIRE body in a super-hot lubricant nicknamed "The Cheese." Think Bengay multiplied by 10. The day before at the expo I found a lube called "DZ Nuts" (no joke). It wasn't quite the same strength as the queso but definitely had some kick. Generally, I would avoid covering the groin region, but figuring temperatures were in the 20s and I was about to jump into lake water in the 50s, extreme conditions called for extreme measures.

The pro cannon went off at 6:30 am and that was our cue to hightail it out of the heated van and to the start line. The "rolling" start consisted of several groups beginning with the self-seeded, sub-1-hour swimmers. I jumped the fence where the 1-hour to 1:10 group was situated. As I settled in, waiting for the age group cannon to go off, I quickly realized "DZ Nuts" were on fire!!! I was now profusely sweating and practically foaming at the mouth. I needed water.

Thankfully, I spotted a spectator holding a half-full water bottle. I literally grabbed it out of his hand then guzzled the entire thing. In case you are reading this, sorry, dude! "BOOM," the age group cannon fired away.

The first 50 yards of the swim were very shallow and filled with all sorts of sand bars that essentially made swimming impossible. Every Ironman that I have done in the past, I have had some sort of euphoric experience that generally happened towards the latter stages of the bike or at some point during the marathon. This time, that experience happened as soon as I crossed the timing mat. Maybe it had to do with the fact I began skipping in the water, which for whatever reason brought out my more sensitive and emotional side? Very tough to describe but I essentially became completely entranced by the snow-topped mountains and steam rising from the water. Everything became quiet; all of the noise around me and the other swimmers became non-existent. As soon as the water was deep enough, I took one final big skip and dove in headfirst. The immediate ice cream headache woke me up from la la land and the reality of the 140.6 miles that lied ahead set in.

The steam made it very difficult to see anything, so my only focus was the next yellow buoy. The first row of buoys to follow was yellow and the turn buoy was red. I swam alongside the yellow buoys, keeping anyone in a kayak or on a stand-up paddleboard to my left. I felt like I had been swimming for a while and still had not found the red buoy to make the turn; that's when I realized I was about to swim into cross traffic. I had followed the yellow buoys but missed the red turn buoy. As much as I wanted to keep going and blend in with the rest of the swimmers, which I could have very easily done, I had to go back. I figured I didn't get to the starting line of my 4th Ironman by cutting corners and I wasn't about to start.

I essentially had to swim about 100 yards to go back around the red buoy and then another 100 to get back to where I was. I was swimming the complete opposite direction of traffic and did my best to avoid head-on collisions; it was kind of like playing Frogger in the water. I eventually made it back on the correct course, completing the first lap in 36 minutes. I was not thrilled with the time, but considering my Magellan route, I wasn't about to complain. I then hammered out the second 1.2-mile loop in 32 minutes completing the entire swim in 1:08. My expectations for the 2.4-mile swim were anywhere between 1:02 and 1:10 depending on the conditions and my questionable navigational ability. I was not surprised at all that my watch read 2.8 miles!

When I got out of the water, it was awesome to see the tremendous crowd support along the beach, including my mom, sister, Aunt Claudia, Aunt Cathy and Uncle Mike, and of course my wife, Tarah, and her two best friends, "Cole Cole" and "Amanda Panda" all standing at the water's edge. It definitely helped me forget how freaking cold it was outside. I headed up to transition, grabbed my bike gear bag, and then went into the changing tent to do my best Clark Kent impersonation. The tent was packed so instead of trying to find a place inside the tent, or a chair to sit on, I just peeled down right at the entrance. Usually I would have worn my tri shorts underneath the wetsuit but because of the cold I wanted to keep everything dry and decided to go commando. I could probably think of better times to expose myself considering the natural shrinkage elements.

I geared up with my tri shorts and top and then covered that up with my tight black long underwear I generally wear under my ski gear. I topped that off with a wind-breaking jacket, full booties covering my shoes, and gloves that I could have comfortably built a snowman in. The last thing was the beanie on the head and I was off.

I got about 50 yards away from the tent, and just as I was digging myself after what I thought was a pretty good transition, some guy from the crowd chimed in. "Dude, where's your helmet?" Sh*t! Backtracking was becoming an all too common theme of this race so far.

I sprinted back to the tent, barging through the other triathletes like a frantic maniac as if I literally lost my head. Before I was eventually on my bike, I had spent over 10 minutes in transition. My boy Mike Breen, who also competed and finished, later asked me if I was checking football scores.

Although my hands and feet were numb for the first 2 hours of the ride, the good part about spending the appropriate amount of time in transition was that I was able to gear up and was actually very comfortable on the bike, despite starting temperatures in the 20s and 30s. I had ridden the course several times and planned to manage my effort by using my power meter. Overall, I wanted to average 230 watts for the ride. I figured if I stayed between 210 and 220 on the flats and around 260 on the hills, I should come in around the 230 number. Of course, like most races I have done in the past, my ego kicks in when some yahoo passes me on the bike, and generally the watt plans go out the window. Although I figured if I rode each 45-mile loop in 2 hours and 30 minutes, I would leave myself an hour to finish the last 22 mostly flat miles to Squaw Valley in order to achieve my under-6-hour bike goal. Unfortunately, I got into a pissing contest on Highway 89 and finished the first loop in 2:24 averaging 255 watts. I quickly realized if I wanted to run the entire marathon I was going to have to scale it back.

All seemed to be going well but then I hit a wall about mile 70 of the bike. I actually started to enter a pretty dark place. My legs felt overly fatigued, my neck was starting to get sore from the extended amount of time in aero bars, and I still had 42 miles to go, including the most difficult part of the bike course. Oh, and there was this little 26.2 mile run that awaited me at the completion of the bike. I quickly refocused on the process and simply put all my attention on continuing to move forward with smooth, clean peddle strokes. I then got a HUGE recharge when I rode by my house climbing through Martis. My entire family, including my 3 kids, were out front ringing cowbells, blowing horns, and holding signs. I am usually very uncomfortable riding my bike with no hands but I could not help throwing both arms in the air to salute their support. It is amazing how that sort of encouragement can take me from thinking, "this is the last Ironman I will ever do" to the thought process of, "when is the next one!" I finished the second loop in 2:36 putting me right back where I had hoped to be, at 5 hours with 22 flat miles to go.

I eventually pulled into Squaw with a bike split of 5 hours and 58 minutes, but I was not feeling great. I could only hope that I did not burn too many candles on the first lap. Regardless of how I managed my watts on the bike, I was hurting and the notion of running a marathon at this point seemed ridiculous. I did just about all my long training runs on the IMLT course so I knew exactly what to expect, but problem was I had no idea how my legs were going to respond after a 2.4-mile swim and 112-mile bike with gnarly elevation gains.

I had done all the training runs of 18 miles or more between an 8:30 and 9-minute pace. To be conservative, I figured I would be about 1 minute per mile slower based on fatigue so I went into the run with the goal of running 9:30 to 10-minute miles. I came off the bike running very comfortably at an 8:30 pace for the first two miles, which were mostly flat and a bit downhill. The 3rd mile took us back uphill and around the Squaw Creek resort, and that's when I knew I was going to slow down.

The next mile was downhill so I went back to around 8:30 then followed it up with a mostly uphill 10-minute mile when we hit Highway 89. All the way out to Tahoe City, I was clocking 9-10 minutes per mile, running slightly up hill and against the Truckee River flowing the other direction.

When I made the turn around, I was hoping to get faster running "down river" as I had during my training runs but that did not happen. My legs continued to get heavier and heavier as the miles piled up. My goal was to make it to mile 16, and then I would dip into the reserve gasoline, Coca-Cola. In my last Ironman, between miles 10-16, my splits dropped off significantly. I finally decided to go for a Coke at the aid station as a move of desperation and what I experienced after that was a game changer. My thoughts became clear, my legs felt fresh, and most importantly, my pace picked up big time and I actually had a negative split the last 10 miles. So, when I finally got to mile 16, pure bliss awaited me and I guzzled down the soda and every mile after that I was like a crack addict looking for his next fix. My times did not improve but they also did not fall off, and considering what I had put my body through since 6:40 am, I was not about to complain as the sun began to set.

Coming up on mile 25 I felt great. I am not sure if it was the Coke, the fact that I did not over-exert myself at any point during the run, or simply because the finish line was 1 mile away. I came into the Squaw Village and spotted my sister holding Pat Tillman's #40 Arizona Cardinal jersey over the rail. For all my IM's, she has been there to pass me the jersey which I have proudly made my Ironman finishing tradition. 11 hours 37 minutes and 5 seconds after the race had begun, I crossed the finish line with Pat Tillman's jersey flying high, completing my 4th Ironman triathlon. I was 155th out of the original 2700 to finish and 22nd out of 270 in my age group. In my first 3 Ironman's, I finished in 11:09, 10:45 and 10:24. I was 1 hour and 14 minutes slower than my personal best, yet at that point it was by far the highest I have placed overall and in my age group.

I can go out on a training run and it feels like it is almost impossible for me to go any slower than a 9-minute mile. My last half marathon I completed took 1 hour and 26 minutes, 6:36 per mile. My last 5k, I finished in 18 minutes clocking 5:50 miles. My last marathon I just completed in January of 2018, I finished in 3 hours and 9 minutes with an average pace of 7:12 and qualified for the historic Boston Marathon. My time in the Lake Tahoe Ironman was 4 hours and 14 minutes, which equates to 9:41/mile. That is the amazing thing about

Ironman. Several times when I had been feeling good and was thinking I am moving along nicely, I have looked down at my watch only to find out I was running an 11-minute mile!

My wife Tarah, and 3 kids, Chloe, age 4, Cali, age 3, and Colton, age 2, were waiting just across the finish line and I literally fell into their arms. I then looked back into the snow-filled mountains and could have sworn I saw my dad with a big-ass grin on his face. When I first got into triathlon and everybody thought I was nuts for wanting to do an Ironman, it was my dad who encouraged what others perceived as insanity. Shoot, I even questioned myself! His explanation was very simple though. He felt that the challenge of IM would help me transition away from baseball and into the next phase of my life as a father, husband, and broadcaster while maintaining the physical and psychological discipline and structure, which I had become accustomed to and essentially needed since my childhood. The passion and drive that he and my mom instilled in me throughout the course of my life is what continues to bring me to the start line. I now relish the opportunity to set an example and pass those same traits on to my children.

In Ironman, each race has its own personality, difficulties, and challenges. Statistically, there has never been a harder Ironman than the inaugural Lake Tahoe. While many people may avoid a race with an average finish time of well over 14 hours (basically an hour slower than any other Ironman), believe me when I tell you, I couldn't wait to do it again.

Human Crash Test Dummy Life Lesson #114

The victory is the process; therefore, the greater the process, the greater the victory. It's up to you whether or not you truly accept the award while in the midst of the process.

Chapter 115
Chase Your Kona

"Our goals can only be reached through a vehicle of a plan,
in which we must fervently believe, and upon which we must vigorously act.
There is no other route to success."
-Pablo Picasso

8 weeks after Tahoe, in November of 2013, I finished Ironman Arizona again, my 5th Ironman in exactly a 2-year period. After Ironman Lake Tahoe was cancelled because of smoke in 2014, I returned to Arizona for the 4th consecutive year and finished my 6th Ironman in a personal best time of 10 hours and 8 minutes. Out of well over 3000 athletes, I finished 100th overall and 14th out of several hundred in the very competitive 35-39 age group. I then spent several months delving into the ultra-marathon world before returning to triathlon and completing Ironman Lake Tahoe in September of 2015. I completed the race higher than I ever had at an Ironman event: 51st overall and 10th in my age group. I followed up IMLT with IMAZ in November of 2015 and finished in a personal record of 10 hours and 1 minute. Keeping with tradition, I completed IMAZ in 2016 in just over 10 hours again and then the iconic Ironman Lake Placid in July of 2017 and IMAZ again in November of 2017, finishing 9th in my age group.

In the triathlon world, the legendary race that just about every triathlete shoots to qualify for is the Ironman World Championship held in Kona, Hawaii every October. There are a few different ways to get to Kona, the first being to get a lottery spot or an Ironman exemption. People pay a premium each year to have their name in the lottery in hopes of being selected and towing the start line with the world's best. The exemption is usually made for people who are going to bring the sport more exposure and are generally highlighted on the NBC broadcast that is so brilliantly put together each year. Former Pittsburg Steeler Hines Ward and celebrity chef Gordan Ramsey were both featured in the 2013 Kona race. Olympic speed skater Apollo Ohno was featured in 2014. Oftentimes you will see inspirational stories about people dealing with some sort of personal tragedy. They are rightfully granted Kona slots so their stories can be told.

In 2013, a triathlete father who always had dreams of competing in Kona lost his 6-year-old daughter in the Sandy Hook Elementary shooting. He completed the race in her honor. Another way to get to Kona is to qualify based on your time at another Ironman event. There is not a universal time that a person needs to get at each race, but rather each race has a certain number of qualifying spots that are distributed based on the percentage of men and women that constitute each age group. To give you a gauge of how difficult it is to qualify, I just received my AWA gold card (All World Athlete), which goes out to the top 5% of all Ironman competitors in the world. The closest I have come to qualifying for Kona was Ironman Arizona in 2017, and I was still 4 spots away. Many of the age groupers that qualify for Kona routinely beat several professional triathletes. The last way to get to Kona is the "legacy" clause. Once a triathlete completes 12 full-distance Ironman triathlons, he or she enters a pool with other legacy members. Then several triathletes who qualified the "hard way" get selected to compete each year.

Of course, I would love to qualify for Kona at some point, but I have no desire to go through the lottery process or take any sort of Ironman exemption. If I am ever fortunate enough to compete in the Ironman World Championship, it will be because I earned it based on my time. Although I have completed 11 Ironman's as of November of 2017, I figure I am too close to qualifying on time to accept the 12 full-distance Ironman legacy entry. No disrespect to any former professional athlete or celebrity who has participated in Kona. No disrespect as well to the people who are granted exemptions because of their inspirational tales. Triathlons need ambassadors to bring the sport into the mainstream world and Kona slots that are given out help do exactly that. The thing with me is that I have completely immersed myself in the sport, so much so that I would feel like I was taking a slot away from a well-deserving age grouper who has worked his or her entire life to get a chance to compete in Kona. I also love the challenge of continuing to do different Ironman events around the world and working to improve as a triathlete. I will by no means consume my life with getting to Kona, but I will not back down from the challenge either. One thing for certain, although it may hurt a little bit, I will continue to enjoy the CHASE.

Ironically, in the spring of 2017, I competed in the half distance Ironman (70.3 miles) in Kona, Hawaii and qualified for the Ironman 70.3 World Championship in Chattanooga, Tennessee. I then raced against the World's Best at the half Ironman distance in September of 2017, an incredible humbling, AWESOME experience.

Human Crash Test Dummy Life Lesson #115

With 11 full-distance Ironman's under my belt, I will continue to strive to qualify for the Ironman World Championship in Kona, but I've also come to realize it's okay to have your "reach" goals. Those are the goals you may not reach and they are the goals that keep you entrenched in the process. I've also realized it truly has very little to do with reaching the actual goal, but rather it is about the process of hunting that goal. It's not the kill that excites; it's the chase. Keep chasing!

Chapter 116
Do Epic Sh*t

"In every walk with nature one receives far more than he seeks."
-John Muir

When I originally received my Spring Training work schedule in 2015 for MLB Network, I became a bit concerned. I was going to have to leave home on the 8th of March and not return until the 26th. My trip took me from San Francisco to NYC to Arizona, back to NYC, then to Florida before finally returning back to San Francisco. My 2 immediate thoughts were that it is way too long of a time to be away from my family and how was I possibly going to be able to get in quality training sessions to prepare myself for an upcoming BEAST of a race, the Miwok 100k? The course entails nearly 12,000 feet of elevation gain over 62 miles of hard-core trails. I quickly scheduled to have the family come out to NYC for a week and began brainstorming about creative ways to accomplish some long runs. As I was dissecting the schedule, I noticed that the first camp I worked in Florida was the Detroit Tigers, located in Lakeland. The next camp was the Houston Astros, located 48 miles away in Kissimmee. BOOM! The solution to my problem just slapped me in the face and kicked me in the nuts at the same time. I decided to run the 48 miles from camp to camp.

Immediately, I began searching all sorts of route options. Unfortunately, not one of them seemed appealing. The best route took me southeast from Lakeland on the US 92/17 and eventually north to Kissimmee. There were various back roads involved as well. I landed in Tampa on Saturday, March 21st and right away headed out to scope the course I intended to run the next day. What I found was essentially what I had seen on Google Maps, and what I had expected: roads with no shoulders surrounded by swamp land and speeding cars. Was the run possible? Of course. Was the run ideal?

NO, not even close.

At the last minute, possibly because my wife Tarah was becoming overly concerned with the idea of the run, my family decided to accompany me on the trip. Once the route was detailed, it confirmed both of our beliefs that the only way to get the run done in any sort of safe manner was to have her drive a support vehicle along the way. We hit up the convenience store the night before and loaded up. Smart waters, Gatorades, Muscle Milks, Cliff Bars, Chips, Reese's Peanut Butter Cups, and 4 Sierra Nevada's for the finish. Other prep items for the run included 3 pairs of socks, 3 shirts, 3 shorts, 3 hats, 2 pairs of shoes, a backpack, a mophie, and 2 headlamps.

Because of my work schedule, which had me arriving at Tigers camp at 7 am and not finishing until 4 pm, the earliest I was going to be able to take off running from Lakeland was 4:30 pm. That undoubtedly ensured there was no way I was going to finish before midnight. I obviously realized the elements and logistics of the run were going to be extremely difficult, but I never expected to endure each one to such an extreme magnitude.

The day started off with a home plate collision demo with Detroit Tigers catcher Alex Avila. Ironically, I have run into him before. Then I had interviews with Brad Ausmus, Joe Nathan, David Price, and capped off the day with a live talk back with the guys in the MLB Network studio. At that point, I thought my day was done, but I was then instructed to make sure I talked with Miguel Cabrera, who had just played in his first Spring Training game following foot surgery. I don't like chasing guys down for interviews, but knowing that I needed to get on the road, I basically turned into a paparazzi reporter as soon as Miggy came off the field. If he had made it back to the locker room, there was a good chance it would be at least another hour before I would have been able to talk to him.

In the morning, there was actually a ton of fog that did not burn off until game time. The projected high was in the low 90s with 90% humidity, but because of the fog in the morning and the breeze in the afternoon, the temperature seemed bearable. I was hoping the wind would continue until nightfall. Wishful thinking. Just about 4 pm, the breeze stopped and the humidity went through the roof. The weather was my biggest pre-run concern. I generally don't do all that well in extremely hot conditions because I have a tendency to sweat more than any other human alive. Losing key salts and electrolytes with my eternal buckets of perspiration make it very difficult to replenish. The furthest I had ever run in my life at that point was 31 miles. I was not only going to ask my body to go nearly 19 miles further than it had gone before, but I was going to do it on a fuel tank that was on the borderline of empty. Not a great combo.

Right after the Cabrera interview, I shot out to the "support vehicle" that Tarah had driven and Superman-changed into my initial running gear. I fired out a tweet announcing my intentions of running from Lakeland to Kissimmee, and then another one indicating that I was going to donate $100 to the Baseball Assistance Team (BAT) for every mile I was able to complete. I then took a "launch video" right out in front of the Tigers' stadium as I began mile 1.

I had sent Tarah the intended route and told her to meet me about 10 miles up the road for my first refuel. The first mile was gorgeous. I was able to run on quiet side streets by the stadium and then along a path that wrapped around a gorgeous lake. I then hit the highway and essentially had to run on the hardened swamp grass. Around mile 3 I was enjoying the scenery as the highway wrapped back around toward the lake, when I looked into the swamp about 20 feet away and a big-ass alligator decided to stick his head out of the water!

I guess you could say this was my first WTF moment of the journey. A couple miles later, I was running along what appeared to be old vacated warehouses and fenced-in tire yards. While passing one, I heard frantic footsteps from behind me, then WHOOF WHOOF WHOOF!!! I was so startled that I literally tripped and just about fell on my ass as two dogs jumped up against the fence in full attack mode. I captured the dogs on video but the video doesn't even do it justice because the dogs had calmed down a ton by the time I was able to pull my phone out of the pack.

The next few miles were spent dodging traffic as if I were playing the 1985 real-life version of Frogger. I basically had to pick my poison. Run on the concrete highway with a solid 8 inches of shoulder or run on the swampy terrain that was right next to what looked like a levy of water that a hungry gator could pop out of at any moment. I watched enough of Steve Irwin, the famous crocodile hunter, to know that I had a much better chance against the gator as opposed to a car, truck, or semi rolling at 70 mph.

There was so much action going on that by the time I reached Tarah at mile 10, I didn't even realize how much I was sweating. My shirt and shorts were both sopping wet and I had no choice but to go for the early change. The back of the SUV looked like something that belonged in some sort of designer magazine. My alternate outfits were laid out perfectly. All of my liquid and food options were very neatly displayed and set up for my easy choosing. Tarah was undoubtedly going for support vehicle of the year. I quickly changed my shirt and shorts, grabbed a fresh water and Gatorade, and then I was off. Miles 10-15 in dry clothes made the journey more comfortable but the road conditions continued to deteriorate. Small shoulders and any sort of sidewalk paths became non-existent. During miles 16-23, the sun began to set and orange groves dominated what I would describe as a gorgeous and somewhat euphoric setting. At mile 20, there was even a dude hosing down the outside of a produce stand that obliged when I asked him for "a little love."

Tarah was waiting at a gas station around mile 23. "Shady" would be the word I would use to describe the atmosphere, but I don't feel as if it would do it justice. There was one guy sitting on the bed of his truck looking at my wife as if he just got out of prison and hadn't seen a female in 15 years. There was another guy leaning up against the side of the car drinking a 40 of Old English and a third dude sitting on the curb smoking a joint. I put a towel around my waist and stripped down my disgustingly wet clothes once again. I then fired on my most breathable and shortest pair of shorts (1980 Dolphin Style). When I wrung out my second shirt of the day and saw the endless stream of water flowing, I decided I was done with shirts for the night.

I shoved my phone into the one small pocket on the backside of the shorts and then held a bottle of water in one hand and the Gatorade in the other. I had lost so much fluid that I knew it was soon going to start taking its toll. Because I had no way to carry my nutrition or pills, I instructed Tarah to meet me every 2-3 miles wherever she could find a safe spot off of the main road. Then, as I began running, I actually back-pedaled the first 100 yards as I made sure my wife got away from the lion's den safely.

With a fresh pair of shorts and no shirt and no pack, you would think I would have been more comfortable at this point. Unfortunately, that was not the case. I had lost so much fluid and was so incredibly depleted I was miserable. I was light-headed and basically every step between mile 23 and 30 was a struggle. Not to mention the towns that I continued to run through were flat-out sketchy. On several different occasions, I had people cat calling me, "Boy, you shouldn't be running through this here neighborhood," "Look at this crazy white dude," and "Run, Forrest, Run" were three of my favorites.

After meeting Tarah at mile 27, she could tell I needed something and needed it in a hurry. When we met again at mile 30 she was waiting with a large pepperoni pizza. As quickly as I mowed the pizza down I would have given any world champion eater a run for their money. I grabbed a Coke and a water, and then immediately took off running again. Somehow, I was completely rejuvenated.

Once I passed mile 31, I entered unchartered territory. I had run two 50 Ks (31 miles) in my life but never before had I surpassed the 31-mile barrier. Believe it or not, my easiest miles were actually 31-40. The pepperoni pizza/Coke combo dialed me in. Just about any endurance athlete will tell you that Coca-Cola is an absolute SAVIOR when the tank is low. The huge amounts of sugar and caffeine serve as a mega turbo fuel source.

The temperature definitely cooled as the time and miles clicked off but the running conditions did not improve one bit. There was one stretch in which I felt like I was running on the 405 freeway in Los Angeles and then another extended area in which I actually had to have Tarah drive behind me with her hazard lights on because the only shoulder was a gator-infested swamp. On at least 3 different occasions, I shined my light into the swamp and witnessed sets of alligator eyes glowing outside of the water.

Somewhere around mile 40, I ran past the Gatorade plant, but I barely noticed because right beyond the plant there was huge amount of police activity. I don't know exactly what was going on, but there was a dude cuffed and stuffed in the back of the police car and a couple other guys sitting on the curb handcuffed as well. Right around mile 44, I saw something on the ground in front of me. I veered to the left a bit and then jumped half way across the highway. A snake with some very interesting markings was smack dab in the middle of the road. I cautiously approached it and realized it wasn't moving. The tail looked like it had a rattle on it, but I didn't think that they had rattlesnakes in Florida. The next day my wife sent me a picture of the exact same snake. The picture was on a caution sign inside a gator farm saying, "Beware of Rattlesnakes."

The final 4 plus miles were run through the streets of downtown Kissimmee and then along a path on the side of the highway before rolling up to the gates of the Houston Astros facility. According to my Garmin, the total distance was 48.12 miles. The total time was 8 hours 15 minutes and 37 seconds. I had gotten into endurance sports 4 years prior. To that point I had completed 6 full-distance Ironman Triathlons and two ultra-marathons. Of all the crazy endurance challenges I had done in my life, once you consider all of the elements, this was by far the most whacked out. The weather, the traffic, the roads, the swamps, the gators, the snakes, and the backwoods Florida towns made it a wild, wild, wild experience.

Human Crash Test Dummy Life Lesson #116

You don't need an organized race to do epic sh*t. Sometimes you don't even need time off work. Implement something active in your life. Bike, swim, run, paddleboard, skateboard, or even walk to a destination you would normally drive. It may take a bit longer, but you will feel a lot better when you get there. Life is about experience and the best way to get experience is to create it!

Chapter 117
Endure the Next Level

"What lies behind us, what lies before us,
are tiny matters compared to what lies within us."
-Ralph Waldo Emerson

In March of 2014 I finished my first ultra-marathon: the "Way too Cool" 50k that featured 5,000 feet of elevation gain across crazy terrain including fallen trees, rocks, and knee-high creeks. I immediately fell in love with the alternative running culture. Imagine a very eclectic group of individuals with an extreme fascination for nature and exercise. Add in a fiery competitive edge, an eternally optimistic vibe, and a blatant disregard for what mainstream society deems normal or even possible and that to me is the ultra-running community.

Ever since I got into the endurance world, there was a race that I kept reading and hearing about that completely captivated me: The Western States 100. Originally, this was a horse race that started at Squaw Valley and covered 100 miles of the Western States Trail, ending in Auburn. The race features nearly 19,000 feet of elevation gain and 23,000 feet of descent with temperatures that typically will start in the 30s as runners crest Squaw Valley and then surpass 100 degrees as they enter the dreaded canyons. In 1974, after his horse went lame, Gordy Ainsleigh was the first to attempt the race on foot. The next year, he returned to prove to his doubters that it was possible a human could run the 100-mile course in a 24-hour time period. Gordy finished in 23 hours and 42 minutes. More amazing is that he has continued to do the race every year since. The Western States has now become known to be one of the most iconic and difficult endurance races in the world. Every year, over 3,000 people qualify at other 100k and 100-mile races around the world, but only 370 get in.

After I got my first taste of the ultra-marathon world, I knew I wanted more. While checking into my first "Way Too Cool," I met a guy by the name of Jim Richards, a staple in the ultra community. Jim was very helpful, providing insight into a world that I knew very little about. After the race, we touched base and I explained to Jim that I had a goal to complete the Western States 100 and ideally do it in 2016, the same year of my 40th birthday. Knowing there would be an arduous preparation process involved, I needed direction. Jim recommended several training runs and race options that could potentially dial me in to race Western States, provided I was able to qualify and also find my way into the race. To help me get more acquainted with the ultra community, via email, Jim introduced me to Julie Fingar, the race director of Way Too Cool, and Tia Bodington, the race director of the legendary Western States qualifier, "The Miwok 100k." I picked both their brains about all things ultra.

In November, after I finished my 6th Ironman in exactly a 3-year period, I put the bike away, ditched the speedo, and fully committed myself to the ultra-marathon world. In December, I secured a spot into Miwok and the training was officially on. Looking at the result times of the 2014 Miwok was definitely an eye-opening experience. Basically, I realized that I needed to somehow train myself to run for over 12 consecutive hours. 62 miles was intimidating, but when you add in 11,800 feet of elevation, the Miwok became flat-out daunting. I had no choice but to attack this new challenge the same way I did playing baseball or racing Ironman Triathlon: work my ass off.

I figured 11,800 feet of climbing over the course of 62 miles roughly works out to 200 feet of elevation gain per mile. Up and away I went. Every treadmill workout contained either a long, steady hill climb or some sort of intense hill intervals. I then took advantage of every opportunity to run some of the Bay Area's best trails. Windy Hill, Purisima Creek, Montara Mountain, and the Dipsea were common training grounds. While working Spring Training in Arizona, I charged up Camelback Mountain daily, and as I mentioned, while in Florida, I ran 48 miles from Tigers camp in Lakeland to Astros camp in Kissimmee. I enjoyed several other "destination runs" that included running from Half Moon Bay to Palo Alto several times as well as a 32.2-mile trip around Manhattan.

In all, I averaged 50-70 miles a week with anywhere between 6 to 12 thousand feet of elevation. Most importantly though, I really learned to enjoy running. I looked forward to hitting the trails, and for the most part, time and miles were simply a result of enjoying the process.

I arrived at the Miwok start line in Stinson Beach at 4:55 am, 5 minutes before the start. I hopped in the middle of the pack with my handheld flashlight and off we went. The first part of the course is up the infamous Dipsea Trail. Within the first 2 miles of the race, we climbed nearly 2,000 feet before heading back down the mountain and into Muir Beach where the first aid station was at the 8-mile mark. I spent the entire first section of the race chatting up a schoolteacher from New York City and another dude from Maryland. We were not even 1/10th of the way into the race and I had already talked more than I had in all of my Ironman Triathlons combined.

In order to get to the Muir Beach aid station, we had to run across a bridge and then backtrack over that same bridge. I passed several runners going the opposite direction on the way in and then several runners on the way out. I am not sure if there was one runner that did not offer some sort of words of encouragement or at the very least flash a big smile on the way by. The overall energy of the Miwok was flat out like nothing I have ever experienced.

Every aid station was basically the same operation. I walloped a PB&J, refilled my water bottle and electrolytes, and was off. Once I got my first glance of the Golden Gate Bridge at mile 17, I basically hit that runner's high, which helped me float all the way to the return to Muir Beach at mile 32. Unquestionably, that 15-mile stretch is the most beautifully epic running trail I have ever seen in my life. When I rolled through Tennessee Valley the second time at mile 26, my entire family was waiting for me with signs, all sorts of different food options, and a change of clothes. I was 4 hours and 20 minutes into the race, had a marathon and nearly 6,000 feet of climbing under my belt, and I had barely broken a sweat. No need for a change of clothes; I blew off the food, filled my bottles, snapped a pic with the family, and cruised away. It wasn't until after the Muir Beach aid station when we headed back up the backside of the Dipsea that I felt any sort of fatigue. This was the first time I completely dried out both water bottles before reaching the next aid station at the top of the mountain.

We then headed north on some pretty sweet trails that took us in and out of redwood trees then exposed hayfields high above the Pacific Ocean. For the most part, the majority of the day was overcast, but once I got to mile 40, there was a thick fog that settled in, only to be quickly replaced by clear skies and sunshine. It seemed as if around every corner I turned, there was a different weather pattern that included a heavy drizzle or even a light rain at some point. If there is such a thing as perfect running weather, this was it. As I approached the aid station at mile 42, Bolinas Ridge, there was a sign that was made by the Half Moon Bay Coastside Runners Club that read "Man Imposes His Own Limitations." Franz Dill, who has run both the Miwok and Western States several times and has been a huge mentor of mine in the ultra world, was manning the aid station. He busted out an ice-cold coke, a few more inspirational words, and I was quickly back on the trail.

I picked up Kyle Hamilton, my firefighter triathlete training partner-in-crime, at the mile-50 aid station. When we immediately began the climb, Kyle started running up the 15% grade hill. Somehow, he must have forgotten I had 50 miles and 10,000 feet of climbing already under my belt. The idea of running the nearly 2-mile climb at that point was unrealistic if not impossible. The last 12 miles hurt in every sense of the word. I could physically feel blood blisters forming on my feet, my calves were tightening up, my quads felt like mashed potatoes, and my hamstrings were basically spaghetti noodles. We walked every incline and continued to run any flat area or downhill. The final 2 miles were straight down and hurt worse than any uphill I encountered the entire day. I must have tripped 10-15 times during the descent. As we approached the finish, I was covered in blood, sweat, and tears of pain and exhilaration.

I spotted my 3-year-old, grabbed him and hoisted him over my shoulders before crossing the finish line 11 hours and 49 minutes after the day had begun.

There is something about trail running that is very calming and peaceful. It is a very euphoric and uplifting experience amongst some of the fittest and most optimistic people in the world. That said, I can say with great conviction that the Miwok 100k was the most painful and difficult race I had ever done in my life. I had officially qualified for the Western States 100-mile endurance run.

Human Crash Test Dummy Life Lesson #117

If there is something that you have a vision of doing in your life, do what is in your power to make it happen. Educate yourself as much as possible and treat each step of the process very meticulously. You need to figure out how to build the house before you start hammering away. Go to construction school and always focus on the task at hand. Small gains lead to big results.

Chapter 118
The World Lines Up

"Once you make a decision, the universe conspires to make it happen."
-Ralph Waldo Emerson

Shockingly, the easiest part of getting into Western States was qualifying for the race at the Miwok 100. Ultra-running has grown so popular that 3500 people qualified for the 2016 race. When it came to getting into Western States, it was damn near impossible. Knowing that I had a vision of competing in Western States in 2016, I began laying the groundwork two years before. I didn't know anybody within the ultra community so I bombarded Jim Richards, who I met at my first Way Too Cool race, with questions about the different ways I would possibly be able to get into the race.

The raffle was my first opportunity to get in. Western States held the raffle in June of 2015 and I took this as my best opportunity to get into the race. I bought 1000 raffle tickets at $4 a pop. The money goes directly to preserving the trails, so I figured a $4,000 contribution was well worth it no matter what happened. I didn't get into the race.

Special Consideration: this was what I thought would possibly be my best chance of getting in. The Western States board of directors usually will grant one or two special consideration spots a year to people whose contributions to WSER are "unusual and substantial." I felt I had 3 things going for me: 1) there has never been a former MLB player or any other player from the 3 mainstream professional U.S. team sports to ever compete in Western States; 2) I held a unique position in the media that would allow me to create a different sort of exposure for the race within the local and national sports media; 3) I was willing to make a significant financial and/or service contribution to the WSER foundation.

I was promptly shut down for "Special Exemption" by the Western States Board.

So, there I was with my fate left up to the lottery drawing; it was not looking good. Every year you qualify and do not get into the race, you receive double the amount of tickets from the previous year. In total, with the 3,000 plus people that qualified, there were over 8,000 tickets. Only 270 tickets were going to be drawn. I had one ticket. I am not a mathematician but I figured my chances of getting drawn were about 3%. Also, if I showed up, I would have another small chance of getting drawn with another lottery for the people that were in attendance. Regardless of the long odds, I took off work at MLB Network and flew into San Francisco arriving at midnight on Friday night. I then drove the family up to Tahoe so the girls would be able to get to ski team, slept for an hour, then headed back down to Auburn with my 4-year-old boy for the drawing. As I was driving past Donner Lake, the sun was rising and I was looking off in the distance at the Sierra Nevada Mountains and the Western States course. I had this weird feeling come over me, a feeling that I was going to be picked.

When I arrived in Auburn, they had already drawn 100 names. I met up with Franz Dill, who had saved me a seat, and he pointed out many of the ultra-running legends and Western States diplomats in the room. As much as I was hoping to get lucky, the main idea to go to the drawing was so I would be able to meet some of the people within the Western States community. I realized that this is a very tight-knit group, and in this day and age of electronic communication, there is nothing more genuine and endearing than face-to-face meetings.

I had just sat down and Franz was giving me the low-down on who was who when I heard Tim Twietmeyer say, "WOW! Not sure how many baseball fans we have in here." My heart dropped. "This guy played several years for the Oakland A's, from Half Moon Bay, California. Eric Byrnes."

I grabbed Colton and immediately hoisted him into the air. I let out a huge WOOOOOOOOOOOOOOOOOO and charged down the aisle as if Bob Barker had just announced my name on "The Price is Right." I hugged Twietmeyer and anybody else around. It was honestly one of the greatest moments of my life. Soon after my wild celebration and the place settled down, somebody in the crowd busted out a, "LETS GO OAKLAND" chant. EPIC!

Human Crash Test Dummy Life Lesson #118

To reach a goal, make a commitment to do what is in your power then let your universe speak to you. No need to take things personal, simply keep a positive attitude of gratitude and you will be shocked how things will eventually play out. You have to BELIEVE.

Chapter 119
40 on 40

"Success in life has nothing to do with what you gain for yourself; it's what you do for others."
-Coach Ben Parks

The reality of running 100 miles with 19,000 feet of elevation gain and 23,000 feet of descent quickly set in. I began every treadmill workout with a 2600-foot climb that simulated the first 4-mile climb from the base of Squaw Valley to the peak. I ran every chance I had and created other fun ways to incorporate massive amounts of training. I turned 40 in February so I figured it would be a perfect time to pick up a birthday mile tradition that was once created by LEGENDARY Coach Parks years ago. Here is the invitation:

40 years ago, Ben "Coach" Parks decided to run 40 miles on his 40th birthday to help raise awareness and money for a variety of causes he held close to his heart. He continued the tradition every February, culminating with 60 miles on his 60th birthday. Coach even added 2 extra miles in his final run just for good measure. Ultimately, Coach Parks raised hundreds of thousands of dollars and motivated hundreds of thousands more... Including myself.

I had an opportunity to train with Coach Parks from the time I was 10 years old all the way through college. He brought discipline into my life at a time I undoubtedly needed direction.

Coach Parks passed away in 2011. This February I turn 40 and figure it's about time somebody picks up the torch and relights the flame. On Saturday, February 13th, to honor Coach Park's memory, I am going to run 40 miles and begin my quest in bringing bring back the birthday mile tradition.

Also in the spirit of Coach Parks, I plan on donating $100 per mile to Fit Kids: A Bay Area organization that provides after school athletic programs and equipment to local under privileged children.

The first 22 miles of the run will take place on the Western States trail and the final 18 will happen on the Placer High School track in Auburn, just off Hwy 80.

I invite you to join me in the last 18 miles to run a few laps or just hang out for moral support and enjoy an adult beverage.

Following the run, we will head to Casa de Byrnes at Martis Camp (about an hour away) for Margaritas, a full-blown Mexican Feast and possible late night illegal gaming activity.

Of course kids are more than welcome at both events...

What: 40 on 40

Where: Placer High School Track, Auburn CA
Byrnes Tree House Martis Camp

When: Approx 12:30-3:30 pm at track
Approx 5:00 pm-5:00 am at Tree House

Other than my electric car dying at the Donner Summit on the way home from the run, and the party I was 5 hours late to, it was a total success. I didn't arrive until 10 pm, but figuring we went till 5 am, I don't think too many people felt shorted on the party time.

On my 41st birthday, I knocked out 41 miles on the treadmill. Yes, that experience was as bad as it sounds, and this year I hammered 42 miles plus 20 more to complete the Black Canyon 100k in Arizona.

Human Crash Test Dummy Life Lesson #119

Find any excuse to get your ass up and do something. You don't have to run 40 miles on your 40th birthday, but maybe you celebrate with 40 laps around a track, a 40-mile bike, or challenge yourself to workout 40 consecutive days?

Whatever it is, get creative, use the beginnings of weeks and months to start new challenges, and try to involve friends. We always get better results when we have other people to push us and hold us accountable.

Chapter 120
It's Not Always Wine & Cheese

"Life should not be a journey to the grave with the intention of arriving safely in an attractive, well-preserved body, but rather to skid in sideways, chocolate in one hand, wine in the other, body thoroughly used up, totally worn out and screaming, 'Woo-hoo! What a ride."
-Matt Fitzgerald

The process of preparing for 100 miles started on a treadmill the day I got selected in the lottery. The first big step was running 40 on 40, and then a couple weeks later in March, I knocked out the iconic Way Too Cool 50k and then ran the Lake Sonoma 50 miler in April. Here is the race recap on a grueling day spent in wine country:

When I had an opportunity to secure a late entry into the Lake Sonoma 50, I instantly re-routed our planned Family Griswold vacation. Despite living just a few hours away from Yosemite Falls, El Capitan and Half Dome, I had waited 40 years to see them, so I figured they could wait a couple more days. Talking to other ultra-runners, I had heard two general things about the Lake Sonoma 50. The first was that it is absolutely beautiful. The second was that as beautiful as it was, it was even more of a ball-buster. The 50-mile course with 10,500 feet of elevation gain has been described as "death by 1 million paper cuts." The entire course is either up or down but only a couple significant climbs so it can be very deceiving. I grew up in the Bay Area and for the most part have lived on the Peninsula my entire life, yet SHOCKINGLY, just as I had never been to Yosemite, I had never been to Sonoma.

So, I packed up the Airstream, loaded my 3 kids, wife, our Spanish au pair, and we were off for an adventure. My preconceived judgments were pretty right on as we rolled into the northern California wine country. There were absolutely gorgeous rolling green hills surrounded by one recognizable vineyard after another. Unfortunately, we missed the pre-race dinner, but we were able to get to the campsite just as the sun was setting and immediately lit the fire pit and crushed a pre-race spread of quinoa, rice, veggies, and a bottle of JCH Pinot Noir; we were in Sonoma, weren't we?

My 7-year-old daughter, Peanut, slept in the bed with me, which I have become very accustomed to, but the issue was that she had the flu and rucky-chucky-ed throughout the course of the entire night. Most likely, from the time I rolled into the rack at 10:00 pm to the time I got up at 5 am, I probably logged a solid 2 hours of shut eye. I usually don't sleep well before races, but obviously this was enhanced by the barfing barrage. Speaking to a few experts over the years trying to figure out how to maximize performance, supposedly it is the sleep you get 2 nights before your race that is the most important; same is true with your carb loading. When I got up, I immediately steamed the water on the pot and put two instant coffee packets into an empty cup and took in the aroma, which always helps start the interior early-morning release system the body is usually not accustomed to at that hour.

I threw down a banana, a yogurt, and a bowl of oatmeal, and then headed for the start line. The race started at 6:30 am sharp so by the time I got to check in it was already 6:15. I imagine it was not by coincidence that I received the number 22; I safety pinned it to my shorts, snapped a quick pic with the lake in the background, found my ultra-running coach Franz Dill, and away we went.

Franz is the President of the Coastside Runners Club based in Half Moon Bay. I first met him a couple years ago on a Western States training run, and we quickly figured out our HMB connection and even that our kids go to the same school. Figuring this was my first Western States training run, I peppered him with questions about ultra-marathons. At the time, I had yet to do an ultra and my first race, The Way Too Cool 50k, was just a couple weeks away.

Franz represents everything that is right with ultra-running. First and foremost, he has an extreme passion for running that you can almost physically see radiate through him. Secondly, he has an incredible willingness and ability to vary his pace and engage both fast and slow runners, answer questions, share his experiences while peppering questions back at the other runner, all while in the middle of slaughtering a 20% grade hill. Lastly, he embodies the perfect blend of running with a competitive edge yet never at the expense of compromising the core community values of the sport. Oh yeah, I forgot to mention, he is ridiculously humble and an absolute badass. He is one of just a couple hundred people to ever complete the Grand Slam of Ultra Running, which is completing the four oldest 100-mile races in the United States all within a 4-month period.

There is nothing like the start of an ultra race. Unlike an Ironman, which will usually have 3,000 competitors, thousands of spectators, super loud music, sponsor banners, and elaborate starting chutes, ultras seem to be a bit more reserved to say the least. Usually it's just a few hundred racers standing around an area who eventually just start running. Other than race director John Medinger, who was flowing knowledge, truth, and a few inspirational messages on the mic, it was a classic ultra send off.

Franz and I ran together most of the race at Way Too Cool, so we figured we would stick together unless one of us started feeling sexy and decided to open it up. It was supposed to rain and temperatures were going to be in the low 60s, so I started the race in a very light jacket. The rain held off for most of the day but it was surprisingly humid. By the time we got to the Warm Springs Creek aid station at mile 11.6, I was freaking drenched with sweat.

Both my wife, Tarah, and Franz's wife, Jen, were at the aid station. When we pulled in, Tarah looked at me like she had seen a ghost. Jen has a tremendous amount of experience crewing for Franz over the years and having Tarah shadow her around for the day gaining intimate crew knowledge was huge, not just for Lake Sonoma but for Western States or any subsequent race I do in the future. Although I was sweating like a pig in heat, I felt fine. Yet when I saw Jen give me the same look Tarah did, I thought I was screwed.

To lose that much fluid barely 20% into the race makes it nearly impossible to replace. Judging by their reactions, I decided to take my time and spend a couple minutes re-hydrating and firing down a PB&J. Franz, who I pulled into the aid station with, bolted a good minute and a half before me. I spent the next 14 miles running alone. I had my headphones but never put them on. The ridiculously beautiful Lake Sonoma scenery completely captivated me as I cruised along the single-track trail situated above the lake. It was almost as if I became one with the mountain. Corny-sounding, I get it, but I was completely blown away.

I pulled into No Name Flat at mile 25.2 feeling surprisingly good. Because of all the fluid loss in the first 11 miles, I was very conservative with my effort while experiencing my zen-like state. I filled my bottles, crushed another PB&J, and slammed an ice-cold aluminum-bottled Coke Tarah had brought for me. It was ecstasy.

Before I got to the next aid at mile 32.8, I had caught up with Franz and a few other runners. We continued to run together but leap frog each other along the way, almost as if we were running a pace line on a bike. There was a pack of us that hit Warm Springs Creek at mile 38 all at about the same time.

There is a point in every endurance race that I've ever done when the "race" really begins for each individual. I don't think you can determine that exact point for any race. I believe it coincides with your current effort at the time, what you feel like you have left in the tank, and who is around you.

To that point, I had run socially with Franz, I had run very comfortably alone, and I had run in a pack that pulled into the aid station all at the same time. All day I had taken my time at the aid stations but I blew through Warm Spring Creek mile 38 and I was gone. I didn't plan on making any sort of move at mile 38 but it just felt right. I had 12 miles to go and figured it was nut-crunching time. When I read Iron Wars by Matt Fitzgerald, I remember Dave Scott talking about pumping his arms and getting up on his toes when he wanted to run faster, so that's exactly what I did.

Over the course of the next 6 miles, I not only dropped that crew I was running with but I proceeded to pass at least another 6-10 people. Then I got to mile 44 and realized I had downed both water bottles and still had another mile and a half to the next aid station. I was naked and it wasn't a great feeling. My pace started to dramatically slow. A couple guys passed me back as I basically rolled into Island View Camp at mile 45.5 with my tongue wagging out of my mouth like a bulldog on a hot day.

There were at least 7 or 8 runners at Island Camp and nobody seemed to be in a hurry. We were just 4.5 miles away from the finish line but the 45.5 miles and 10,000 feet of relentless climbing and descent had definitely taken its toll. I cruised out of there slamming another Coke and a half and decided I was going to test my limits. I got up on my toes once more and began pumping my arms. I was cruising, right up until the point I felt a small cramp in my right quad. I slowed down a bit but that didn't help. The cramp continued to escalate and shot up to my groin. It then wrapped around my hamstring. I had no choice but to stop and let it dissipate. I couldn't move.

Thankfully, it subsided in under a minute. I was now just 2 miles from the finish line and I could hear at least a few runners hot on my ass. My only choice was to live on the QGH (Quad, Groin, Hammy) cramping edge. I crossed the finish line in 8 hours and 35 minutes, 43rd overall.

In the grand scheme of things, I really don't give a rat's ass where I place in a race. This is not my profession, and fortunately, I don't have to rely on endurance sports to feed my family. Yet, I do feel I have a responsibility to myself and my kids to put forth my best effort that I have in me on that given day. I constantly preach to my children the single most important thing in any sport is effort. I was never the most talented baseball player at any level, but there is no doubt in my mind that my effort afforded me an opportunity to make a career playing a game.

The only way for us as human beings to realize our true potential is to push limits and not just find boundaries; sometimes we need to cross them.

The combo of the finisher jackets, tamales, and ice-cold beer at the end of the race was probably the greatest post-race trifecta I have ever received. All in all, Tropical John and his crew put on an incredible race. If you ever have the desire to run 50 miles and see if you can survive the 1,000,000 paper cuts, Lake Sonoma is definitely for you.

Human Crash Test Dummy Life Lesson #120

Don't be afraid to go where you have never gone before. We all think that we know our limits but our limits are actually determined by our minds and not our bodies. Our mind will always shut down before our bodies. The question then becomes how far are you able to push your mind before you force your body to quit. It's not always wine and cheese.

Chapter 121
Channel The Energy

"The will to succeed is important,
but what's more important is the will to prepare."
-Bobby Knight

The next step of the process and the final race before Western States was my second bout with the Miwok 100K, which at 62 miles and 12,000 feet of elevation gain was the longest distance and most amount of elevation I would run before States.

My first Miwok experience was the most grueling endurance challenge I had ever faced. Round 2 was a test of how far I had come, but more importantly, it was an indication of how far I was going to be able to go.

I typically don't like to arrive at races until I absolutely have to. The pre-race tension is by far and away the worst part of race day. Pre-race is usually a bunch of people standing around with all sorts of nervous energy jockeying for a dumb-ass position on the start line that means absolutely jack sh*t over the course of a ridiculously long day. I always try to arrive as close to the start time as possible, but I have never taken it to the absolute extreme as I did on that Saturday. My arrival time: 4:59 am. The race started at 5 am. I snapped a quick video of the runners, and in standard ultra running fashion, people just started running and that was it. We were off.

There is a single-track trail about a tenth of a mile up the road, so literally one minute into the race, it is basically 450 runners all trying to fit into the top of a Tabasco bottle. A big-ass line formed and came to a complete standstill. I've never seen nearly 500 people so eager to go head on with the ball-busting 2.8-mile climb straight up the Dipsea. Unless you are in the absolute front, the only option is to be patient and realize it is going to be a long-ass day.

I figured whatever energy I save at the beginning is energy I will have plenty of time to exert over the course of the next 62 miles. Of course, there were a few jackasses who thought they were Prefontaine running a 5k and bullied their way up the trail, literally nudging runners out of the way in the process. I targeted two that I remembered passing me and not shockingly flew by both before I got to the Muir Beach aid station.

When we got toward the top of the Dipsea, it was still dark but definitely lighter than when we began the race. There was thick fog that was scattered in patches and covered the hilltops off in the distance. Then all of a sudden, I started to hear the faint sound of a bagpipe playing. I wasn't sure if I was tripping or it was an actual bagpiper. Mile 3 seemed a little early to start hallucinating. As I continued to approach the summit, the pipes continued to get louder. When I reached the top, I came within feet of the bagpiper's silhouette, which was immersed in a cloud. Ironically, the last time I was that close to a dude wearing a kilt blowing into the bagpipes was at my dad's memorial service a few years ago. Now here I was, with 59 miles still to go, experiencing an incredibly euphoric and emotional moment.

Reality set back in quickly when I began the descent down the mountain. I was now spaced apart from the other runners and realized that the light on top of my head was not working. All of a sudden, every step was a leap of faith. I literally could not see anything. Luckily, and I mean luckily, I made it to the bottom with just a couple small trips that I was somehow able to catch.

I had done Miwok the year before and my man Franz Dill sent me a text that had all of my times into the aid stations from last year. My goal was to stay on roughly the same pace at the beginning of the race. In my first Miwok, I absolutely crashed and burned at mile 50, so with my increased training load, I had no doubt that I could run the last 13 miles a lot better than last year's crawl to the finish.

I rolled into Muir Beach aid station about 5 minutes ahead of schedule. Quick bottle refill and I was off to Tennessee Valley where my wife and kids were supposed to meet me at mile 13. I rolled in about 10 minutes ahead of schedule and they were nowhere to be found. I called them as I made the climb up toward Bridge View to see if they needed anything. They were pulling in just as I had left.

The next 6 miles or so are some of the greatest trail miles in the world. After the climb up the fire road, it is all single-track with gorgeous rolling hills with ridiculous views of the city of San Francisco, Alcatraz, and the Bay Bridge. Then you come around a corner and it feels as if the Golden Gate Bridge pops out of a mountain and is going to swallow you up.

After the Bridge View aid station, there is an extended downhill that was basically made for me. Being a big dude in comparison to other ultra-marathoners, climbing up hills is definitely not my strength. Being that I am relatively new to the sport, super steep technical descents are not really my strength either. But give me a gradual downhill grade where I can let my legs go without worrying about eating a face full of rocks and I will freaking CRUSH it. I had found my happy place.

62 miles is obviously a long day, and considering the course, which contains 12,000 feet of elevation gain and descent, you can imagine the variation in times per mile. I had one mile that took nearly 20 minutes, and in this case at mile 19, I ran one that took 6 minutes and 20 seconds.

Very unusual for a race with almost 500 runners, but after the first 6 miles, I was basically running alone. When I got back to Tennessee Valley at mile 26, the family was there waiting with an ice-cold towel, a Coke, and some inspirational signs. After I slammed a couple PB&Js and snapped a family portrait, I was headed back to Muir Beach.

The one thing that I am able to digest well when I am running is gel blocks. I started with 3 packs on me and had munched 1 pack an hour. I had meant to reload at Tennessee Valley but I simply forgot. I now had no nutrition on me at all. Oh yeah, I also had forgotten my salt pills too.

The part of the race that torched me the year before was the climb back up the Dipsea to the Cardiac aid station. I ran out of fluids and nutrition. I was okay immediately after hitting the aid, but by the time I got to mile 50, I paid the price.

The Muir Beach aid station was the next stop before the long Dipsea climb, and when I arrived it was as if an angel was dropped from heaven. My 5-year-old daughter stood there with my gel packs and salt tabs!!! At the same time, it slowly started to rain.

Every runner is different; some prefer it hot, some cold, some wet, and some dry. If I were to describe my ideal day this was it. Temperatures in the 50s, a pretty aggressive breeze, and what started as an overcast day turned into torrential downpours at times.

As I rolled up the Dipsea, I finally had a couple dudes to run/hike with. The first guy was a very competitive runner and finished top 10 at TRT 100 last year and the other dude was a 2:50 marathoner who happened to tell me his boy from Inside Trail magazine said, "No matter what you do, don't let the baseball player beat you!"

At that point, I knew two things: I was in good company with some fast runners, and I was going to do everything in my power to make sure the baseball player came out on top. I am generally very non-competitive against other people in the race. My goal going into the day and up to that point in the race was to beat my time of 11 hours and 50 minutes from the year before. I was well on pace to do that. Now, this dude lit a fire under my ass. He wasn't being rude nor did I think he was talking sh*t, but I was out to prove a point to my man, whoever that may be at Inside Trail mag, that there are actually a few baseball players who can run further than 90 feet!

They continued to charge the hill and I slowly faded back. The flashbacks of the previous year were too strong to attempt to redline up the Dipsea. I also knew exactly who my target was, and if I was going to take down a very good runner, I was going to have to make my time up on the flats and down hills.

When I got to the Cardiac aid station at the top, I felt terrible for all the volunteers. They looked soaked and freezing. The rain was at its hardest point all day and the wind was howling. As far as I was concerned though, I felt great.

I charged out of the aid station, and by the time we got to the ridge, which is an exposed single-track trail along the top of the hillside, I had my guy back in my sights. I felt like a lion stalking a gazelle. With every corner I turned, I gained more and more ground. What was a 2-minute lead slowly dissipated to a minute 30, then a minute, then 30 seconds and next thing you know, I was on his ass. I started up some small talk and then when we hit a slight downhill I made my move. "On your left here." I blew by and continued straight on the trail. Then immediately I hear him shout from behind me, "Wrong way, dude!"

I couldn't do anything but laugh. There was another trail that veered to the right that I missed. Because of the rain and wind, the ribbons were either on the ground or pretty far immersed in the bushes. Regardless, my guy was back in front and the chase was back on. I eventually passed him again on the next downhill and that was it. I cruised into Bolinas Ridge aid station run by my man Franz Dill, his wife Jen, and the rest of the Coastside Runners Club located in the HMB.

I am biased, but in my 4 years now in the ultra running world, I have never been to a better aid station. It starts a quarter mile away with an inspirational sign: "Pain is temporary, quitting is forever." Then another sign: "Don't throw in the towel, use it to wipe your face."

Finally, I could hear the music bumping and I freaking motored in just AMPED. Franz and Jen helped get my Solomon water bottles off my hands and passed them to volunteers, who immediately filled them up. Jen then delivered an ice-cold Coke; I crushed 3 PB&Js and went sprinting out of there ready to run through a brick wall.

At the time, Franz had said I was around 40th place but I was concerned about 2 things and 2 things only: solidly beating my time from last year and laying the hammer down on my Inside Trail guy.

After I left the aid station, more signs for the next quarter mile: "Man Imposes His Own Limitations."

When I headed toward Randall aid station at mile 49, I tried to keep the stoke of the Coastside Runners Bolinas Ridge aid station by bumping some music of my own. Problem was I couldn't get my headphones working because they had been absolutely soaked by the rain. I then pulled my phone out, which is protected by a Life-Proof case and began playing DJ. Spinning anything from TODO to Jay-Z, to Timberlake to Kenny Chesney, to the Grateful Dead. I eventually hammered the downhill into Randall passing several people in the process.

When I got to the bottom of Randall, my main man and pacer Rob Dean was there and ready to go. It was freezing balls and still raining hard. Rob had been standing in the wind and the rain for a while and was geared up to the nines: rainproof sweat pants, rainproof jacket, warm hat. Then we started trekking up the 1.6-mile hill. About halfway up the mountain, Rob ditched the jacket and hat. I felt like we kept the effort relatively light and talked shop about the Giants on the way up.

Then we got to the top. At the same spot I had fallen apart the previous year, I was scuffling again. My legs were thrashed so I simply tried to focus on my hip swing and using my core. I still felt like sh*t for the next 3-4 miles but what could I really expect at mile 55. There is a downhill that leads back to the Coastside Runner's Club Bolinas aid station and as soon as I saw the sign, "Age wrinkles the body, quitting wrinkles the soul," I took off.

Rob had been running in front or beside me, but I wanted to take the lead, so we fired through the aid station with a huge "Coastside" call and quick fill-ups. I was pumped to see Tarah, who earned Comeback Crew Member of the Day. After missing the first spot, she made every other aid station the rest of the way and fully stocked me up with gel blocks, cold towels, salt tabs, Coca-Cola, and a final French kiss to get me home.

Rob and I then hit the ridge and picked off a few more runners along the way before making the turn down the hill for the finish line. That was the first point since mile 26 that I looked at the overall time on my watch. I was at 10 hours and 50 minutes. Originally, I was STOKED, realizing I was going to take nearly an hour off my time from the previous year. Then it dawned on me that I had a chance to break 11 hours. I put it into another gear. In the final descent, we passed 4 more people as I watched the clock tick away. At 10:55, then 10:56, and I got to a point where I was sure I was at the bottom at 10:58 but a turn back the other direction said otherwise. I wasn't giving up hope. When the clock hit 10:59, I moved into a reckless all-out sprint. I could hear the people cheering and the announcer on the mic. I could smell the mac and cheese and sausages at the finish; I could taste a Headlands Double IPA (8.8% Alcohol). 10:59:30... 10:59:45... 10:59:50... I am now completely anaerobic, my quads are shivering, and I am literally foaming at the mouth.

10:59:51, 10:59:52, 10:59:53, 10:59:54, 10:59:55, 10:59:56, 10:59:57, 10:59:58, 10:59:59...

I crossed the finish line in 25th place out of a field of 450 bad-ass runners and a good margin ahead of my man who was specifically instructed by Inside Trail run mag guy to not let the "baseball player" beat him. I guess there are a few of us old ballplayers who can run a little further than 90 feet. My official finishing time: 11 hours and 1 minute, always something to bring you back.

I finished off my last huge training weekend over Memorial Day by running 75 miles of the Western States course over a 3-day period. I couldn't officially say I was ready because there was still the mystery of how my body would respond running 100 miles for the first time. But I had taken care of everything I perceived to be in my control. The work was complete, the wood was chopped, the hay was stacked, and the cows were in the barn.

Human Crash Test Dummy Life Lesson #121

Take the energy you would spend over being anxious for an upcoming event and transform it into working towards preparing yourself for that day. That will release whatever anxieties and tension you may be holding and give you the peace of mind in knowing that you did everything within your power to prepare for the upcoming moment of truth.

Chapter 122
No Judgment Necessary

"Don't judge a man until you have walked a mile in his shoes."
-American Proverb

In December of 2015, I had the opportunity through a mutual friend to play golf with Lance Armstrong. I had never met him before the round. He knew I had competed in Ironman's and had just got into Western States, so we hit it off talking trail running and endurance sports. He told me he was in town for the Woodside Ramble and through the course of the day convinced me to toe the line with him. I had done Ironman Arizona less than a month before and had only run a few times since, but I was not going to pass up an opportunity to run with arguably one of the greatest endurance athletes of all time.

Before the race, there was one guy that came up to him saying he was a big fan and asked for a picture. Lance could not have been more pleasant and took the picture just seconds before the start. Other than that, it seemed as if nobody had any clue he was there. I ran the first mile with him, and then he took off as soon as we hit the hills. The next time I saw him was about a mile before the turnaround for me, and a mile after the turn around for him. He was in the lead.

"Byrnesie!!! You're killing it!!!" Then he threw me a big high five.

As of April of 2018, I have competed in 10 half Ironman's, 11 full distance Ironman's, three 50Ks, two 50-milers, 4 100Ks and a 100 miler. I have never had the leader of any of those races say a word to me, let alone toss me a high five. And none of their names were Lance Armstrong...

I played a sport for a living in a time that performance-enhancing drug (PED) use was wide spread. Although I made the decision not to use PEDs for fear of shriveling testicles, premature balding, and "backne," I saw many of my best friends make the decision to do what they felt was necessary to keep up with an unfortunate culture that had been created.

In my opinion, cyclists who used PEDs are no different than baseball players who used PEDs. Both are simply by-products of an environment that was very much facilitated by the two sports themselves.

I am not making excuses for PED users. Ultimately that is a decision that some athletes make in their careers and the consequences are generally immeasurable.

What separates ultra-running from any other sport that I have been involved with is that I truly feel as if it is a counter culture that doesn't care about your past or even what your future holds. It seems to be a sport that is very much in the moment. So long as you love and respect the trails, the trails and the people that navigate the trails will show you the same love and respect.

In professional sports, it is no secret that athletes are driven by money and fame. Occasionally, you will run across somebody that tries to convince you he or she is solely into the sport for the love of the game and has no interest in the riches that accompany it. In my opinion, they are typically full of sh*t.

In the very rare case of Lance Armstrong and trail running, I can promise you that it is neither money or fame that he is after. Ultimately, it is very simple. The dude loves to compete and he loves the endurance world. Two things that should be celebrated, not detested.

More than any other sport I have been involved in, trail running is less about results and much more about community. It's about a group of people that continue to push limits and redefine what is possible. In many different ways, it involves runners that are looking for some sort of escape.

In Lance's case specifically, I am not exactly sure what led him to the trails. I am not sure if there is something specific that he is running from or possibly something he is running towards. Regardless, I have never been one to judge somebody on their past or negative things that other people have to say. I have always made my own assessment on personal experience and people's actions going forward.

We have all made decisions in our life that we are not proud of. Personally, I realize I cannot change some of those actions, but I take solace in knowing that I can learn from my wrong doings and do my best to help others, including my own children, from making the same mistakes.

There is no doubt baseball players who used PEDs did cheat their peers out of potential financial prosperities. Yet like I mentioned earlier, I blame the culture of the sport much more than the individuals themselves. That does not mean I clear these individuals of any wrongdoing but to treat them as outcasts to society and ostracize them for life is ridiculously over-the-top. In the case of the ultra-running community, that sort of "holier than thou" attitude is everything the ultra-world seems to stand against.

Seeing some of the running communities' response to Lance racing made me sick. Those individuals' negative reactions are a gross representation of what I would consider an otherwise awesome and loving group of people.

Human Crash Test Dummy Life Lesson #122

You don't have to ignore past mistakes, but if you want to get the best out of yourself and other people, don't assume the opinions of others are truly indicative of who that person is. Spend time to really get to know somebody and look beyond the surface to understand who that person is. Assumptions are the kryptonite of society that have caused anything from petty fights to world wars.

Chapter 123
Game Plan

"Your ability to think concisely, your ability to make good judgments is much easier on Thursday night than during the heat of the game. So we prefer to make our decisions related to the game almost clinically, before the game is ever played. ... Without question you can make more objective decisions during the week as to what you would do in the game than you can spontaneously as the game is being played. To be honest with you, you are in a state of stress, sometimes you are in a state of desperation and you are asked to make very calculated decisions. It is rarely done in warfare and certainly not in football; so your decisions made during the week are the ones that make sense."
-Bill Walsh

Bill Walsh, who is widely recognized as one of the greatest coaches of all time, would script his first 20 plays of the game. He would do so because he didn't want to emotionally overreact to unforeseen circumstances. Going into a 100-mile race, there undoubtedly was going to be unforeseen circumstances, so I took a page out of Walsh's playbook and laid out a race plan:

*"Western States F*IT List"*

Gear...

Oils and Creams... Glide, Hemp cream, Sunscreen, bug spray

Clothes... Solomon shoes, 2XU Compression socks, black Solomon tight shorts, black Solomon Shirt, Mission cooling sleeves, Mission cooling towel, mission cooling cap and bandana, HUSTLE hat...

Nutrition... Solomon backpack, 2 17 oz water flask bottles, 2 packs gel blocks, 2 nutrition bars. 8 Salt tabs and altoids.

Solomon 17 oz hand held filled with electrolyte drink.

Electronics... Flash light, iPhone 6 with life proof charging case and downloaded music. iPhone 6 plus with case

Apple head phones, monster head phones

Below are 4 critical categories to mapping out the 100 miles:

Aid Station... MILE... Estimated 24 Hour Pace Time... Estimated Time to next aid station

Lyons Ridge... Mile 10.5... 7:10 AM... 1:20

Standard Non Crew Nutrition Plan

Refill Water Bottles, Electrolytes
Watermelon with salt
PB and J
Pay Day
Chips
Gel
Reload on blocks

Red Star Ridge... Mile 16... 8:20 AM... 1:30

Standard Non Crew Nutrition & Hydration

Duncan Canyon... Mile 23.8... 9:50 AM... 1:30

Standard Non Crew Nutrition & Hydration

Robinson Flat... Mile 29.7... 11:20 AM... 55 min

Standard Crew Gear, Nutrition & Hydration

Crew... Solomon White Shirt, Solomon Red Shirt, Solomon shoes, Solomon shorts, HOKA Shoes, 2 short socks, 2 2XU compression socks, sanitary sock filled with ice, HEMP Lotion, Sun Tan lotion, bug spray.

1 new hand held ready to go filled with water, 2 Fresh Solomon bottles water, 1 Fresh bottle electrolytes

Peanut Butter and Jelly Pancakes
Chips
Avocado
Ice Cold COKE

Nothing beats an OPPO TACO crew stop :)

Miller's Defeat... Mile 34.4... 12:15 PM... 45 min

Standard Non Crew Nutrition & Hydration

Dusty Corners... Mile 38... 12:55... 1:00

Standard Non Crew Nutrition & Hydration

Last Chance... Mile 43.3... 1:55... 1:20

Standard Non Crew Nutrition And Hydration Including
Drop Bag with extra 2 water bottles Iced Over

Devil's Thumb... Mile 47.8... 3:15... 1:05

Standard Non Crew Nutrition And Hydration

El Dorado Creek... Mile 52.9... 4:20 .... 55 min

Standard Non Crew Nutrition And Hydration

Michigan Bluff... Mile 55.7... 5:20 ... 1:25

Standard Crew Gear, Nutrition and Hydration

Forrest Hill... Mile 62... 6:45 PM ... 45 min

Crew Surplus ... Solomon White Shirt, Solomon Red Shirt, Solomon shoes, Solomon shorts, HOKA Shoes, 2 short socks, 2 2XU compression socks, sanitary sock filled with ice, HEMP Lotion, Sun Tan lotion, bug spray.

1 new hand held ready to go filled with water, 2 Fresh Solomon bottles of water, 1 Fresh bottle electrolytes

In N Out Burger/Pizza
Chips
Avocado
Ice Cold COKE
Protein Drink

Refill Water Bottles, Electrolytes
Watermelon and Salt
PB and J
Pay Day
Chips
Gel
blocks

Cal 1... Mile 65.7... 7:30... 1:15
Standard Non Crew Nutrition and Hydration

Cal 2... Mile 70... 8:45... 40 min
Standard Non Crew Nutrition and Hydration

Cal 3... Mile 73... 9:25 ... 1:15
Standard Non Crew Nutrition and Hydration

Rucky Chucky... Mile 78... 10:40 ... 40 min
Standard Crew Gear, Nutrition and Hydration

Green Gate... Mile 79.8... 11:20... 1:30
Standard Non Crew Nutrition and Hydration

Auburn Lake Trail... Mile 85.2... 12:50... 1:15
Standard Non Crew Nutrition And Hydration

Browns Bar... Mile 89.9... 2:05... 1:05
Standard Non Crew Nutrition And Hydration

Highway 49... Mile 93.5... 3:10... 1:00
Standard Crew Gear, Nutrition And Hydration

No Hands Bridge... Mile 96.8... 4:10 ... 30 min
Standard Non Crew Nutrition and Hydration

Robbie Point... Mile 98.9... 4:40... 20 min
Crew... Tillman Jersey, Lets go home.

Obviously, there is going to be deviation from the plan but the blueprint for the race was laid out right in front of me. I had a playbook to follow, which more than anything eased my mind going into the race.

Human Crash Test Dummy Life Lesson #123

When you have a big event or even a big day, lay out a plan of attack. Know what you are going to start out with, so if you have to make adjustments, you can make them without judgment or reservation.

Have a plan, but flexibility and the ability to adjust in the moment is the key to successful execution. The F*IT List will lead you in the right direction, but ultimately, the execution will be up to you and how you are able to deal with unforeseen circumstances.

Chapter 124
Spread The Love

"Try not to become a man of success,
but rather try to become a man of value."
-Albert Einstein

I am not sure if I ever had a month fly by as quickly as June did, but before I knew it, race week was here. My man Robert Rhodes, an ultra-runner from Woodside who runs the Trails in Motion Film Festival, introduced me to a guy by the name of Myles Smythe over the training run weekend. Myles is a film producer and shot a kick-ass film called "This is Your Day" following the 2015 Western States. The last thing I was thinking about leading into my first 100-mile race was having a film crew follow me around to document my experience. Yet, the more Myles and I talked, the more it started to make sense for both of us.

In its 43 years of existence, there had never been a mainstream athlete make the transition to competing in the Western States 100, or any other 100-mile race for that matter. Why not? I figured it was a question worth exploring.

Why do so many former professional athletes fall victim to obesity and depression?

Could running be a possible outlet to prevent both?

The thought of being able to compare and contrast Major League Baseball and the ultra-marathon world also seemed very intriguing to me.

Yet what drew me to the idea more than anything was to hopefully further explain to the average sports fan what exactly it means to be an ultra-runner and what exactly the ultra-running community represents and stands for.

Unfortunately, ultra-runners are still looked upon as freaks by many people. They are often stereotyped as outcasts that seem to be running away from whatever problems they may have in their life. As far as I am concerned, that could not be any further from the truth.

Ultra-runners that I know don't run to escape problems; they run to face them head-on. They run for mental clarity that directly impacts every other aspect of their life, a mental clarity that quite frankly allows them to live their life on a very different level. They achieve a Zen-like state that brings a peace, calmness, and focus to everything that they do.

Human Crash Test Dummy Life Lesson #124

If your story can inspire somebody, don't be shy or timid about getting it out there. So long as it's authentically done, it will resonate with many different people for many different reasons. The inspirational value that you can ultimately provide to other people is worth whatever headaches you may endure along the way.

Chapter 125
Work It

"Physical labor not only does not exclude the possibility of mental activity, but improves and stimulates it."
-Leo Tolstoy

More than anything, the best way to describe the ultra-running community is: a group of people who enjoy running endless miles and are not afraid to push the limits of what others may consider not humanly possible. It is a group of people whose number one priority is to preserve and maintain the trails that they navigate. In what other sport would you see the greatest players and legends of the sport prepping the field before the game? Imagine Michael Jordan sweeping the court before the NBA Finals, or Derek Jeter raking the infield before the World Series, or Tom Brady mowing the lawn before the Super Bowl. The Saturday before the race, I was out on the Western States trail with several other runners clearing and restructuring a section of the trail between Red Star Ridge and Duncan Canyon. The two runners that were leading the trail work just happened to be two of the greatest ultra-runners in the history of the sport, Tim Twietmeyer and Ann Trason.

As a matter of fact, every single runner who runs Western States, from elite to bottom-barrel age-grouper, is required to do 8 hours of trail work; otherwise, they will not be allowed to race. The Western States Trail Service Team, led by Elke Reimer, who has dedicated a large portion of her life to this, have several organized campouts and trail cleanup sessions throughout the course of the year.

Human Crash Test Dummy Life Lesson #125

The reward of manual labor is one of the greatest things you can experience in life. In order to truly get the most out of your experience, become a master of your craft by learning and experiencing the tools of your trade. If you are a runner, take a trash bag with you and dedicate a run to cleaning up trash either on the road or trail. Every single run I do, I make sure to pick up at least one item of trash. Some days I will bring the bag and fill the entire thing. If you ride a bike, learn how to change a tire or better yet put an entire bike together. If you play baseball, learn to lace a glove, carve a bat, or try dragging the infield dirt or mowing the lawn. The more you are able to intimately understand the dynamics of your craft the more you will be able to exude gratitude, which is the gateway to success.

Chapter 126
Respect History

"We are not makers of history, we are made by history."
-Martin Luther King

Following the trail cleanup session, I headed to our home in Truckee where I got in a couple last-minute trail runs and daily sauna sessions. On Thursday, I met Myles and his film partner, Damien, on top of the escarpment at Squaw for the flag-raising ceremony. The one thing I wanted to do was completely immerse myself in the Western States culture and learn as much as possible about the history of the race. I wanted to truly understand how and why this specific race is so special and so sought after. It didn't take long to find the answers.

At the flag-raising ceremony, two members of the Western States family who had recently passed away, Dr. Bob Lind and emeritus race director Greg Sunderland, were honored. I did not personally know either one but to hear friends and colleagues speak about them showed me how close and special the Western States community is.

I had an opportunity to hike down the mountain with Mo Livermore, who headed the ceremony and is one of the original founders of the race. It was fun to hear her perspective on how the race has evolved since its infant days.

My one big take-away was that Western States is more than a race; it is a family of runners, past and present, that are continuing to do everything in their power to preserve its authenticity.

Human Crash Test Dummy Life Lesson #126

Learn about the history of whatever endeavor you are undertaking. Talk to people associated with the endeavor and you will get a much better understanding and appreciation for everything and everybody involved. Ultimately, it will give that endeavor an authentic significance only attainable through your own experience of taking the time to learn.

Chapter 127
Brian Morrison

"If you want to lift yourself up, lift up someone else."
-Booker T. Washington

The day before the race, there was a huge meeting where they went over race details and introduced the elite field of men and women's runners.

One of the runners introduced was a guy by the name of Brian Morrison. I had done several interviews about my transition from baseball to ultra-running. A common question that had come up was how did I hear about Western States? I didn't really have the answer. I know I heard about it when I was a kid but I dismissed it as something that was so incredibly crazy that it was tough for me to even comprehend. I also knew that when I got into triathlon, there was a girl who trained at the same cycling studio that I went to that was preparing for the race. Being an endurance athlete at that point, I had a much better grasp and understanding of what the Western States 100 was: a 100-mile foot race from Squaw Valley to the historic gold mining town of Auburn by way of climbing 19,000 feet and descending 23,000 feet through the Sierra Nevada Mountains. Temperatures typically started in the 30s and reached well over 100 degrees in the deeply nested canyons along the 100-mile course. If you complete the journey in under 24 hours, the reward is a LEGENDARY silver belt buckle that reads "100 MILES ONE DAY." The race definitely had me intrigued.

Now here I was, just days away from competing in my first Western States, and I was reading the program of the "runners to watch." I read through all the elites and I came across #133, Eric Byrnes. It explained my transition from baseball to ultras and mentioned I had just recently gotten into the sport. I was almost embarrassed to be on the same page as the other runners but definitely honored that they would even mention me.

Then, I came across the next runner to watch for, Brian Morrison. It talked about how Morrison was coming back for the first time in 10 years since he was leading the race, collapsed 3 times running around the track, and ultimately crossed the finish line on what they determined to be assistance. He was disqualified from the race.

The year was 2006 and I was playing baseball for the Arizona Diamondbacks. I was sitting in the locker room at Chase Field in Phoenix when I ran across an article that explained the Brian Morrison situation. I remember marveling at the fact that the dude ran 100 miles, had a 20-minute lead on the second-place guy, and couldn't make it around the track on his own power. I shared the story with whoever was within earshot; then I remember thinking how incredibly impressive of a feat that was, even if the dude did not "officially" win the race.

Looking back, I can say I TRULY learned about the Western States 100 because of Brian Morrison. The incredible ball sack and pain tolerance he displayed was nothing short of heroic. The fact that he put everything he had into the race to the point of complete and utter exhaustion mesmerized me. I may not have known it that day, but subconsciously that was the day I decided I was going to one day compete in the Western States 100. Ten years later, I got my shot.

Ten years later, Brian Morrison returned.

When Tim Twietmeyer announced Morrison's name, he deservedly got a bigger ovation than any other runner. Obviously, he seemed very emotionally moved. Then the runners went back to sit down in the huge auditorium that probably had at least 1,000 people. Ironically, Morrison was sitting with his wife right next to where I was standing. As soon as the meeting ended, I went straight up to Brian, introduced myself, and told him my entire story of following him 10 years ago when I was still playing baseball and how inspirational his effort was. I basically continued to tell him how much giving every last ounce of his energy to reach the finish line resonated with me, and how I believe it ultimately had somehow brought me to the start line. He could not have been a more humble and cool guy.

Sometimes in life we are put in certain situations for certain reasons. Without looking too deeply into it, I felt like meeting Brian had more to do with the alignment of our universes than a random chance.

Human Crash Test Dummy Life Lesson #127

Draw inspiration from others and hold that inspiration with you. If you have a chance to share what inspired you with that person, don't hold back! The most rewarding moments of my life come when another person shares with me that something I have done has inspired them to take action in a positive direction.

Chapter 128
It Takes a Team

"If you want to go fast go alone, if you want to go far go together."
-African Proverb

I rolled back to the house and we had almost the entire crew there for the big pre-game meal. MiMi and my boy Kowalski from Arizona, Franz and Jen Dill, Max and Eli, Hao, my mom, sister Shea, brother-in-law Justin, cousin Amy, Tarah, and the 3 munchkins. Lance and Kyle were coming in on race day. A mountain of vegetables and gluten free pasta was served, but before we dug in, we circled around the center island to say a prayer. I had every intention of keeping it simple by thanking everybody for being there, and then handing it off to Tarah to bless the food. When I looked around at everybody there holding hands, I felt this overwhelming gratitude pulsate my body. In the process of thanking everyone for coming, I broke down. I can't really explain why other than the fact that I felt incredibly selfish. Everyone was there on my behalf to help me chase an individual dream. I was completely overwhelmed with gratitude and it made me realize how lucky and blessed I am to have these people in my life.

After dinner, I went to lie vertical and stare at the ceiling with hopes of falling asleep at some point between 8 pm and my wake-up call of 3 am. It was probably around midnight when I was finally out. 3 am rolled around seemingly minutes later when my wife's alarm went off. Without asking her, she had set it as a back up. Good thing because the phone that I set my alarm on went dead. I thought I had plugged it in but apparently not. I rolled out of the rack, took a big whiff of eucalyptus oil, let the film crew (Myles and Damien) in the door, fired down a yogurt, poured myself a cup of Joe, crushed an oatmeal/granola combo with a banana, and embraced the fact that the next 24+ hours would be the most physically and psychologically challenging of my entire life.

I lubed up with chafe cream, tiger balm, sunscreen, bug spray, and hemp jelly, and then fired on my cooling vest and got out the door at 4:15 am. It takes about 25 minutes to get to Squaw, but I then realized when we were half-way there I had forgotten my watch. I called back to the house to have my sister and brother-in-law (hopefully) bring it to the start line before the gun went off. I arrived at Squaw about 4:40 am, where it was a balmy 41 degrees. The very first person I saw was none other than Brian Morrison. I gave him a big hug and wished him luck, and then scurried to go get my number. I went for one last potty break where I ran into Jim Wallmsley, one of the pre-race favorites and the baddest runner I have ever seen. Incredible to think what adventures would lay ahead for that dude on that day.

Wallmsley led the race by a wide margin and was on pace to break the course record until he lost traction crossing the American River at Ruck a Chucky, where he went floating down the river. He needed to be rescued by the water safety patrol. He somehow recovered to still have the lead but made a wrong turn a few miles later and went 4 miles off course. He went from breaking the course record to 14th place. Nonetheless, he showed why he is and should be one of the best ultra-runners in the world for years to come.

I still had 10 minutes before the race so I rolled back into the truck for some last-minute seat-heater action and some final Kowalski words of encouragement. Kowalski, who I originally met when he worked for a triathlon store in Scottsdale, has become an EPIC friend and training partner with more one-liner inspirational phrases than Tony Robbins. Dude will always keep a smile on your face. I bolted for the start line at 4:55 am. Five minutes later, the shotgun went off and the 2016 Western States 100 Mile Endurance Run began.

Human Crash Test Dummy Life Lesson #128

Rely on the people you love. Your love will be reciprocated through their actions and you will have an opportunity to send the love right back to them through your own actions. Show gratitude for the sacrifices that each of your team members make, big or small. Life's experiences are a lot better, easier, and more rewarding when shared with others. The right team will allow you to endure unimaginable distances.

Chapter 129
Let's Go

"...we rejoice in our sufferings, knowing that suffering produces endurance, and endurance produces character, and character produces hope, and hope does not disappoint us..."
-Romans 5:3-5

The run starts with a 2550-foot climb within the first 4 miles to the top of the escarpment at Squaw. I ran/hiked up a good portion of the climb with Karl Hoagland, the editor of Ultra Running Magazine, his fiancé Erica Lindland, and Scott Dunlap; 3 people who I have gotten to know pretty well and have helped me better understand the intricacies of the sport. Eventually, I backed off. My number one goal on the initial climb was to not put out any sort of big effort. When I got to the top, the scene was unreal. There was a slew of people going nuts cheering while the sun was raising over Lake Tahoe behind us and the entire Western States course view laid in front of me. I took a minute to capture it on video and then began the trek through the high country to Lyons Ridge, which was the first aid station.

10 miles in, we hit the Lyons Ridge and I could not have felt better. The views up in the high country were phenomenal and just about all the snow had melted so the trail was smooth and very easy running. Then after the Red Star aid station I found a groove. I had broken away from a pack of runners I was with and began to open it up on some of the slight down hills. There was one point around mile 20 where I completely hit a running bliss. I was on a ridge with a view of a huge canyon to the right and another killer view of a canyon and crystal blue shining lake to my left. I was floating.

Just as I was becoming comfortable in the euphoric la-la fantasy running land, my right toe clipped a rock. Throughout the course of my Major League career, I became known for making diving catches that resembled Super Man flying through the air. This was not any different. I literally was launched forward and went FLYING through the air.

I headed (literally) off the right side of the trail and landed in a huge bush. The branches kept me suspended without ever hitting the ground. Wooooooooooooo Hoooooooooooooo!!!!! I was f*cking alive. I had a cut on my knee and shin, but other than a little blood, I was good to go. I immediately got my ass up and got right back into my groove. As I was headed down to the Duncan Canyon aid station there was a section that was completely exposed. At this point, I was dropping altitude with every stride, and the temperature was increasing by the minute. Duncan Canyon aid was at mile 25, and for whatever reason, most likely the heat or lack of calories, I felt like sh*t.

I iced up my arm sleeves for the first time, got some watermelon and salt in me, crushed a PB&J, and was on my way. The next mile after the aid was terrible. Overall, it was downhill and pretty easy terrain but there were a few mild ascents that I should have had no problem running. Yet the nauseous feeling I had brought me to a slow walk on even the easiest of up-hills.

I felt like in order to break 24 hours, I was going to have to run all of the flats and downhills and power hike the up-hills. If I was at mile 25 and I was already walking the easiest of up-hills, what did that mean for the next 75 miles? I had no choice but to go directly to my Western States mission statement, "One foot in front of the other." When I got to the bottom of the canyon, there was a small creek crossing that I decided to capture on video. I took my time, let my feet soak in the cold water, and did my best to get my sh*t together.

I started the race with Solomon S Lab Speed shoes. They are light, durable, fast, and the most water-resistant shoes I have ever put on. I ran 62 miles at Miwok in the pouring rain and had absolutely no issues, so I was not afraid to get the shoes wet. I then made the long hike up to Robinson Flat trailing 3 elite female runners. I figured I was in good company with Erica Lindland, 9th overall woman in 2015, leading the charge.

When I got up to Robinson, I felt much better. Tarah and the crew were there. I got my water bottles replaced then added two more. In total, I was now carrying 4 Solomon soft flask bottles as I headed into the hottest part of the race. I had 2 bottles strapped to the back of my hands and the other 2, which were frozen, I held on to. I also had a baseball sanitary sock filled with ice wrapped around my neck.

Miller's Defeat was next, and then Dusty Corners where I met my sister Shea and brother-in-law Justin, who were waiting with a fresh sanitary sock filled with ice. Next stop was Last Chance and the name could not be more perfect. It literally is the last chance to refuel, recharge, and find some way to cool down before hitting the absolute depths of the canyons and climbing up to Devils Thumb.

The Last Chance aid station crew was AWESOME. I snapped another video upon the exit, and then was on my way to thumb-wrestle the Devil. I have always struggled in the heat in every race I have ever done since entering the endurance world. By far and away, my biggest concern of the entire race was how I was going to be able to manage the scorching hot weather in the canyons.

The thought of using a baseball sanitary sock filled with ice came to me from watching numerous pitchers use them to ice their arms over the years. The socks are very light, very durable, and are very easy to tie up and keep tight from both sides. The only time I had actually tried it was in the sauna a few days before. It worked perfect then and it worked even better on the course. I could make an argument that the baseball sanitary sock saved my race. Despite consistent temperatures in the mid-90s that climbed well into the 100s in certain parts of the canyons, I never once felt overwhelmed by the heat. I find it a bit ironic and even more humorous that a piece of baseball equipment happened to be my SAVIOR in a 100-mile endurance running race.

Once I got to the bottom of the canyon and began the climb up to Devils Thumb, I began noticing some weird sh*t. There was somebody on my ass running right behind me, but every time I turned around and went to let him pass, he was gone. Then there was a guy that was positioned about half way up the climb. He was in the bushes on one knee taking pictures with a huge extended lens camera. Yet, when I got closer to the cameraman, he was gone. Also, along the course throughout the canyons, I saw a woman, an enthusiastic older lady, that was clapping and cheering words of encouragement, but when I got closer to thank her for her support, she was gone. I also kept hearing a constant ruffling in the bushes; I was certain that I was getting stalked by a mountain lion. I would slow down and swiftly turn to the direction of the noise, but when I did, the noise stopped; it was gone. I was certain that I saw a baby cub just off the trail to my right, but once again as I got closer, it was gone. I finally realized my vision and mind were obviously playing tricks on me when there was an orangutan swinging from a tree to my left as I approached the top of Michigan Bluff. I am not an expert on hallucinations, but I imagine it had something to do with the heat, fatigue, and possibly even my kick-ass old school Blue Blocker sunglasses tossing out images in crazy high definition.

When I arrived in Michigan Bluff after the two gnarliest climbs of the day, my watch read 59 miles. I knew that Forrest Hill was at mile 62, so I figured just 3 miles until the next aid station where I would be able to see the entire crew. When I rolled into Michigan Bluff, I kept thinking how weird it was that there were 2 crew aid stations just 3 miles apart. I took a total minimalist approach. I dropped 2 water bottles, slammed a Coke, and wanted to take off. The crew started yelling at me to eat more, take in more salt, drink more, etc. I told them, "I'll dial it in at Forrest Hill in 3 miles." Then Jen Dill broke the bad news. "UMMMMMM, Eric... Forrest Hill is 7 miles away, not 3."

I felt like I just got kicked in the nuts. I was then out on a desolate road in between Michigan Bluff and Forrest Hill all by myself, nobody within sight in either direction, when I heard footsteps rapidly coming up behind me. I figured once again I must have been hearing things so I didn't even bother to turn around. The footsteps kept getting louder. Then I heard heavy breathing that got more intense with every step. Now sh*t was really getting trippy.

I finally turned around. From behind me came a furry four-legged figure running at MACH 3 full-speed up the hill. I thought it was a mountain lion and I was ready to take him on. He flew right by me and then was gone. I began uncontrollably laughing when I realized the mountain lion was a yellow lab.

Here I was, somewhere in between mile 56 and 62, with no idea exactly how far I had gone because of a watch malfunction. I was feeling sorry for myself and here comes a dog that looked like the purest and most natural runner I have ever seen in my life. He didn't care about what zone he was running in, how hot it was, or what the reading was on his GPS watch. He was running for the simple joy of the sport. Ironically, that was the exact same reason I was running. Once I took a minute to fully comprehend the parallels, I could not take the smile off my face.

When I was making my way out of Volcano Canyon, I saw Myles waiting for me with the camera. He immediately told me, "All your boys are waiting for you at the top." I did not expect to see them until Forrest Hill so to hear that was MUSIC to my ears. Speaking of music by the way, I started the race with wireless headphones in my pocket and was now approaching mile 60 and I had yet to take the headphones out. I didn't necessarily plan to listen to music but I did not plan not to listen. The bottom line was I became so involved in each and every moment and dynamic of the race that I did not feel as if I needed any other sort of stimulus.

Waiting at the top of Bath Road was what I like to refer to as the pacer dream quad.

The leader of the "Bobby Malibu Overachievers Multi Sport Life Optimization Group" is Michael Kowalski. I have a lid I rock all the time and people will ask me what it is. The answer is exactly how it reads, except the name "Bobby Malibu" is spun off of the old iconic character on American Gladiator and he has absolutely no affiliation with our group other than being the legendary and humorous team mascot.

The next dude was my original Facebook stalker and endurance sports mentor, San Rafael fire fighter, Kyle "Chief" Hamilton.

Also waiting was Franz Dill, five-time Western States finisher, finisher of the Grand Slam of Ultra Running, my official pacer from mile 80-100, and my neighbor in Half Moon Bay.

Last, but certainly not least, and without a doubt our most controversial member, seven-time Tour De France champion, amateur ultra-runner, WEDÜ founder, and a typical adrenaline junkie who fits in perfectly with the rest of the pacer dream squad, Lance Armstrong.

The entire 2 to 3-mile section I got to run with the whole squad was the most invigorating of the entire race. We talked gear, strategy, nutrition, fluids, and energy consumption, but most importantly, we talked exactly what I needed to talk at that time: a whole lot of F*CKING SH*T.

MiMi, a good friend of Tarah and I from AZ, joined us as well when we got to Forrest Hill Road. Forrest Hill is by far and away the biggest aid station and one of the few points of the race where it is an absolute spectacle; people line the street on both sides for about a mile. As we made our way down parade chute, people were going nuts, and I actually just got the chills thinking about the euphoric feeling that I had as we marched down the street, shoulder-to-shoulder, 6 men deep. It wasn't about me; it was about our squad. My wife had dubbed us Team Oppo Taco. We were unified; we were in this SH*T together! It was AWESOME.

One of the most rewarding sights of the entire day was seeing former Western States president and 10-time finisher John Trent on the side of the road at Forrest Hill, cheering loudly for our group as we rolled through town.

When we met up with the rest of the crew at the end of the street, a few of the realities began to set in. First and foremost, my feet were wrecked. The crew wanted me to change shoes and socks but I knew that we had the big river crossing at mile 78, and I only had one other pair of shoes that I wanted to change into, my softly cushioned Hoka's. The problem is I know that the Hoka's do not do well in the water, so I decided to suck it up the next 16 miles and hold off on the shoe change until after the river.

I did everything I could to down an In-N-Out double double and fries but it didn't work out all that well.

Lance, now my official pacer, and I took off and started to make our way down to the river. About a mile into the run, we heard something coming from behind.

"HEY!!!!! HEY!!!! STOP!!!! STOP!!!!!"

We both looked at each other, shrugged, and kept rolling. Finally, about a mile and a half from when we left Forrest Hill, my brother-in-law Justin comes FLYING from up behind us. "Dude, you forgot your light!"

From mile 60-80, I don't think I could have asked for a better pacer. Lance and I bullsh*tted the entire time. We talked life, cycling, baseball, family, and just about everything else you could imagine. Nothing was off the table. In all there may have been a total of 2 minutes of dead air in our 4 hours of running together. Break Lance out of the hard shell that he can appear to have at times and this dude is fun to hang with, but more importantly, he's got a HUGE heart.

By the time we rolled into the last aid station before the river at mile 73, we had absolutely hit our stride. I had felt as good as I had all day. The sun was down and the darkness had settled in. The dude greeting us at the aid station even commented, "Man, you guys look good." Unfortunately, he followed it up with, "Just think, all you got left is a marathon." I then became consumed with the fact that I still had a marathon to go. Not just your average street marathon, but 27 miles over incredibly rocky unstable terrain, through a roaring river, then up and down several thousand feet of elevation gain. F*CK.

Before we bolted, I probably had one of the most unusual requests of the day; I needed a hair tie. I had taken my cooling skullcap off from under my HUSTLE hat because I was no longer hot enough to wet it or put ice in it. Yet, my head was actually the only part on my body that I felt like was trapping a significant amount of heat. I wanted to ditch the hat but my hair was so long on top that my bangs would fall into my face without something to tie it up. Hence the mini man-bun look I occasionally will rock. There were 3 women there and not one of them had a hair tie. Then out of nowhere a big, burly, cowboy-looking dude rolled up and said, "Boy, you need a hair tie?"

"Yes, sir."

He the proceeds to reach into his pocket, "I got 3, which color would you like, purple, pink, or black?"

"I am not much of a purple or pink guy, so I'll pick black, sir, THANK YOU!!!"

Much like the pioneers who blazed the Western States Trail, you just never know where you may strike gold. I quickly tied the hair knot and the man pony express was off.

We had one big last climb and then it was a dash towards the lights of the historic river crossing at Rucky Chucky. When we got there, we refueled at the aid, and then made our way about 40 yards down to the middle fork of the American River. Because of the massive amount of snowfall we got that winter, the water level of the river was higher and flowing much better than the past few years. They actually put a cable that starts on one side and stretches all the way across the river. Runners had to hold onto the cable as they navigated their way through the chest-high water across slippery rocks and boulders. The AWESOME volunteers came up HUGE once again. They fired life vests on both Lance and I, and there was a team of at least 10 people that were in the water staged along the path of the cable. I grew up surfing in Half Moon Bay where the ocean water typically hovers in the low 50s. Generally, cold water does not bother me one bit. I don't know what the temperature of the American River was at that point of the night, but I can say from experience, it was F*CKING bone chilling.

When we arrived at the other side, I was shocked to see the entire crew waiting at the bottom. We then began the 2-mile hike up to the top of Green Gate. We were rolling 10+ deep, shoulder-to-shoulder, bullsh*tting about the day that had taken place. We also had a chance to strategize about the last 20 miles. My feet were toast and we had to figure out a way to get them through the last 20. Everybody was telling me to change my shoes and socks but the thought of taking off my socks and exposing my dawgs was gut wrenching. I knew my feet were slaughtered but I wanted to deal with them after the race. I also knew exposing them would freak everybody out almost to the point where they would not want me to continue the race.

When we finally got to the top, I flew through the aid station, and then went and sat down for the first time all race. Hao was Franz's friend and crew guru in many of his races. I met Hao for the first time that morning. Now here we were, several hours and 80 miles into the Western States 100, and Hao is peeling off my compression socks and pedicuring my feet that looked like they just went through the meat grinder.

After the spa treatment, I fired on a fresh pair of compression socks and Hoka shoes. I felt like I went from running barefoot across hot coals to doing the moonwalk. My feet had never been so happy in my entire life.

Originally, Franz was going to pace me from mile 60-80 and Lance was going to take me 80-100. We eventually decided to switch it up at the last minute. Figuring Lance and I were both relatively unfamiliar with the course, it would be better to have us run in as much light as possible. As far as Franz, he basically has so much knowledge of the trail that he literally could run the trail backwards, blindfolded, and with one of his legs tied behind his back.

Franz and I shot out of Green Gate invigorated. As we made our way toward the mile-85 Auburn Lakes Trail aid station, we hit a happy place. It also didn't take long to realize how incredibly knowledgeable Franz was with the terrain. We would be coming up on a section and Franz would say, "We have about 400 feet of technical rocky descent coming up. Watch your step and take it easy." We then would roll around the next bend and Franz jumped in again. "We have a slight downhill of nice hard packed dirt, we can open it up a bit." Then shortly before the next uphill section, "We have about a 2-minute climb coming up, good time to take in your fluids and get some calories in you."

I have not been in the sport very long and I am not sure what constitutes a GREAT pacer, but between Lance and Franz, I am not sure I could have asked for two better dudes. Running with Lance was like going on a jog with a buddy. There is no doubt that we opened it up and pushed the pace together but Lance's greatest asset was that he kept me entertained from start to finish with basic bullsh*t conversation. Franz was a technician, an engineer on the course. He knew absolutely every turn, every descent, and every ascent well before we approached it.

As soon as Franz and I got rolling at mile 80, my headlight was dying and dying fast, so I figured I was screwed. Franz quickly pulled out a hand-held light and proceeded to shoot the light in front of me on the trails at an angle. It was better than I could have ever lit the course myself. I have joked around about having the "pacer dream squad," but between Lance, Franz, and the crew, this was no joke.

The Auburn Lake Trails aid station is run by the Coastside Running Club. Franz just happens to be the president of the Coastside Running Club. When we were approaching the aid, Franz let out his signature howling call, and immediately, the Coastsiders were howling back like a pack of wolves. Franz, his wife Jen, and the rest of the Coastsiders run by far and away the best aid station at Miwok, and Western States was not any different. They had a Christmas-themed aid station so starting about a quarter mile away from the aid was a plethora of green and red lights. All the volunteers were dressed in Christmas-themed garb and they basically delivered like Santa Claus. Outside of the normal aid station fixings I had grown accustomed to in the first 85 miles, the Coastsiders actually had bacon and eggs on the griddle.

As tempting as it was to sit down and have a full diner breakfast, Franz kept me on schedule. I walloped down chicken broth, a Coke, and we were gone. For most of the race I was hovering right on the 24-hour pace and even fell behind at some points. For a good 20-mile portion after the watch miscalculation, I paid no attention to the time.

Between mile 85 and mile 90 there was very little interaction between Franz and I. We both knew my main goal was to finish in under 24 hours and we were hammering.

When we rolled up to Brown's Bar at mile 90, you could hear the aid station from nearly a mile away. It sounded like we were in a 1980s hair band club with AC/DC and Metallica headlining.

We were in and out in a hurry, and as we were leaving, I saw the 24-hour pace sign that read 3:30 am...

I then turned to Franz and asked, "Yo dude, what time is it?"
He gave me a blank stare then responded... "2:30 am."

Tough to describe the feeling that came over me at that point because we still had 10 miles to go, but this became the very first time I allowed myself to think about the finish.

We were an hour ahead of the 24-hour pace but obviously that meant under 23-hours became the new mark. We continued to push the pace. At no point in the entire race had my effort level been as high as it was between mile 90 and 94. We were doing everything in our power not to have to make a sprint to the finish on the track in Auburn to break the 23-hour mark.

Before we reached Highway 49, apparently Franz had texted the crew with our new goal and basically instructed them to keep the pit stop to a minimum. According to everybody in our crew at the Highway 49 aid station, I appeared to be a bit loopy. Supposedly I asked Justin, "Where are the babies? Despite the fact it was past 2 in the morning, and though I still dispute this one, apparently I called my Mom JU JU Pants.

We bolted out of the aid and we were right on the 23-hour pace. It was on. We power-hiked the first hill and then busted our asses on the ensuing flats and downhills that took us to No Hands Bridge. I would love to give you a more detailed account to this section, but to be honest, I don't really remember it all that well. When we got to No Hands Bridge at mile 97 we had just over 3 miles to the finish. We basically blew through the aid station and were now running up-hill sections that I undoubtedly would have been walking earlier in the race.

We got to a point where there was a turn that went up to the right and another that would continue forward. There were 2 runners that had stopped and had no idea which way to go because there was no visible ribbon in place. Without hesitation, Franz yells out, "This way, boys!" We finished the climb up to Robbie Point, exerting as much energy as possible. We then got to the famous mile 99 sign where Tarah, Shea, Justin, Mila, Kowalski, and Kyle were all waiting to charge the final mile.

I looked at the clock for the first time and realized we had about 20 minutes to get through the last 1.2 miles. I then told the runners behind us to go ahead so they didn't have to share the track with the #TeamOppoTaco small army.

I then proceeded to run the most rewarding mile of my entire life. Whatever pain I had felt over the first 99 miles was gone. I was floating. I was giddy. I was running the last mile of the oldest and most prestigious 100-mile race in the world with the most important people in my life. When I reached the track, my mom and kids were waiting to run as well. Cali and Colton were both tired and I am pretty sure not exactly aware of what was going on. I pulled off the track and onto the grass infield to try to get Cali to run with us, but she wasn't having it. We then continued to make our way around the track. I had told everybody that I wanted nothing more than for everybody to cross the finish line together. The entire crew was still there until the last straight away, and then everybody peeled off.

The reason why I wanted everybody in the entire crew to cross together is because it took everyone in that entire crew for me to complete the 100.2 miles across 19,000 feet of elevation gain and 23,000 feet of descent. This was truly a team effort and I wanted to celebrate as a team. I saw my mom so I pulled her out to the track, and Chloe, my 7 year old, came sprinting out of nowhere. Then Tarah came running from behind with Colton and Cali. I took the Pat Tillman jersey my sister had passed to me and hoisted it above my head and then sprinted the last 90 feet. I crossed the finish line at Placer High School in Auburn 22 hours, 50 minutes and 55 seconds after the day had begun at the base of Squaw Valley in Lake Tahoe.

I played 11 seasons of Major League Baseball. As of March of 2018, I have completed 11 Ironman's and multiple ultra-marathons. The Western States 100 was the most difficult, grueling, humbling, and rewarding thing I have ever done in my life.

I finished 73rd overall and was one of 102 silver belt buckle award winners who finished in under 24 hours. There are no words I can speak or emotions I can express that will show the gratitude I have for my entire family and group of friends that helped me throughout the journey.

I don't think there is any doubt that a common theme of the Western States 100 is realizing the value of "paying it forward."

I have and will continue to champion Pat Tillman and the foundation that bears his name in hopes of teaching the future generations about who Pat was and the ultimate sacrifice he made for something that he deemed much larger than himself.

As far as my own pursuits in life, I hope through my work I am able to continue to influence kids to play baseball and live life with an effort and passion that will ultimately inspire future generations.

I hope to help people of all ages realize the physical and psychological value of exercise.

I hope to inspire anybody who has been diagnosed with ADD that there is an outlet and focus that is obtainable that will allow you to thrive in the classroom, at home, in the office, and with whatever sport you choose.

I get it, doing Ironman's or running 100 miles is not for everyone. Some people simply don't have the time to dedicate to the training hours involved. Yet, if there is a person who is willing to commit to the training demands, there is not a doubt in my mind that person has the ability to complete whatever his or her mind is able to dream up.

The question simply becomes are you willing to pay the price? Are you willing to make the necessary sacrifices in order to achieve your dreams?

The next day, after I completed the Western States 100, Cali, my 6-year-old daughter, who wanted nothing to do with the final lap around the track before crossing the finish line, came up to me while I was laid up on the couch downstairs. She sat on my lap, wrapped her hands around my neck and said, "Daddy, when I turn 40, I am going to run the Western States 100."

Human Crash Test Dummy Life Lesson #129

Even when your children may seem uninterested, realize they are always watching. Your influence as a parent or mentor is far greater than you will ever know. It is our responsibility to continue to instill values, work ethics, and beliefs that there are NO limits as to what is attainable.

10 years ago, a dude drove himself to exhaustion trying to win a race, and ultimately, he was disqualified. 10 years later, Brian Morrison officially crossed the finish line of the Western States 100, carrying his two children.

43 years ago, a man on foot lined up next to hundreds of horses in a quest of running 100 miles in a 24-hour period. That man, Gordy Ainsleigh, completed the quest and became responsible for the creation of modern day ultra-running. Once again, just as he has done practically every year since, Gordy stepped up to the same start line just as he did 43 years prior.

Now is probably a good time to ask... What do you plan on doing with your next 43 years?

Closing Time...

"A life is not important, except for the impact it has on others."
-Jackie Robinson

In the winters of 2017 and 2018, my daughter Chloe began ski racing at a very competitive level. She was on the mountain 5 days a week and skied with the same coach each day: Chris 'Moose' Anderson. From the very first time I met Chris, I knew there was something special about him and I had no doubt that my daughter was in great hands. Watching Chloe's development throughout the winter was an incredible experience and absolutely none of it would have been possible without Chris' selfless dedication. Chris was Chloe's ski coach, but he was much more. He became a buddy and a mentor to all 3 of my kids and a good friend to our entire family. In January of 2018, while driving to the work, Chris was just a mile away from the ski mountain when a drunk driver swerved into his lane and hit him head on. He was killed.

As far as we know, we get one shot at this beautiful gift called life. Just as Chris did, make sure to use your time on earth to positively influence others. Chris is gone, but because of the overwhelming positive influence he had on others, his spirit is alive and well.

It is our responsibility to live our lives in a way in which our actions will inspire others. Just as my Dad ingrained in me, let your behavior reflect your commitment. Your thoughts and words are forever influencing your reality, yet it is your actions that truly reveal your character.

We all will be faced with many obstacles along the way. Learn to love the obstacle. Learn to love the challenge. Learn to say F*ck It. The freedom you will experience is life changing. Ultimately, your ability to say F*ck It will have a direct impact on the way you live your life, which in turn will have an incredible impact on others.

"Yesterday's gone; learn from it, then forget about it. Tomorrow's only on its way; plan for it, but do not worry about what it may bring. Today is here; however, live in the moment. Don't let it pass by unnoticed because once it's gone, it's gone forever. SEND IT."

-Chris 'Moose' Anderson

If you somehow made it this far, **thank you.**

To show our appreciation for your commitment to the F*It lifestyle:

- Go to **EricByrnes.com**
- Click on 'Documentary'
- Punch in the promo code **PROCESS** to get 50% off Diamond To The Rough.
- Also download the **Daily F*It List PDF**: 22 life hack items that will help you live a more fit and active lifestyle.
- Check out the **Resources** section of website, which has recommended readings that will help aid your quest to authentically live your life.

Snap a Pic with *The F*It List* on Social Media!

(Be sure to tag Eric and include **#TheFItList**)

About the Author

Eric James Byrnes is a San Francisco Bay Area native who grew up in Woodside, CA and attended St. Francis High School (Mountain View) where he excelled playing both football and baseball in the prestigious West Catholic Athletic League. Byrnes regularly competed against fellow Major Leaguer Pat Burrell (Bellermine Prep) and future NFL Hall of Fame'r Tom Brady (Serra) in both sports. After his senior year Byrnes was selected by the Los Angeles Dodgers in the 1994 Major League Baseball draft but elected to attend UCLA on an athletic scholarship.

At UCLA, Byrnes was an All American outfielder and multiple time recipient of the Bruin Academic Award, given to the player with the highest GPA. After a trip to the College World Series in 1997, Byrnes was drafted by the Houston Astros but again chose to put professional baseball on hold in favor of education. In 1998, after his Senior year, Byrnes was drafted for the 3rd time and eventually signed with the Oakland Athletics. Byrnes was elected into the UCLA Athletic Hall of Fame in 2013.

Byrnes made his Major League debut with the Oakland A's against the Cleveland Indians on August 22, 2000. Byrnes was part of the 2002 Oakland A's "Moneyball" team that broke a modern day record with 20 consecutive wins. In 2003, Byrnes hit in 22 consecutive games and while playing against his favorite childhood team, the San Francisco Giants, Byrnes became the 1st player in AT&T Park history to hit for the cycle. Byrnes played parts of 6 seasons with the A's and was a member of 4 playoff teams.

During several winters throughout Byrnes' Major League career he played for the Licey Tigres of the prestigious Dominican Winter League. In 2002 Byrnes became the 1st American player in over 20 years to win the league's Most Valuable Player award. Byrnes played a total of 5 winters between 2002 and 2010 and won 2 Dominican League championships with Licey. Along the way, Byrnes, who is bilingual, immersed himself in the Dominican culture and became somewhat of a cult hero. He earned the nickname "Captain America" from the Dominican faithful with his all-out style of play. Although, his teammates simply called him "Loco."

In 2005, Byrnes was traded to the Colorado Rockies and then 2 weeks later was traded to the Baltimore Orioles. He was released by the Orioles at the end of the 2005 season.

Byrnes signed a free agent contract with the Arizona Diamondbacks in 2006 and went on to hit 26 home runs and steal 25 bases. While playing for the Diamondbacks in 2007, Byrnes became the 11th player in Major League history to hit 20 home runs and steal 50 bases. That same year he won the "Fielding Bible Award," handed out to baseball's best defensive left fielder. During Byrnes' time with the Diamondbacks, he hosted and co-produced the Emmy award winning "Eric Byrnes Show" on Fox Sports Arizona. The 30 minute once a month show provided viewers with an in depth look into a major leaguers life on and off the field.

Byrnes went on to play parts of 11 big league seasons with the Oakland A's, Colorado Rockies, Baltimore Orioles, Arizona Diamondbacks and Seattle Mariners. He compiled 109 career home runs and 129 stolen bases.

In 2010 Byrnes walked away from baseball and began a career in broadcasting. He has since worked for ESPN, FOX, SiriusXM and KNBR. Byrnes is currently an analyst with MLB Network. His unique and straightforward approach has helped him become one of the most entertaining and polarizing broadcasters in sports television.

Ever since his playing days, Byrnes has always been progressive in his thinking on ways to improve the game of baseball. Committed to progress in the game, Byrnes has partnered with the San Rafael Pacifics and Sports Vision to pioneer implementing an automated strike zone and was featured on HBO Real Sports for their experiment.

In 2011, Byrnes completed his first full distance Ironman triathlon and as of November of 2017 he has completed 11 full distance Ironman's. In June of 2016 Byrnes completed the grueling Western States 100 Mile Endurance Run where he was the subject and executive producer of the award winning documentary "Diamond To The Rough."

On April 21st, 2018, as part of a fundraiser for non-toxic lymphoma treatment research, Byrnes competed in the Napa Valley 12 Hour Ultra Speed Golf Competition and set a new WORLD RECORD by completing 245 holes.

Byrnes is an avid supporter of the Pat Tillman Foundation, Challenged Athletes Foundation and Fit Kids. He resides in Half Moon Bay, Truckee and New York City with his wife Tarah, a former Miss California USA 2002, and their 3 children, Chloe, Cali and Colton.

For more from Eric Byrnes,
visit **EricByrnes.com**